INTERCULTURAL SKILLS
FOR INTERNATIONAL BUSINESS AND
INTERNATIONAL RELATIONS

A PRACTICAL INTRODUCTION WITH EXERCICES

One must carefully study the commercial customs of the lands where one travels. It is essential to know commercial law. To be successful in trade, one must know foreign languages ...
(*Speculum regale*, Norway 13th c., in Gourevitch 1989: 270; my translation).

A toutes les disparues

S. Paul Verluyten

Intercultural Skills for International Business and International Relations

A Practical Introduction with Exercices

Acco Leuven / Den Haag

Teaching aids and a teacher's manual to the exercices are available at the website of Uitgeverij Acco: www.uitgeverijacco.be/interculturalskills

First edition: 2010
Second edition: 2012
Third edition: 2013
Fourth edition: 2014

Published by
Uitgeverij Acco, Blijde Inkomststraat 22, 3000 Leuven (België)
E-mail: uitgeverij@acco.be – Website: www.uitgeverijacco.be

For the Netherlands: Acco Nederland, Westvlietweg 67 F, 2495 AA Den Haag

Cover design: www.dsigngraphics.be

© 2010 by Acco (Academische Coöperatieve Vennootschap cvba), Leuven (België)
No part of this book may be reproduced in any form, by mimeograph, film or any other means without permission in writing from the publisher.

D/2010/0543/269 　　　　　　　　　NUR 780 　　　　　　　　　ISBN 978-90-334-8053-9

Table of Contents

Chapter 1. *Introduction* — 11
1.1 What is the use of this book? — 11
1.2 Resistance to intercultural training — 12
1.3 A costly example: Sephora's failure in Japan — 14
1.4 The need for intercultural training — 17
1.5 Cultural units: countries, religions, languages — 19
1.6 Cultures as partially overlapping entities — 22
1.7 The ecological fallacy — 23
1.8 A definition of culture — 26
1.9 Values and practices — 26
Notes — 29

Chapter 2. *Basic mechanisms: SRC, attribution* — 31
2.1 SRC, the Self Reference Criterion — 31
2.2 Attribution — 32
2.3 Reversibility and transitivity of attributions — 34
Notes — 36

Chapter 3. *Time* — 37
3.1 Temporal structure of a conversation — 38
    3.1.1 Backchannelling — 38
    3.1.2 Turn taking — 40
    3.1.3 Tolerance of silence — 42
3.2 Punctuality — 43
3.3 Temporal structure of a negotiation — 46
3.4 Short vs. long term orientation — 54
3.5 Time and tasks: polychrony vs. monochrony — 57
3.6 Some philosophical aspects of time — 60
    3.6.1 The arrow of time — 60
    3.6.2 Event-linked time (procedural time) — 62
    3.6.3 The past and the future — 64
Notes — 69

Chapter 4. *Space*	71
4.1 Proxemics: interpersonal distance	71
4.2 Haptics: physical contact	73
4.3 Office space	74
Notes	74
Chapter 5. *Verbal communication: language*	77
5.1 English as a foreign language	77
5.1.1 Avoid idioms and check for understanding	77
5.1.2 Some common pronunciation problems	79
5.1.3 Working with interpreters	80
5.2 Loudness of voice	81
5.3 Expressing oneself	82
5.3.1 Verbal exaggeration, overstatements and superlatives	82
5.3.2 Verbal rhetoric and expressing emotions	84
5.3.3 Conflictual tone of voice	85
5.3.4 Honorificals and social stratification	86
5.4 High/low context communication	90
5.4.1 High context communication, face saving and preserving harmony	91
5.4.2 Low context communication	105
Notes	108
Chapter 6. *Non verbal communication*	111
6.1 Facial expressions	112
6.2 Eye contact	114
6.3 Gestures	116
6.3.1 Nodding and shaking your head	116
6.3.2 The 'OK' sign	117
6.3.3 Beckoning	118
Chapter 7. *Etiquette*	119
7.1 Greetings	120
7.2 Gift giving	120
7.3 Dining, smoking and entertainment	122
7.4 Hands, feet, the head and other taboos	127
7.5 Belief systems and 'superstition'	129
Notes	132
Chapter 8. *Hierarchy*	133
8.1 Power Distance in Hofstede's Work	133
8.1.1 What does Power Distance mean?	133
8.1.2 The Power Distance Index: country scores	136
8.1.3 The origins of cultural dimensions	137

	8.1.4	Power Distance in business and organizations	138
	8.1.5	Power Distance and professional class	139
8.2	Hierarchy in the workplace		140
8.3	Beware of oversimplification!		142
Note			143

Chapter 9. *Individualism* — 145

9.1	Individualism: a Western and historically recent 'invention'	145
9.2	Hofstede's Individualism Index values and their implications for work-related situations	147
9.3	Individualism – Group Orientation: discussion and further examples	149
9.4	Related and correlated concepts	153
	9.4.1 High vs. low context communication, vagueness and tolerance of silence	153
	9.4.2 Shame vs. guilt cultures	153
	9.4.3 Face saving and harmony	154
	9.4.4 Indebtedness	154
	9.4.5 Getting acquainted and being part of the in-group	156
	9.4.6 Dependency relations	157
9.5	The correlation between Hofstede's Power Distance and Individualism	158
Notes		159

Chapter 10. *Work, ambition, career-orientation vs. leisure, family and vacation* — 161

Chapter 11. *Uncertainty Avoidance: stress, anxiety and fear of the unknown* — 167

11.1	Country scores on the Uncertainty Avoidance Index (UAI)	168
11.2	The UAI Scores in the workplace	168
11.3	Uncertainty Avoidance: discussion	171
Notes		171

Chapter 12. *Research methodologies* — 173

12.1	Sociology	173
	12.1.1 Geert Hofstede	173
	12.1.2 'Dimensions', 'value types', values: terminological and conceptual issues	175
	12.1.3 Authors inspired by Hofstede	177
12.2	Anthropological approach	180
	12.2.1 Qualitative vs. quantitative research	180
	12.2.2 An example: Philippe d'Iribarne, The Logic of Honor	181
12.3	Cross-cultural psychology	186
12.4	Linguistics: discourse analysis and conversational analysis	187
12.5	Cases and examples	189

12.6 Cultural clusters	191
12.7 Stereotypes and how to deal with them	193
12.8 Change and evolution of cultural values over time	198
Notes	200

Chapter 13. *Attitudinal issues and ethics* — 201

13.1 Ethnocentrism	201
13.2 Universalism and cultural relativism	202
13.3 Minimizing and normalizing differences	207
13.4 Cultural bias	211
13.4.1 Cultural bias in publications	211
13.4.2 Hofstede's survey and the Chinese Values Survey (CVS)	212
13.5 Tolerance	214
13.5.1 Religious (in)tolerance and syncretism	214
13.5.2 Tolerance and openness today	218
13.6 Nationalism vs. multiculturalism	220
13.6.1 A homogeneous society?	220
13.6.2 Nationalism	221
13.6.3 A multicultural society	224
13.6.4 Diversity	228
Notes	230

Chapter 14. *Adaptation strategies: who should adapt to whom?* — 231

14.1 An often ignored issue	231
14.2 Some preliminaries and a research program	233
14.2.1 A typology of adaptation strategies	233
14.2.2 No Communication	233
14.2.3 Communication without adaptation	234
14.2.4 Bilateral adaptation: compromise	235
14.2.5 Unilateral adaptation	235
14.3 Predictive factors	236
14.4 Evaluating adaptation strategies	237
Notes	239

Chapter 15. *Globalization?* — 241

15.1 Convergence	241
15.2 Divergence	243
15.3 Cultural features and economic growth	247
Notes	249

Chapter 16. *Further explorations* — 251

16.1 Intercultural negotiations	251
16.2 Expatriation	253
16.2.1 The failure rate of expatriates	253

		16.2.2 Selection of appropriate candidates for expatriation	254
		16.2.3 Pre-departure training and repatriation training	255
16.3	International management		256
16.4	Cross-cultural marketing		257
		16.4.1 Pictures and names	257
		16.4.2 Colors, sounds and smells	257
16.5	Intercultural communication in general		259
16.6	Area studies		260
Notes			262

Exercises 263

References 329

Index 345

Chapter 1

Introduction

1.1 What is the use of this book?

Take a look at the following, real-life story.

> **Mr. Adams goes to China**
>
> Mr. Adams works for one of the largest transshipment agencies in the port of Antwerp. After various assignments in Brazil which went smoothly, Mr. Adams is sent to Shanghai, China, where he is to instruct port executives in modern transshipment techniques. He lectures in English, and an interpreter translates what he says into Chinese for the people present. At one point, Mr. Adams, referring to the development of a computer program, wishes to say that a particular way of writing the program should be avoided because it would take too long for the results to appear on the screen; there are better ways of writing the program, which produce faster output. But rather that saying just that (e.g., 'Don't write the program this way, it will take very long for the results to appear on the monitor'), he says: 'Don't do it this way, because then, *you might as well get up and have a cup of coffee.*'
>
> Once the sentence is translated, the Chinese start getting up and leaving the room. It is not difficult to guess what has happened: the interpreter misinterpreted Mr. Adams' expression and announced a coffee break (or a break in any case) to the audience.
>
> Mr. Adams, becoming aware of what has happened, calls the audience back, explaining to them that this is all a misunderstanding and that the interpreter made a mistake. The interpreter translates this into Chinese. People pour back into the room, and the course resumes where it had been left.
>
> And the interpreter? He was never seen again. The next session, he had been replaced by a new interpreter.

After having read this book, you are likely to avoid the mistakes Mr. Adams made in China.

You will have learned that, when dealing with non-native speakers and when using interpreters, it is advisable not to use expressions the meaning of which is not transparent, such as 'you might as well get up and have a cup of coffee'. This simple expression raises various culturally relevant questions. Do the Chinese have coffee breaks? If they do, do these breaks have approximately the same length as a Western coffee break? Will the Chinese interpreter understand the expression as synonymous to 'it will take more than five minutes to...'?

You will also have learned that, in a country such as China, face saving is essential. In the story above, the interpreter was humiliated in public. Mr. Adams calls the participants back, and he can only do this through the interpreter who has to admit that he made a mistake in his translation, a professional error. This is so shameful that the interpreter literally cannot show his face any more in front of these people, and that is the reason why he did not show up the next day.

In business, cultural insensitivity costs companies millions of dollars. In international relations, intercultural skills may make the difference between straining or smoothening relations between people and countries.

The classic example of intercultural blindness causing a business venture to lose hundreds of millions is the case of Eurodisney (now Disneyland Paris) which, the first few years after opening (in 1992), was losing so much money that Disney Corporation started to think of closing down the theme park altogether. In 1993, losses stood at approximately one billion US dollars; they were still at around US$ one million *a day* in 1994-5.

Cultural blindness was one of the main reasons, if not the most important, of this initial failure. One simple example: the parking lot followed the design of the parking lots of Disney parks in the US; they had simply forgotten that many more Europeans travel to such a theme park by bus, rather than by private car. The first days, ten buses were arriving for every available bus parking space.

As the Eurodisney example has been described in detail in many textbooks, I will develop another case below (1.3): the failed venture of the Sephora in Japan.

1.2 **Resistance to intercultural training**

For a long time, communication problems in business, industry and administration that could have been tracked down to intercultural differences were overlooked because those intercultural differences were not recognized as such. It was simply assumed that, in international business, everything would go the Western (and mainly the American) way.

This attitude is not tenable anymore today, and anyone who is involved in contacts with people from other cultures (i.e., virtually all of us) can no longer adduce ignorance as an explanation for intercultural mistakes or blunders, now that training materials are readily available.

Nevertheless, resistance to intercultural training is still rampant in the business world, in some countries more than in others. In a survey one of my students (Grieten 1994) carried out among approximately sixty Belgian companies involved in trade with Central and Eastern European countries, it appeared that not one of them organized any intercultural training or briefing for its employees who were in contact with those countries. Large companies may organize in-house training for their personnel, but small and medium-sized companies do not, and independent training and consulting agencies are not widespread as yet. The situation seems to be different in the Netherlands, where intercultural training is provided by several agencies and institutions, including the respectable Royal Institute for the Tropics in Amsterdam.

A first reason that is commonly adduced is that experience is what counts in this domain, rather than theoretical knowledge as it could be gathered in training sessions. This argument could, of course, equally well be applied to learning how to handle a new machine, how to use a computer program, or to learning a new language. The argument is spurious, because just as it make sense to learn a new language by taking classes rather than sending everyone who wishes to learn it immediately off to a country where it is spoken (which is totally unrealistic), and just as it makes sense to train employees before they use the new machine or the new software that is being installed, it also make sense to provide training in intercultural communication before launching employees into contacts with other cultures.

Having employees learn how to handle a new machine through experience only, and without any previous training for it, could prove a costly and dangerous exercise. Things are no different with respect to the acquisition of intercultural skills. No-one will deny the role experience plays in becoming an expert intercultural communicator. But preparatory training is essential in providing people with the necessary tools to start, and in avoiding costly mistakes. How easily Mr. Adams' blunders in China could have been avoided by a simple intercultural training session, or by reading some appropriate materials! One cannot even begin to calculate the cost of Disney Corporation's mistake when they overlooked cultural factors while planning for Eurodisney. According to the newspaper *The Guardian* (19 August 2004), Microsoft "lost hundreds of millions of dollars in lost business and led hapless company employees to be arrested by offended governments", sometimes simply because of lack of knowledge of basic geography, such as distributing software in the respective countries where Kurdistan is separate from Turkey, Kashmir from India or Taiwan from China, but also because of other cultural blunders, such as using chants with Coranic verses in a game software program.

A more insidious reason for not facing intercultural issues and problems, and one which is not always stated openly, is that some may be afraid of opening Pandora's box, and that things may come out of it which run against the prevailing ideology.

For a long time, the European Community, now European Union, has avoided addressing intercultural issues. By refusing to acknowledge that intercultural differences between the member states played a role in the decision making processes and their implementation, one could officially keep up the pretense of a common European culture with little or no internal variation on the level of politics, administration and business. Only in 1995 did the European Union put out a bid to organize large-scale intercultural training sessions for its personnel. Fortunately, more and more institutions and companies are following that trend.

Finally, in some cases people may be worried about the implications of an intercultural diagnosis to a problem, and they prefer to refuse the diagnosis itself, like the proverbial ostrich which puts its head in the sand in order to avoid facing the danger. For instance, Hofstede argues, as we shall see later, that the culture of many (though not all) South-East Asian nations strongly values *Long-Term Orientation,* and Hofstede explicitly correlates this to economic success in the modern world. But then conversely, the economic failure of many African countries could be traced back to the fact that their cultures are much more Short-Term Oriented. If one assumes in addition that most deep-seated cultural values only change very slowly over time,[1] the implication could be that there is little hope for African countries to improve their economic situation dramatically in the near future.

In fact, things are never that simple in real life, and many other factors undoubtedly intervene in explaining a nation's economic success or failure; it would be naive to trace it down to one theoretical dimension only. Besides, why should *economic success* be the only yardstick we use to measure a society's standing in the world?

But even if it were the case that cross-cultural research arrives at pessimistic conclusions in certain cases, the diagnosis that comes out of the cross-cultural investigation should be heeded if one wishes to change things for the better. Refusing the diagnosis is like shooting the messenger who brings the (bad) news, or refusing to go to the doctor because she possibly might discover that you are ill and need treatment...

1.3 A costly example: Sephora's failure in Japan[2]

Sephora is a French chain of cosmetics stores, with over 400 outlets in Europe, including Central and Eastern Europe, and a large number of stores in the USA and now also in China. Its parent company is LVMH, "the largest luxury group in the world" (www.sephora.fr, 2009).

In 1999, Sephora opened its first store in Japan: it was in Ginza, the luxury shopping district of Tokyo. Sephora had ambitious expansion plans for the country: it intended to open several dozens of stores in Japan over a 5-6 year period.

Yet in November 2001, exactly two years after opening that first store on Tokyo, Sephora decided abandon its Japanese operations entirely because of blatant lack of success in conquering the Japanese market. At that time, they had nine stores already open in Japan; they closed them down and left.

What went wrong? LVMH, the parent company, blamed the failure of Sephora in Japan on "the faltering Japanese economy". It is true that a recession, or at least economic stagnation, hit Japan at the time Sephora was opening its first stores in the country. It is equally true, however, that luxury goods typically resist the onslaught of recession rather well; and Luis Vuitton stores, also part of the LVMH group, did not close down in Japan.

Several analysts believe that Sephora's own strategy is to blame for its failure in Japan.

Above I wrote that Sephora is a chain of cosmetics stores. But even today, on its website, Sephora defines itself as a "chaîne de parfumerie", i.e. a chain of *perfume* stores. Of course Sephora sells other cosmetics besides perfume: make up products, hair care and skin care products, and more. But its own definition reveals that perfume is the central product in Sephora's assortment; and that is so because in Western countries, perfume is the core product in a line of cosmetics, the product consumers will most identify with. Companies spend a fortune on designing a new bottle for a new perfume; they do not spend the same amount of money on the new shampoo flask!

Take a look at this picture of a Sephora store, taken in a shopping mall in San Diego, California.

Figure 1. Sephora at a shopping mall in San Diego, California.

Above the shelves, you notice two photographs of a model holding a perfume flask in her hands; it would be hard to imagine she would be holding a deodorant stick, or any other cosmetics product for that matter, wouldn't it?

The picture also shows that when looking inside the store from outside, the only products that are visible on the shelves are perfume (we use this term here for fragrance in general). As consumers presumably identify with perfume primarily, the visual attraction of this product will be greater than if, say, the shelves would show hair conditioner, skin cream or deodorant; it will attract them inside the store, and they may be tempted into buying various products then.

In the Ginza store in Tokyo, the ground floor was devoted to perfume only. For all other cosmetics products, the consumers had to go one floor up.

What's wrong with that, you may ask? Take a look at the share of various segments of cosmetics in sales figures in Japan:

- Skin care   39.1%
- Hair care   31.3%
- Make-up   25.4%
- Other   3.6%
- Perfume and cologne   0.6%

(Source: 2000, Japan Cosmetics Industry Association)

Figure 2. Cosmetics in Japan.

In the USA and in Europe, the most important segment is make-up; fragrance is a very close second, accounting for some 30-40% of cosmetics sales. While Japan is the world's largest cosmetics market (on a par with the USA), sales are dominated by skin care, hair care and make-up products. Perfume and related products account for less than 1% of total sales in Japan, even if the figure may be rising slowly. "Perfume is not a major market in Japan" says Tomoo Inoue in a headline article in the *International Herald Tribune* (November 30, 2001) about the failure of Sephora in Japan. The same article states:

> Sephora committed a fatal error by putting its perfumes section on the all-important first floor [i.e., the ground floor] of its stores.

Thus, the layout of the Sephora stores in Japan was similar to that in picture F1 above. In other words, Japanese women walking past the Sephora stores and looking inside would only see products they would never, ever buy. It is impossible to quantify how much this error contributed to the failure of Sephora in Japan; the least we can say is that it did not do them any good...

The majority of our readers will find it inconceivable that the Sephora executives were not aware of the fact that the vast majority of Japanese consumers do not buy or use perfume. If so, they were presumably hoping to change the behavior of the Japanese (female) consumer: OK, women here have not been using perfume up to now, but our concept and our products are so attractive that they will modify their behavior and start buying perfume from now on. Of course, sales should pick up within a reasonable time span; a commercial company is normally unwilling to wait for many years before becoming profitable in a new market.

Even so, the Sephora people have not done their homework about Japanese culture. If they were hoping that Japanese consumers would change their habits, they should have asked themselves: what *motivates* Japanese women not to use perfume? If the motivations are superficial and accidental, it may be reasonable to expect changing their behavior. If the motivations are profound and strong, this hope is illusory. Even with the best concept and massive advertising, it is not advisable to open a chain of liquor stores in a strongly Islamic country: you are unlikely to convince devout Muslims to start drinking whisky or wine!

On the basis of many interviews I did with Japanese people, I believe the reasons for not using perfume include the following.

- *Cleanliness and naturalness.* Take your shower every morning, and you're clean: no bodily odors! If you add something to that, such as perfume, it is suspicious: perhaps then you *didn't* have time to take your shower this morning? After all, cologne and perfume were originally invented to mask the bodily odors of Europeans at a time (17th-18th c.) when no-one took a bath.
- *Modesty.* A 'proper' Japanese woman is supposed to behave in a modest way. Anything that enhances one's attractiveness goes against this norm.
- *Individualism.* If five Western women gather at a party, the normal situation is definitely not that they would all be wearing the same perfume. Perfume is supposed to express and enhance your individuality. However, this goes against the group orientation of Japanese culture, where one wants to merge with the group rather than stand out from the crowd.

- *Social class.* According to my Japanese informers, perfume is also low class. A barmaid might wear perfume, but, some of my Japanese students say, 'my mother, a respectable woman, will not use perfume'.

Figure 3.   Japan: merging with the group.

How much money did Sephora (and LVMH) lose in this failed business venture? We will never have a precise figure, but we are clearly talking about many millions of euros, or dollars. Recall that they had already opened nine stores in Japan: renting the premises, decorating the stores, putting in the supplies, hiring and training the staff (and subsequently firing them again), ... One million euros per store seems to be a very conservative estimate. Sephora's loss may well amount to 10 million euros or more, – apart from the operational losses they incurred during the two year period they were in business in Japan.

Below we will explain the basic pitfalls of relying on your own SRC (Self Reference Criterion) and not taking cultural differences intro consideration.

1.4   The need for intercultural training

Global trade and international relations are not a recent phenomenon. Bronze and terracotta Greek and Roman oil lamps have been found as far as South-East Asia (Batiste & Zephir 2009: 21). There were international exchanges even in prehistoric times, though the speed of transmission was, of course, slower then.

But now more than ever before, economic success means doing business internationally and globally. And now more than ever, international relations between interconnected countries become essential for our planet. As I am writing these lines, a UN Climate Change Conference is about to open in Copenhagen; others will follow. Hundreds of delegates from governments as well as observers and journalists will exchange ideas and emotions, and each of them brings his or her cultural background and culturally defined frame of reference to the venue.

International negotiations, expatriation processes, international marketing, international joint ventures, mergers and acquisitions, or, simply, welcoming foreign visitors in your own country: the list of situations where intercultural skills are needed involves almost everyone nowadays.

One word of warning. There is still the naive idea that intercultural skills are easily acquired 'on the spot' through travel and experience. The *Contact Hypothesis,* dating back to Allport (1954) states, in its simplest form (which may not correspond to Allport's position), that more contacts between cultural groups lead to better understanding. But there is ample empirical evidence that simply exposing people to different cultures does not automatically lead to mutual sympathy and improved understanding.

During the political unification of Italy, in the 19th century, naïve attempts were made to create a sense of common feeling among the soldiers from the various regions:

> One of the peculiarities of the Italian army was the obsession of trying to minimize municipal or provincial loyalties by [...] making sure that each regiment was made up of troops drawn from all over the peninsula. [...]
>
> Whether soldiers really did feel more 'Italian' as a result of being thrown together with men from other provinces is extremely questionable. There are good grounds for believing that the policy had exactly the opposite effect, with soldiers from the same region ganging together and [...] persecuting, harassing and tormenting soldiers from other regions, as one observer noted, with 'quarrels, brawls and bloody scenes' (Duggan 2007: 288).

More recently, attempts to improve mutual understanding between racial groups in the USA by simply putting, say, African Americans and Caucasian Americans together equally resulted in failure (Van Oudenhoven 2002: 143). The available evidence also suggests that self-reported intercultural skills bear no relationship to real intercultural effectiveness (Herfts, van Oudenhoven & Timmerman 2008) and that intercultural sensitivity typically lags far behind language skills (Jackson 2008).

If you throw someone into intercultural situations unprepared he or she may suffer emotional distress and the company may lose millions of euros, before getting it right, if ever; and most of this could rather easily have been avoided through basic intercultural training.

Intercultural skills are needed as soon as you do any of the following:
- Having contacts with people from different cultures, whether professionally or privately
- Buy and sell abroad: international negotiations and contracts

- Represent your country at international conferences and meetings
- Welcome foreign visitors to your country or company
- Market goods or services internationally and adapt them to foreign markets
- Work as an expatriate, including in diplomatic service or on UN missions
- Getting into a joint venture or a merger with a partner from another country
- Better integrate migrant workers and minorities into the work force.

For expatriates, failure rates range from 10 to 40%: in other words, at least one in ten expatriates returns home prematurely, and in some companies almost half of them do! The cost of one expatriate returning home prematurely is likely to be higher than the cost of a fully-fledged intercultural training program for all future expats, which might have helped avoiding some (though not all) of those premature returns.

Similarly, in the case of joint ventures and mergers and acquisitions, companies sometimes spend vast amounts of money on the harmonization of their accounting procedures or their product assortment, and fail to spend one penny on potential intercultural trouble spots which might arise between the two companies. According to Magala (2005: 116-7), in almost 75% of mergers no attention is paid to cultural aspects. Estimates are that at least half of all joint ventures and mergers either fall apart or do not work as expected (Van Oudenhoven 2002: 166), and here also paying attention to intercultural differences and misunderstandings is likely to reduce the failure rate by a substantial percentage. A good illustration of the effects "special efforts devoted to intercultural communication" have on the success of a Chinese-American joint venture can be found in Newman (1992: 74, 1995). For the impact of culture on mergers and acquisition, see for instance Jöns, Froese & Pak (2007).

It may well be that the failure of the Daimler-Chrysler merger is partly due to not taking cultural factors into consideration. In the Air France-KLM merger on the other hand, cultural factors were explicitly addressed; up to now, the merger is successful.

1.5 Cultural units: countries, religions, languages

In most publications in the field of intercultural communication for business, culture is equated with *national* culture, the culture of a country or nation state: Japan, India, Australia, and so forth. This is the case in virtually all the research frameworks we mention in chapter 12: Hofstede, Trompenaars, Schwartz, the Globe study, d'Iribarne, and many many more. A look at the articles published in *International Journal of Intercultural Relations,* the leading journal in this field, will confirm this impression.

It is legitimate to express doubts about the appropriateness of the equation *culture = nation state,* in view of the fact that many modern nation states are themselves culturally varied. Does it make sense to refer to 'Belgian culture', when there are two linguistic communities in the country which often define themselves as culturally different one from another, plus a number of other cultural groups (an orthodox Jewish community in Antwerp, Turkish and Moroccan Belgians in many of the large cities, civil servants from different parts of Europe who work for the European Union administration, and more)?

Some arguments, however, plead in favor of using country membership as a primary cultural group.

- *A convenient number.* There are about 200 countries in the world, and substantially less if we leave out the very small micro-states. This is a manageable number. Surveys can be carried out in 50 to 100 countries, as is illustrated in chapter 12. Other groupings may be either too large, or too small. It is possible to study religious groups rather than countries, for instance. But there are at most half a dozen major religions in the world, and many of them group people together that are culturally very heterogeneous. Catholicism encompasses the majority of the population in Bavaria as well as in Mexico; Islam, most Syrians as well as most Indonesians... Linguistic groups, on the other hand, may well be too numerous to study culturally: estimates are that some 3,000-5,000 languages are spoken in the world.
- *Clear membership.* Countries usually have clearly defined borders and clearly defined membership. I am a Frenchman living in Mulhouse, or a Swiss living in Basel, usually not both.
- *A clearly defined societal framework.* The bureaucracies of nation-states exert dominant influence upon individual creation of cultural software and 'identities' (Magala 2005: 73). Countries typically have their own unique legal and political framework, educational and judiciary system, economic strengths and weaknesses, etc.
- *Empirical evidence.* The work of many researchers substantiates the idea that countries are relevant cultural groupings. Hofstede's seminal work is an indirect tribute to the relevance of nation-state (Magala 2005: 2), which was not obvious at the outset:

> ... [although] we could even wonder whether modern nations possess national characters [, t]he present book shows that modern nations do have dominant national character traits which can be revealed by survey studies and by the comparison of measurable data on the society level (Hofstede 1980: 38).

If nation states were primarily collections of subcultures that do not have more in common with each other than with other subcultures inside other national borders, Hofstede and others would never have been able to ascribe different specific, culturally defined characteristics to the neighboring countries that are included in various studies.

This is not to say, of course, that other levels of cultural grouping are irrelevant and should not be taken into account. Many if not most nation states are composed of more or less clearly defined *subcultures* which may differ with respect to language, religion, ethnic background, etc. It is then quite possible to refer to cultural features of those subgroups separately whenever the need arises, provided the required empirical knowledge about those subgroups is available.

For the purpose of scientific study, working with national cultures has the advantage of using a clear, well-known concept and an often unambiguous definition of membership. These advantages may outweigh the disadvantage of amalgamating different subcultures within one larger group. Simplification of a complex reality is inherent in any scientific or pedagogical effort, and is acceptable as long as the amalgamated picture is still accurate and close enough to observable reality for it to yield an insight and understanding which may, in fact, be blurred in the more complex picture where the stress is mainly on decomposing cultures into subgroups.

In addition, as we will see later, any characteristics ascribed to a cultural group only make sense if interpreted as a statistical truth. They do not apply to individual cases with any certainty. Therefore, understanding that people differ with respect to their sense of hierarchy (see chapter 8) and that this may explain some of their behavior in front of their boss, for instance, is more important than ascribing stronger hierarchy to France than to Great Britain. To be sure it is more likely for a French person to possess a stronger sense of hierarchy than for a Brit; but that does not necessarily apply to the next French person, the one you have an appointment with tomorrow. Ascribing characteristics of groups to all individuals belonging to that group is called the *ecological fallacy*, an error that will be discussed in more detail below.

The Sapir-Whorf hypothesis. An examination of the potentially strong relation between language and culture is not complete without a discussion of the widely quoted *Sapir-Whorf hypothesis* (see for instance Crystal 1980: 311-2). In essence, this hypothesis states that the (native) language we use shapes the way in which we view and categorize the world, including deep-seated cognitive categorization related to the way we view space, time, etc. If this hypothesis were correct, then the equation *culture = language* would be true in the most absolute terms, because the entire cognitive system which equips a human being would then depend on the native language that human being grew up with.

At a superficial level, it is true that, for instance, the color terms that are available in the language we use will influence our perception of reality. If a language does not have a separate term for *blue* and *green*, but uses one term for both (as is the case in many languages, including Gaelic, Japanese and Chinese), then the native speakers of that language may perceive the color of the leaves of the trees and the color of the sky as belonging to the same category (though this is debatable in itself). But to conclude from there that there is a one-to-one relationship between the linguistic categories that exist in our native language and the cognitive categories we are equipped with, is another matter altogether. After all, native speakers of Gaelic are able to learn English which does have separate words for green and blue, and, as Crystal points out, 'the fact of successful bilingual translation weakens the force of the theory's claims'.

The prevailing opinion in contemporary linguistics is to reject the Sapir-Whorf hypothesis, and it is in any case too controversial to be used as a definitive proof that our native language strongly determines our cognitive structures, including the value system we absorbed as part of the culture we grew up in (for a good critique, see Pinker 2007: 124).

1.6 Cultures as partially overlapping entities

The Netherlands and the Flemish part of Belgium share a common language (Dutch) and a good part of their 'high culture': literature, theatre, historical heritage, and more. Historically, the two regions belonged to the same cultural entity:

> There was certainly no 'Dutch', or specifically north Netherlands identity before 1572, nor any specifically southern Netherlands awareness. Indeed, it is questionable whether either of these existed before the late eighteenth century (Israel 1998: vi).

At the same time empirical evidence shows that many of the current values and practices of the Dutch and the Flemish differ widely.

The table below (F4) illustrates this. While the Dutch and the Flemish share a substantial part of their 'high culture' (art, literature, historical heritage), Hofstede's data show that they differ with respect to their sense of hierarchy (Hofstede's Power Distance) as well as on two other cultural dimensions that will be explained later, Uncertainty Avoidance and Masculinity. In fact, as one can see, on these three cultural dimensions the Flemish score much closer to francophone Belgians and to the French, than to the Dutch.

	'High culture'	Hierarchy	Uncertainty Avoidance	Masculinity
Netherlands	Dutch	38	53	14
Belgium Flemish	Dutch	61	97	43
Belgium French ('Walloon')	French	67	93	60
France	French	68	86	43

Figure 4. High culture vs. Cultural values and behavior.

In other words, many Flemish belong to one cultural group with respect to their 'high culture', which coincides with their native language; and to another cultural group (a French or catholic European cluster) with respect of some other cultural features they possess.

These partial overlaps may be quite complex. In a documentary on Belgian television about a predominantly Turkish area in Brussels, many (though not all) of the first or second generation Turkish people who were interviewed defined themselves as 'Turkish and Belgian' (or vice-versa) at the same time, and explicitly saw themselves as endowed with features of Turkish culture (such as being a Muslim or having a stronger sense of loyalty towards their family and relatives) as well as with features of the host Belgian culture (such as being involved with Belgian politics and working within the Belgian economic structures). Similarly, in the UNPD report 2004, *Cultural Liberty in Today's Diverse World,* a survey shows that the vast majority of Catalans define themselves as both Catalan and Spanish, the vast majority of Flemish as both Flemish and Belgian.

A Moroccan Belgian might well claim membership, depending on the situation, of (a) Morocco, (b) Belgium, (c) Islam, (d) Berber, and more.

1.7 The ecological fallacy

Many authors (Hofstede 1980: 29, 51; Lane, DiStefano & Maznevski 2000: 44; etc.) rightly warn against the error that consists in applying characteristics of groups (such as cultures) to individual members of those groups. This is called the *ecological fallacy* because it is based on the assumption that people will by necessity exhibit the characteristics that are typical of the place they inhabit (or originate from): if this person comes from France, then he/she must exhibit all features that are known to be typical of that country (some are described later in the present book), such as accepting high Power Distance (hierarchy), using interruption as a turn-taking strategy, or easily adopting a sarcastic, conflictual tone in a discussion.

Now there can be no doubt that the culture one belongs to is one of the defining dimensions for any human being. If I had been born and had grown up in Uganda, the United States or Japan my values and my behavior would each time be very different from what they are now, and that is true over and beyond individual characteristics that are obviously also at stake. The reason for many differences in values and practices can easily be traced back to the cultural characteristics of the countries and societies involved.

On the other hand it would be naive and dangerous to interpret a human being's behavior in terms of cultural origin only, and it is essential to warn against that danger. Culturally defined characteristics represent statistically established sociological tendencies, and cannot be blindly ascribed to individuals belonging to a particular culture. If I learn that Japanese women tend to be shy and keep their eyes down, I cannot infer from there that a particular Japanese woman I meet later today necessarily exhibit these characteristics; she may well be loud and outspoken.

In the same way, even though hierarchy is stronger in France than in Great Britain, you are likely to meet one day a French person (F) whose sense of hierarchy is weaker than that of the Brit (GB) who is also with you.

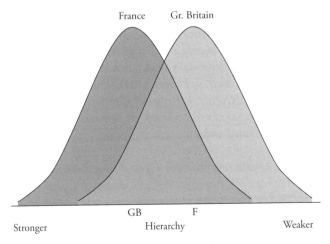

Figure 5. Hierarchy: country characteristics vs. individual.

Applying culturally defined characteristics to individuals may lead to a form of racism ('all Russians are...'). While one should warn in the strongest terms against this danger (which is inherent in any sociological description), serious scholars do not fall into this trap. Hofstede (1980: 40), for instance, clearly states that he is involved in ascribing properties to *societies,* and not to individuals.

Figure F6 illustrates the fact that a human being must be defined in a multidimensional space. Many dimensions other than the person's cultural background intervene in defining the unique human being we are communicating with. Some of these other dimensions are briefly mentioned here.

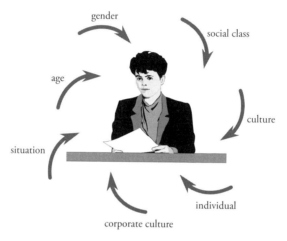

Figure 6.   Multidimensional(wo)man.

- *Social class.* Just as the Japanese have a different set of values and practices from Belgians, people's values and practices are partially defined by the social and professional class they belong to. To put it more concretely: does a Pakistani executive share more values and practices with a Pakistani worker in his factory (same culture, different social class), or with a British executive (different culture, same social class)? The answer to this question, inasmuch as it is answerable, seems to be that both factors are of about equal importance. Hofstede (1980: 105) has shown that the difference, along a particular dimension such as Power Distance, between the culture with the highest score and the culture with the lowest score is about the same as the difference, along that same dimension, between members of the highest professional class and members of the lowest professional class in the company.
- *Gender.* Similarly, within one culture a person's values and practices are to a certain extent determined by gender. In all cultures on earth, there exists variation in values and practices observed among its male and its female members. Perhaps gender is more of a differentiating factor in some cultures than in others; but it would be naive to think that gender-linked differences in values and practices are minimal or non-existent in Western cultures.

- *Age.* As every marketing professional knows, the values and practices of people also depend on their age: young and old people do not behave in identical ways, they buy different clothes, spend their vacation differently, listen to different kinds of music; nor do they have identical ideas about life and death, love and marriage, politics or art.
- *Professional culture.* Values and practices also differ depending on the corporation or institution where one works. Other things being equal, they will not be the same, for instance, in an advertising agency and a bank, or in a civil service administration and the army.
- *Corporate culture.* Each company develops its own corporate culture. In one software company (such as Google), informality may prevail; in another one, relations may be more formal and more hierarchical.
- *Situational factors.* The same person may exhibit behavior that differs widely depending on the situation he/she is in: someone who attaches high value to hierarchical structures at work may be egalitarian during leisure time spent with family or friends, or vice versa. There is also good evidence that bilingual-bicultural individuals switch between cultures depending on the language they are speaking (Van Oudenhoven 2002: 45, 95). Bilingual Hong Kong Chinese react in a more Western way when speaking English, in a more Chinese way when speaking Chinese; they are bicultural, depending on the situation (Nisbett 2005: 118).
- *Individual features.* Over and above the various sociological factors which define human beings, a large part of the variation observed in them is purely individual. Two persons sharing the same culture, gender, working in the same corporation in similar positions, and so forth, will not be identical. Individual variation is by definition beyond the scope of sociological-type investigations. Keeping in mind that individual variation is important will prevent us from falling into the trap of overgeneralization ('all such-and-such are so-and-so').

The risk of falling into the ecological fallacy should not lead to the opposite extreme, where the existence of culturally determined characteristics is denied. When I (European) am going to meet a man from Japan, I *can* make a substantial number of predictions on the basis of that person's cultural background, with a variable degree of probability (though never with absolute certainty): that his native language is Japanese (probability of nearly 100%), that he is more used to eating with chopsticks and sitting on the floor than me (probability also nearly 100%), that his diet includes more fish and less meat than mine (very probable), that he does not change employers during his career (probability around 80-90%) that he will find it harder to openly reject a suggestion or proposal (probable), etc. The fallacy here would consist of turning these probabilities into certainties, which they are not. On the other hand, undeniably the more I have learned about culturally defined features of Japanese people (as they are described in this book and elsewhere), the less likely I am to misinterpret some of my Japanese partner's words and deeds the first time I meet him.

To sum up: use the knowledge you will have gathered in this book to *understand* other people better, to avoid misinterpretations; never ever use it to make predictions about an individual you meet!

1.8 A definition of culture

In the early 1950s already, over 300 definitions of culture were collected by two authors (Kroeber and Kluckhohn 1952; see Victor 1992: 6). We are obviously not going to discuss all of them here. There is in fact no particular difficulty in understanding intuitively what is meant by *culture* in the context of intercultural studies.

In this book we are normally not using the term 'culture' to refer to the arts, literature, music, painting, etc., and to the intellectual life that goes with these, to some kind of 'refined ways of thinking, talking, acting, etc.' as Webster's dictionary puts it. Whenever we need to refer to this meaning, we will use the term 'high culture', as in 1.6 above.

The word 'culture' as it is used here refers to the *values* and *practices* (Hofstede 1991: 9) that are acquired and shared by people in a group. A key attribute of culture is that it is by definition something *shared* with other members of a group; it cannot be a property of individuals (Kincaid 1996: 288).

A nice metaphor, also from Hofstede, is that culture is the *software of the mind*. The hardware all human beings are equipped with, i.e. our brain, is similar, apart from individual variation. But the programming that is put inside that brain depends on the culture we grew up in.

Another good way of putting it is to say that culture refers to *the particular solutions which societies give to universal problems*. Thus, feeding oneself is a universal problem; but what is considered edible and what is actually used as food varies from one culture to the next, and ranges from bird's saliva to caterpillars, from live oysters to marshmallows. Finding shelter is also a universal problem, but, as everyone knows, the size, shape, interior lay-out, etc., of the dwellings of humans vary widely, from yurts to concrete 30-story buildings. Children's education is yet another a universal problem to be solved, and here again the solutions range from experiential learning through observing adults and participating in their activities, to being immobilized for many years in a room every day with a number of other children and listening to abstract, verbal explanations by one adult person.

Culture permeates every aspect of our life. Whether we shake hands or not, how we hold our fork in our hands (if there are forks in our culture), the amount of eye contact we establish during a conversation, the amount of moral authority our parents have over us, what we think about the causes of illness and death, and a myriad of other thoughts and activities are, to a certain extent (but not completely), determined by the culture we grew up in.

1.9 Values and practices

Various authors have proposed an 'onion model' to illustrate the relationship between *values* (underlying, invisible as such) and *practices*, i.e. behavior which is visible. This is Hofstede's version of it:

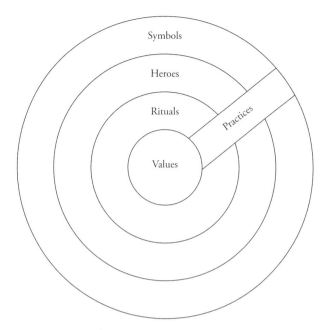

Figure 7. The onion model (Hofstede 2001: 11).

Such a model suggests (as does its variant, the 'iceberg' model, with a large invisible part and a smaller emerging part) that the core of a culture are its values. Values express themselves in practices, in behavior. I cannot look into someone's brain to detect if he is a Jew, a Christian or a Muslim. But if I see that person entering a synagogue, I may surmise that he is Jewish.

While it is undoubtedly the case that underlying values manifest themselves in visible behavior, I wish to formulate two caveats.

Firstly, values may remain hidden and not manifest themselves in any clear way for a long time. A person may be racist or xenophobic, and be afraid to openly admit that. He may express his xenophobic feelings only in the intimacy of the voting booth.

More importantly, the above model suggests that *all* practices emanate from underlying values. This leads to the naïve idea that once you understand the underlying rationale of a culture, you will be able to cope with virtually all unforeseen situations that may arise. This is variously referred to by different authors as 'understanding the principles' (Peterson 2004: 108-9), 'breaking the code', etc.

> To put it in a nutshell: having 'broken' the code of a given culture, one should be able to generate creative statements and perform acceptable acts in social situations one has never faced before (Magala 2005: 29).

In reality, a large number of practices cannot be traced back to underlying values. In some of these cases, there may have been an underlying value at the outset, but it is lost in history.

At a typical business meeting in many countries, the men will be wearing a colorful neck scarf called 'a tie'; the probability that businesswomen in the same room are also wearing a tie is extremely low. In this situation, ties are nearly obligatory for men, while they are a rare option for women. What is the underlying principle or value behind this superficial set of norms? I cannot detect anything especially deep underneath it (though a psychoanalyst might, I guess). In fact, the rationale has been lost to us many generations ago. The French word for tie, 'cravate', is etymologically the same as 'Croat'. It referred to a scarf which Croat mercenaries (in the 17th century, possibly earlier) wore around their neck. However, the businessman who puts on his tie in the morning is unlikely to know this, and even less likely to have decided he would wear a tie because he is trying to look like a Croatian warrior.

In other words, many traits of behavior are simply arbitrary, and it would be vain to try and search for a 'deep' explanation of them.

I therefore disagree with Peterson (2004: 108-9) who claims that understanding 'the principles' behind the ritual exchange of business cards in Japan is preferable to 'do's and don'ts' and will allow one to properly perform this operation.

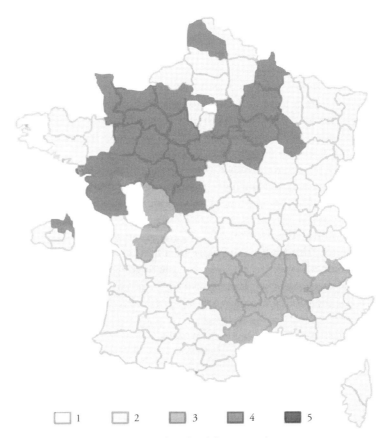

http://strangemaps.wordpress.com/2007/12/02/210-french-kissing-map/

Figure 8. French kissing map.

Good luck to anyone who tries to explain the following by referring to deeper, underlying values:
- Americans typically hold their fork in their right hand (except when cutting), Europeans in their left.
- Women have the option of wearing shoes with high heels or low heels; men do not (at least in most situations).
- When greeting, in some cultures people take each other's right hand and shake it vigorously (appropriately called a 'handshake'); in other cultures they don't. Fox (2005: 177) has a picture of an Athens gravestone around 410 BC featuring a very modern handshake. The presumed historical origin of the handshake, i.e., extending the open hand to show one is unarmed, may well have been lost already at the time.
- Depending on the region, French people exchange one, two, three or four kisses when greeting (see F8): an expression of underlying differences in value systems?

For a more detailed discussion of the terms involved such as 'values', 'practices', etc., see 12.1.2 below.

Notes

1. Not all scholars would agree on that, but I think it is fair to say that it is the majority view, and it is certainly Hofstede's own view.
2. This account is partly based on an article in the *International Herald Tribune* (30 November 2001), 'Analysts Blame Sephora's Strategy for Japan Failure'.

Chapter 2
Basic mechanisms: SRC, attribution

2.1 SRC, the Self Reference Criterion

When you have to decide which course of action is appropriate in a given situation, you rely on a set of norms, a frame of reference that will guide your decision. The obvious, default choice is to rely on the set of norms that is stored in your mind: your own frame of reference. You enter a bank in Bogotá, Colombia and *assume* that cashing a check there will be done in the same way it would be done back home; you want to motivate your workers in Korea, and *assume* that what motivates people back home (money, perhaps) motivates them everywhere; etcetera. In an intercultural situation, this default option is bound to create problems, as the frame of reference of the other person or party may well be very different from yours.

A simple example. When George Bush, then president of the United States of America, visited Prime Minister Koizumi of Japan in 2003, the two gentlemen exchanged gifts, as is usual on such occasions. The gift President Bush received from Koizumi was a robot dog, symbol of Japanese state of the art technology: the dog is supposed to respond to voice commands. However,

> [a]board Air Force One from Tokyo to Manila, Bush and his staff tried to bond with this new pet – only to discover that the dog understands only Japanese... (Newsweek 3 November 2003).

In other words, the Japanese person, whoever it was (probably not Koizumi himself), who selected this robot dog as a gift for the President of the United States, has not been able for one moment to put himself in the positions of the person (a speaker of English who does not speak Japanese) who would receive the gift. He has decided on the choice of the gift on the basis of criteria that work for him, rather than getting out of his own frame of reference: he has relied on his SRC.

In this case, there were no dire consequences. In other cases, relying on your SRC and not taking into consideration that other people may have different norms, values and habits may lead to political or business decisions that are extremely costly. That is precisely what happened to Sephora and its failed Japanese venture I described above: they relied on their own set of certainties about the layout of their stores (corroborated by their success in Europe and North America) rather than asking themselves what would work in a very different country such as Japan.

In the following example, the strength of one's SRC overrides the possibility of observing that things are different: the SRC is so strong that it makes the participants blind.

> **Relying on the SRC when ordering a meal in a restaurant**
>
> At the Centre for European Studies of the University of Maastricht I regularly teach courses to groups of American (US) students from various schools who are on their study abroad program.
>
> One of the first things many students do after arriving in the Netherlands is to visit a local restaurant. When waiting for the waiter to take their order as well as when waiting for the meal to arrive, students rely on the SRC (what is acceptable in the US) in order to assess what are reasonable waiting times. Invariably, these are exceeded in both cases; it takes 'too long' for the waiter to arrive at their table, and it takes 'too long' for the meal to be served. Often, the students' conclusion is that this is perhaps because 'they don't like foreigners (or Americans) at this place.'
>
> When the meal is finished, they again rely on the SRC when assuming that the waiter will bring the bill to their table spontaneously as is common in the US – which the waiter does not, as that would be considered rude in Europe. In many cases, students wait for up to thirty minutes for the bill to arrive, so strong is their assumption that things must work the way they work back home. So strong also is the SRC that they completely fail to observe that all other customers in the restaurant ask the waiter for the bill: *they don't see* what is happening at another table perhaps one or two meters away from them.
>
> In this case as in many others, the strength of the SRC actually overrides exposure to easily observable cultural differences.

Opening your eyes, developing your sense of observation, is a crucial skill in intercultural situations. At the end of this book, the reader will find a set of observation exercises that may help in developing one's observation skills. The amount of relevant information that is contained in a simple street scene with a couple of buses, some cars, storefronts and people on the sidewalk is absolutely astonishing – provided one learns to look for it.

Opening one's eyes should also lead to opening one's mind: escaping from one's own SRC, which is like a mental prison that prevents us from accepting that, in another culture, things may be totally different from what we deem normal. Learn to expect the unexpected!

2.2 Attribution

The term *attribution* is used by different authors with related but different meanings (Blom 2008: 71, Van Oudenhoven 2002: 175-6, etc.). In this book, attribution means: attributing a meaning, ascribing an interpretation to what people around you say and do.[1]

Within our own culture also, we need to do this constantly. When someone says to you 'I love you', you will try to figure out what that person really means:
a. he/she really loves you
b. he/she just wants you to feel good
c. he/she wants to have sex with you
d. he/she wants to get married with you because you are rich or powerful or can provide him/her with the necessary papers to stay in the country

Even in our own culture, we sometimes make *attribution mistakes:* we ascribe to the other person's words or deeds a meaning which does not correspond to the intended meaning. Readers who have been married for many years will probably agree that a misunderstanding may occasionally arise even between two spouses who have been together for a very long time.

It is obvious, however, that the danger of attribution mistakes is much higher between individuals who are more different from each other, such as individuals belonging to different cultures. In that case, if you rely on your SRC, i.e., use your own, familiar (but culture-specific) framework to interpret the other's behavior or words, the result may well be that your interpretation of someone's behavior on the one hand, and that person's intended meaning on the other, are totally at odds with each other. Needless to say, repeated attribution errors will seriously strain the intercultural communication process.

The following is a typical example of an attribution mistake. In Iraq, locals tend to complain about the behavior of US soldiers who frequently sit in their jeeps, trucks and helicopters with the soles of their shoes showing:

> Whenever the Chinook helicopters flew overhead, Jassem said, the American soldier stationed at the back of the helicopter always hung his feet out of the back door – a sign of disrespect in the Muslim world (*The New York Times,* 4 November 2003).

Is it the intention of the American soldier to insult the Arabs down there? Probably not, as showing the soles of your shoes is perfectly normal in the USA. Americans frequently sit in their office with their feet on the desk, even when a visitor is coming in. In the frame of reference of Jassem the Iraqi however, showing the soles of your shoes is considered an insult, as is anything that has to do with shoes in many countries around the world.[2] Jassem relies on his SRC to interpret the behavior of an American, who is operating within a very different frame of reference. Jassem thereby misinterprets the behavior of the American soldier: he is making an *attribution error.*

Mistaken attribution with non-verbal behavior: two more examples

A Dutch nurse is working in a field hospital somewhere in East Africa. Her task consists, quite simply, of showing the patients in: they are all sitting on the floor in a tent, and she needs to signal to each of them that it is his/her turn to go into the doctor's cabinet.

> Although the nurse's task is apparently simple and straightforward, the local people seem to hate her, and don't want to have anything to do with her. They say: 'she treats us like dogs.'
>
> At first view, there is nothing in the nurse's behavior that could cause such a strong reaction. Until it is discovered that she indicates the next person to be seen by the doctor by *pointing with her finger.* This simple gesture was the cause of the local people's reaction: in many countries, you can point at animals, but it is extremely rude to point at people with your finger (Pinto 1990: 112).
>
> Therefore, the local people *attributed* to this gesture the meaning which it has in their culture: if you point at someone, you convey the meaning that this person is nothing but a dog to you.
>
> The second story happens inside an airplane bound for a central African country. An African passenger wants to catch the Belgian stewardess's attention, but she is not looking in his direction. The passenger then uses a means to catch her attention that is common in his culture: he hisses at her. Furious, the Belgian stewardess turns around and says to him: *Je ne suis pas votre chien, Monsieur* ('I am not your dog, Sir').
>
> Here also, the stewardess uses her own, familiar framework to interpret the behavior of the African passenger: you don't hiss people in Europe, though you could hiss your pet.

The attribution mistakes made by the East Africans and by the Belgian stewardess are strikingly similar to one another, including the strong (and identical) wording they use: both feel as though the other party treats them as a dog, i.e., as less than a human being.

The two incidents also show that seemingly innocuous behavior (such as using your finger or making a certain sound between your teeth) can lead to extremely strong reactions. No-one is immune against attribution mistakes, which will be made by educated people as well as by illiterate villagers. Attributing a meaning is largely carried out unconsciously, and in order to lower the risk of making attribution errors we need to know and understand how the interpretative frameworks in other cultures differ from our own, and become aware of what is considered normal, unmarked behavior in other cultures.

The story with the Belgian stewardess also illustrates a point we made before: exposure to and experience with intercultural encounters (which the stewardess undoubtedly possessed) do not necessarily lead to fewer attribution errors and to the optimization of intercultural communication skills.

2.3 Reversibility and transitivity of attributions

Imagine an encounter of a European or American businessperson with an Arab on the one hand, with a Japanese person on the other. Chances are that, among many other culturally defined traits, the communicative behavior of the Arab and the Japanese will differ from the European's in the following aspects: interpersonal distance, eye contact, loudness of voice (we will develop these in more detail below).

	Arab	European	Japanese
Interpersonal distance	±25 cm	55-65 cm	±90 cm
Eye contact	>50%	35-40%	15%
Loudness of voice	Loud(er)	Mid-range	Soft(er)

Figure 9. Interpersonal distance, eye contact and loudness of voice in three areas.

Just imagine a conversation with someone who is standing a lot closer than what you deem normal, who is speaking much louder and who looks you into the eyes 'all the time'. You can simulate this with a friend, and observe what will happen almost inevitably and automatically, but unconsciously: the Westerner will back off in order to restore the interpersonal distance that seems normal to him/her; after which a real Arab is likely to come closer again to restore the distance that is normal to *him*... The impression the Westerner may have during and after the conversation is that his/her interlocutor was pushy or even aggressive. Needless to say, attributing 'pushiness' to the Arab's behavior is an *attribution error,* because it corresponds in no way to the intentions of the Arab: he is simply exhibiting behavior that is normal for a business conversation to him.

Now put yourself in the shoes of your Arab partner: which impression the Westerner will make on him? Every time the Arab is at a distance he feels comfortable with in order to have a conversation, the Westerner backs off; in addition, he seems to avoid eye contact; and his voice is too soft for normal conversation, from the Arab's point of view. In brief, the Arab is equally likely to attach a mistaken attribution to the Westerner's behavior, but one which is exactly the reverse of pushiness: he is likely to feel that the Westerner is cold and aloof, avoids real contact and communication. Every attribution error in an encounter is *reversible:* person A may get a mistaken impression of B, while B may get the reverse mistaken impression of A.

Attribution errors are also *transitive*. Which impression will the Westerner get from the Japanese, who is standing so far from him, avoids eye contact and is speaking so softly? The same as the Arab will get from the Westerner, i.e., 'cold and aloof.' And conversely, the Japanese will feel that the Westerner is pushy and loud – just what the Westerner was thinking of the Arab! F10 illustrates all this.

Figure 10. Reversibility and transitivity of attributions.

Notes

1. Some authors use the term *attribution* for ascribing an underlying motivation to observed behavior, or attributing a person's behavior to a given set of factors (for instance, Shadid 1998: 166, Gudykunst & Kim 1992: 30). For example, it has been shown that people tend to attribute negative behavioral traits of someone from their own culture to individual, exceptional factors ('John is so...'), whereas they tend to ascribe negative behavior of someone from a different culture to this person's cultural background ('This Japanese woman is so...' – with the implication: '... because she is Japanese'); and vice-versa. A definition which is closer to the one I give above is endorsed in Fisher 1980: 15.
2. In many variants of Arabic (Sudan, Iraq), when mentioning shoes or feet one commonly adds an expression of 'excuse me' (for using such a dirty word); this is also the case in Thailand (Welty 2004: 157). In Thailand you should never use your feet for anything other than standing or walking (Segaller 1993: 69).

Chapter 3
Time

> ... in the ordinary course of life the Balinese never 'date' anything in our sense of the term (Geertz 1973: 398)

Time underlies human activity in a broad variety of ways and has been the object of innumerable treatments, ranging from physics to psychology (for a classic overview, see Reichenbach 1958; also Evans 2003).

Time is not a physical feature of an objective world (Evans 2003: 7), but a psychological construct in our mind. Everyone knows that spending an hour of time in different situations (in a doctor's waiting room, having dinner with friends) does not feel as though it is the same length of time.

Experiencing time is an extremely basic human cognitive mechanism, yet at the same time it is culture-specific. Psychological experiments and neurological evidence suggest that perception is fundamentally temporal in nature:

> ... a temporal code, cognitively instantiated, may ultimately ground event perception (Evans 2003: 23)

But at the same time, normative temporal awareness (what is considered the normal length of a conversation or a speech, for instance) is acquired through socialization and is culture-specific (Evans 2003: 19).

The reader will find many fascinating cross-cultural aspects of time described and analyzed in several books by Edward T. Hall. Of course we cannot provide a full treatment of the time dimension in various cultures in this book. We will limit ourselves to some aspects that are of potential interest to a person engaging in international business or international relations.

The time dimension as it relates to human beings ranges from 'microscopic' (seconds, minutes) to 'macroscopic' (weeks, months, years, centuries). Below, I discuss a selected number of topics relating to the microscopic time scale and to the macroscopic time scale.

3.1 Temporal structure of a conversation

In this section we will concentrate on three mechanisms that play a role in conversational structure: backchannelling, turn taking and tolerance of silence.

3.1.1 Backchannelling

Backchannelling refers to the feedback signals the listener provides to the speaker in a conversation in order to communicate that he/she (the listener) is listening and basically understands what the speaker is saying.

Backchannelling is probably universal: it exists in every culture. It can be done through nodding your head, saying 'mm' or 'yes', etc.

If backchannelling in itself is universal, the frequency with which people emit those signals is culture-specific, as well as the way in which backchannelling is carried out. In similar situations, Japanese backchannelling frequency is substantially higher than what happens in Western cultures. In one study (Miller 1991: 111-130), Japanese were found to emit backchannelling signals (called *aizuchi* in Japanese) approximately three times more frequently than Americans, with an average interval between backchannelling signals of 4.75 seconds, against 15 seconds for the Americans. A number of typical characteristics of many culturally determined features are present here, such as the following.

- Backchannelling frequency is not learned consciously, nor are people in a given culture aware of their own behavior in this respect; without training, one may never become aware that people from other cultures have a different backchannelling rate, even if one perhaps feels that there is something odd in the conversation.
- The choice of a certain backchannelling frequency in any given culture is arbitrary and seemingly trivial: there is no deep significance to the fact that the Japanese emit these signals every four or five seconds, Westerners every ten or fifteen seconds, and no-one would argue that one is intrinsically better than the other.

Yet this superficial and trivial factor may in itself already lead to mistaken attribution.

> For a foreigner, *aizuchi*, can cause confusion when he/she is speaking. The speaker may misconstrue the expressions by his/her Japanese audience as a sign of agreement where none is intended. Ironically, a lack of *aizuchi* by a foreigner can lead a Japanese speaker to feel that he/she is not being understood (Kaori Tajima, on his internet website).

Suppose a Japanese passenger at a European airport has a problem with his ticket, and is now explaining this to a European airline agent. The airline agent is likely to acquiesce every 10-15 seconds, thereby (in his/her mind, unconsciously) conveying the message that he/she is listening carefully. But the Japanese passenger, who (unconsciously) expects backchannelling signals to be forthcoming much more frequently, may easily infer that the Westerner is not listening carefully:

the Japanese mistakenly attributes 'inattention' to the Western person's behavior. This example is based on my own observations at Brussels airport when preparing intercultural training seminars for an airline company.

Conversely, the higher frequency with which the Japanese emit backchanneling signals may be mistakenly interpreted by Westerners as agreeing, in particular when translated into English:

> [T]hree 'hais' in a row, when interpreted, sound pretty decisive: 'Yes. Yes. Yes.' (Engholm 1991: 110).

Several accounts confirm that Westerners frequently think that the Japanese have agreed with their proposals or even think they have an order (as in the Lestra Design case reproduced in Usunier 1996: 161-71) whereas in fact that is not so. The word *hai*, literally 'yes', may in fact be used more often as a token of backchannelling than as a sign of agreement (Miller 1991: 124). In a telling anecdote in an article by the Hungarian japanologist Judith Hidasi (1995b: 18), a Japanese stage manager receives detailed instructions from the Hungarian conductor of an orchestra, replies with *Hai, wakarimashita* 'Yes I understand', then does not carry out the instructions at all.

In reality, the difficulties will be compounded because backchannelling frequency is not the only factor that differentiates speakers from different cultures: there are dozens of such factors, small and large, that may be the cause of mistaken attribution and therefore result in less than optimal understanding, sometimes even in almost total breakdown in communication.

Similarly, the *way* in which people emit backchannelling signals is not universally the same. Americans of European descent and African Americans appear to have different backchannelling styles, and this leads to miscommunication due to an attribution error in the following instance[1]:

> American students from black communities have frequently complained that white American teachers, counsellors, and employers insult them by talking down to them. Harvard professor Frederick Erickson investigated the problem and offered this explanation: Because the black students do not give a speaker the same non-verbal feedback that white students do, white teachers think that they don't understand. While receiving instruction, a white student will nod emphatically and murmur 'uh-huh.' Blacks nod almost imperceptibly or say 'mhm,' seldom both. As a result of this difference in feedback, speakers from purely white American cultures tend to overexplain to blacks, thereby insulting them by treating them as seemingly incapable of understanding the first time (Victor 1992: 195-6, based on M. F. Vargas).

Above, we only discussed backchannelling. Obviously, there are other *regulators* (Victor 1992: 195) in a conversation, with which the listener may convey to the speaker that he/she (the listener) is puzzled or does not understand well, that he/she wishes to take the floor, etc. All these are likely to vary from one culture to another, and therefore they are a potential source of attribution errors if not interpreted correctly.

3.1.2 Turn taking

In a conversation, at one point person A is speaking, and a few seconds later person B is speaking: B has taken turns. On what basis does B (unconsciously in many cases) decide that at one point in time it is appropriate to take turns, while it was preferable to allow A to continue speaking a few seconds earlier? Turn taking mechanisms are largely unconscious. We have been involved in turn taking since we started to speak, yet most of us would be at loss to explain how turn taking works.

Turn taking is only seldom called for explicitly. Person A does not usually say to B something like: 'I am finished now, please you start speaking.' Many subtle clues may indicate to B that this is an appropriate moment to take turns. We limit ourselves here to examining two basic options B has for taking turns:

a. B may wait for a moment of *silence* in A's discourse to take turns (that does not necessarily mean that A was really finished talking)
b. B may *interrupt* A in the middle of a word or a sentence

The acceptability of these two basic strategies, not surprisingly, varies with the culture. For example, Dutch scholars (Van der Meijden, adapted by Hendriks & Ulijn; see Ulijn 1995) studied differences in turn taking strategies between Italian, Dutch and German interlocutors. We shall not concern ourselves here with the two types of silence they distinguish ('rest', under half a second, and what they call 'silence', over half a second). The difference in making use of the interruption strategy between the Italian, the Dutch and the German speaker they studied is striking:

Taking the floor:	Successful Interruption	Rest (<0.5 sec) or Silence (>0.5 sec)
Italian	30.6%	
Dutch	15.3%	
German	5.3%	
Dutch	4.3%	

Figure 11. Turn taking

As can be seen, the Italian interlocutor takes turns in almost one case out of three by interrupting the other person; it is a common turn taking mechanism for the Italian, even if it appears that, in the majority of cases, the Italian also 'prefers' a pause or silence to take turns. The interruption strategy plays only a marginal role in the conversation between the Dutch and the German interlocutor: one case out of twenty, approximately. Notice also that the Dutch person adapts his behavior to the situation: he interrupts more frequently when speaking with the Italian than with the German.

It is easy to see how this cultural difference is a frequent (and documented) cause of intercultural attribution mistakes during a conversation or negotiation. Take a person from a culture where interrupting the other as a strategy for taking turns is rare (say, Germany or Holland) and suppose this person is having a conversation with someone from a culture where interrupting is much more acceptable (say, an Italian or French interlocutor). The first person is likely to be interrupted much more frequently than what he/she is used to and finds acceptable, and may mistakenly attribute rudeness, impoliteness to his/her interlocutor's behavior.

It is tempting, when you come from a non-interrupting culture, to assume that interrupting is not only less polite, but also intrinsically less conducive to real communication and exchange of ideas. I used to teach business French at my university and I recommended my Flemish, i.e. Dutch speaking students to watch French television as often as they can to improve their French. But many of them came back to me and complained that they can't stand watching some programs on French television: typically, debates and discussion programs. The Flemish students qualify these as total disorder and chaos, people yelling and shouting all at the same time. The observation is partly correct, yet the attribution (that the French are not communicating with each other during a public debate such as this) is obviously mistaken.

I recorded several discussions and debates on British and French television respectively, on comparable topics and with comparable participants and audiences (see also Gallien 1996: 60-66 for a comparison between British and French turn-taking in a pedagogical perspective). Even without a detailed quantitative study of those programs, it is immediately clear to any observant that turn taking does not work the same way, and that other conversational mechanisms also work differently, in the two countries. French discussants frequently interrupt the others, and there is a lot of overlap (several people speaking simultaneously) and fighting for attention and for the floor (this is related to the concept of polychrony discussed below). All these will be significantly less frequent (while not altogether absent) in Britain. Yet there is little indication that debates (political or other) are less fruitful in France than in Britain. If the British, like my Flemish students, are likely to find the French style of debates chaotic and disorderly, and may conclude from there that no real exchange of ideas is taking place, the reverse is equally true. Most French people are likely to find British debates boring: there is no fire, no sparks, the discussants seem to be good pals rather than opponents defending contradictory ideas; there is no real debate, no real exchange of ideas. Recall what we argued above: A will attribute a value judgment to the behavior of B, while B attributes the reverse value judgment to the behavior of A.

Interrupting as a turn-taking strategy may be even less acceptable in some Asian cultures such as Japan than in the US or Northern Europe (see also Tanaka 1999):

Engholm (1991: 166-7) reports the following quote from Hiroshi Ishi of Nippon Telephone & Telegraph:

> In my own experience, I found that turn taking is most difficult for me to learn to adapt to, in discussions with Americans. Situation-oriented non-verbal cues for turn taking in Japanese meetings are much more clear to me. In Japan, it is very rude to interrupt other persons' speaking. We have been taught to be patient, to listen until others are finished talking.

The Japanese are likely to find it even more difficult to adapt to the turn-taking strategies that are common in France or in Italy than in the USA!

In addition to the different strategies that are commonly used for taking turns (interrupting vs. using a moment of silence), it is likely that turn taking *frequency* is also different from one culture to the next. Peterson (2004: 149) reports the case of a video camera at video conferencing not being able to follow speakers who take turns (too) rapidly in Brazil.

3.1.3 Tolerance of silence

Suppose a worker (we will call him Pete) in the office asks a co-worker a simple question in the course of a conversation: 'What do you think, Joanna, couldn't we do it this way?' How much time does Joanna have before providing an answer? If your students or colleagues believe a period of silence of five seconds does not seem too long, organize a simple role play: one student or colleague will play Pete and ask the question stated above; the other, playing Joanna, must wait five seconds before replying something like 'I don't know Pete, I'll have to think about it'. It will come as a revelation to many that those five seconds will seem extraordinarily long, and all will agree that the role play does not reflect a realistic scenario in an everyday conversation.

In many Western countries the amount of silence that is tolerated in such a situation is extremely small, two-three seconds at most. If Joanna cannot think at once of an utterance to reply to the question, she may say 'uuh' to fill up the unbearable silence, but she must say something or make some noise. More generally, tolerance of silence is low in Western countries.[2] In France as in many other European countries, when people are together (in a bar or restaurant for instance), conversation is supposed to go on virtually uninterruptedly. In French there is an expression to refer to the situation where suddenly, no-one is speaking any more: *un ange passe,* i.e., 'an angel passes by.' This expresses the feeling of uneasiness, of something odd going on when there is even a short moment of silence.

Cultures where silence does not make people feel uncomfortable but is on the contrary valued positively include China, Japan and many Native American ('Indian') cultures. E.T. Hall's various books provide us with several examples of the latter; I will quote one from Pinxten (1994: 95, my translation):

> When an anthropologist discusses an arrangement with a Navajo or an Apache, the Indian will take the time he deems necessary to reach a decision. It is not uncommon to wait for two hours in silence for a reaction to an invitation to cooperate. No alternative proposal, no talk or no attempt whatsoever, no time pressure can change anything to this long, silent reflection.

Uninformed, untrained Westerners will most often attempt to fill this uncomfortable period of silence by talking again themselves. In certain cases, the result may be a virtually complete breakdown in communication, where in addition both parties see their respective negative stereotype of the other reinforced: the white person feels that the Indian is dumb and unable to answer even the simplest questions, the Indian feels that this is again one of these arrogant whites who do all the talking and don't even allow him time to think and reply. Watson (2005:

450 and note p. 781; also Watson & Hill 1984) discusses the concept of what is called 'Apache silence': Apaches observe silence when meeting strangers, during the initial stages of courtship, or with relatives after a long period of separation.

Many documented cases attest that in China and Japan, periods of silence are a common occurrence in the negotiation process (see for instance Chen 1993: 155, Fisher 1980: 55). Conversely, Westerners will often appear in the eyes of Asians as people who never stop talking, and therefore how can they have time to think?[3] A typical scenario of negotiations between a Western and a Japanese or Chinese negotiating team is that the Westerners make an offer, then feel so uncomfortable with the silence that follows that they take turns again, paraphrase or reformulate their offer, or even lower the price because they cannot tolerate the ten or twenty seconds of silence before the reply would be forthcoming.

> During negotiations in Asia, North Americans generally feel so uncomfortable with silence that they make unnecessary concessions. Fear of silence costs Westerners millions of dollars! One Westerner negotiating in Japan dropped his prices, because he took silence to mean a rejection of an offer. On one deal, he dropped his price $750,000 because he couldn't wait out 30 seconds of silence. His Japanese counterpart had thought his first price was fine. In Japan, and among ethnic Chinese, I've seen negotiations in which *10 minutes of silence* followed an offer (Engholm 1991: 141-2).[4]

Mistaken attribution (in this case, erroneously attributing the meaning of disapproval or rejection to silence by the other party) can be a very costly affair!

In addition, the more a Westerner presses the Japanese for a clear and direct answer, the longer they may remain silent, because they are thinking of ways to avoid giving a direct answer (Condon 1984: 41; see also 5.4 below). Then the Westerner may press even more urgently for an answer, and a vicious circle of misunderstandings and irritation may arise.

3.2 Punctuality

> **India: an invitation to a dinner party**
>
> Two Polish diplomats, husband and wife, arrive in New Delhi, their new diplomatic post. A few days later, they are invited by a wealthy Indian businessman for a dinner party. When they ask at what time they are expected to arrive at their host's house, he replies that they can come around seven o'clock.
>
> On the given day, they decide not to have any snacks after lunchtime, for they expect a lavish dinner and want to be able to honor it properly. They calculate with precision how much time they need to travel to their host's house, and they arrive there at 7 p.m. sharp.
>
> They ring the doorbell, and a servant opens the door. He stares at them in disbelief, and they immediately feel that something is terribly wrong. Their first idea is that, perhaps, they got the date wrong; they ask the servant if this is the day there is supposed to be a dinner party in the house.

> 'Oh, yes, yes, he replies, please come in.'
>
> They are shown into a large room where they can take a seat. Some time later, the host enters the room, greets them, and then disappears again. The next guest arrives at nine o'clock, i.e., two hours later. Most people arrive at the party between 9: 30 and 10: 00 p.m.
>
> Drinks are served (mainly an expensive brand of scotch whisky), but no food. The Polish couple, who have not had anything to eat for eight to ten hours now, feel obliged to participate and drink several glasses of whiskey on their empty stomach.
>
> Around midnight, a lavish buffet dinner is served. All the guests rush toward the food and start eating. As soon as the meal is finished, everyone leaves immediately, and the party is over.

The story above illustrates the fact that people in different parts of the world structure the chronological unfolding of a simple event such as a dinner party very differently. Firstly, there may be a *time lag* between the stated time and the time an event is really to start or take place. Many parameters influence the extent of this time lag: it will not be the same for an airplane leaving, for a business appointment, or for a dinner party. But overall, the degree of punctuality will not be identical in different cultures (I use the term 'punctuality' descriptively, without attaching any positive or negative connotations to it).

In some countries, including the United States and Switzerland as well as many but not all South-East Asian countries (Engholm 1991: 97), there is virtually no time lag between the stated time and the real starting time of the event. When invited to someone's home in these countries, guests are expected to arrive at the stated time, and they can be perhaps five minutes 'late' at most. In Belgium, it is entirely acceptable to arrive some 15-20 minutes or so after the stated time for a dinner party; in France (Paris), the time lag is probably between twenty and thirty minutes for this situation. If the foreign guests were to arrive at eight o'clock sharp for an eight o'clock dinner in Paris, this would cause some embarrassment, for the hosts would not be ready to receive their guests: they might still be in the kitchen, or setting the table, or getting dressed.

Of course figures such as those I mention here have no mathematical precision, and situational factors no doubt play a major role: someone's punctuality may be very different at the office and during leisure time, and standards may not be the same for a business meeting as they are for a dinner party.

One should also beware of stereotypes, here as elsewhere. Some accounts describe the Polish as not being punctual, but I suspect that these accounts are based on a stereotype rather than on real observation in situ. Richmond (1995: 66) describes Poles as not being punctual in private, when receiving in their home. In my experience, the Polish people *are* punctual. On an official visit to NATO headquarters in Brussels, President Lech Walesa of Poland was the victim of a minor diplomatic incident: when his motorcade arrived, strictly on schedule, there was no NATO official at the door to welcome him. They had all assumed that, being Polish, he was bound to arrive late...

In the previous edition of this book, I wrote that I knew of no culture where it is consistently acceptable and appropriate to arrive earlier than the stated time. As soon as the book was in print, I found out I was very probably wrong. In several South-East Asian countries, including Japan (Hidasi 1995b: 34), Vietnam and China, it appears to be polite for guests to arrive five minutes early or more. This may be due to the face saving factor which we will discuss in detail below: arriving later might convey the meaning that you were not very keen on honoring the invitation, that you had more important things to attend.

Cultures where the time lag is very large (two hours or more) include countries as diverse as the Philippines, Brazil and India. The example of the dinner party tells us a number of things about the way culturally acquired features work, such as the following.

Many (though not all) culturally defined features are acquired and implemented unconsciously by the members of a given culture. French children are never taught by their parents, or at school, that they are expected to arrive some 20-30 minutes after the stated time for a dinner engagement; they learn it through immersion in their native culture. French guests do not decide consciously (by looking at their watch, for instance), to be 20-30 minutes late; it just happens 'automatically.'

In other words, the temporal framework is rarely made explicit in a specific culture. There may be some exceptions. In Mexico, Seelye & Seelye-James (1995: 26) claim, two frameworks exist side by side and can be referred to explicitly. When a time is stated, one can specify whether this is to be taken according to *hora mexicana,* meaning that a time lag is tolerated, or according to *hora americana*, meaning that punctuality is expected. I have to add, though, that my Mexican or other Latin American students say they never use this system.

Not only is the time lag between the stated time and the real starting time of the event different depending on the culture (ranging from a couple of minutes to two-three hours), the way in which a complex event is structured also differs. We can decompose a dinner party into three basic subparts:
a. pre-dinner talk and drinks
b. the dinner itself
c. after dinner conversation and drinks

The average duration of each of the subparts varies widely depending on the culture, and some subparts may be virtually absent. In France, (a) will take perhaps one hour, (b) two hours or more, and (c) may go on for a long time in certain cases. As the story above showed us, in India (a) is very long (approximately three hours), (b) brief (perhaps one hour), and (c) almost non-existent.[5] Combined with the fact that the entire event starts later in India, the result is that in India one will start eating at a time when dinner is long over in France:

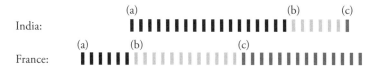

(where a = pre-dinner, b = dinner, c = after dinner; 1 square = 10 minutes)

Figure 12. temporal structure of a dinner party in India and France.

If the guests in India come from some other Western countries such as Germany or the US, the discrepancy will be even larger between the time they expect to eat and the time food will really be served. Every reader can determine how the dinner party event is likely to be structured in his/her own culture, and what the respective duration of the subparts will be.

3.3 Temporal structure of a negotiation

Other, more complex events can be analyzed in the same way as we did for the dinner party above. Let us consider a business negotiation. We can decompose the process into four basic subcomponents:
a. getting acquainted with the other party
b. negotiating and consulting
c. deciding
d. implementing the decision

Here also, the relative importance and the duration of each of the subparts will vary widely depending on the culture.

Getting acquainted

There is no culture on earth where one starts talking business without at least some preliminaries. The very first sentence you utter when you meet your business partner will not be something like 'Our asking price is...'. When two American or Dutch businesspeople meet, these preliminaries are likely to be limited to a couple of sentences, such as 'did you have a nice flight?', 'how is the weather back home?', and the like. As soon as they settle in the office, the two parties may start discussing business, i.e., move to stage (b). Stage (a) is limited to a number of minutes, nothing more.

In France, the situation is different. Before they start talking business, the two parties who meet for the first time are likely to have an extended lunch together, lasting perhaps two hours or more. The function of the business lunch in France has been described by Vincent Merk (1986, 1989). It serves to probe the background of the other party, in particular his/her educational and cultural background – not to talk business, except sometimes at the very end.

In Arab countries, the process of getting acquainted which precedes business negotiations may last for weeks or for months.

> [T]he best salesmen [in Kuwait] were not necessarily the most dapper, eager, or efficient. The most successful ones were those who were relaxed, personable, and patient enough to establish friendly personal relations with their clients (Nydell 1987: 25).

Arabs may want to probe the character and the moral standing of their business partner extensively before they decide they can do business with him/her:[6] respectability and trust are crucial. If a company changes negotiators in midstream, the process of getting acquainted will have to start all over again.

In Arab countries it is almost always necessary to be introduced by someone your partners already know and trust. This intermediary will be a first guarantee of your own moral standards and respectability. In many South-East Asian countries as well, an intermediary who introduces you vouches for your trustworthiness. This means that introducing someone is not done lightly, for the introducer's personal integrity and reliability are at stake:

> To save his own face, [an] Asian introducer was impelled to pay back all of the losses incurred by the Asian associates (friends) to whom he had introduced [an] American [who bungled a real estate deal] (Engholm 1991: 86).

In many Latin American, Asian and African countries, building up trust is essential in a business relation and may take a long time. At the very least, a number of days will be spent getting acquainted with the other party. This may consist of taking the visiting party on a sightseeing tour, having lunch, dinner or organizing banquets, taking the party to meet government officials, etc. Western delegations may feel that they are made to lose valuable time. In fact, toasting and speeches at banquets, luncheons and dinners are an essential element of the process of getting acquainted in most East and South-East Asian countries (Engholm 1991: 193-4). The Japanese like the Chinese will open with long speeches expressing goodwill and hopes for the future (Chen 1993: 152). In the People's Republic of China, excursions and sightseeing tours organized by your Chinese hosts often take up 30% to 50% of the time you spend in the country.

In many African countries, getting anything done depends almost entirely on knowing the right people. You may have all the necessary documents to get your goods through customs, but if you do not know anyone at the customs office, chances are that the goods will never arrive at their destination. It is absolutely essential to build up networks of people (held together by mutual indebtedness; see below) you can rely on for information and help.

Looking for links: an African passenger at Brussels airport

One of the check-in agents at Brussels airport is from the Indian subcontinent: he has dark skin, but his physical features are anything but African.

When confronted with an African passenger with excess luggage, the check-in agent applies the rules, i.e., tells the passenger that he will have to pay a surcharge for the overweight luggage.

More than once the African passenger reacts as follows: 'How can you do this to me, you are my brother, we have the same skin color!'

To people coming from cultures where being acquainted with the other is more important than rules and regulations in getting things done, the Western way of doing business will seem cold and impersonal: how can you deny a favor to a friend because of a rule that is written on a piece of paper?

The refusal to enter into a personal relationship may seem equally strange. Pinto (1990: 160) tells the story of a Moroccan migrant worker who receives friendly help from a clerk at city hall in a Dutch town in filling out the necessary documents. When the Moroccan worker returns with a small gift for the clerk, the latter refuses to accept it. To the Moroccan worker, this reaction is like refusing to acknowledge a human relation which was established the first time they met.

The importance of establishing networks of people you know and can rely on is equally essential in most Asian countries. With ethnic Chinese, these are called *guanxi* ('webs', 'networks'). Guanxi, as often described, provide the Chinese entrepreneur with anything from business opportunities to credit lines, help in need and protection against outsiders (Luo 1997, Tsang 1998). It is obvious that in such a culture, 'cold calling' potential customers will not work: no-one accepts to do business with a person one does not know, let alone with a person one has never met. Engholm (1991: 86) rightly says that cold-calling potential customers is a strictly Western business practice; there are few other places in the world where it might be effective.

In Japan also, the relation between supplier and customer is slowly built up over time. A customer may place a small order first, and then gradually place larger orders as the relationship builds up (Yoshimura & Anderson 1997: 220). In such a long-term relationship, price is not the most important criterion when placing a new order (Engholm 1991: 72).

Westerners who embark on business ventures in other parts of the world will be forced to accept that it may take a very long time to close a deal in many, many cultures, ranging from Central and Eastern Europe to the east of the Asian continent, and elsewhere:

> Transactions between people are made on a personal basis after credibility and trust have been established. That requires time and explains why it takes weeks, months, and sometimes years to get things done [...] (Richmond 1995: 7, about East Europeans)

> In Asia, the business courting process that precedes substantive contract negotiations can take months or even years (Engholm 1991: 285).

Lane, DiStefano & Maznevski (2000: 12) quote real-life cases where it took one company nine years to close a deal in the USSR, another (General Motors' Diesel Division, which manufactures diesel locomotives) seven years to make a sale to Indonesia. Not surprisingly, the longest delays are to be expected when dealing with governments and authorities. In China also, negotiations may last for months or years (Chen 1993: 154).

Historical links may be considered important in establishing a working relationship. In many Asian countries including Japan and China, business negotiations are likely to begin with a general presentation of the company, including, if possible, references to historic links between the two countries or companies. It is recommended that you do some research on such possible links before you travel to these countries, and you may be surprised to discover that your company has done business in Shanghai around the turn of the 20th century, or that one of your uncles worked in Vietnam in the 1920s... How many Belgians are aware of the fact that King Chulalongkorn, who modernized many aspects of Thai society around the turn of the 20th century, relied very heavily on his 'General Advisor' Gustave Rolin-Jaequemyns, a former Belgian government minister, for his reforms between 1892 and 1901, and that virtually all of the King's advisers involved in the legal reform which was crucial to preserve Siam's independence, were Belgian (see for instance Tips 1996)? My own University of Antwerp, then School of Commerce, played a crucial role, in the early 20th century, in setting up the first major business school in Japan, now part of the prestigious Hitotsubashi University in Tokyo. If you really look for historical links, you may well be surprised to find them.

Negotiating and consulting

There exist (at least) two basic ways to structure the timing of the negotiation process itself, which we could call respectively
a. 'zooming in': start with the general idea and then gradually move towards closer detail
b. 'zooming out': start with the details and work your way up to the general agreement.

Procedure (a) appears to be more typical for Japanese and Chinese culture, (b) for many Western negotiators. As a first serious step during the negotiation process, the Japanese will often suggest that both parties sign some kind of statement of intent, a letter of mutual co-operation. For the Japanese, this statement engages the honor of both parties, and once it is agreed, the technical people can be relied upon to work out the details of the contract itself. The drafting of the written contract, and especially bringing in lawyers, should be left for the final phase, and the contract is likely to be more informal, shorter and less worked out in detail anyway (Pye 1992; Chen 1993; Engholm 1991: 71, 159-60; Hendry 2003: 238).

For many Westerners, signing such a statement of intent may seem meaningless, for how can we be assured that we will really cooperate on this venture before we have worked out the details? And besides, this letter of co-operation is not legally binding anyway, so what is the use in signing it? Westerners will want to discuss price, payment and delivery terms, warranty and all else, and when there are no further disagreements about all these, then we have a contract (in fact, all these details together *are* the contract). The two procedures, zooming in or zooming out, are incompatible, and the different views on how to start the negotiation process may cause irritation and frustration between Japanese and Western negotiators.

In China also, negotiations start with general principles, and the details are to be filled in later. Americans (and Europeans) may feel at the beginning that they are losing their time with 'mere rhetoric' (Pye 1992). The Chinese are 'more interested in long-standing sincere commitment to working together than [...] in seemingly perfect contract packages' (Chen 1993: 148).

> The biggest difference in the negotiation process between Americans and Asians is the motivations of the parties to enter into negotiations. Americans meet to make a deal while East Asians meet primarily to establish and develop a relationship (Paik & Tung 1999: 115).

Once the negotiations have really begun, how do you proceed from the starting point to the end? Judith Hidasi (1995a: 73) compares the Japanese approach to business negotiations with a *spiral,* circling around the core issue and moving gradually closer, but not in a linear, straight-to-the-point kind of way. General considerations, side issues, vaguely related points will be explored first, the grounds will be probed. One of my trainees who does business with Japanese frequently described the first conversations in the negotiating process as 'woolly'. In cultures where face saving and harmony are essential (see below), this is a way of avoiding open confrontation and possible loss of face. If the core issues (price,[7] warranty, payment terms, and the like) were to be addressed directly and openly, it is almost inevitable that disagreements between the parties would arise, and this must be avoided at all cost. As a result, in particular in the first stages of the negotiation process in Japan, Western negotiators will frequently be under the impression that they are getting nowhere, that no progress is being made. In China also, confrontational issues will be held off (Chen 1993: 151), though possibly to a lesser extent than in Japan. Koreans are reported as being more straightforward and forthright than both Japanese and Chinese negotiators (Paik & Tung 1999).

In addition, Japanese presentation style is 'explanation first' (Kameda 2005: 36). The origin of something, side considerations, etc. will be presented, and this may take quite some time, before the core issue or the conclusion is addressed.

On the other hand, in Japan the consultation process is more extensive than in the West. A new proposal will be discussed at many levels of the hierarchy in the company, and gradually a consensus will be built where everyone's opinion is considered and if possible taken into account. Whenever a manager formulates a proposition, this will be discussed informally, often after work, and everybody's concerns should be taken into consideration in order to produce a document *(ringi-sho)* which reflects a decision to be taken. The ringhi-sho is a document that everyone has to sign, and this process starts at bottom of the decision-making hierarchy and is based on consensus. Japanese decision-making is therefore often described as bottom-up decision making. Yoshimura & Anderson (1991: 165, 179, 233) describe this process well, yet question how 'democratic' it really is. In any case, when the ringi-sho is circulated to department managers and top-level executives for approval, consensus about the decision to be taken has already been established. At the highest meeting where the decision needs to be approved, there will not be any reservations about it in anyone's mind (Varner & Beamer 1995: 204). In fact, top management will often go where middle management (where the decisions originate) wants it to go.

Because of all this, negotiations which to a Western delegation are likely to last a couple of days or weeks may in reality go on over a period of months or even years. Usunier (1996: 261-271) describes the case of a French manufacturer of duvets (comforters) who explores the possibilities of importing his product into Japan. The first contacts with the Japanese take place in 1983, and the Japanese seem to be genuinely interested in the French product. *Seven years* and many episodes later there is still no deal, but it is still possible that one day in the future the Japanese will be satisfied and start importing the product.

In brief, the very long time (in Western eyes) it takes for the Japanese to decide is caused by a combination of (at least) four factors.
- Japanese negotiating style: spiraling around the issue rather than going to the core problem in a straight line (because of the need for saving face and preserving harmony).
- The emphasis on process as against result: in Japan, doing things 'the right way' is as important as achieving results, and subsequent evaluation may focus more on the process than on the results that were obtained, such as achieving targets or goals (Yoshimura & Anderson 1997: 88, 163).
- The consultation process in the Japanese company, as described above.
- Japanese perfectionism and the process of incremental improvements *(kaizen)*.

In the case of the duvets, the French company is asked many times over to modify the product: first the size (for obvious reasons: Japanese beds are smaller), then the colors, etc. Then the Japanese complain about the fact that when you shake the duvet, some dust falls out through the pores in the fabric. With Japanese (and German!) duvets, this does not happen. After various improvements, the amount of dust that falls out diminishes, but does not disappear completely. The French are willing to put their product on the Japanese markets as it is, confident that the Japanese customer may buy it; but the Japanese partners refuse to go along with that. The Japanese are unwilling to put on the Japanese market a product with the label 'made in France' which would be less than perfect. In fact, they seem more worried about the long-term damage this might cause to the label 'made in France' than the French themselves!

If the other party seems slow, pressing for a speedy decision may have the opposite effect. The other party may grow suspicious (Nydell 1987: 61, about Arabs), or else, the arguments used to press for a decision may fall flat because the other party does not share the same time frame. In the West, time is seen as a commodity with a limited supply, but in the Middle East, there is no idea of scarcity attached to the time it takes to negotiate (Faure & Rubin 1993: 11). In international negotiations, many Westerners are literally handicapped by their representation of time as something which is always in danger of being 'lost' if not allocated in the most efficient way (Biguma & Usunier 1991: 111).

Pressing for a decision in an Arab country

When a European delegation attempted to sell a turnkey hospital in an Arab country, one of its members tried to press for a speedy decision by arguing that the present health facilities were seriously inadequate in the town where the hospital was to be built. The Arab answer was: 'Sir, we have been living here for centuries without your hospital; a few more years won't make that much of a difference.'

In addition, in many cultures the process is as important, or more important, than the results one achieves during the negotiation (Faure & Rubin 1993: 9). The negotiation process then becomes some kind of an aim in itself, and signing an agreement as well as its subsequent implementation are only one, possibly minor, element in that process.

Deciding

In many cases, the decision itself will take the shape of a written contract: a piece of paper with signatures at the bottom. However, this is not always so, even today. In cultures or groups where trust is high, striking a deal may take the form of a handshake (as with cattle dealers in some European countries) or an oral promise. In the close-knit circle of diamond traders in Antwerp, very expensive diamonds are often lent to other brokers (for a potential customer to examine the diamonds); usually nothing is written down, no receipts are issued.

Even if there is a written contract, it does not necessarily have the same value in other cultures as in the West. The relationship and trust between the parties may prevail over the text of the contract. In many countries in the Arab world and in Asia, the contract is better considered as a declaration of the intent of a mutually fruitful co-operation than as a text which is legally binding in all its details. The contract may be seen as marking the end of the first stage in business dealings, not the final agreement (Chen 1993: 148, about China; Fisher 1980: 47, about Japan). If the situation changes, if something unforeseen happens, it is expected that (parts of) the contract can be modified or renegotiated.

In Japan, 'unforeseen circumstances' are a legal concept that makes renegotiating an agreement compulsory, if requested by the other party (Naoki Kameda, personal communication). Hendry (2003: 238), as many others, stresses that Japanese contracts are much more informal that in the West and the agreement between the negotiating parties is based on 'goodwill'.

In general, renegotiating (Engholm 1991: 159-60) is in almost all cases preferable to forcing an unwilling partner (who, if you act that way, will try to find another way out and will never do business with you again in the future) to implement the letter of the contract that was signed earlier.

The term 'decision making' itself may imply a Western approach to the whole process. The president of a Japanese corporation suggested to an American audience that 'decision making' is not applicable to the Japanese and that something like 'direction-taking' might be better (Fisher 1980: 32).

When there is a dispute, bringing the case to court may not be a realistic option in many countries. Courts may tend to favor the locals over the foreign company, as in Saudi-Arabia. In Japan, court cases involving disputes between companies are extremely rare. The two parties will do everything to find an arrangement among themselves because going to court is too shameful for all parties involved. In that country, bringing a case to court may even lead to social ostracism (Hendry 2003: 237). Bringing a lawyer to a business negotiation may be seen by the Japanese as a sign of mistrust, certainly in the initial stages. For an overview of the issues of *compliance with agreements* in cross-cultural transactions, see Thompson (1996).

Implementing the decision

Once the decision is made, it still needs to be implemented. In Western culture, implementation must start as soon as possible and must be completed speedily. In Japan, even if the negotiations may be lengthy (in Western eyes), implementation can take place at the speed of light once the decision is reached (see also Fisher 1980: 33).

This conception, however, runs counter to what is common in many other countries throughout the world. Western companies often complain about the fact that deadlines are not kept, and completing a project may drag on seemingly endlessly.

In Latin cultures (such as in Latin America), there is the well-known concept of *mañana* (literally: 'tomorrow'). What this means is that deadlines are not taken as literally as in the West; but eventually, the work will be completed. Because of the fact that *mañana* means something like 'sometime in the future', it is vain to try and pin down people in Mexico, for instance, on a precise date; this simply will not work (Seelye & Seelye-James 1995: 167-9), even if you offer money to the person involved. Offering money to a Mexican customs agent does not modify the definition of *mañana* that is stored in his brain.

A comparison might be helpful here. Suppose you arrive at an appointment you made with someone, and the person who is waiting for you says: 'hey, you are thirty seconds late!' While this may actually be *true* (you arrived at 2: 30: 30 for your 2: 30: 00 appointment), the remark will seem absurd, because such a small breach of the deadline, you feel, is immaterial. But if a delay of 30 seconds seems immaterial to you, in some cultures the same may be true for 30 minutes, or three days, or thirty days...

Latin America: setting up a computer system demonstration

A Latin American country showed interest in buying the computer software system that was used successfully by the Belgian central government. The Belgians decided to send a team of computer specialists over to organize a demonstration of the system. This involved a complex operation of setting up and connecting the necessary computers for a realistic demonstration, then installing the software.

As the Belgian team would only be in the country for five days (Monday to Friday), they wanted to be sure that the necessary hardware was set up *before* they arrived. In that way, they would have two days for installing and testing the software, and three days for the actual demonstration. They gave very detailed instructions as to the necessary computers and their hook-up, and they got clear assurances from their hosts that all the hardware would be ready to use when they arrived.

Upon arrival, it appeared that their hosts had not even started putting the necessary computers in a room. The Belgians were on what they themselves described as a 'forced vacation': they were housed in a very nice hotel, taken on sightseeing tours, and generally taken very good care of by their hosts.

By Wednesday evening, the hardware had been set up. The Belgians rushed into installing and testing the software they had brought with them, and the demonstration, originally planned to go on for three days, took place on Friday afternoon, just before they left the country.

A similar attitude may prevail in Arab countries:

> Frequently, an Arab shopkeeper or someone in a service trade fails to have something done by a promised time. Be flexible; everyone expects delays. You will appear unreasonably impatient and demanding if you insist on having things finished at a precise time (Nydell 1987: 60).

Many projects around the world remain unfinished, and that is not always because the necessary funds are missing. In extreme cases, the concept of 'closure' (finishing off a task that was started) may be entirely absent. Hall (1983: 32-3) describes how the Hopi Indians in the United States used to leave many of their houses unfinished: the walls would be built, the windows inserted, the material to put the roof in place is there, but the roof is never put on top of the house, so the house is not inhabitable.

> Everything was ready – waiting for what looked like three weeks' work on the part of two or three men – and there the house would sit for years. Questions by whites as to when the house would be finished were treated as non sequiturs – which they were to the Hopi.

It is not that the Hopi are incapable of following precise schedules. As Hall points out, their ceremonies are clearly scheduled: a Hopi marriage includes as many as twenty-six different events spanning an entire year (Hall 1983: 39). Rather, it is that completing buildings is not an important issue for them: they are not living entities, 'therefore have no inherent schedule'; in the past, 'a house could have taken twenty years to build' (Hall 1976: 145).

The conclusion is clear. A deadline for a particular task or event (clearing goods through customs; finishing a report; paying an invoice) may have zero built-in flexibility in some cultures such as the US or Switzerland, where, if payment of an invoice is due on September 30, paying it on October 1st means *you are late.* On the other hand a deadline for completion may have a flexibility extending to infinity, as in the Hopi example described above.

If both those extremes are attested, chances are that we will find cultures that are located, in this respect, anywhere between these two extremes. For example, in France the flexibility for a deadline which involves paying an invoice is a couple of weeks or a month after the date due; this causes a lot of the dismay to the Dutch or German supplier where the flexibility in this case is near zero.

3.4 Short vs. long term orientation

> When Zhou En-lai, then Minister of Foreign Affairs of the people's Republic of China, was asked whether the French Revolution (1789!) had been being beneficial or not, he replied: "It's too early to tell" (Nisbett 2005: 13).

The teachings of Confucius stress the importance of the family as the prototype for society (with aspects such as harmony, dignity and face saving) and virtuous behavior such as working hard, thrift, patience, perseverance and moderation. In the *Chinese Values* Survey (Bond, in Hofstede 1991; see also Hofstede & Bond 1988), both poles of the fourth CVS dimension are composed of values that seem to be inspired by Confucius; but on one pole, we find values that are more concerned with the short term, and on the other pole values more concerned with long-term orientation (Hofstede 1991: 166):

Long-term orientation	Short-term orientation
Persistence, perseverance	Personal steadiness and stability
Ordering relation by status and observing this order	Protecting your face
Thrift	Respect for tradition
Having a sense of shame	Reciprocation of greetings, favors and gifts

The scores of the 23 countries that were surveyed with the CVS are given in the chart below (F13).

Score rank	Country or region	LTO score
1	China	118
2	Hong Kong	96
3	Taiwan	87
4	Japan	80
5	South Korea	75
6	Brazil	65
7	India	61
8	Thailand	56
9	Singapore	48
10	Netherlands	44
11	Bangladesh	40
12	Sweden	33
13	Poland	32
14	Germany FR	31
15	Australia	31
16	New Zealand	30
17	USA	29
18	Great Britain	25
19	Zimbabwe	25
20	Canada	23
21	Philippines	19
22	Nigeria	16
23	Pakistan	00

Figure 13. Long term vs. Short term orientation: country scores.

The following tendencies are clearly visible in those scores.
- Three Chinese territories occupy the first three positions with respect to long-term orientation: China, Hong Kong and Taiwan.
- Many Asian countries, and in particular, East Asia, exhibit higher long-term orientation. Asian countries represent eight out of the ten top scores, and most of them are East Asian. Notorious exceptions in this respect are the Philippines and Pakistan.
- Anglo-Saxon countries score lower than other Western countries: Australia, New Zealand, the United States, Great Britain and Canada have lower scores than the Ne)therlands, Sweden, Poland and Germany. There is ample inde-

pendent evidence that the lower LTO scores of countries like the US and the UK reflect the truth. Lane, DiStefano & Maznevski (2000: 29), among many others, mention that little long-term planning goes on in United States companies. Beldona, Inkpen & Phatak (1998) find that Japanese managers are more long-term oriented than US managers.
- Although only two African countries were surveyed, it is no accident that they exhibit low scores. Independent evidence suggests that African countries (and West and Central African countries even more than East and Southern African) are geared towards the short term.

> *Ancestors planted the trees, descendants enjoy the shade* (Chinese proverb)

Hofstede (1991: 167) explicitly establishes a correlation between the long-term orientation of several East and South-East Asians nations (their 'Confucian values') and their economic growth in recent years.

> The correlation between *certain* Confucian values and economic growth over the past decade is a surprising, even sensational finding.

A high savings quote, companies' strategic planning which is oriented towards the long-term (with more emphasis on increasing market share than on quick profits) and the capacity to integrate Western technology with traditional values are supposedly typical of the rapidly emerging economies of several South-East Asian countries. These cultural values may give South-East Asian countries a competitive advantage in the modern world.

Hofstede contrasts this with the dominant cultural values in many Muslim countries.

> Contrary to what happens in East Asia, many opinion leaders in the Muslim world seem to interpret modern technology and Western ideas as a threat rather than as an opportunity (Hofstede 1991: 172).

The East and South-East Asians' tendency towards integration and synthesis rather than mutual exclusion of different systems and sets of ideas may explain why they react so differently to modernism and Western influence from cultures whose ultimate truth is based on the Book (the Bible, the Koran).

According to Tobin (1994) the Japanese *domesticate* foreign customs [...]. The Japanese are not passive receptacles of Western influence, but active shoppers in a global bazaar, picking what they want, before turning it into something of their own.

We will discuss be possible link between certain cultural features and economic growth under 15.3 below.

Some key differences between short-term and long-term orientation societies are summarized in the chart below (after Hofstede 1991: 173).

Short-term orientation	Long-term orientation
Social pressure to 'keep up with the Joneses' even if it means overspending	Thrift, being spare with resources
Small savings quote, little money for investment	Large savings quote, funds available for investment
Quick results expected	Perseverance towards slow results
Concern with 'face'	Willingness to subordinate oneself for a purpose
Concern with possessing the Truth	Concern with respecting the demands of Virtue

3.5 Time and tasks: polychrony vs. monochrony

The concepts of monochrony and polychrony were introduced by Edward T. Hall (1983: 44-58 and elsewhere). Put very simply, in a more monochronic culture people will tend to engage in only one activity at a time, and move to the next task only when the previous one is finished; in a more polychronic culture, people will tend to spread their attention over the different tasks or activities that present themselves before them, and move from one to the other, back and forth, in rapid succession.

My best chance of experiencing polychrony without travelling is to pay a visit to my Moroccan butcher's store in Brussels. In a Belgian (or American, or Dutch...) grocery store, customers are being helped in order of arrival: A, who arrived first, will get all the items she orders, then she pays, and only then the grocer will turn his attention to B; who arrived second; after B has been helped and has paid, he turns to C, and so on. In fact, often customer B does not even get any eye contact from the shopkeeper as long as he is busy with A; in a way, before it is your turn you do not exist. In the Moroccan store, however, chances are that the temporal structure of the process of helping customers will be very different. My Moroccan butcher tends to spread out his attention over the customers who are in his store. Customer A may order one item and get it, but then the butcher will ask B what he needs, then he moves back to A or to C, etc. Once, when I was finished ordering, I paid with a large bill; between taking this large bill from me and returning my change, the butcher helped another customer! In other words, even a sequence of two actions that are as closely related as paying and getting back the change may be broken up by another, unrelated action.

The difference between polychronic and monochronic structuring of time permeates many aspects of life, ranging from standing in line (go skiing in France one year, in Germany the next, you will notice the difference when you are standing in line, together with twenty other skiers, to take the ski lift) to keeping and appointments and sticking to schedules.

Mediterranean cultures, including France and Italy, tend to be more polychronic than Northern European or North American cultures.[8] Take a German office worker, confronted with the following tasks: making four telephone calls, writing two letters, reading a report. He or she will *order* these tasks, and then perform them with minimal overlap: start writing the second letter only after the first one is finished, etc. A French office worker may have two word processing files open, and move from the first to the second letter several times, while at the same time the report is also open on his or her desk and the office worker reads a section of it from time to time, and, while reading, dials the telephone number of one of his/her correspondents, who may have to wait a couple of seconds when answering because our office worker finishes reading a sentence in the report...

Extreme cases of polychrony are frequently reported to occur in the Arab world. An Arab official may actually receive two delegations who are competing for the same government tender in his office at the same time, and he will discuss your competitors' offer with them for a couple of minutes, then turn to you, but meanwhile his secretary comes in and he needs to sign some letters, and then suddenly he picks up the telephone and starts a telephone conversation while saying to you: 'please continue, I am listening', and then tea and biscuits are being served to everyone in the room, and then... You will rarely have this person's undivided attention for more than a couple of minutes at most, and there is no way you could give him a 15-minute presentation of your bid.

> Arabs have a great tolerance for noise and interference during discussions […]. Businessmen interrupt meetings to greet callers, answer the telephone and sign papers brought in by clerks (Nydell 1987: 104).

There are accounts of overlapping meetings in Arab countries: two meetings about different topics take place in the same room, and some of the attendants participate in both meetings at the same time. There are even accounts of a medical doctor seeing two patients at the same time – while at the same time engaging in small talk with those patients he knows personally (Varner & Beamer 1995: 157).

Polychronic experiences tend to be stressful and frustrating for people from monochronic cultures, because they feel as though they are losing their familiar reference points: there is no clear order in the store or in the line, 'whose turn is it now?' Is a meaningless question, no proper attention is being paid to what one says, etc.

> In Latin America and the Middle East, North Americans[9] can frequently be psychologically stressed. Immersed in a polychronic environment in the markets, stores and souks of Mediterranean and Arab countries, one is surrounded by other customers all vying for the attention of a single clerk who is trying to wait on everyone at once. There is no recognized order as to who is to be served next, no queue or numbers to indicate who has been waiting the longest. To the North European or American, it appears that confusion and clamour abound (Hall 1983: 47).

It goes without saying that from an intercultural point of view, one way of structuring time is not superior to the other, and to my knowledge there is no evidence that the monochronic way of structuring time is more efficient than the polychronic way; it might as well be the other way around, or else there might be no difference at all in terms of productivity. Some Western experts recommend *multitasking,* and this seems closely related to polychrony. Hall (1983: 49) rightly points out that monochronic scheduling may be counterproductive in some cases. Nonis, Teng & Ford (2005) acknowledge that some studies suggest polychrony is negatively related to performance and that monochronic time management is superior; however, they also present clear evidence of cases where polychronics perform better, and cases where there is no measurable differences between the two styles. Leonard (2008) finds that in the three countries she surveyed (the USA, India and Venezuela), as polychronicity increases, job satisfaction also increases.

If polychrony is stressful to a more monochronically oriented person, the extreme monochrony of some Western cultures may seem absurd to a more polychronically oriented person, as in the story below.

> A Turkish graduate student, shortly after arriving in Belgium, went to a travel agency to pick up some brochures, as she was planning on visiting different cities in Europe. However, the brochures were on shelves behind a counter where the travel agents were sitting, and they were all busy with customers who were booking trips. The Turkish woman thought that it was absurd she would have to wait for perhaps 15 minutes or more just to get some brochures, so she attempted to interrupt the proceedings between a travel agent and a customer: she wanted to say something like, "Excuse me, could you just give me some of those brochures that are sitting on the shelf behind you?" But before she could finish her sentence, she was thrown back to the end of the queue with a: "Madam, you have to wait your turn!"
>
> To get 10 seconds of attention, she'd have to wait for 15 minutes…

Patricia Wibaut (2009), one of my students, interviewed a number of Indian people living in Belgium, among whom a Mrs. Shah, who declares:

> In a store in India, several customers are being served at the same time. In Belgium and in most Western countries, customers are used to waiting their turn, until the storekeeper finally turns his attention to them. Mrs. Shah had the feeling that she was being ignored by the storekeeper here. In India, he would quickly lose his customers [my translation].

As the story above illustrates, polychrony and monochrony are not only about structuring time, but also concern relations between people; that makes these concepts different from simple multitasking (Leonard 2008). In a monochronic time structure, the schedule, the queue, are sacred; in a polychronic time structure, the needs of people may take precedence over the schedule. Let us suppose you are desperate because you have to go to a very formal party tonight and you have to get your hair done, but you forgot to make an appointment with your hairdresser. So you call him in panic and explain the situation; but he happens to be fully booked. If your hairdresser is monochronic, he will say "Sorry Madam, I'm fully booked, I cannot take you today"; if he is polychronic, he might say "Well, in fact I'm fully booked, but why don't you come by around 11 o'clock and I'll fit you in somewhere." In the latter case, the schedule will break down a bit, but a human need takes precedence over the inviolability of the schedule.

> **Dominican Republic: monochrony or polychrony?**
>
> The following story was offered to me by a Brazilian who lived in the Dominican Republic for several years. It illustrates how people, when confronted with cultural change, may sometimes 'revert' to the old system quite suddenly.
>
> In small stores in the Dominican Republic, polychrony prevails: there is no clear order in which customers are being served, and the order of arrival is immaterial as to when you will be served. Yet in the large, modern supermarkets, the well-known system with numbers has been installed: you take a number when you arrive, and when your number is called, it is your turn to place your order.
>
> Most of the time, the Dominicans abide by the new system. But sometimes, someone tries to catch the attention of the salesperson before his/her turn. When that happens, all at once the other customers also discard their numbers and 'revert' to the old system, all trying to vie for the attention of the salesclerk simultaneously.

3.6 Some philosophical aspects of time

3.6.1 The arrow of time

Human beings are not born with some kind of innate feeling of time, they acquire it with their culture (Biguma & Usunier 1991: 97).

In Western cultures, a drawing that seems close to representing the intuitive feeling of the time dimension is a line or an arrow. The line is commonly subdivided into three parts: past, present and future.

Figure 14. The arrow of time (Western).

The arrow as it is drawn above represents well the naive[10] Western representation of time, which exhibits the following properties.
a. It is linear and uninterrupted. For Westerners, it goes without saying that time never stops regardless of what they are doing, and that it elapses continuously at the same rate. My clock or watch does not stop ticking at certain moments of the day, nor does it sometimes slow down or accelerate. But of course, *we* build the clocks, and it would not be difficult at all to build one which does run at a variable pace or stops altogether at certain times.
b. Time has three distinct parts, the past, the present and the future, and no overlap between those three is possible. A past event cannot take place again in the future. Also the past is gone forever, and while we can study it historically, we can never go back there.

c. In modern Western society, the emphasis is on the future. It is no accident that the arrow points toward the future, and very hard for Westerners to conceive that it could point toward the past. The future is *ahead of us*, the past is *behind us*. This conception is also interpreted spatially: when asked, people will locate the future in front of themselves and make a gesture pointing to an area in front of their body, and they will locate the past with a gesture pointing toward an area behind their back.
d. The future is open, whereas the past is closed forever. Human beings can (and should) shape their own future, and mankind is responsible for making the future better (and equally responsible if we make it worse). The implicit idea of *progress* is perhaps not as strong any more in the West today as it was in the late 19th century and the beginning of the 20th, with people now perceiving growing threats to the environment, world-wide overpopulation, and so forth. Nevertheless, many values and activities of Westerners are still based on the idea that future progress is possible, from building cleaner cars or financing research against cancer to 'helping' the Third World.

While the above properties of time will seem so obvious and natural to Westerners that it may be hard for them to conceive how they could be otherwise, in reality none of them are universally shared. In fact, the concept of linear time, as well as the idea of progress that now goes with it, are relatively recent, even in the West.

The famous anthropologist Clifford Geertz describes in detail how time in Bali is totally different from our Western view on it:

> Balinese social life lacks climax because it takes place in a motionless present, a vectorless now. Or, equally true, Balinese time lacks motion because Balinese social life lacks climax (1973: 404).
>
> Details aside, the nature of time-reckoning this sort of calendar facilitates is clearly not durational but punctual. That it, it is not used (…) to measure the rate at which time passes, the amount which has passed since the occurrence of some event, or the amount which remains within which to complete some project: it is adapted to and used for distinguishing and classifying discrete, self-subsistent particles of time – "days". The cycles and supercycles are endless, unanchored, uncountable, and, as their internal order has no significance, without climax. They don't tell you what time it is; they tell you what kind of time it is. (1973: 393)
>
> … in the ordinary course of life the Balinese never 'date' anything in our sense of the term. (1973: 398)

Possibly the oldest, and perhaps also the most widespread concept may be that of a cyclical or circular time. Most phenomena that we observe in nature are in fact cyclical and return at regular intervals: the tides, the seasons, the movements of the sun, the moon and the planets (Coveney & Highfield 1990: 25). From there, most cultures including the classical Greeks

> have clung to the comfort of time's cycle, where the past is the future, there is no real 'history' and mankind is resigned to rebirth and renewal (Coveney & Highfield 1990: 26, based on Mircea Eliade).

Evans (2003: 202) also confirms that in classical Greece time was cyclical; according to her, linear time originates from the Hebrew tradition.

According to Shaughnessy (2005: 6),

> [...] like the movement of the dragon, in China time is considered to be cyclical: when what is below moves up, what is above moves down, ready to rise again. This marks a stark contrast with Western notions of time moving in a straight line. It is perhaps easy for us to see that future time eventually becomes past time. Less clear, however, is the notion in Chinese thought and culture that past time also becomes future time, yet this is what lies behind the famous saying of Sima Qian (ca. 145-86BCE), China's first great historian: "Those who do not forget the past are the masters of the future."

In Hinduism also, time is cyclical. In fact our era, the *kali yugua,* is the worst of all eras, and this era of 432 000 years will be followed by a Golden Age (Narayanan 2004).

According to Lewis (2008: 12) Zoroaster's philosophy is probably the first example of linear (vs. cyclical) time. Only with the Judaeo-Christian tradition does linear, 'irreversible' time become firmly established in Western culture (Coveney & Highfield 1990: 26).

The idea of progress and a better future is much more recent still. Medieval Europeans lived with the idea that progress was either vain or impossible. In medieval Europe, innovation was sinful, invention immoral, and reference to the past obligatory (Le Goff 1982: 299). The idea of linear progress originated perhaps with the 'discovery' of the world which Europeans started in the 16th century, but is in fact not attested before the 18th century,[11] and is mainly a product of technical progress (steam engines and railroads, telegraph and telephone, vaccines and medicines, etc.) achieved during the 19th century.

'Progress' in the early 20th century

'This belief in fatal and continuous 'Progress' had, in those days, the strength of a religious creed. Some already believed in 'Progress' more than in the Bible, and this gospel seemed to be irrefutably confirmed by the ever new wonders of science and technology.'

Stefan Zweig, *The World of Yesterday* (autobiography) [my translation]

Before we discuss the past and the future in more detail we shall consider another aspect of the time dimension: event-linked time.

3.6.2 Event-linked time (procedural time)

Biguma & Usunier (1991: 100-5) distinguish three basic culture-specific concepts of time.

a. Traditional procedural time: time is shaped by events, no arrow of time.

b. Traditional circular time: polychrony, geared towards the present, no 'economic' dimension of time, dominant in 'Latin' countries.
c. Linear-separable time: monochrony, geared towards the future, interpreted in economic terms, dominant in 'Anglo' countries.

In what follows, we examine the contents and implications of type (a) as exemplified in Bantu (Central African) culture.

Of course acculturation (partial adaptation to a foreign culture) takes place everywhere, and pure examples of the Bantu conception of time and its consequences in real life may be rare nowadays. Yet many of my African friends, some of whom have lived in Europe for years, retain aspects of the Central African philosophy of time to a surprising degree, and I only started to comprehend and appreciate some of their puzzling behavior after having studied the Bantu concepts related to time, and only then did I cease to be irritated by it. More than once, after a lecture about event-linked time as it is explained below, some people in the audience exclaim: 'Now I understand why my Africans friends act the way they do!' This is not only a corroboration that the analysis I propose has a degree of accuracy; it also illustrates the main function of intercultural training as I see it: bringing people to a better understanding of the other, and thereby eliminating sources of irritation, frustration and conflict.

In the Bantu culture of Central Africa, time is not an abstract dimension ticking away continuously and at the same rate regardless of what we are doing or not doing, and intrinsically quantifiable and measurable. Rather, time is linked to activities or events that relate to you.[12] When I am performing some action or when there are events that relate to me, time (as it relates to me) is elapsing, as when I am writing a letter, or fixing my car, or watching someone else fix my car. But whenever I am not performing any action or referring to any event, time becomes irrelevant or non-existent. This will be the case, for instance, when I am simply sitting in my living room, or outside under a tree, and not engaging in any conversation or other intercourse with others. As there is nothing related to me going on by which time could be measured, the time dimension then ceases to exist or becomes immaterial.

Obviously, in such a culture, 'waiting' does not carry the same meaning as in the West – insofar as it has a meaning in Bantu culture at all. In the West, waiting means losing time, as time elapses continuously whether we are engaging in any activity or not. Westerners are therefore likely to become quickly impatient or annoyed when they have to wait for long. But in Bantu culture, time is not an independent commodity which you can use or lose; it is linked to events or actions taking place. Therefore, when you are 'waiting' (inaction), you are outside this time dimension, and the 'length of time' (in Western eyes) you are 'waiting' (in Western eyes) becomes equally irrelevant.

'Waiting' in African culture: two examples

- While preparing a training seminar for check-in agents of an airline in Brussels, I interviewed a number of agents of the company. More than one expressed surprise at the behavior of Africans when a flight is delayed. While most Western passengers quickly become impatient and start complaining, most Africans remain impassible and do not get upset by the delays.

> - When I was in Bukavu (Congo ex-Zaire) with my African wife in 1993 on a visit to my parents in law, one day around 9 a.m. a repairman came by to fix the refrigerator. My father in law, however, was not home, and the repairman needed his instructions before he could start the work. The repairman then said 'OK, I'll wait for father to return,' and sat down in a chair in the living room. In the middle of the afternoon, close to 4 p.m., the repairman was still sitting in the same chair, without eating or speaking, virtually without moving at all.

It is worth comparing the stories above with some of Hall's observations:

> As a young man working on Indian reservations, I often saw Navajos and Hopi patiently waiting around at trading posts at the agency in Keams Canyon, Arizona, or at the hospitals in Keams and in Winslow. I realized that it was not possible to imagine myself in their shoes. There was a different quality to the Indian's waiting from my own. In this respect I was no different from other white men. We were all impatient, always looking at our watches or the clock on the wall, muttering or fidgeting. Yet an Indian might come into the agency in the morning and still be sitting patiently outside the superintendent's office in the afternoon. Nothing in his bearing or demeanour would change in the intervening hours. [...]
>
> Later, as a grown man working and visiting in other countries, I encountered the same difference. It was quite evident that my time was not their time. Arab men who spend hours on end – in fact, all day – talking to their friends in coffee-houses still amaze me. Even people in Paris cafés exuded a different air from what I had experienced at home. In Paris the same people could be seen sitting day after day watching the world go by (Hall 1983: 132-3).

In cultures where 'waiting' and 'losing time' are less relevant or even meaningless, punctuality is likely to be equally irrelevant, and keeping appointments may not be as crucial as in more time-conscious cultures. But another factor intervenes in that, which we shall examine now.

3.6.3 The past and the future

Kilani (1992: 117) describes Polynesian and Melanesian cultures where

> the future is located behind a person's back, because it is totally unknown, while the past is in front of you because it is very much alive in the present (my translation).

A similar view appears to be present in a totally different region of the world: in Aymara, a language spoken in Andes, the future is behind one and the past in front (Pinker 2007: 192; Evans 2003: 194). In the Chinese worldview, Shaughnessy (2005: 6) writes, "[...] time is visualized as moving up before one's eyes, with past time already above the horizon and future time below it."

There are many cultures on earth were the future is totally unknowable. In others, it is largely irrelevant, or perhaps even non-existent.

> To the Navajo, the future was uncertain as well as unreal, and they were neither interested in nor motivated by 'future' rewards – a foundation on which many of our government programs were based. Sheep and stock reduction programs were planned and sold to the Indians in terms of future rewards, 'when the range recovers from overgrazing' twenty years hence, which the Navajo took as a ludicrous joke – simply one more example of white perfidy (Hall 1983: 29).

Many of the arguments Western salespeople use, whether they are trying to sell a washing machine or an industrial plant, are based on the implicit idea of making the future better: the new washing machine will do your laundry better and in less time, the new industrial plant will develop the economy of that region in your country, and so forth. In cultures where the future is not the first priority, such arguments are largely irrelevant.

Bantu culture of Central Africa may be a prime example of a culture where the future almost does not exist, and where the past and the present are what really counts. An African scholar, John Mbiti, contends that

> ... according to traditional [African] concepts, time is a two-dimensional phenomenon, with a long past, a present, and virtually no future (1969, quoted in Ferraro 1994: 94).

This is, of course, a serious overstatement. The Africans Mbiti is referring to are agriculturalists, and agriculture is impossible without projecting oneself in the future: sow today, collect the harvest in several months. Still, there is some truth in Mbiti's words.

Remembering and retracing the past is essential, and the way the ancestors did things is an important yardstick for future action. Many Central African peoples such as the Lega (Barega) of Eastern Zaire have several epic songs which are thousands of lines long, and which were (and still are) transmitted orally from father to son in certain specialized families of poets or bards. Research has shown that these epic poems are historically accurate to a surprising degree and trace back events that happened several centuries ago. Central African tribes also possess a vast collection of *proverbs* (over 3,000 in the case of the Shi in Eastern Congo; see Ntabaza 1992) which embody the traditional, ancient wisdom of the people and which are used in the course of argument. Some discussions among the elders about important decisions to be taken may be made up almost entirely of an exchange of such proverbs, i.e., of references to wisdom acquired in the past.

Westerners will have difficulty understanding the decision-making base of someone who, when confronted with a choice between two options, might ask himself something like: 'what would my grandfather have done under similar circumstances?' For many Africans, the past is an important guide for present behavior (Ferraro 1994: 95).[13]

> In these societies, where an event is perceived as being identical to its original, the past, such as it is laid down in myths, legends and foundational

narratives, constitutes a vast reservoir of possible action schemes. The past is a dynamic representation which makes action in the present possible. Referring to the past consists in going from event to myth and from myth to event (Kilani 1992: 117; my translation).

The present is also important to Bantu Africans: enjoying the present moment, especially in the company of friends, has high priority. The future, on the other hand, while perhaps not absent altogether, is vague and relatively unimportant; and in any case, *it does not exist (yet)*. These philosophical aspects of time may sound abstract, but they are directly relevant for the way society works and for the way business is structured in those cultures.

Saving and investing vs. spending and enjoying

A Chinese or Japanese businessman, when asked why he is working so hard and saving the money he is making rather than spending it (by taking a vacation and more generally enjoying the good side of life), may well answer: 'For my grandchildren to have a better life.' In other words, he may project future events that are twenty or more years away, and he thinks in terms of generations. A survey I carried out in Bangkok (Verluyten 1997) shows that Thai people commonly save money for their grandchildren; the same is true in various other East and South-East Asian countries. Many South-East Asian countries, including those that are still poor, have a high savings ratio (APS, average propensity to save, sometimes also called savings rate). Household savings in countries like China, Vietnam or Thailand are typically between 20 and 30%: people save 20-30% of their disposable income. Even people with low incomes put money aside for the future. Finding capital for investments (or for lending money to countries with very low savings rates!) is relatively easy in such cultures. In continental Europe, the savings rate is typically between 10 and 15 %; it is lower in the UK (5-6%) and even lower in the USA (below 2%). It appears difficult or impossible to find reliable figures for many developing countries in Africa, but their savings ratio is likely to be very low also.

In Central Africa, the first priorities of a businessperson who makes money are likely[14] to be different from those of his Asian counterpart. He will want to enhance the way he enjoys life and for that purpose be willing to spend a great deal (or all) of his money on food and drinks, cars and clothes, and more. In addition, he will also give away much of what he earned to relatives, friends and acquaintances, – or be morally obliged to share it with them.

Keeping appointments

I often present my students with the following dilemma. Suppose you have two appointments of equal importance, one with person A at 2 p.m., and the other with B at 3 p.m. Your 2 p.m. appointment goes well, but three o'clock is approaching fast and you realize that you will never have finished your work with

A before that time. Assume also, to keep the story as simple as possible, that you cannot call or inform B. You now basically have two options.
a. *Interrupt:* tell A that you are very sorry, but you have another engagement at three, and you will have to leave it at that for today; you may suggest having another meeting with A at some later date; then you go and honor your 3 p.m. appointment with B.
b. *Continue:* as the conversation with A is going well, you continue with A even beyond 3 o'clock, until you are finished; in that way, however, you ignore your appointment with B, who will presumably be waiting for you in vain.

In Western countries (US, Europe), the vast majority (almost always over 90%) of the people I survey opt for (a):[15] they will tell A they are sorry, then go to their second appointment. Although I have not carried out surveys with large groups of Central Africans, I am confident to predict, on the basis of my African friends' behavior, that the vast majority of them would go for option (b). (Choosing option (a) or (a) does *not* necessarily mean that the person involved, whether Western or African, is making his choice consciously, of course.)

Why is that so? Westerners (and many Asians even more), as we have seen above, put high emphasis on the future. They feel responsible for their own future as well as for their children's future many years from now, they may make detailed projections and scenarios of future events and developments, etc. In that way, future events may take on a character of *reality* that puts them almost on a par with events that are actually taking place; although strictly speaking, we would agree that future events are nothing, at this point, but projections in our mind. Keeping an agenda with appointments for future dates and times is a small example of that: an agenda is little more than a list of future, projected events. These events are almost as real, and may certainly be as important, as events that are taking place now, and planned future events may receive priority over what is happening now: if you have an appointment at 3 o'clock, then you must go.

In cultures such as Bantu culture, as we have seen, the present will normally take priority over the future rather than the other way round.[16] You are having a fruitful conversation (or other activity) in the present with person A. Your 3 o'clock appointment, on the other hand, is nothing but a few words on a piece of paper, for instance in your agenda; it is a statement of intent concerning a future event which does not have any reality at present. Even beyond the 3 o'clock limit, it will be difficult for the Central African to give up something that is real and fun and useful for an abstraction, for something that does not exist as yet. Therefore, most Central Africans will continue their conversation with A, and ignore their appointment with B.

How can Central Africans then stick to a schedule for the entire day, when they have several things to do? The answer is simple: often they don't. Frequently, the person with whom you had an appointment either does not show up at all, or else arrives much later than planned. Maybe the Bantu way of interpreting time is not efficient in running a modern economy – though it could be argued that, in some cases, continuing the work with A may be economically more profitable than interrupting it and going to see B. On the other hand, Central African people who interpret time in the way I described have a quality of life that most people in the West have lost completely: they are *never under time pressure,* never in a hurry or stressed, they live their lives with a serenity many Westerners can only dream of.

> **'I Will Get There When I'll Get There'**
>
> A South African relates how he once gave a lift to an old farmer who said he was going to visit his daughter. 'How far does she live?' the driver asked. 'Three days' travel,' answered the farmer. 'When did you leave home?' 'When I left,' answered the old man. 'And when will you get there?' 'When I get there.' 'Does your daughter know that you are coming?' 'No.' 'And what will she say when she sees you?' 'Oh, you are here.' (Richmond & Gestrin 1998: 109)

In fact there are few cultures where appointments are binding to the same degree as in the West, even if the Bantu way of looking at them is at the other end of the spectrum.

In real life, interactions between people are of course seldom regulated by one parameter only, such as the relative priority of the present and the future as discussed here. Other factors that are relevant in understanding how appointments are set up and kept (or not) include the following (some of which were mentioned before).

- The concept of *event-linked time* (in Bantu culture) reinforces the way Central Africans keep or do not keep appointments as described above. If person B is 'waiting' and A does not show up, B is unlikely to become 'impatient': as we have seen, to a person who is doing nothing (what Westerners would call 'waiting'), the time dimension is irrelevant or ceases to exist.
- In some countries such as Japan, people tend to move gradually closer to specifics in a circular way, rather than going straight to the core. This applies to business negotiations, as we have seen above, but equally well to a person taking a taxi or to someone setting up an appointment (Hidasi 1995a: 72). In the taxi, the passenger will not give the final destination to the driver at once: he/she will first define a broad area where the taxi needs to take him/her, then get more specific about the location, and only at the end the precise address will be specified. When setting up an appointment, people will first keep it vague ('we should meet sometime soon, this month I suggest'), and here also the period will gradually become more specific, until eventually a precise date for the meeting is specified – only when it is clear that this date will suit both parties.
- In addition, in cultures (such as in many Asian countries) where face saving is an important consideration, one should be careful in refusing a suggested date for a meeting. Judith Hidasi (1995a: 72) tells a story where a Japanese friend in Tokyo suggested they meet in the evening the day after, and she replied she couldn't make it that day because she had bought tickets for a concert. She felt that she had made a cultural mistake with her reply, because it was like saying that going to the concert was more important to her than meeting with her friend, like saying that she preferred music to his friendship.

Notes

1. As I mentioned earlier, I will refer occasionally the level of *subcultures* when the explanation of a phenomenon is situated at that level. Black and white Americans (US) undoubtedly, at one level, share a number of values and practices which distinguishes them from, say, Europeans or Japanese. At the same time, at another level they may hold different values and exhibit different practices, as is illustrated here.
2. As usual, there may be exceptions to this like to any other generalization. Several accounts describe people in Finland (or Finnish males?) as having higher tolerance of silence. C. Hall (1996: 44) describes Finns as accepting longer pauses both within and between turns, as a result of which they are more frequently interrupted and thereby frustrated, 'while the other party thinks it odd that they have nothing to say.'.
3. In addition, when negotiations start, Westerners want to talk first, Japanese and Chinese last (Varner & Beamer 1995: 118). The Japanese value *listening* more than Westerners do (see also Miller 1991: 114-5).
4. A similar story, where the Americans lower their price because they feel uncomfortable with a certain period of silence, is reported in Victor 1992: 155, based on McCaffrey and Hafner.
5. The reason for this may lie in the fact that food is cheap, while imported alcoholic beverages are expensive. The host therefore shows his high social status by offering the latter, not the former.
6. Related to this is the *specific-diffuse* dimension which Trompenaars (1993) 'borrowed' without acknowledgement from Parson (1951; see Gudykunst & Kim 1992): in a 'specific' culture, your partner can concentrate on one specific aspect of you as a person (such as the business aspect); in a 'diffuse' culture, your partner needs to know your personality as a whole, including aspects unrelated to business, before he/she feels comfortable engaging in business with you.
7. Lin (1993) shows that in advertising also, explicit references to price are eschewed in Japan because they are felt to be too direct, too 'rude'.
8. Again these properties are relative, not absolute. No culture is 100% monochronic (never any overlap between tasks) or 100% polychronic (doing everything at the same time), but some cultures tend to be more polychronic, others more monochronic. Even in a very monochronic culture, some situations may call for a high degree of polychrony, and vice-versa. A housewife with three children who has to get them all washed and dressed in the morning, cook their breakfast and make them eat it, and get them on their way to school is operating in a polychronic fashion, no doubt!
9. And Northern Europeans as well, – my footnote.
10. Obviously physicists, and some philosophers, will not share this naive representation of time, which certainly does not correspond to the time of 20th century physics; see for instance Hawking 1988, Reichenbach 1958. It does not correspond to our own psychological perception of time either. We 'pretend' every hour has the same length as every other hour, but we very well know that under certain circumstances an hour may seem endless, under other circumstances it may fly by all too rapidly.
11. Before the 18th century, in Europe, progress only seems to have been accepted as a restoration of a previous, better period, which is the contrary of linear progress.
12. In linguistics, Lakoff and Johnson defend an *Event-comparison hypothesis* of time («We cannot observe time in itself [...]. We can only observe events») as opposed to a 'durational' view of time (where time cognitively exists outside events taking place); see Evans (2003: 63-65). These authors do not address the issue, however, of possible intercultural differences related to this.
13. My own research (Verluyten 1997: 12) has shown that the past is also more important as a yardstick for present decisions in Thailand than in the West. Similarly, Yoshimura & Anderson (1997: 157) write that history is a source of inspiration for managers in Japan. In Burma, all the proposals of administrative reform put forward by the British were judged according to the criterion: 'does it conform to our custom?' (D.G.E. Hall 1995: 770).
14. Once again, beware of the ecological fallacy (see above): this obviously does not apply to every individual. Some Central African businessmen will save money and invest, some Asians may spend it all. There is no doubt, however, that the general tendencies as explained in the text are accurate.

15. I carried out a survey with over 100 executives in Bangkok (Verluyten 1997), and there the figures are as follows: 23% prefer to continue with A, 77% would interrupt what they are doing and go to B. Not surprisingly, most Thai executives in a business setting act in the same way as most Westerners. What still needs explaining, however, is the substantial percentage of them (approximately one quarter) who would stay with A. This difference between the Thai and Westerners can be explained by Asian *face saving* (see below): it is more difficult for the Thai to say to A that they have something else to do (which takes priority), for this may make A lose face. The Thai stay with A for reasons that are very different from those of the Africans I refer to here.
16. Here as elsewhere, the reader needs to put things in perspective and avoid oversimplification. (Central) Africans may have more difficulty than Westerners sticking to a tight schedule over a day, and they may have more difficulty planning ahead for the future. But African cultivators *do* plan ahead for planting their crops, harvesting them, etc. (Richmond & Gestrin 1998: 109).

Chapter 4
Space

4.1 Proxemics: interpersonal distance

Figure 15. Interpersonal distance: African Americans standing in line (left, from: Desmond Morris, *Manwatching);* Nigerians standing in line to vote in 2007 (right).

How far do you stand from another person when talking to him/her? How close to another person do you sit on a bench in a waiting room? The answer depends on a number of parameters, such as the degree of intimacy you have with that person: you will stand furthest away when talking to a stranger, closer when you talk to someone you know, and even closer to your spouse or lover.

Along with other parameters, however, the culture of the people involved will also play an important role. For normal conversation, middle class white North Americans (US) stand at a distance of approximately 46-51 cm from one another.[1] African Americans (US) usually stand a bit farther away from each other. When I ask my Belgian students to stand opposite each other and imagine they are having a conversation together at a cocktail party, the average distance I measure is 60-65 cm: Belgians, probably like other Northern Europeans, stand a bit further apart than Americans (US). In Thailand, I performed the same test with many classes of Thai students, and the average distance is considerably higher, some 80-85 cm. This is close to the figure Engholm (1991: 136) gives for Japanese, i.e. 91 cm.[2] The Navajo Indians of North America stand several meters away from one another when having a conversation (Pinxten 1994: 63-4). On the opposite end of the spectrum, Latin Americans may stand at a distance of some 36-38 cm, and in some cultures in the Middle East people may stand at only some 23-25 cm from one another. In some areas of the Arab world, there is a saying that in order to really be talking with someone, 'you have to feel the breath coming out of his mouth'. Nydell (1987: 44) confirms that Arabs "tend to stand and sit closer and to touch other people (of the same sex) more than Westerners do." Typically, Arabs may stand close to you in an elevator rather than moving to the opposite corner, or choose to sit beside you on a bus or on a bench rather than going to an empty seat or space.

Here again, people are usually not aware of their own normal interpersonal distance. However, commonly

> [c]onversational distances [are] maintained with incredible accuracy, [.] to tolerances as small as a fraction of an inch (Hall 1983: 154).

Here as elsewhere in this book, the point is obviously not to learn by rope what the average interpersonal distance is in various cultures. Individual variation may be more limited than one might think, but it is still there, and many other parameters interfere: degree of intimacy, age, gender, social class, etc. Therefore, predicting the interpersonal distance at which the person you are to meet will be standing (or try to stand) from you is pointless and impossible. The point I want to make is the need for awareness. If you are not aware that interpersonal distance is culture-specific, this trivial, seemingly unimportant dimension (no-one will claim that a certain interpersonal distance is 'better' than another) may lead to mutual mistaken interpretation of the other person's behavior, and thus to irritation and suboptimal communication.

Imagine a conversation between a person from Latin America or the Middle East on the one hand, an American or Northern European on the other. When the person from Latin America or from the Middle East comes closer in order to restore the conversational distance which is normal to him, the American or Northern European will back off until he/she is at the distance which is normal to him/her; the other person will again come closer, the second will again back off, and so forth:

> If a person gets too close, the reaction is instantaneous and automatic – the other person backs up. And if they get too close again, back we go again. I have observed an American backing up the entire length of a long corridor while a foreigner whom he considers pushy tries to catch up with him. This scene has been enacted endlessly – one person trying to increase the distance in order to be at ease, while the other tries to decrease it for the same reason, neither one being aware of what was going on (Hall 1959: 176).

The entire process happens unconsciously, but this does not prevent mistaken attribution from arising, as explained in more detail above: the American or European will feel that the other is intruding into his/her personal sphere, is obnoxious, pushy, and perhaps even aggressive. Needless to say, this does not correspond at all to the intentions of the Latin American or Middle Eastern person. The latter, in turn, may feel that the American or European is cold, aloof, reserved, and does not really want to enter into a conversation.

4.2 Haptics: physical contact

Cultures where people stand closer to one another also tend to be those cultures were touching the interlocutor is more common. In an analysis of negotiations which involved Japanese, American (US) and Brazilian negotiators, one study found that the Japanese and the Americans never touched, while the Brazilians touched an average of 4.7 times per 30 minutes, i.e. approximately every 6 minutes (John Graham, quoted in Adler 1992: 210). Within Europe, there is a marked difference in this respect between Northern European (such as German and Scandinavian) and Latin (such as French or Italian) cultures. Vincent Merk, a Frenchman, recalls the astonishment of one of his German professors when he lightly touched his shoulder during a conversation.

Most East and South-East Asian cultures are typically low on physical contact. People do not shake hands, but bow (in Japan) or *wai* (in Thailand).[3] They almost never touch one another during a conversation or a discussion. In Bangkok, one almost never bumps into another person or even brushes against someone's shoulder or arm. Even in the most crowded streets, people usually manage to maintain a couple of centimeters between each other. In a television program I saw recently, a young Chinese woman from Singapore said that she could not remember being touched by her mother. When she walked up to her mother with a problem, her mother would sit on a chair opposite her and comfort her like that, without ever touching, let alone hugging her.

> From the middle of the Ming period onwards, [...] families who claim to have high educational standards consider that persons of different sex should never touch each other except in situations of the strictest and conjugal intimacy. Men and women therefore live separately [...]. According to recent inquiries, these ancient prohibitions subsist in residual form in contemporary [Chinese] society (Eliseef 2003: 119).

> Today, in north-eastern Thailand, boys are still fined if a charge is brought and proven involving the 'touching' of a girl. Incidentally, the fine varies according to the part of the body touched. [...] The *farang*[4] gentleman often finds himself an innocent victim of either his politeness or his feelings as his outstretched hand is avoided even as he is helping a young lady from a car (Klausner 1993: 260; this text was first published in 1976).

Here also, other parameters such as intimacy or friendliness may blur the picture to some extent. On *one* occasion, during my various stays in Thailand, an older Thai professor I had become really close friends[5] with lightly touched my knee; but that happened literally just once in the course of our many meetings, and it never happened with any other Thai colleague during several stays in the country.

In a mixed class of US-Japanese students I had in Maastricht a few year ago, I asked my students if they were hugged or kissed by their parents at the airport when saying goodbye. All the Americans confirmed their parents hugged and/or kissed them. Of the four Japanese girls in my class, one got a kiss on her cheek from her mother, but not from her father who was also there; in the three other cases, there was no physical contact whatsoever between parents and daughter.

For an overview of numerous studies on proxemics and haptics, presenting sometimes conflicting evidence, see Remland e.a. (1995).

4.3 Office space

In Western countries, anyone in the company who has some importance will insist on having a private office space: you need to have your own cubicle. In addition, office size is correlated to the person's rank in the company: the more important the person, the larger the office.

In Japan, however, the manager typically sits in the same large room together with his workers; only upper management may have private offices (but not always). In many cases, the manager even sits at the same large table together with his workers. This is related to the stronger group-oriented nature of Japanese culture. It also makes for a different communication process between the manager and his workers: as they share the same space, it is easy for manager and worker to discuss a problem together as soon as the need arises for it (see also Varner and Beamer 1995: 158-9).

The way space is structured inside an office room is also culture-specific. For instance, if you need to share your office with co-workers, in the West the preferred location would be next to the window, in particular if the window looks out to a garden or park. In Japan, however, the senior person who is in charge and who shares a room with other workers will want to be in a position where he looks *at them*, not outside through a window. In some cases, an older man who is not on top of things any more will be deprived of responsibilities and subordinates, and he may be put close to a window; he is literally called a 'window-gazer' in Japanese (Yoshimura & Anderson 1997: 76). In other words, sitting near the window does not convey a message of power in Japan at all.

In very polychronic cultures, as described above, office space involves little privacy, as many people are usually present in the office and others are entering and leaving all the time.

Notes

1. These figures and some others below are based on a review of the literature in Ferraro 1994: 77 and on Engholm 1991: 136. Some of the data are based on E.T. Hall. See also Van Oudenhoven (2002: 95-6). Desmond Morris (1979), in his book *Manwatching*, shows fascinating pictures of the way interpersonal space is structured in various cultures.
2. Ferraro (1994: 78) quotes studies showing that 'Asians' and people of the subcontinent of India choose conversational distances 'that are midway between Arabs and Northern Euro-

peans' (i.e., some 45 cm, presumably). In my experience, this is either mistaken (or another parameter was overriding 'normal' interpersonal distance) or else it does not apply to East and South-East Asians such as the Japanese and Thai. In my opinion Engholm is much closer to the truth in putting interpersonal distance in Japan as very high (91 cm), and I am sure the same is true for Thailand. However, according to Engholm interpersonal distance is considerably closer (61 cm) with Koreans and Chinese.

3. The *wai* consists of putting the palms of your hands together somewhere in front of your chest. As with the Japanese bow, the precise way of executing this gesture depends on the rank of the people involved. The *namaste* in India looks similar to the Thai *wai*.
4. *Farang* is the word used in Thailand to refer to a foreigner, i.e., a non-Thai person [my footnote].
5. Close friends, that is, in the sense the Thai give to that word; the actual substance of close friendship is very different in Europe.

Chapter 5
Verbal communication: language

5.1 English as a foreign language

5.1.1 Avoid idioms and check for understanding

In international business as well as in international organizations, when people do not share the same native tongue, they will most often use English. However, in many areas of the world, fluent mastery of English is still a rare thing. This includes China and Japan as well as various Latin American countries. In one Chinese university where I spent some time, the professor who is head on the international office, i.e. the person who is in charge of all relations with academic institutions outside China, does not speak or write one word of English: every e-mail he writes or receives has to be translated by someone else.

Surveys have shown that very often, the major obstacle in intercultural communication settings is, simply, the fact that the parties who would like to communicate with each other do not share a common language.

Even if both parties use a common language, say English, the fact that most businesspeople spend their life communicating in a language which is neither their own nor that of their interlocutor is bound to create specific problems. If some of the participants are native speakers of English, the problem is compounded, because they may not be sufficiently aware that the non-native speakers' skills in English, even if they sound quite fluent in it, are always more limited than their own.

Using an interpreter helps, of course, but it also creates additional constraints that should be taken into account. A number of simple precautions can be taken by both native and non-native speakers to limit the risk of miscommunication with (other) non-native speakers and/or when using an interpreter. These precautions include the following.

- Speak slowly and clearly and eliminate background noise (such as a noisy air conditioner, traffic noise, etc.) as much as possible. The faster the rate of speech and the lower the channel to noise ratio, the more difficulty non-native speakers will have to understand. And even the most skilled interpreters cannot adequately perform their difficult job beyond a certain rate of speech.

- Avoid long sentences and complicated syntax such as many subordinate clauses, double or triple negatives ('it is *not* altogether *un*true that we do*n't* believe that...'), counterfactuals ('if it were the case that...'), etc. This advice holds true for business communication in general, but even more so when communicating with non-native speakers. The shorter and more direct your sentences, the easier it will be to get the message across.

> **Speaking English in Thailand: avoid counterfactuals!**
>
> I am sitting in a bar in Bangkok with an English speaking Canadian colleague. When taking orders for drinks and conversing with us, the bartender seems to speak English reasonably well, and this makes my colleague unaware of the fact that outside his narrow professional field (cocktails and other drinks, small talk with the customers), the bartender's English vocabulary and grammar are, in fact, very limited.
>
> At one point a photographer comes into the bar and asks if we want our picture taken, which we decline. Several other people (tourists) in the bar, however, accept and are happy to pay the photographer for their picture.
>
> My Canadian colleague then says to the bartender: "Too bad you don't have a camera, *if you had one* you could take the customers' photographs yourself and earn some money with it."
> The bartender immediately calls the photographer back and tells him we have changed our mind and want our picture taken.

- Repeat the same information more than once, paraphrasing it in a different way or with different words. Summarize periodically what has been said and discussed, and check for understanding frequently:
  - 'So, if I understand it correctly I believe we agree that...'
  - 'Please correct me if I'm wrong, I understand that...'
  - 'Let me summarize in my own words what I think you are saying, to avoid any misunderstandings...'

  Here also, the advice of frequently summarizing and testing for understanding holds for any negotiation, but is even more necessary when communicating with non-native speakers.
- Avoid idiomatic expressions, proverbs and expressions that refer to culture-specific features. The latter include, for instance, references to the Bible ('We all bear our cross') or to Christian practices ('You'd better say your prayers before you enter his office'): they will not be universally understood. The same is true for references to Greek or Latin mythology and history ('he is a real Croesus') and for sports terminology (such as 'he is totally off base', from baseball: Europeans will not understand what this means[1]). Proverbs are often language-specific and difficult to translate or to understand in another language. Even the simplest idiomatic expressions can be a cause of misunderstanding, as the mishaps of Mr. Adams in China illustrate (see chapter 1 above). Engholm (1991: 122) reports another striking and funny example, given by Diana Rowland, of a misunderstanding caused by using an idi-

omatic expression. An American and his Japanese associates are on a cruise together on a yacht and the conversation is about high taxes. The American says, complaining that taxes are high everywhere: "Well, in that [i.e., taxes], we're all in the same boat." The Japanese are astonished: they have concluded from his remark that he wanted to do the cruise on a different yacht from them...

'Are we on the same page?'

At the train station in Prague I was looking at the complicated schedule the Czech receptionist was showing me in order to try and make me understand which connecting trains were available, but I could not follow her explanations and we were getting nowhere. After yet another misunderstanding I said, "OK, we have to make sure first that we are on the same page." Irritated she responded that we had both been looking at the same page of the schedule since the beginning, so what was I talking about? (M.H., USA)

5.1.2   **Some common pronunciation problems**

It is impossible in this volume to discuss in depth the many types of grammatical errors that non-native speakers of English may make and which are partially influenced by their native tongue. Insight into some common cases of mispronunciation, however, may turn what is otherwise nearly unintelligible into discourse which it is possible to understand.

- **The sounds [l] and [r].** These two sounds are nearly indistinguishable to native Japanese and Thai speakers, among many others. Whether someone says *law* or *raw*, *lack* or *rack*, *loyal* or *royal*, most Japanese and Thai will hear the same word twice. This may sound surprising, but many readers will equally hear twice (or three or four times) the same word when confronted with identical syllables that are distinguished by the tone they carry, as in Thai, Chinese, Vietnamese. In Beijing Mandarin, the 'word' *ma* has four different meanings depending on the tone with which it is pronounced:

    -*ma* (level tone) = mother
    -*ma* (rising tone) = linen
    -*ma* (rising-falling tone) = horse
    -*ma* (falling tone) = to call a bad name

    (there are four tones in Mandarin, more in some other languages; Crystal 1980: 356).

When they speak English, Thai people tend to replace [r] by [l]. The Royal Rose Hotel where I used to stay in Bangkok usually comes out as *Loyal Lose Hotel*. In one instance, someone in the hotel called housekeeping and said "I have some *laundry*, could you send someone to my room please to pick it up" and was surprised to find a prostitute knocking on his door. The reception thought he had said 'I am *lonely*, could you send someone to my room...' In Japan, on the other hand, [l] tends to become [r]. An office worker is called *sarariman* in Japanese

(from s*alaryman*) and *Rosu Angeresu* is the name of a large city in Southern California. In Rwanda also, typically, [l] will become [r].
- **The sounds [p] and [f].** In some languages such as Filipino and Korean, the sounds [p] and [f] are not distinguished: *copy* and *coffee* are phonetically identical. In addition, Filipino and Korean as most languages in the world do not have articles, so 'do you want a copy?' and 'do you want coffee?' may well come out the same.
- **The sound [ü].** The sound [ü] which we find in French *tu* or German *Brücke* does not exist in many languages, including English, Italian, Spanish or Portuguese; native speakers of such languages may not be able to pronounce it. They will replace it by a sound that is close, such as [u] (as in English *soon*) or [i]. Most speakers of those languages we mentioned will replace [ü] by [u], and say *too* for the French *tu;* some Africans, however, who also do not have [ü] in their native tongue, replace it by [i]: *tu as une voiture,* said by someone from Rwanda or some areas of Congo, will become *tee a een voiteer.*
- **Final consonants.** Many languages in the world have only open syllables or syllables closed by a nasal *(m, n)* or *l* or *r*. Syllables closed by other consonants may therefore be impossible to pronounce, and the consonant may be dropped: *soup* will become *soo,* etc.
- **Consonant clusters (groups).** Groups of several consonants may also be unpronounceable. Many Western Europeans will have difficulty with Russian consonant clusters as in *Dnepropetrovsk,* while some Asians including Japanese and Thai in turn have difficulty with the simpler, English clusters: *spring,* with three initial consonants, may be nearly unpronounceable for them. Once I ordered *deep fried spring rolls* from room service in my hotel in Bangkok, and the person downstairs repeated my order to be sure there was no mistake. It came out *dee fly ping loh*: the final consonant of *deep* and *fried* were dropped, the initial *spr* of *spring* was simplified to *p*, and the two remaining *r* were replaced by *l*. In Japan, consonant cluster may be broken up by inserting a (voiceless) vowel, often [u]: *free* may become *furii,* etc.

Knowing these phonological problems may allow one to understand which phonological rules have applied (such as $l \rightarrow r$) and to mentally 'undo' the rules in order to re-establish the correct pronunciation.

On two occasions, my wife asked a waiter and a bartender for 'Perrier' in Bangkok, and what she got was a glass of Baileys. Firstly, in the Thai language the distinction between [p] and [b] does not work in the same way as in English, therefore Thai people may not hear the difference between 'our' [p] and [b]; second, as we have just seen, they may not hear the difference between the middle consonant [r] or [l] as in *Perrier* and *Baileys* respectively; and thirdly, they may not hear the final [s] in the latter word. If you add it all up, *Perrier* and *Baileys* truly turn out to be nearly impossible to distinguish.

5.1.3 Working with interpreters

Translating is an arduous task and simultaneous interpretation even more so. Though it may be costly, in a negotiation it is always advisable (a) to use *two* professional interpreters, (b) to bring your own interpreters rather than relying on those that are provided by the opposite party.

Some words and expressions are particularly hard to translate, if the concept itself does not exist in the target language or if it has entirely different connotations. In several group-oriented cultures (see chapter 9 below), 'privacy' does not have the same positive connotations attached to it as it has in individualistic cultures and, when translated, it may come out as 'loneliness' or something similar.

A Chinese dictionary will translate 'privacy' as *yin si* (yin3 si1 with the appropriate tones). But the two Chinese characters involved, 隐私, mean 'to conceal, to hide' and 'selfish, private, secret, illicit' respectively. In other words, contrary to the English word 'privacy' which has positive connotations attached to it ('I value my privacy', 'I need more privacy'), *yin si* has negative connotations, or, at best neutral ones at present.[2]

In Arabic, the same word, خَلْوَة *(khilwa)* is used for 'loneliness' and for 'privacy', two very different things in English; and the Oxford English-Arabic Dictionary defines privacy as 'the state of being able to be alone or away from other people who may disturb you', – probably not a definition a native speaker of English would subscribe to. Neither Dutch nor French have their own word for privacy. In Dutch, the English word 'privacy' is used; in French, privacy is translated as *vie privée* ('private life'), but this expression cannot always be used in the same context as the original English word.

Different Connotations in Translation

When Kurt Waldheim, then Secretary General of the United Nations, arrived in Tehran for a mediation attempt in the American hostage crisis, he announced 'I have come as a mediator to work out a compromise'. The trouble is that the word used in the Farsi (Iranian) translation for 'compromise' had negative connotations (think of the English 'he has been compromised'), and the translation for 'mediator' suggested 'meddler'.

Waldheim's mission was not a success (Fisher & Ury 1981: 34).

5.2 Loudness of voice

The average loudness of voice with which one speaks varies with culture, and may easily lead to attribution errors, such as thinking that the person who simply speaks louder is obnoxious or even aggressive.

In certain Asian countries people speak very softly (so softly, in Bangkok, that I often can't hear what the speaker says when I'm sitting somewhere at the back of the room and the air-conditioning is running). One of the first pieces of advice for a foreigner visiting a country such as Thailand should be: never ever raise your voice, never shout or get angry (Welty 2004: 147).

In addition, the same people may lower their voice for emphasis. That is the opposite of what people do in the West, where they speak louder when they wish to emphasize a point.

> The loud voice – and the uproarious laughter – of the typical Westerner is probably the characteristic that most offends Asians. North Americans' habit is to raise their voice when they are not being understood or not getting their way. The Asians understand *what* was said only after the interpreter's rerun. *How* it was said may make them recoil and become quiet, to avoid a confrontation. The higher an Asian's status, the less volume is used in speech. A gentle, soft-toned voice should be used for normal speech; as the importance of the topic increases, the speaking volume should *decrease*. A *quiet* voice gives emphasis, not a loud one. Even if asked to repeat a point for the tenth time, the speaker should not turn up the volume, for clarity. It will shatter the mood of the meeting (Engholm 1991: 122, 124).

Loudness of Voice: Dutch Military Officers in Cambodia

A number of Dutch Army officers were sent to Cambodia, under the umbrella of the United Nations, to help negotiate an agreement between warring factions at the end of the civil war. They had prepared themselves thoroughly for this mission and had been familiarizing themselves, as much as possible, with various aspects of Cambodian mind and culture. They were totally unprepared, however, for what appeared to be the major problem during their first meeting with Cambodian authorities and Army staff: they simply could not hear what the Cambodians, who were seated on the other side of the negotiating table, were saying.

Arabs, on the other hand, tend to speak louder than Westerners, as we have seen above.

> *Loudness of speech is mainly for dramatic effect and in most cases should not be taken as an indication of how definite the speaker feels about what he is saying.*
>
> In a taxi in Cairo once, my driver was shouting and complaining and gesticulating wildly to other drivers as he worked his way through the crowded streets. In the midst of all this action, he turned around, laughed and winked. 'You know,' he said, 'sometimes I really enjoy this!' (Nydell 1987: 104).

5.3 Expressing oneself

5.3.1 Verbal exaggeration, overstatements and superlatives

The *loudness of voice* parameter seems to be correlated with the understatement-overstatement dimension. Many South-East Asians tend to understate their point and, in particular, to describe their own abilities in self-depreciating terms. Varner & Beamer (1995: 23) call this *antipraxis*.[3] Western expatriates in East or

South-East Asia may be puzzled when they interview applicants for a position in their company. The Asian applicant will play down his/her qualities and past performance rather than try and explain why he/she is the best person for the job. The danger of a mistaken interpretation is clearly present once again.

> China: downplaying your own merits
>
> In China, when praised for an achievement, one *must* answer something like 'my success is mainly based on the help and instructions of my teachers: both are inseparable'.

> Thailand: don't overdo it!
>
> I was present when a Belgian brewer gave a sales presentation in Bangkok in front of an audience of potential Thai importers of his beer. I immediately felt that something was terribly wrong in the brewer's tone. His presentation seemed to me to be too boastful, overwhelming and loud; how much more would the Thai have felt that way! The Belgian brewer did not manage to convince his audience to import the beer. Possibly he lost the market mainly because of his inappropriate sales presentation. Modesty is valued in most Asian countries, not bragging.

Hofstede (1991: 79) tells of a job interview he once did with a potential employer who was American, and where he felt his 'polite and modest' behavior conveyed the wrong impression to the American manager and lost him the job. Within the English-speaking word, Americans may tend to overstate their merits, British and some others (including New-Zealanders: Varner & Beamer 1995: 170) may understate them. A British person might say 'I think we have a bit of a problem here' when a machine is on the verge of exploding and destroying a large part of the installations.

> If you want to give a present, then in Eastern and Southern Europe you have to mention its merits. You say what you think of it, or what you want your partner to think of it. Something like: *This is a bottle of very fine old wine; I hope you'll like it.*
>
> In England, you would use some slight understatement: *I wonder whether you'll like this: most people think it's quite good.*
>
> A Japanese speaker however, is expected – according to Japanese language usage etiquette – to belittle the present he wishes to give: *This is poor quality wine, I'm afraid you won't like it; still, please accept it.*
>
> (Hidasi 1995b: 15; I omitted the Japanese sentence and I modified the layout of the text somewhat).

In the United States, a widespread form of overstatement is the use of superlatives and exaggerations. A remote town in the middle of nowhere may well call itself 'artichoke capital of the world'. This form of rhetoric goes back over 100 years in the country: it is the way Barnum advertised at the end of the 19th century: "the world's largest, grandest, best amusement institution", "the greatest show on earth", etc. (Corbin 2005: 288-9).

Some years ago we received a letter from an American student who was seeking admission at the University of Antwerp's program for foreign students, of which the reader will find some excerpts below.

> **Statement of Proposed Study**
> **R.H., the University of Kansas**
>
> Intelligently creative, organized, perspicacious, dominant, tangy and an enigma just about sums up my personality traits. My favorite flower is the daisy.
> [...]
> Although I am dissatisfied with my classes, the University of Kansas has proven to be one of the top-rated journalism schools in the nation.
> [...]
> With my experience on the number one rated college newspaper in advertising and editorial content, I received not only an understanding of the importance of interpersonal communication, print production, and the creative rules of advertising, but I was also honored as Advertising Representative of the Semester, and honored with the Most Outstanding Single Ad Campaign.
> [...]
> I think by propelling myself constantly into leadership roles, I've gained insight on the importance of commitment, responsibility, group interaction, respect, and I've been able to understand how to harmonize different incoming personalities in order to create a successful environment.
> [...]

The letter contains a vast number of superlatives and ratings (top-rated journalism school; number one rated college newspaper; Most Outstanding Single Ad Campaign) as well as other expressions of self-congratulation (intelligent, creative, organized, perspicacious, dominant; propelling myself constantly into leadership roles; create a successful environment). To someone from a culture with a weaker tendency to overstatements, the person who wrote such a letter may give the impression of being extremely boastful and arrogant. In fact, we admitted the student at the University of Antwerp and he appeared to be a kind, friendly person: yet another potential attribution error!

5.3.2 Verbal rhetoric and expressing emotions

In Arab culture, and in the Arabic language, there is a tendency toward verbal rhetoric. If an article from the Arabic-language press is translated into a Western language such as English, many expressions will seem shocking because they are too strong in Western eyes. About the Israelis, Arab newspapers might write things such as 'we will drink their blood' or 'we will use the bones of the Jews to open the doors of Paradise'. While acknowledging that many Arabs do not like the state of Israel and its inhabitants, in other cultures people do not write like this even about their worst enemies. In the same vein, Saddam Hussein of Iraq called the Gulf War 'the Mother of all wars' and promised the desert would run red with blood (Varner & Beamer 1995: 129).

Ferraro (1994: 53) reports a study by Prothro that shows that Arabs were more likely to overstate their point than North Americans, and

> [w]hat would be an assertive statement to a North American might appear weak and equivocating to an Arab. Even though verbal threats are commonplace in the Arabic language, they tend to function more as psychological catharsis than as an accurate description of the speaker's real intentions.

In addition, Arabs tend to express their emotions more than Westerners, and they may attribute lack of involvement to the typical, emotionless tone of voice of many Northern Europeans or Americans. Add the display of emotions together with verbal rhetoric and a louder voice, more intense eye contact and closer interpersonal distance: it is easy to see that the Westerner may easily mistake for anger or aggressiveness what is in fact merely the strong expression of sincere feelings.

> [O]ne of the most commonly misunderstood aspects of Arab communication involves their 'display' of anger. Arabs are not usually as angry as they appear to Westerners. Raising the voice, repeating points, even pounding the table for emphasis may sound angry but, in the speaker's mind, indicate sincerity. [...] *Emotion connotes deep and sincere concern for the outcome of the discussion* (Nydell 1987: 38).

5.3.3 Conflictual tone of voice

> **'A Fat Cow like You'**
>
> At Brussels airport, a French passenger got into an argument with the Belgian check-in agent of the airline. The (female) check-in agent tried to explain to the French passenger that he was too late for the next flight, and told him what he ought to do in order to catch another plane later, to which the furious Frenchman replied: *Je ne vais pas me laisser dicter la loi par une grosse vache comme vous*, 'I am not going to let a fat cow like you dictate to me what I should do'.

I am not claiming that calling someone 'a fat cow' is a compliment. However, in cultures such as France where a conflictual tone of voice is commonplace even between colleagues and friends, the use of expressions such as this (and stronger ones as well) has to be put into proper perspective: they are often quickly forgotten and do not leave a permanent trace of hostility. The French themselves call this *soupe a* lait, 'milk soup': when left unattended, milk may suddenly boil over; but when you cut off the heat, it falls flat as it was before. The French passenger in the story above, though undoubtedly angry, may be less angry at you, or less permanently, than the smiling Japanese passenger with a similar problem; the latter may hold a grudge against the company forever and swear never to fly with this airline again.

Philippe d'Iribarne (1989: 28-35; see also 12.2.2 below) describes very well the nearly continuous confrontational atmosphere in the French industrial plant he studied.[4] Conflicts are open and occur frequently; people yell and shout at each other easily. Getting angry may convey sincerity or the strong feelings of the person who expresses his/her anger. Most often, getting angry also produces results: the other party may yield. If you do not raise your voice from time to time, people may tend to ignore you. Yet this strong language does not leave a permanent trace: "The atmosphere was rather tense. [...] This lasted for fifteen minutes, and then it was over" says a worker quoted by d'Iribarne. And a foreman in the plant says something like "These verbal fights are inconsequential. They are rather inevitable and usually happen in a good-humored way." [my translation in both quotes; I also shortened the text somewhat]. D'Iribarne qualifies the situations he describes as a *ritualization of verbal confrontations*.

> **Open conflicts: France vs. Thailand**
>
> When a French oil company opened an office in Bangkok, most of the clerical workers they hired were Thai, most of the executives came from France. The French bosses had a habit of yelling at their secretary when something went wrong; to them, this was a spontaneous reaction which would not leave any permanent trace or damage the relation between them and their assistant. For the Thai, however, it was extremely traumatizing, even after the boss had explained that yelling at people was a habit in France and should not be taken too literally. Sometimes, when a Thai secretary had been shouted at, she would not show up any more for work the next day and never return.

5.3.4 Honorificals and social stratification

Honorificals are grammatical devices for expressing respect to people you address. Many European languages have a rudimentary honorificals system, usually two- or three way, for the second person singular pronoun: in French you say *tu* or *vous* depending on the degree of familiarity you have with the person; analogous systems exist in Spanish, Portuguese, Italian, German, Dutch, and many more. Contemporary English[5] does not have such a system any more: one uses the word *you* whether addressing a five year old child, an unskilled worker, or the President (of your company or of the country).

Several Asian languages have an honorificals system that is vastly more developed than those we may know from Western languages. Thai as well as Japanese are a good case in point; Javanese has an even more elaborate honorificals system in its grammar.

The Thai language has some twelve different forms of the second person singular pronoun 'you', and some seven forms for first person 'I'; their use depends on the degree of formality and the social status of the interlocutors involved (Cooper & Cooper 1982: 99; for more details, see Klausner 1993: 308-10). When speaking to a person whose position in the social hierarchy is very much higher than one's own, the noblest part of one's body, i.e. the (top of the) head or hair, is used to refer to oneself, and the lowest part to refer to the other person, something like: 'May the hair on my head ask the dust under your feet to...' (rather than: 'may I ask you to...').[6]

In Japan, a suffix you add to a person's name indicates his or her status. The default is *-san*, hence *Taro-san* is the equivalent of 'Mr. Taro'. But for a person of much higher rank, *-sama* is needed, for teachers it is *-sensei*, etc. Referring to oneself with one of these suffixes, including in English and by mistake, is extremely arrogant and inappropriate in Japan: if your name is Johnson, don't introduce yourself by saying 'I am Johnson-san'!

Of course, most non Thai or non Japanese persons will not use the Thai or Japanese language, and therefore will not have to worry directly about the proper way of addressing someone. If you are a visitor or an expatriate, your Thai or Japanese colleagues are likely to speak English with you. The honorificals system, however, illustrates the way society is structured in many Asian cultures.

In his own culture and language, a Japanese or Thai person cannot address anyone without properly assessing first that person's position the social hierarchy: is the person socially very superior, slightly superior or equal to me, or slightly below, a bit more below or very much below me? And how familiar am I with that person?

In many cases, the socially superior person is the oldest male. In Japan, in particular, age, seniority and position in the hierarchy (in a company which provides life-time employment to its male workers) go together. The following example illustrates a rare case where a younger person is hierarchically superior to a one year older person, the result being that the honorificals system with the proper way of addressing superiors and inferiors gets blurred because of a clash between age and hierarchical position; it also illustrates that high importance is attached to the proper way of addressing another person:

> I was assigned to be the deputy branch manager in London, where the branch manager was one year younger than I. The branch manager had been promoted at the top of his *doki*[7] while I was two years behind the top of our *doki*, so I was his deputy although I had joined the company a year earlier than he had. Our families had known each other for a long time, and when my wife happened to meet his wife on the street in London, my wife started to talk to her as she always had. The wife of the branch manager replied, 'In our company, does seniority prevail over positions?' (Yoshimura & Anderson 1997: 197-8).

Even when speaking English, your Thai or Japanese interlocutor will not easily shed this culturally defined feature: he will want to know as precisely as possible what your place is in the social hierarchy as soon as he establishes contact with you. The reason is that your respective social rank will regulate the 'protocol' in nearly all activities you might carry out together, ranging from having dinner to organizing a meeting. At the dinner table, the most important person has the most prestigious seat (in the center, facing the door if possible), to his right will sit the number two and to his left the number three in the social hierarchy within the party, and in that manner we work our way down the dinner table up to the lowest (usually youngest) participants at the dinner. The order in entering a room, the order of speakers at a meeting, of starting to drink or eat, virtually everything is regulated with a high degree of precision by the respective social rank of the people involved. Even going home from work reflects the social hierarchy: in Japan, it is unthinkable to go home before your boss does, even if you don't have anything more to do in the office that day (Yoshimura & Anderson 1997: 168).

Thailand: the Order of Speakers at an Intercultural Communication Seminar

In August 1995 I was invited by the alumni of the Graduate School of Business of the National Institute of Development Administration in Bangkok to be the main speaker at a one-day seminar they were organizing on intercultural communication in business. I was taking charge of the middle part of the day, but before as well as after me, they wanted to invite a number of well-known local (Thai) persons whose names could attract a larger audience. The first speaker was Dr. Supachai Panitchpakdi, a well-known MP, former negotiator for Thailand at the GATT-negotiations: so far, so good. But when they wanted to close off the seminar with some testimonials by Thai businesspeople who would talk about their own intercultural experiences in business, the organizers were stuck with a problem. They wanted well-known people on the one hand, but on the other hand these people *must* be socially below the foreign university professor, otherwise they could not speak *after* him, only *before* him. This ruled out quite a few possible names of famous business leaders that were suggested. At the end, they managed to come up with some speakers who appeared to be at the same time relatively well-known, yet also socially lower than the foreign professor. Fortunately, the high social status of teachers in Buddhist countries, including Thailand, may have eased the task somewhat.

Thailand: the Correct Way of Handing out Napkins in a Restaurant

I am having lunch at an outdoor restaurant in Bangkok in the company of three other guests: an older Thai professor, a Thai businessman about my age, and the wife of the latter. The waiter forgot to put napkins on the table, so we ask him to bring these, and after a few minutes he returns with four napkins. These have to be handed out (there is no doubt about that in the waiter's mind) in the proper social order. It is clear that the older professor will get his napkin first, and that the wife will get hers last (because she is a woman and/or because she is the youngest). But the waiter is stuck with an insurmountable problem: the Thai businessman and I look about the same age, and he does not know either of us. After a clearly visible hesitation, he hands the second napkin to the Thai businessman. The older Thai professor immediately corrects him, and points in my direction: I should get a napkin *before* the Thai businessman. Presumably an *ajarn* or teacher, who is also a foreign guest, is socially higher than a local businessperson.

It would be a mistake to believe that, because of all this, everyday life must be terribly complicated and oppressive in countries such as Thailand or Japan. In fact, both the Japanese and the Thai will feel *more* comfortable when the social hierarchy is clear and unchallenged. In that case, everything proceeds smoothly, because we all know who goes first, who comes second, etc. Social equality, on the other hand, makes them feel uncomfortable (Cooper 1991: 168). Between equals, a simple act such as drinking tea may become problematic in Japan: who will drink first? (Yoshimura & Anderson 1997: 188).

> Asians feel more comfortable in relationships between persons of unequal status, with one person deferring to the other. Westerners are just the opposite. They feel uncomfortable in unequal relationships and at ease dealing with social equals. Westerners must adjust to being treated either as royalty *or* as inferiors (Engholm 1991: 61).

In these cultures where social stratification is so strongly expressed in everyday actions,[8] the presence of a *gaijin* or *farang* (foreigner, in Japan and Thailand respectively), whose rank is not always clear, may make the locals feel uncomfortable, because they run the risk of behaving either too humbly or too superior with respect to that Western person (Yoshimura & Anderson 1997: 207). If the (male) foreigner brings his wife with him to Japan, difficulties are compounded, because it will be even harder for the Japanese to place her at the dinner table, etc. (Varner & Beamer 1995: 183).

How is it possible to assess in a split second the social rank of the person you have in front of you? You may rely on age, gender and dress, but that is not always sufficient. The main instrument that is being used for the purpose is both simple and effective: the business card. As soon as you meet someone, the ritual exchange of business cards will take place before anything else. You take the other person's card with both hands and look at it carefully and respectfully; you hand him/her your card with both hands, in such a way that he/she can read the text when taking your card. Apart from your name and your company's name and address, it is crucial that your card mention in the clearest and most explicit way possible your position in the company. It is on the basis of this description that your East or South-East Asian interlocutor should be able to determine your rank. After having looked at the other person's card carefully, you may put it away respectfully: don't fumble with it or put it casually in your pocket! In Asia, most businesspeople have leather or silver holders for business cards. If you are at a meeting, it is acceptable to spread the business cards you received in front of you on the table in an arrangement that represents the seating locations: this will make it easier to identify and address each person around the table (Engholm 1991: 89-90); but writing on them is inappropriate. It is recommended to have business cards specifically made for the country you are going to visit, with English on one side and Japanese, Thai, Chinese or another language as the case may be on the other side; or alternatively, an all-English card but with a translation of your name and title on the same side (Engholm 1991: 100-1). The translation should be done by a trustworthy and skilled translator, as some Asians, and the Chinese in particular, attach special importance to the way names sound and/or are written.

> **China: the effect of a business card**
>
> A few years ago *Export Flanders* organized a mission to China to introduce Flemish companies to the Chinese market. One of the companies represented was *Stow International,* a firm specialized in storage systems and a novice to the Asian market.
>
> The CEO of the company knew that in order to please Chinese partners he had to have his business cards as well as the company brochure translated and that it is customary to offer a small token of appreciation to all the members of the delegation he would meet. He realized that he would not immediately close any deals, but he felt that he had to give the Chinese something to remember him by. He decided to have a small diamond-like gem inserted into his business cards. As expected, there were no immediate results. Apart from the fact that the Chinese will not do business overnight with a new partner, the local market was not ready for his products yet.
>
> A few years later he accompanied another mission to China and even though he had not followed up on those initial meetings he discovered to his surprise that all the parties he had met on that first occasion still remembered who he was and what his intentions were. His business cards had left a long-lasting impression on the Chinese businessmen, and to the Chinese it was as if the time span between their first and second meeting had only been a few weeks rather than a few years.
>
> Stow International went on to sign a letter of intent and later on set up a successful representative office in Shanghai.

5.4 High/low context communication

> A Japanese student receives a telegram with the text: 'There was a storm on Shinji Lake'. He understands he has failed his exams (Finkelstein, Imamura & Tobin 1991: 180).

In various publications, Edward Hall[9] introduced the now widely used concepts of *high and low context cultures.* A message is typically made up of text (words uttered or written) as well as (non-verbal) context. Linguistics will tell us that an utterance can usually be interpreted only if the situation in which it is uttered is taken into consideration. But in some cultures, there is relatively less text, hence one needs to rely more on the context, the situation, for interpretation: the message is then more implicit, less direct. In other cultures, more words or more explicit language is being used, and the context carries less weight in reaching an interpretation of the message.[10]

In many cases, the following terms can be (and will be) used interchangeably:

indirect communication	direct communication
implicit communication	explicit communication
high context communication	low context communication

5.4.1 High context communication, face saving and preserving harmony

Some cultures tend to favor harmonious relations between people, at the expense of frankness and directness; other cultures give higher priority to frankness and directness, and pay the price of exposure to open criticism and of a tenser general atmosphere. In East and South-East Asian cultures where saving face is essential, messages, especially negative ones, will tend to be less explicit for fear of involving loss of face.

SIR or smooth interpersonal relations are of the highest value. A Filipino will go along with the group decision *(pakikisama)* rather than trying to impose his own, personal views, but does not feel that as an attitude of submission, but rather as a way to preserve harmony within the group.

In maintaining harmonious relations between people, the concept of *face saving* is essential in East and South-East Asia. Any negative remark or answer, any form of open criticism could make your interlocutor lose face and thereby create a degree of tenseness or worse, humiliation.

Let us apply this to some simple examples. Good tourist guides warn the Western tourist that in Bangkok, if you ask a local person for directions, say, to a famous monument, and if that local person does not know the way, he or she may send you the wrong way rather than admitting that he/she does not know: admitting that would be too shameful and would make him/her lose face, and you too, because you asked an embarrassing question.[11]

Similarly, if you extend a direct invitation to a Thai (or Japanese) person, something like 'We are having a dinner party next week Saturday at our house, could you join us?', the answer will almost invariably be 'yes'. Saying 'no' is nearly impossible, because it would imply 'no, I have something else to do on Saturday that I prefer to your dinner party', and thereby make you lose face. If a Westerner extends such a direct invitation, his Thai friends will probably accept it, but if they had planned another activity for that evening they may simply not show up. According to Welty (2004: 146), the number of people who do not show up for an invitation they had verbally accepted may reach 50% in Thailand.

At this point, the Westerner is bound to object: yes but if I discover after ten minutes that I was sent the wrong way, or if I cook dinner for a number of people who never show up, isn't that a much worse form of losing face than receiving a mere negative answer to a question? In fact, it is not, because at that point *you are not facing each other*. Face saving is a means to preserve harmonious relations between people, and therefore it plays a role mainly (though not exclusively) when you are facing the other person. It may play less of a role over the telephone, and even less when you are not in contact with the other person.

> [I]nvitations are often accepted, but attendance is another matter. It is felt that an abrupt initial refusal would be more psychologically and culturally disruptive than not attending the function where quite a few others will be present (Klausner 1993: 391).
>
> How many *farang* have been initially puzzled by their secretaries either suddenly bursting into tears or developing a splitting headache that requires a half-day's leave after being 'mildly' rebuked by their boss; by the dinner party with empty places though all those invited had accepted [...] (Klausner 1993: 252-3).

Face saving is not an aim in itself. The ultimate value that explains its importance is the need to preserve harmony. Harmony can be broken in various ways. Disagreements, denying requests and saying 'no' to someone, criticism and negative remarks in general, unfortunate events even, all threaten the harmony.

> **Bangkok: a dispute over price would threaten harmony**
>
> I am standing at the cashiers' desk of a supermarket in a suburb of Bangkok and I hand the check-out clerk a box of biscuits I want to buy. She enters a price at the cash register which is higher than what I thought the biscuits costs. I let her know that I disagree by gesturing 'no' with my hand and writing the lower price I thought I had seen on a piece of paper. Rather than discussing things over with me or calling the supervisor or in some way checking whose version is correct, she immediately puts the box away on a shelf, smiles and pretends the 'incident' never happened. I left the supermarket without the box of biscuits I wanted to buy.

> **Japan: a harmonious dinner party at a cost**
>
> All through the dinner party we were invited to in Tokyo, the Japanese lady of the house seemed cheerful and relaxed. We were surprised to see her a few days later wearing an impressive bandage around her hand, under which it appeared that she had a serious wound on her finger that was stitched. Only after we pressed her a lot she admitted what had happened. When she had been preparing dinner on the evening of that party at their house, as she was cutting up some vegetables with a sharp knife, the knife slipped and she cut the tip of one of her fingers off. She wrapped her finger up in a towel to slow the bleeding and she finished preparing the dinner and served it, without showing any pain or suffering. Only when her guests had left did she drive herself to the hospital to get treatment for her wound (J.A., USA).

In some Asian countries, the emphasis on preserving harmony at all cost is so strong that there is a tendency to deny the existence of any problems, to pretend that nothing went wrong. "In troublesome situations, one acts as though nothing had happened" (Hall 1976: 161). One of the first phrases good tourist guides teach visitors to use in Thailand is *mai pen rai* or 'it doesn't matter'. Suppose there is a mistake in the bill you get at the end of your dinner in Bangkok: the waiter inadvertently overcharged you 100 baht. Many Thai people will knowingly pay the erroneous bill and pretend the error is not there, rather than calling the waiter and ask him to correct the mistake, because that would create tenseness and threaten harmony.

Klausner (1997: 25) reports the case of a Thai student in the US whose bicycle gets stolen one day. His American friends become extremely distraught and angry by the incident, but he accepts the theft with great equanimity. The Americans find his approach incomprehensible, but at the same time they cannot help but be captivated by his cheerful calm.[12] Around the turn of the century, Gustave Rolin-Jaequemyns, the Belgian General Advisor of King Chulalongkorn of Siam

(Thailand) is astonished to discover innocent people who spent up to four years in prison without complaining about it, "due to the Oriental attitude of patience" (Tips 1996: 251-2).

The foreign visitor should be aware that any negative remark he or she might innocently make about the heat, the rain or the traffic jams might threaten the harmony between him and his local partners in East and South-East Asia. Uttering such a remark is almost like saying 'I don't like being here'.

For the same reasons that we just described, court cases between companies are extremely rare in Japan. Bringing a case to court is of course a clear breach of harmony and would be shameful for both parties.

> The Japanese are among the least litigious of cultures. In Japan, a nation with roughly half the population of the United States, there are under 15,000 lawyers, less than in the state of Illinois alone. In the United States,[13] there are over 650,000 attorneys; at one point (during its divestiture) a single US company, AT&T, maintained an in-house legal department of over 1,000 lawyers. Such practice is incomprehensible in Japan (Victor 1992: 125).

Bringing a case to court in Japan is terribly shameful; it will lead to social ostracism (Hendry 2003: 237). A particularly strong form of loss of face in Japan is being forced into an apology, and many Japanese would prefer paying compensation to having to apologize (Hendry 2003: 238). All this does not mean that there are no disputes or disagreements in Japan or in other cultures where saving face and preserving harmony are important; of course there are! But the disputes "are *wrapped* and the wrapping should not be removed" (Hendry 2003: 122).

In South-East Asia, harmony and face saving are traditional values that can be traced back many centuries. For instance, after the loss of Laos to the French in 1893, King Chulalongkorn of Siam (Thailand) "could no longer face his people in public" and remains indisposed for a long time (Tips 1996: 60). Charles Buls, former mayor of Brussels, on a visit to Siam in the year 1900, reports that a Westerner in Bangkok

> in order to make his [Chinese] valets obey him better, had drawn up the following graded tariff of punishments: breaking a plate would result in a shortening of five centimetres of the [hair-]tail; forgetting a letter in his pocket, ten centimetres; theft, fifteen centimetres and so on. Nevertheless, I believe that he has never dared to apply this scale of penalties. The humiliation would have been too sensitive for these boys. He would risk that they would declare 'they had lost face'. If a Chinese no longer has his face, there only remains one thing for him to do: to kill himself in front of the door of the cause of his dishonour (Buls 1994 [1901]: 22).

SIR (smooth interpersonal relations) and group harmony are, not surprisingly, more prevalent in group oriented societies than in individualistic ones (see also chapter 9 below). Some authors conclude from there that group oriented societies necessarily attach high importance to saving face. In my opinion, however, the correlation between collectivism (group oriented), harmony and face saving is not always present.

In the Arab world, preserving harmonious relations is no doubt of the utmost importance, and care must be taken not to issue direct criticism (Nydell 1987: 27). In one instance, an American supervisor reprimands a Tunisian employee in front of others, including some of the Tunisian's subordinates, for arriving continually late:

> The Tunisian flared up in anger and responded: 'I am from a good family! I know myself and my position in society!' Clearly he felt his honour had been threatened [...] (Nydell 1987: 28).

But this incident also points to a difference between face saving as it is practiced in South-East Asian countries on the one hand, in the Arab world on the other. The Arab is mostly concerned with *his own* pride and honor being threatened by the criticism (see also Feghali 1997). For South-East Asians, face saving is primarily (though not exclusively) a device to ensure that *the other person* not lose face, if need be even at the expense of putting oneself down. When the Japanese play golf with a customer, they may play badly to make the customer look good (Yoshimura & Anderson 1997: 191). In this book, I will reserve the term *face saving* for the 'Asian' variant, and use 'preserving one's pride and honor' or a similar expression for the other variant (contrary to Feghali 1997 who uses the terms 'honor' and 'face saving' more or less interchangeably when referring to Arab values in communication).

Accept to lose to allow others to save face

In most West European countries you can only practice and advance in the martial arts until you reach a certain level. In order to obtain the degree of 'Shihan' or just to train on a very high level it is necessary to participate in training programs in Japan.

On his first stay in Japan, a Belgian judoka was being beaten continuously by the Japanese judokas who were technically much better.

Sitting at the side of the tatami were some masters in the martial arts of a very respectable age, who watched the training sessions. Sometimes they picked out a younger Japanese man for a fight. Amazingly, the old men always won those fights.

After about two weeks, one of the old masters invited the Belgian for a fight. The Belgian, glad that he could finally win a fight, immediately floored the old master. As a consequence, he was expelled from the training program and he had to return to Belgium (M.E., Belgium).

I also question the idea that face saving is important throughout Africa, as several authors write (for instance, Varner & Beamer 1995: 100). This may seem like a natural inference, at a theoretical level, from the fact that African societies are group-oriented, therefore maintaining group harmony must be an important value, and therefore face saving prevails. However, while there is certainly a statistical correlation between group orientation and harmony, face saving and high context, in my experience this correlation is not present in some or possibly in many African societies.

My late wife was from Central Africa (Congo, ex-Zaire), and my Africans friends can be (what appears to me) extremely open and blunt with each other, in particular among equals (they will normally defer to superiors). They may sarcastically poke fun of someone who is unemployed and lives at his friends' (or his wife's) expense, they may laugh at physical defects and obesity ('You were so pretty before, look how fat and ugly you have become! Do they make you pay for two seats when you take the bus? Your arms look like hams!') and all this is received with a smile or a laugh by the addressee. It sometimes makes me feel uncomfortable, and a Thai or Japanese person who overheard such a conversation would probably wish he/she could disappear instantly.

Face Saving in Africa: Really?

My (African) wife and I are shopping in Antwerp and in the street we meet a newly wed African couple whose wedding party we had been to a couple of months before. That wedding party had been rather poorly organized: it was hard to get food or drinks, and the waiting times were incredibly long even for African standards (that is, *very* long: the bride disappeared around 10: 00 p.m. to change to her evening gown and returned around 1: 30 a.m.; only then could dancing begin).

When asked by the young couple how the wedding party had been, my wife replied: "Yours was absolutely the most awful, chaotic wedding party I have ever been to in my entire life!"

Face saving?

We have just seen that direct, explicit messages, especially when they are negative, are not acceptable in cultures where face saving is of high importance. Indirect, less explicit messages are less hurtful, do not create tenseness, and are thus a means to save face, and ultimately to preserve group harmony.

$$\text{indirect communication} \rightarrow \text{face saving} \rightarrow \text{harmony}$$
(where the arrow = 'is a means to preserve')

How to ask a question without asking it

After the previous section, readers have probably already asked themselves: how can I invite someone for dinner, or formulate any request or suggestion, in a country such as Japan or Thailand? How can I tell a worker he has made a serious mistake?

What is already clear is that the local people may formulate a question or request implicitly and indirectly rather than explicitly and directly: an important part of the message is implied (in the context) rather than spelled out (in the text).

> **Invitations to Taste the Local Food: Japan and Thailand**
> - An artist from Poland had been invited out to dinner by his Japanese colleagues. Three of them picked him up at his hotel and on the way to the restaurant they were talking in the car. They asked him what sort of food he liked, and he explained that his favorite was Italian cuisine, but that he liked Chinese food as well. 'And what about Japanese sushi?' they asked him. 'Well, you know, I've tried it but since I don't very much like fish, it's difficult for me to eat raw fish.' All the three of his hosts roared with laughter, but he had hardly finished speaking when they landed up at an exclusive sushi bar (Hidasi 1995a: 73-4).
> - Two Thai professors, both female, were inviting another Belgian academic and myself to a restaurant in Bangkok to taste some of the local delicacies. My Belgian friend and I are both fairly adventurous in trying out new kinds of food, and we were ready to taste whatever our Thai colleagues would suggest. One of the local specialties we had heard about but never tried is *fish gut soup,* i.e., soup made with the entrails of fish. While we were driving toward the restaurant, the two ladies asked us: 'Do people in Belgium eat fish gut soup?' We gave a factual answer to what we took to be a factual question: 'Oh no, in Belgium people do not eat fish gut soup.' Upon arrival in the restaurant, we were served a different kind of soup and no further reference was ever made to the fish gut soup, although we would have been willing to taste it if they had only asked us about it. Or had they?

The two stories above illustrate how things will go wrong when indirect communication is interpreted by Westerners as direct communication. In Japan, the European interprets the question 'Do you like sushi?' as a direct question and provides the Japanese with a direct answer. In a face saving country such as Japan, however, this question is very unlikely to be a 'yes-no' question about whether or not you like sushi, even if it looks like it on the face of it. It cannot be a 'yes-no' question because to the Japanese, 'no' is not a possible answer to it. Saying 'no, I don't like sushi' amounts to saying you don't like Japanese food, therefore you may not like the country, or the people you are with: it certainly is face threatening to the Japanese. In reality, when the Japanese in the car said 'What about Japanese sushi?' they were not asking a real, direct question. Rather, they were *informing* their Polish colleague that they were taking him to a sushi bar, but they did so indirectly: it would have been too direct, it would have sounded too much like an order, to say something like 'we are taking you to a sushi bar.'

Many Western readers will still wonder if it is at all possible then, in a country such as Japan, to verbally inquire whether a person likes, say, sushi or not, or whether or not he/she can come to your dinner party on Saturday. Suppose the Japanese had not yet made reservations in a sushi restaurant, and now they really want to find out whether you like sushi or not. How could they do that without asking you if you like sushi? The second story above, which happened to me in Bangkok, may give us a cue to the answer. Our Thai hosts did not ask us 'Do you want to try fish gut soup?', because in their eyes this is a question we could not have replied 'no' to, lest they lose face. They therefore phrased the question in a way which sounds merely factual and unrelated to us or to them, leaving out words like *you* or *to like:* 'Do people in Belgium eat fish gut soup?' Unfortunately, my Belgian friend and I interpreted this erroneously as a direct question, and we provided them with a direct and factual answer: no, in Belgium people do not eat fish gut soup. It was only afterwards that we figured out that in reality the question was meant to probe indirectly whether or not *we* were willing to try it, and that the two Thai ladies took our answer to mean we were not. If we had wanted to make clear that we were ready to try the fish gut soup, we should have said something like 'No, in Belgium we don't have it, *but we would be happy to try it with you today if that is possible.*'

There is perhaps an even better (because less face-threatening) procedure to put in a request or inquiry, without asking a question at all: simply bring the topic up in a conversation, and wait for reactions. In a culture where people are used to indirect, implicit communication patterns, they will pick up your slightest hints and they may respond to them positively if they can. If no reaction is forthcoming, that is probably the equivalent of a negative answer.

> **Thailand: Requesting a Ride to the Airport**
>
> I am leaving Bangkok at the end of the week and it would be very convenient if one of my Thai colleagues could pick me up at my hotel and drive me to the airport. However, I put in a direct request for a ride early in the morning once before, and the person who had replied 'yes' to my request never showed up; I learned my lesson then and there. So when I am sitting in the communal faculty room where we all share lunch every Tuesday, I bring up the topic of my departure: 'On Saturday I am leaving already, time goes by so quickly when you are enjoying yourself!' – then I wait for a reaction: is anyone picking up the hint? Insisting (rather heavily) would consist of adding something like 'Last year I had a very hard time finding a taxi to get me to the airport, I hope this won't happen again this time.' If no-one present reacts to that, you'd better draw the conclusion that no-one is free or willing to drive you to the airport next Saturday.

Another device that may be used (if enough time is available), certainly in Japan, to avoid the danger of a negative answer, is to begin in a vague way and only very gradually move closer to the core issues. For an invitation to dinner, this could consist in suggesting a broad period during the first conversation ('We should get together sometime.' – 'Good idea! I am very busy at the moment but next month should be possible'), then some time later 'zoom in' to a more specific time span (perhaps a week or a fortnight), and so on. A specific date will be mentioned only when it can be reasonably assumed that this day will suit both parties, because their availability has been extensively (but indirectly) probed before (see also Hidasi 1995a: 72). Recall the section on negotiating and decision making, where we applied the concept of 'zooming in' to Japanese negotiating style.

How to say 'no' without saying it

In the workplace, it may not always be possible to avoid putting in rather direct suggestions and proposals to someone, even in Japan. In that case, if the addressee disagrees, he may not literally reply 'no' or 'I don't think so' or 'I disagree with what you just said', but convey his negative response in a milder, less explicit way.

Hiromitsu Hayashida, a Japanese scholar, lists sixteen strategies the Japanese use in order to avoid saying clearly 'no' (in a presentation at the 1992 convention of the Association for Business Communication) I list some of the most commonly used strategies below.

1. Vague 'no' (mumbling something between the teeth)
2. Silence
3. Counterquestion ('Let me ask you, in turn, what do you think of...')
4. Tangential responses or changing the topic
5. Equivocating or making excuses: sickness, previous obligations, etc.
6. Questioning the question itself ('Why do you ask me that question?'; 'Do we really have to answer that question now?')
7. Refusing the question ('I am sorry, I can't answer that question')
8. Conditional 'no' ('It would not be possible if...')
9. 'Yes, but...' ('It would be a good idea provided that...')
10. Delaying answers ('We will give due consideration to that'; 'We'll write you a letter')
11. Apology ('I am sorry.')

In fact the Japanese word for 'no' is primarily used only when filling out forms and the like ('Are you married?' – 'No').

Engholm (1991: 111; based on Draine & Hall) similarly lists seven strategies Indonesians use to convey the meaning 'no' without using the word itself.

> AMERICAN: You said yes.
> CHINESE: That doesn't mean I agree.
> (Ge Gao 1998)

Most East and South-East Asian cultures share the overall concern for harmony and face saving with Japan and China. That should not be taken to mean, of course, that all aspects and details of the communication process are identical everywhere. Vietnamese communication patterns are probably less implicit than the Thai are; the Chinese are reported to be less indirect than the Japanese; etc.

Ge Gao (1998) presents a fine overview of Chinese communication patterns, based on the following five characteristics:
1. implicit communication
2. listening-centeredness
3. politeness
4. focus on insiders
5. face-directed communication strategies.

Clearly, this list overlaps largely with the East and South-East Asian communication patterns we have presented above.

Criticizing

It should be obvious that in cultures where loss of face or loss of pride and honor are important, extreme caution should be exercised when criticizing someone. In

Arab and Latin countries, the risk is high that overt criticism will hurt the person's pride and honor. In many Asian countries, it will cause loss of face, and the worker may not show up again the next day because he/she has been shamed too much to 'face' the others.

> In Thailand, face-to-face criticism is seen as a form of violence. It hurts people and threatens superficial harmony. [...] Open criticism is therefore rarely, if ever, entered into with any positive intention of improving a conflict situation. The act of criticism is at best a sign of bad manners,[14] at worst a deliberate attempt to offend (Cooper & Cooper 1990: 134-5).

Cooper and Cooper discuss the following example (1990: 138-140). Suppose you have a secretary who does her job reasonably well but shows up late for work almost every morning. In a Western country, on the day when she gets in late once again, her boss might reprimand her immediately. In a country such as Thailand, it is probably better to wait until the afternoon or the next day to talk to her, and extreme care should be taken not to hurt the person's feelings and not to disturb the harmony between her and you. The following basic precautions should be taken according to Cooper & Cooper (similar advice is given by Engholm 1991: 318).
1. Avoid public confrontation at all cost.
2. See the person yourself.
3. Pick the best time for the talk, preferably when things are going well, never when you are angry.
4. Balance any criticism with praise using a ratio of ten parts praise to one part criticism.
5. Be indirect and diplomatic, offering criticism as suggestions if possible.
6. Be nice all the time and buy lots of cream cakes for everybody.

How indirectly should the criticism be expressed? In the case of your secretary being late, Cooper & Cooper (1990: 138) suggest something like:

> Is everything all right at home? Has the baby recovered? Are you still living at the same place? That's a long way, isn't it? And, if you really need to drive the message home, nothing stronger or more sarcastic than – how long does it take you to get to work?

In fact, even this may upset the harmony between your secretary and yourself, and you should wonder if it is not preferable to put up with the situation as it is, and accept that your secretary arrives late, rather than running the risk of creating a situation which is worse than before by criticizing her. When criticism is issued, it also helps to 'pass the buck', i.e., to hold your own superiors responsible for it, and say, in this case for instance, that *you* will be in trouble if she keeps being late. In that way, the harmony between you and her is not broken as much.

Westerners not only have a hard time being as indirect as is described above; they will also have major difficulties in interpreting and understanding indirect, high-context communication. Suppose you, Westerner, are the secretary, and your boss is Thai. Your boss calls you into his office, repeatedly tells you how good a worker you are, offers you a box of biscuits and says something like 'Are you still living at the same place? That is a long way, isn't it?' There is a good chance that, upon leaving your boss's office, you won't have the slightest idea why you were called in in the first place, – let alone understand that you were being criticized for arriving late!

In 1995 I carried out a survey among over 100 executives in Bangkok, and in the questionnaire I asked my respondents to describe strategies their boss might use to criticize them indirectly. These are their answers.

1. Mention the point of criticism through a colleague
2. Mention a related situation and take that as an example without referring openly to the case at hand; leave the interpretation to me
3. Refer to a future task or assignment and explain how he/she would like it to be done, without mentioning the case at hand
4. Insist that I be cautious in general terms, without mentioning any specific case
5. Show me the correct way without any blame or criticism
6. Point out the problem during a training program
7. Criticize but at the same time stress that I clearly do my best and that there are always many factors involved when something goes wrong
8. Correct the document where I made a mistake, then pass it to his secretary who will forward a copy to me
9. 'Let me learn from experience'
10. Comment on other things that are in my favor...

As one can see, various means are explored to achieve indirectness:
- using an indirect sender of the message, as in (1), where the message is delivered to the addressee by a person other than the criticizer (so that they are not *facing* each other), or in (8)
- choosing an indirect addressee, as in (6), where the error is pointed out during a training program in which the identity of the real addressee is blurred among other participants
- indirectness of the message itself, where another message is delivered than the one which is really intended: a hypothetical or future error in (3), a related but different case in (2).
- Other examples of delivering the message indirectly are based on vagueness, such as in (4).

In those cases where the message is delivered more directly, it is mixed together with praise in order to soften the blow, as in (7) (recall the 'recipe' of Cooper and Cooper (1990) above: 'balance any criticism with praise using a ratio of ten parts praise to one part criticism').

Terms like 'error' or 'mistake' are virtually never pronounced, and even less something like '*you* made a mistake here'. In almost all cases the addressee has to draw his/her own inferences on the basis of the indirect messages he/she receives. Note also that, as in (10), excessive praise should make the addressee suspicious ('why does my boss start praising me like that just now?') and should set him/her thinking that, perhaps, he/she made a mistake.

The context may be all that is left

A respondent in my survey in Thailand says that, when her boss is dissatisfied with something she did,

> I feel it by myself, such as the way the boss treats me has changed, he avoids direct contact with me, some of his attitude is different from normal. These are the warning signs, and let me find out what happened.

In this case, as also in (9) above, there is no verbal message any more. In other words, the entire message is conveyed by the context, the 'atmosphere': when something is wrong, 'you feel it in the air'.

Thailand: indirect communication

When discussing the topic of face saving and high and low context communication with some of my students in Bangkok, I asked them what they would do if an absent-minded teacher wrote an obvious error on the blackboard that could easily be corrected: would they point it out to him/her? The unanimous reply was: no, they would not. When I further asked whether there wasn't, then, any way in which they would inform the teacher about the error he/she made, one of the students replied with a wonderful expression: 'yes, there is: our face would show a question mark.'

Obviously, Westerners who are less used to detecting indirect, contextual messages may have a hard time 'feeling in the air' that something is wrong, or reading the question mark on someone's face.

People from cultures with less explicit communication patterns are likely to detect such non-verbal message more easily:

> When the Tokyo branch manager of an American company heard from New York about potentially serious problems that might befall his office, he was careful to tell no one until he had more information. Nevertheless, within days he got the clear impression that others in the office knew something was up and, if anything, were even more worried than he was. He was baffled as to how the report might have leaked out, until a Japanese co-worker had the courage to ask about the problem. The American explained what he had heard and then asked, 'But how did everybody here know something was wrong?' 'Oh, that was obvious. For the past week you have come to the office with a sad face. That scared us.' (Condon 1984: 44-5)

A Japanese man would feel that his wife is upset if he comes home and a flower is askew in the flower arrangement. If his wife serves him half a cupful of lukewarm tea, the message is even clearer: something is wrong in the household (Stewart, reported in Varner & Beamer 1995: 124).

> [I]n China in the spring of 1983, foreigners who hoped to do international business there were (indirectly) given to understand their hopes should not be too high. Visitors in the Beijing Hotel noticed suddenly, overnight, not a single waitress was wearing makeup. When they asked about this change,

they were told that the woman who read the nightly news on Beijing television had appeared without makeup the night before. Thus the change of policy toward the West was signaled, although a formal statement of the cooling toward the West didn't come for several months. Businesspeople unaccustomed to reading contextual signs were at a disadvantage; those with context interpreters who were able to decipher the signs had information earlier than their competitors who relied on 'hard' facts and published sources (Varner & Beamer 1995: 198).

The need to rely more on non-verbal signals in high-context communication cultures also helps explaining why Japanese (Yoshimura & Anderson 1997: 230), Chinese and South-East Asian people prefer conducting business during face-to-face conversations rather than over the telephone.

Denying the existence of problems

Another strategy which is common in face saving cultures is to (verbally) deny the existence of a problem rather than addressing ('facing') it (see a good example that happened with a group of Chinese in Varner & Beamer 1995: 128). If there is a problem, the supervisor or boss will have to discover it by reading the context, not by relying on verbal information provided by the workers.

> **Thailand: denial of problems and saying 'yes'**
>
> I was sitting next to a Belgian engineer on a plane bound for Bangkok. The engineer worked for the Belgian subsidiary of an American manufacturer of air conditioning and cooling equipment. One of their large cooling devices had been installed in the polyvinyl chloride plant of a Belgian company near Bangkok. The cooling device, however, kept breaking down, and the Belgian engineer was now flying for the fourth time to Thailand to fix it and get it operating properly. It was clear that the Thai workers did not always operate the machine correctly, and that this was the cause of the repeated breakdowns. In order to be able to brief them properly and correct possible manipulation errors, the Belgian engineer asked the Thai workers how exactly they had operated the machine, who was responsible for doing what and when, but he only got evasive answers and denial of any problems (even though the machine was not working). Discouraged, he explained for the umpteenth time how to operate the machine and asked the workers afterwards if they had now understood his explanations; to this question they replied 'yes' unanimously.
>
> As soon as he was back in Belgium, the engineer was called up because the machine had broken down again.

Sad to say, the story above is still typical of a good part of the communication between Westerners and Asians. The Belgian engineer has never received any intercultural training; after repeated visits to the country, he is still unaware that communication in Thailand works differently, and that the probing questions he normally uses back home will not work here. The Thai workers will keep replying 'yes' whenever he asks them if they understand his explanations: to them, saying 'no' would be an insult to their trainer, it would be like saying 'no, your explanations were not very good.'

In addition, the expression 'do you understand?' is frequently used in Thailand, but as an end-of-explanation marker rather than as a real question, and the answer 'yes' to it means nothing at all (Cooper 1991: 75).

To check for understanding, a better strategy would be to ask the Thai person to repeat your instructions or order, but that of course also has its limits:

> Asking for a repetition of words does not guarantee understanding, but it is a lot safer than asking if somebody has understood you. The problem here is the embarrassment involved in grown people behaving like children. Never ask for such verification in anything but a one-to-one situation. Instructions might be repeated perfectly, but it could look as if you do not have full confidence in the poor repeater. [...] If you feel it is necessary to use such tactics, do so sparingly and make it clear that you distrust your own ability to explain something new and important and need to make quite sure that you are both thinking along exactly the same lines (Cooper 1991: 75-6).

The strategy which consists of hiding or denying problems rather than acknowledging them is also exemplified by the fact that Japanese people who do not speak English will often not be introduced. Pretending the person is not present is less embarrassing, less face-threatening than that person being introduced to an English-speaking foreigner and not being able to respond to a simple 'Hello Mister Suzuki, how are you?' At a reception, senior Japanese executives who do not speak English may actually seek to hide themselves (Yoshimura & Anderson 1997: 50). Japanese wives who do not speak English may be present (though this will occur only rarely), but will not be introduced.

Beware of what you say

In cultures with implicit, indirect communication patterns people are used to searching for a 'hidden' meaning behind the words that are spoken. This also implies that when a Westerner utters what he believes to be a direct message, a person from Thailand, Japan or the like might look for a second-order meaning behind the façade of the words that were spoken. Engholm (1991: 193) reports that "[r]ice may be conspicuously absent from today's Chinese banquet table." However, if you happen to express your surprise at this or ask why that is the case, your hosts will interpret this as an (indirect) request for rice and "it will be brought out immediately. If you don't want it, don't ask about it."

> An Innocent Question...
>
> I am sitting in a plane bound for Chiang mai, the second largest city of Thailand, located in the North of the country. At that time, I had never been outside the larger Bangkok area, and as I wanted to know if widespread prostitution is limited to Bangkok or also exists in other areas of the country, I ask my Thai colleague who is sitting next to me: 'Is there a large red light district in Chiang mai as there is in Bangkok?' His reply was: 'When do you want to go there?'

> **An Innocent Joke…**
>
> Last year I met some Japanese at Concordia University, Illinois, USA. One day these Japanese invited my friend and me (we are both Spanish) to have dinner in their apartment. As we entered their apartment, according to the Japanese tradition we took off our shoes. While I was doing that I made a joke, saying to my Japanese friend that it was a very nice and comfortable tradition but that it would be a problem if your feet do not smell very well. My Japanese friend suddenly seemed to be very worried, he disappeared and after few seconds he brought me some deodorant for my feet. (D.B., Spain)

Playing a role or 'true self'?

In the strongly harmony-oriented cultures we have been describing above, there is nearly always a kind of 'emotional distance' and 'surface friendliness' (Klausner 1993: 139) that, Westerners may feel, makes any spontaneity and sincerity nearly impossible. The anthropologist Niels Mulder, after having spent many years of his life in Thailand, shocked Thai people by declaring upon his departure from the country, "I shall leave without having developed a single deep friendship" (Cooper & Cooper 1990: 43).

In fact this simply means that spontaneity and sincerity are valued less highly than preserving harmonious relations.

> We, focusing upon psychological traits as the heart of personal identity, would say they have sacrificed their true selves to their role; they, focusing on social position, say that their role is of the essence of their true selves (Geertz 1973: 386, about Bali).

Every human being to a certain extent plays a role in social situations, is 'on stage', rather than totally being one's own true self; but in the harmony-oriented cultures we described above, the extent to which role-playing overshadows showing one's true feelings, one's true personality (if there is such a thing; see the quote above) may reach nearly 100%.

Geertz (1973: 402) points out that in Bali the concept of *lek,* often translated as 'shame', corresponds more accurately to something like 'stage fright': "… a diffuse, usually mild though in certain situations virtually paralyzing, nervousness before the prospect (and the fact) of social interaction, a chronic, mostly low-grade worry than one will not be able to bring it off with the required finesse.

> What is feared – mildly in most cases, intensely in a few – is that the public performance that is etiquette will be botched, that the social distance etiquette maintains will consequently collapse, and that the personality of the individual will then break through to dissolve its standardized public identity (Geertz 1973: 402).

In Confucian philosophy also, a human being is considered a totality of roles (Nisbett 2005: 5).

5.4.2 **Low context communication**

Most Western cultures are on the direct, explicit, low-context side of this communicative dimension. However, the difference on this scale between two variants of Western culture, the United States and Europe, is still large enough for Europeans to be surprised by the extreme explicitness of many messages in the US, where so little is left to context or interpretation by the listener or reader.

In many instances the reason for this very explicit communication style is the American legal system (which is of course itself an emanation of the culture). In the US, it is much more common and easy to sue a person, company or organization for damages in case the information which would have prevented those damages was not spelled out, or not spelled out clearly enough.[15] Most readers will have heard of the story, apocryphal or not, of the old lady who had dried her cat (or was it a dog?) in her new microwave oven after giving it a bath (she had done so previously in a conventional oven, leaving the door open) and then sued the microwave oven's manufacturer when the cat died: she was awarded damages, because the instructions for use of the microwave oven did not tell her not to put live animals inside.

The instructions for use of an iron I bought when I arrived in the US told me not to put it away in its cardboard box while it is still hot. If the company does not inform the user of this precaution explicitly, and one user does put the iron away in its box while it is still hot, and as a result of that the box catches fire, and his entire house burns down, there is little doubt that user could sue the company successfully: they did not instruct him how to use the iron properly. A European, on the other hand, is likely to feel that the *context* (a hot iron and a cardboard box) is sufficient to tell anyone not to bring those two objects into contact, and that words are superfluous in this case, or even ridiculous.

Once I stayed in a hotel room in New York City where there was a list of six numbered instructions in the bathroom as to how to enter the bathtub (which handles to grasp, which foot to put in first, etc.). Clearly, management was worried that someone who slipped in the bathtub, and as a result hit his head against the wall, might sue the hotel for damages (and would likely be awarded those).

In the US, some fold-up cardboard screens you put behind the front window of your car to prevent the sun from heating up the interior, carry the following message: 'remove before driving'. When reading such messages and warnings, Europeans will feel they are taken for stupid. Of course I'm not going to drive off with the cardboard screen still behind my car's windscreen! Of course I know that bathtubs tend to be slippery! I don't need words (text) for that. Americans, on the other hand, feel that you cannot be too explicit in preventing potential accidents and misunderstandings from happening.

But the American cultural characteristic of extreme explicitness now goes beyond legal reasons, even if perhaps these were at its origins. Somewhere in Northern California I took a picture of this sign on a secluded beach area where there is a small reservation for seals, surrounded by a fence (F16).

Figure 16. California: do not disturb the seals.

As one can see, five quasi-synonymous verbs are used *(harass, bother, interfere with, frighten, tease)* to refer to the concept of 'disturbing'. In European usage, the sign would probably read: 'Do not disturb the seals.' I checked with an American lawyer whether it would make any difference if one of those five verbs, say 'harass', was left out on the sign. Could someone who is disturbing the seals and gets caught by the police then claim that he was not bothering, interfering with, frightening or teasing them, but harassing them, and that harassing is not explicitly prohibited? The answer is no. In fact, using one verb more or less has little if any legal significance, and the extreme explicitness of the message is not only due to legal considerations but has become part of a more general US communicative pattern.

Another example of extremely explicit, low context language where virtually nothing is left to interpretation by the reader can be found in the safety instructions of an airplane (F17). The core message on the page I reproduce is the following: *if you are sitting in a row which leads to an emergency exit, you should, in case of an emergency, be able to follow the instructions by the crew and open the emergency door; therefore, if for some reason you feel you would be unable to do that, please ask for another seat.*

What would be a couple of sentences in Europe becomes a full page in US usage. As one can read, (a) aspects of the issue are typically decomposed into subparts that are expressed and addressed separately, and (b) like in the previous example, lists of quasi-synonyms are used:

- the idea that emergency exits are difficult to open is expressed with two adjectives and four verbs that refer to the successive actions involved in opening the door: *emergency exits are often heavy, awkward to lift, push, pull and maneuver when opening*
- someone not being physically able to open the door is expressed by four nouns: *if you think you lack the strength, mobility, dexterity or balance required to open the exit...*

- various possible reasons for not being able to follow and give instructions are addressed separately rather than taken together: (a) not being able to hear commands because one is hearing impaired, (b) not being able to issue commands because one is voice impaired, (c) not being able to read the instructions because one is visually impaired (that is why there is a message in large characters at the top of the card, for those who forgot their glasses or cannot see well enough)
- the possibility that someone may not understand English is also addressed: a message in six languages (Japanese, Chinese, Korean, German, French, and Spanish) warns such people, if they are sitting in a exit row, to inform the crew.

Figure 17. Safety card in a US airplane.

> **Writing an Exam for US students**
>
> I regularly teach Intercultural Communication classes to groups of US students at the University of Maastricht. I soon learned that I cannot phrase the exam questions in the same way for them as for my Belgian and European students. I need to put limits on what they write, otherwise theirs answers are, in my opinion, long and verbose. I first did this by limiting the space they write their answers in, but that does not work well: many of them then write in very small characters in order to be able to cram as much information as possible in the available space.
>
> The best way is to express the limitation by stating the maximum number of words, as is common indeed in the US. But the first time I did it this way, I still made a mistake.
>
> I wanted the students to define monochronic time and polychronic time respectively, and I added between parentheses: maximum 2 x 20 words. Clear enough? Of course not! Several American students raised their hand and asked me what this meant: Is it maximum 20 words for each answer separately? If I use only 16 words for monochronic time, am I allowed to transfer the four remaining words to my definition of polychrony? Or is it simply 40 words maximum altogether, and am I entitled to decide how many I use for my definition of monochrony, and how many for polychrony? Etc.
>
> Similarly, when I request my students to write a paper and tell them that it should be approximately 5 pages long, many Americans will immediately ask if this is single-spaced or double-spaced: Europeans students seldom ask this question, if ever.

American (US) low context communication patterns extend into the intercultural literature. For example, in a book called *Culture Clash. Managing in a Multicultural World,* Seelye & Seelye-James (1995: 177, 179) advise expatriates to (a) buy a ten or twenty dollar radio, (b) eat well and sleep well, (c) write to family and friends. Europeans may find this type of advice too trivial and obvious to be mentioned in words, while Americans (US) find it normal to express it verbally.

Fisk (2006: 939) reports that even some weapons manufactured in the US carry a disclaimer; he found Pennsylvania gas cartridges used by the Israelis in Bethlehem with the following text:

> Federal Laboratories will assume no responsibility for the misuse of this device.

Notes

1. For a list of sports expressions many American businesspeople might use (and should avoid), see Varner & Beamer 1995: 56, Varner 1996.
2. Gruzinski (2004: 436) notes that when Christian missionaries arrived in China, it proved impossible to sinicize scholasticism because Chinese did not have the terms required for it.
3. Cooper (1991: 94), however, reports that in Thailand 'some candidates have the initiative to exaggerate their skills somewhat'.

4. When there is an emergency in the company, however, feuds will be moderated and in a move of solidarity everyone will work together to redress the situation.
5. Previously English also had a honorificals system with two forms for the second person singular: the familiar *thou* and polite *you*. Because *thou* has become archaic and obsolete, speakers of English may now mistakenly feel that *thou* is the polite form. It is used for instance when addressing God, in some variants of Christianity.
6. For the royal family, *rachasap* or royal language has to be used, a complete grammatical system where most words receive a specific rachasap prefix (Segaller 1993: 15-18).
7. The group of university graduates who graduated in the same year [my footnote].
8. This does not necessarily mean that the objective distance between social classes is also higher. In Japan, in particular, the wage differential between the highest and the lowest paid people in a company is narrower than in many Western countries (Yoshimura & Anderson 1997: 186).
9. For a theoretical model of the *explicit/implicit* ratio in communication, see Haworth and Savage 1989.
10. Do I need to stress once more that these terms refer to tendencies, not absolutes? There is no such thing as an absolute low context communication culture (where you say everything you feel or think and never leave anything implicit), nor does there exist an absolute high context culture (where everything would be implied, nothing said).
11. Nydell (1987: 59) reports that in Arab countries also, if you ask directions people may try to give you an answer even if they do not know. This even worked with a fictitious address (in Riyadh), for which 'the crowning moment came when [someone] asked two policemen, who simultaneously pointed in the opposite directions'. However, in Arab countries the motivation to do so might be somewhat different from Thailand: it seems to spring primarily from the desire not to be seen as unhelpful.
12. In Klausner's story, the Thai student considers the bicycle as a gift to the thief, to whom he might very well have been tied in a karmic embrace forged in a former life. 'It was certainly in the realm of possibility that our friend might once have stolen something from the present-day urban thief in a previous existence.'.
13. The United States is, of course, at the extreme opposite end of the spectrum; European countries are somewhere in between these two extremes [my footnote].
14. To a certain degree, this extends to criticizing the authorities. Criticizing your own government strongly (a common practice in the West) may be unsettling to Asians (Engholm 1991: 296) [my footnote].
15. It is of course beyond the scope of this book to elaborate on the legal risks and on the precautions that anyone should take when entering the US market, but I cannot emphasise strongly enough the need for extensive (and expensive!) legal counsel in those cases.

    The sums that are awarded as compensation will appear astronomical to Europeans. After a mortal accident in Cavalese, Italy, where an American fighter plane cut through the cables of a mountain cable car, the US authorities were offering US$ 2,000,000 for every person killed. In New Mexico, a woman was awarded US$ 1,000,000 because she burnt herself when she spilled a cup of hot coffee she had bought at McDonald's over her thighs. It was proven that the coffee was a couple of degrees *too* hot, therefore McDonald's was held responsible for the burns she incurred.

Chapter 6
Non verbal communication

Non-verbal communication refers to means of expression that are non-linguistic, such as gestures, bodily posture, facial expression, eye contact (or the lack of it), etc. In the communication process, the non-verbal part should not be underestimated. In many cases, human beings convey more meaning non-verbally than verbally. Experiments have shown that when the verbal and the non-verbal signals contradict each other (such as when someone says she likes your application for the job but her face tells otherwise), people tend to rely on the non-verbal signals more and give priority to those.

As we pointed out before, a good part of our non-verbal communicative behavior is unconscious: we are not always aware what our facial expression conveys, how much eye contact we establish, which gestures we make with our hands, etc. There is also little documentation and training material available in this field. I can easily find grammar books, dictionaries, study methods for, say, the Turkish language, but finding a dictionary or study method of Turkish *gestures* will be another matter: they probably do not even exist. This situation is changing gradually: gestures and others means of non-verbal communication are being studied scientifically nowadays (for examples of how this can be done, see, for instance, Poyatos 1992, Burgoon, Buller & Woodall 1996), and some dictionaries are starting to be published.

Klausner (1993: 315-318) gives a good description of the intricacies of body language in a single culture, i.e., Thailand.

- The way in which the greeting sign or *wai* is carried out must, just like bowing in Japan, correctly reflect the respective social position of the people involved.
- It is advisable to always sit with both feet on the ground, because sitting cross-legged involves the risk of pointing with your foot at someone, and that is considered particularly rude. Segaller (1993: 69) warns against kicking a door shut or similar actions which a Westerner might use his foot for; Engholm (1991: 138) in my opinion correctly says that using feet or referring to them is worse in Thailand than elsewhere, even if in other Asian countries it is not advisable either.
- For sleeping, in Thailand, the head should face West.

- Staring and intense eye contact will make Thai people (and many other South-East Asians) extremely uncomfortable and/or may be interpreted as a threat. Touching occurs rarely or never.
- Bodily contact between monks and women is absolutely taboo, and the Thai manage to avoid it even in a crowded bus. And so forth.

We mentioned above that in cultures where high context, indirect communication patterns prevail, people are more geared toward reading and interpreting non-verbal cues than Westerners are. According to Hall (1983: 161) Hispanics are also 'more attuned to the significance of subtle body cues' than whites, and black Americans even more than Hispanics.

We already discussed several instances of non-verbal expression in the previous chapters: proxemics, haptics, etc., which we will not repeat here. Below I will concentrate on facial expressions, eye contact and gestures.

6.1 Facial expressions

Here as elsewhere, when considering human behavior the first question one should ask is: is this feature universal or culture-specific? If it is universal, i.e., if all human beings behave in this respect in identical or similar ways, then it is innate and genetically defined. If the feature varies from one culture to the next, then it is something we have learned through immersion in the culture we grew up in.

Research has established that, contrary to gestures which are culture-specific, a human's basic facial expressions are universal. There are supposed to be six, or for some authors seven or more, basic facial expressions which every human being will recognize (see various publications by Ekman & Friesen (1969, 2003), who are pioneers in this field):

1. Anger
2. Fear
3. Disgust
4. Surprise
5. Happiness
6. Sadness
7. [Contempt]

My students interpret these with more than 95% accuracy, regardless of the culture of the student involved. See if you can identify them in the following pictures (F18).

Unsurprisingly, as we are dealing with the complexities of human behavior, nothing is totally clear-cut. Even if basic facial expressions are universal, there may be some culturally-induced variation. A recent study at Glasgow University (referred to on the BBC News website 14 August 2009) has discovered that East Asian subjects focus more on the eyes whereas Westerners scan the whole face. As a result, East Asians are more likely than Westerners to read

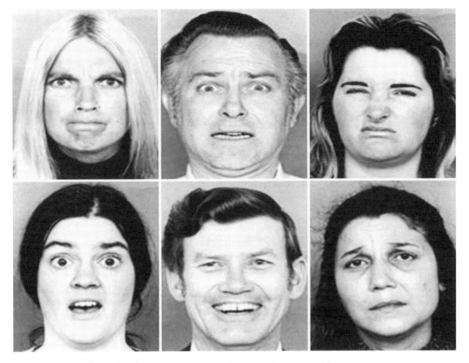

Figure 18. Six basic facial expression (from: Ekman & Friesen 1969).

the expression for 'fear' as 'surprise' and 'disgust' as 'anger'. Interestingly, the emoticons Chinese and Japanese people use in messages illustrate this difference:

Emoticons	West	East
Happy	: -)	(^_^)
Sad	: -(	(;_;) or (T_T)
Surprise	: -o	(o.o)

As one can see, in the Western emoticons the only feature that changes is the shape of the mouth; in the East Asian emoticons, what changes most are the eyes.

Laughing universally signals happiness, openness, friendship. But here also there may be some cultural variants. In many Asian countries, to be sure people smile or laugh when they are happy, but also when they are embarrassed. Recall the story, above, of the Japanese who are taking their Polish colleague to a sushi bar. The Japanese start laughing, not because they find the situation funny, but because they are terribly embarrassed by the answer the Polish man gives: he does not like sushi, yet they are taking him to a sushi bar. Imagine you are negotiating in Japan and push your Japanese partners into a corner. They would like to say 'no' because they fundamentally disagree with what you propose, but they cannot, for face-saving reasons. If then they start giggling or laughing, it is not because suddenly the atmosphere has become more relaxed; it is because they are so stressed they do not know how to react otherwise.

> **Thailand: Laughing to hide embarrassment**
> - A young female student in one of my business communication classes in Bangkok decided to give an oral presentation about prostitution and sex tourism in Thailand. She gave her entire presentation smiling and laughing, because she was rather embarrassed to talk about the topic although she had chosen it herself. I had to warn her that if she acted like this in Europe or America, people would think she considered prostitution and sex tourism to be funny.
> - I am sitting on the back seat of one of those motorcycle-taxis that are common in Bangkok. They bring you to your destination quicker than a regular taxi (car) in the congested city. The driver (inadvertently, I believe) enters a deserted one-way street in the wrong direction and, bad luck, only a couple of meters around the corner a policeman is standing next to his motorcycle. The policeman shouts a warning that I can clearly hear but that is ignored by my driver. The policeman jumps on his motorcycle in hot pursuit of the taxi man, who eventually is made to stop. As soon as the policeman dismounts and verbal contact is established between him and the driver, the taxi man starts laughing and he continues to do so during the whole process where he is given a ticket and a stern warning by the policeman.
> - A Belgian student at the Asian Institute of Technology (AIT) in Bangkok had gathered a large number of newspaper clippings he intended to use for his term paper. Unfortunately, the Thai chamber maids who cleaned his room thought this was all rubbish and threw all the clippings away. When the Belgian student decided to complain about this to various people such as the head of housekeeping and even the head of AIT himself, he was astonished to discover that his complaints were met with laughter in all cases and did not seem to be taken seriously. A few weeks later, however, when entering his room he discovered that someone had placed on his desk a pile of photocopied articles representing an extensive bibliography on the topic of his term paper.

6.2 Eye contact

Sustained eye contact is almost a precondition to communication in many Western countries. To many Americans and Europeans, avoiding eye contact is a sign that you have something to hide, that you are not being straightforward. One of my American colleagues asks her students, when she suspects they have been cheating, to 'look her straight into the eyes', the assumption being that this makes it harder for them to lie.

In a popular magazine I picked up in an airplane, the author of an article on body language writes

> Eye contact is a big "tell" (to use the poker term). If they're breaking eye contact, that might mean they're hiding something. Downturned eyes might mean lying (Sophia Dembling in *Sky Magazine*, Delta Airlines, October 2007).

Interviewing Colonel Qaddafi of Libya

At the time when Colonel Qaddafi of Libya was depicted in the Western press as one of the leaders of world terrorism, an American female journalist went to interview him in Tripoli. As usual, Qaddafi received her in a tent rather than in his presidential palace. After she returned, the journalist declared that he did not refuse to answer even her most probing questions, but that he would never look her into the eyes during the interview. To her, this clearly implied that Qaddafi was not honest and straightforward, that he was lying. In reality, the most likely interpretation is that Qaddafi, as a Muslim man sitting close to an unveiled woman who was not his legal wife, avoided eye contact as much as possible out of respect for her.

In many cultures in Asia and elsewhere, on the other hand, the subordinate or socially lower person should not look his superior straight into the eyes, but is expected to lower his eyes out of respect. Victor (1992: 207) quotes an assistant superintendent of a school in Michigan, USA:

> I made a major intercultural error. While disciplining an American Indian student for skipping school, he took his eyes off me and put his head down. I said, 'When I'm talking to you, pick up your head and look me straight in the eye.'
>
> Later, from the father I discovered it was a sign of respect when an American Indian responds by lowering his eyes. It meant he was accepting his responsibility in this situation. When I forced him to look me into the eye, it went against his cultural and historical customs.
>
> I created a situation of confusion and probably hostility.

Absence of Eye Contact: Mistaken Attribution

A common complaint of school teachers in Belgium (and probably elsewhere in Europe) is that their students of Moroccan origin do not look them into the eyes when they are talking to them. To the Belgian teacher, this means that the student refuses to enter the communication process and listens only passively. To the student, it is a mark of respect for the teacher, and looking the teacher into the eyes would convey defiance and hostility.

Pinxten (1994: 63) notes that Navajo adults, when conversing, not only stand several meters apart, but also avoid eye contact almost totally when speaking to each other. African Americans (US) are reported to establish less eye contact than whites (Shadid 1998: 151).

Westerners who look Japanese and many other Asians straight into the eyes for relatively sustained periods of time will make their interlocutor uncomfortable: the Asians will feel that their private sphere is invaded. Japanese women are likely to keep their eyes down even more.

In the Arab world, on the other hand, between equals eye contact is likely to be more intensive than in the West. Also, after shaking hands "an Arab may continue to hold the other person's hand while talking" (Nydell 1987: 44); and men (as well as women, but only among members of the same sex) may kiss in public, embrace and hold hands.

So may Latin Americans. A study by John Graham quoted by Adler (1992: 210) and Engholm (1991: 134) showed that during a negotiation (a) Brazilians touch the other person on average approximately every 6 minutes, while Japanese and Americans (US) do not touch at all, and (b) Brazilians carry out facial gazing for 5.2 out of 10 minutes (i.e., slightly over 50% of the total time), as against 3.3 minutes for the Americans and 1.3 minutes for the Japanese. The figures for the British and Germans are close to those for Americans (US): they look their interlocutor into the eyes around 30% of the time.

6.3 Gestures

6.3.1 Nodding and shaking your head

Nodding one's head (up and down) to signify 'yes' and shaking it (left to right) for 'no' is so widespread that one might well think that this gesture is universal. However, that is not the case. In some parts of the Balkans (Bulgaria, Greece), a quick movement upwards of the head means 'no'. And in India, among other countries, the characteristic *head wobble* is used to express agreement.

Contrary to facial expressions as seen above, the vast majority of gestures, if not all, are culture-specific. That also entails that they are prone to potential misinterpretation.

In addition, until relatively recently gestures were rarely studied scientifically. Every language has its dictionaries, but where are the dictionaries of gestures?

Khrushchev's gesture: victory over the Americans?

On his first visit to the United States, in the middle of the Cold War, Nikita Khrushchev put his hands, clasped together, above his head as soon as the door of his plane opened and he showed himself to the journalists. The American and international press took this gesture to mean 'victory', 'I come here as a winner'; it was interpreted as a sign of arrogance by many.

When teaching intercultural communication to an international group of students, I had the chance to test what I had read in the intercultural literature about the Khrushchev incident and the mistaken attribution it gave rise to. *All* my students, including those from Poland and the Czech Republic, shared the same interpretation of Khrushchev's gesture: victory. There was only one exception, but that was, interestingly enough, a student from Russia. To her, the gesture meant 'friendship': the clasped hands above the head symbolise a handshake, in Khrushchev's case presumably a handshake between the American people and the Russian people. The interpretation of Khrushchev's gesture by the American and international press and public was mistaken, and could even have led to negative political consequences.

On a more general level, Westerners should train themselves to refrain from wide gestures in Asia, where such gestures may give an impression of anger (Engholm 1991: 139).

In what follows, we limit ourselves to a brief discussion of two commonly used gestures: the 'OK' sign and the hand motion for beckoning.

6.3.2 The 'OK' sign

One of the first scholars in the field of the comparative study of gestures is Desmond Morris. Readers may know Morris from his more popular books such as *The Naked Ape,* but he also did scientific research in the field of gestures, published in books such as *Gestures* and the more popular *Manwatching.* In order to draw maps of the geographical spread of gestures, Morris had his assistants show plates with drawings of several dozen gestures to people in many parts of the world, asking (a) if the gesture means something and (b) if so, what does it mean.

Take the example of the American 'OK' sign, where you form a circle with your thumb and forefinger.

 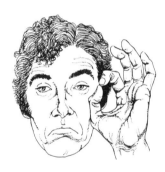

The Circle-sign made by forming a ring with the thumb and forefinger of one hand. It carries different messages for different people. An Englishman knows only one meaning for this sign: for him, both drawings (above carry an 'OK' message. But for many Frenchmen only the smiling picture is signalling 'OK', while the other signals 'zero' or 'worthless'. To a Japanese (below) the same sign may mean 'money'.

Figure 19. The OK sign (from: Morris 1979).

We have quite a bit of information about the origin of this gesture, its history, and its geographical distribution. With the 'OK' meaning, the gesture originated in the US. It carries the meaning 'OK' because originally it consisted of pressing the thumb and the forefinger together, showing that something was thin or fine (like a sheet of paper). In English, the word *fine* has the literal meaning of 'thin' as well as the figurative meaning of 'good'; the latter is the meaning the gesture has acquired now.

The OK-sign was brought to Europe with the American GIs at the end of World War II: it did not exist in Europe with that meaning before. In Great Britain, the only meaning it carries is the imported, American meaning: OK. On the continent (such as in France), however, it clashed with another meaning of the same gesture that already existed before: 'zero', 'you're worthless.'

Nowadays the positive and the negative meaning co-exist in France, and the context, such as facial expression, will signal whether the gesture means 'OK' or 'worthless.' The same gesture has yet two other meanings in other parts of the world: in Japan, it means 'money' (presumably because the gesture resembles a coin); in many Latin American countries, the gesture is strongly obscene (it is the non-verbal equivalent of 'Fuck you!'), and should therefore be avoided.

6.3.3 Beckoning

Beckoning consists of making a gesture with the hand to call someone to come closer. In Northern Europe (England, Holland, France; also Belgium), it is carried out palms up, most often with the index finger sticking out in a hook and moving back and forth. In Southern Europe, including most of Italy, part of Spain, etc., it is done exactly the other way round: palms down (Morris 1979). The same is true, in my experience, in most of Asia and Africa. According to Morris, beckoning palms down prevails in Tunisia (almost 60%, as against slightly over 20% palms up); Nydell (1987: 46) also describes the Arab gesture 'come here' as palm down, while acknowledging that there exists regional variation.

To add to the confusion, the opposite gesture strongly resembles the 'farewell' gesture in both cases: in Northern Europe waving farewell is done palms down; around the Mediterranean it is done palms up. As a result of this, the risk of misinterpretation is particularly high. One day I witnessed a scene on television where during a football (soccer) game, the Brazilian referee beckoned a German player to come to him (palms down); the German took the referee's gesture to mean that he should move away from the referee, and that is what he did.

Chapter 7
Etiquette

In any foreign country you visit, even as a simple tourist, the first problems you may have to tackle are issues of etiquette: how do I greet other people, when is it recommended to bring a gift and which gifts are appropriate, how do I behave at a dinner table and how do I eat and drink, and so forth. Many of these conventions are arbitrary and seemingly superficial, yet mastering them may open the door to fruitful contacts with people from other cultures. In matters of etiquette, knowing as many facts as possible may be more important than insight and understanding, and lists of *do's and don'ts* may be more useful here than elsewhere in intercultural communication issues.

Rules of etiquette are by no means universal. In Japan, it is polite to make slurping noises when eating soup, in the West it is not. Westerners may be dismayed when Chinese spit on the ground, while Indonesians, Japanese and also Brazilians will find the Western habit of blowing your nose in public, in a handkerchief which you then carry around, horrible (see also Ferraro 1994: 33). Japanese consider sitting in a bathtub where the water is not running dirty, and they find it incredible that the toilet is located in the bathroom in many Western homes. In several Asian countries, including Japan, some people might sleep during a presentation or in a restaurant while others are still eating, without this being considered impolite. And so forth.

In many cases the origin of conventional behavior is completely lost in time, even to those who practice it in everyday life. For instance, the origin of the handshake presumably lies in the fact that the extended arm with the open hand meant that a person comes unarmed, therefore has friendly rather than hostile feelings with regard to you. But this explanation is irrelevant to the present practice of handshaking, and many of us are not even aware of it.

In this book, it is obviously impossible to discuss etiquette throughout the world in depth, even less to provide advice on do's and don'ts for all cultures around the world. A good tourist guide, or a search on the Internet, can provide a first introduction to rules of etiquette in the country or countries you are to visit. As etiquette is visible and its rules often consciously held, it is usually possible to ask natives of the country about what is appropriate behavior and what is not; you can even do that before you leave. Attentive observation of the native people's behavior (in the street, in a restaurant, etc.) is also a good guide.

Below, I will briefly treat a few major aspects of etiquette: greetings, gift giving, food and dining; I will also discuss some cases of taboos, i.e., behavior that is to be avoided at all cost.

7.1 Greetings

In any culture, people who meet each other or are introduced to each other will perform a greeting ritual. In Western countries, greetings often take the form of a handshake. The amount of handshaking that goes on, and the way it is carried out, are culture-specific. Most Europeans shake hands vastly more than Americans. In many offices in Belgium, a worker who comes in in the morning or who arrives at a meeting will shake hands with all those who are already there. In the US, on the other hand, two persons may shake hands when they are introduced to each other, then never exchange handshakes any more. The variants of the handshake are innumerable, ranging from a weak touch to a vigorous shake. In parts of Africa, special affection is shown by a triple handshake: a handshake, then grasping the other person's thumb, then a second handshake. In certain cultures, such as some Muslim countries (or groups), men do not normally shake hands with women. Many cultures where originally handshakes did not exist took them over from the West: when a Westerners visits India, Thailand or Japan, his hosts may well shake hands with him/her. Observing what people around you engage in is usually a safe guide for determining what is appropriate.

The traditional Japanese greeting ritual is the bow; in Thailand, it is the *wai*,[1] which consists of holding your hands vertically, palms together, in front of your chest (the Indian *namaste* looks similar to the *wai*). In Japan as well as in Thailand, however, the precise way in which greeting is carried out must reflect the respective social position of the two or more people who are involved, as said above. In Japan, the person who is socially lower will bow more, the superior bows less: there is an exact correlation between your social status and the angle at which you bow. In Thailand, the person who is socially lower (such as a subordinate with his/her boss, or a student with a professor) will lower his head and place his hands in the *wai* position higher up; the superior will simply hold his hands in front of his chest, without lowering himself. In Japan as well as Thailand, a Westerner who does not master the intricacies of the local social hierarchy and the way it is reflected in greetings is well advised to refrain from bowing or using the *wai*. Doing it wrong may convey arrogance (if you do not bow or *wai* deeply enough to a person who is socially superior) or may be absurd and ridiculous (such as the tourist who extends a 'deep' *wai* to a waitress, who is obviously socially inferior to him/her).

7.2 Gift giving

Exchanging gifts is a way of establishing good relations, sometimes leading to real friendship. In many Western countries, this ritual is not very important, and the value of business gifts, if any, is very limited. Sometimes there are legal restrictions with respect to the maximum value of gifts, lest they might be considered as bribery.[2] In Asia, however, exchanging gifts with business partners is an essential element of building a good relationship, and the value of the gifts that are exchanged may seem high in Western eyes.[3] It is difficult to give precise indications, because it all depends on the professional and social level of the people involved, the type of contacts they have, etc. Nevertheless, figures that are often quoted for Japan concerning the value of business gifts are in the area of US$ 200-500, vastly more than what is appropriate in Western countries. A typical business gift for a Japanese partner might be an expensive, exclusive bottle of old cognac or whisky of US$ 500, or British men's clothing (such as an expensive Burberry raincoat) worth US$ 500. Some Thai executives have confirmed to me that occasionally they offer business gifts worth up to US$ 1,000. In Thailand also, these gifts include expensive to *very* expensive bottles of aged whisky of cognac, which are then normally not drunk, but exposed at the receiver's home in a glass display cabinet (it is said that some people drink the liquor and then replace it with coffee or coke in the bottle on display, but I have not seen any evidence of that...).

Once again, carefully informing oneself in advance of what is appropriate and what is not, is essential. The Japanese will choose the gift they offer very carefully (see also Kumayama 1990). They may call your secretary to ask about your tastes, reading habits, the kind of music you like, etc. In Japan more than anywhere else, the wrapping of the gift is essential: it should be absolutely perfect, with no wrinkles in the paper, well-chosen colors, etc. Lin (1993) shows that even Japanese commercials emphasize the wrapping and packaging of the product, likened to an ancient art form.

In Asia, unlike most of Europe and America, gifts are traditionally not opened in front of the giver (for fear of both parties losing face in case it becomes clear that the gift is not well chosen), though Asians may now sometimes take over the Western habit of opening the gift immediately.

Gift Giving: China and Japan

- An American consultant brings an American educational institution together with a group of twenty businesspeople from the People's Republic of China. He purchased expensive photo books of the Pacific Northwest for each of them, has them wrapped appropriately, and permits the Chinese to take the gifts home unopened.
'At this moment, the members of the [American] educational institution announced that they too had gifts for the Chinese. After passing out 20 additional gifts, they urged the Chinese to unwrap them. The mood in the room turned icy. The Chinese balked, but finally gave in and started unwrapping. Out came 20 inexpensive laminated photographs mounted on wooden plaques. 'It looked like something you'd find at a carnival' recounted the consultant. The Chinese were instantly embarrassed, and found it impossible to feign appreciation in order to save face for the givers of such chintzy gifts. The earlier good mood of the evening was irretrievable.' (Engholm 1991: 221-2).

- Two Dutch businessmen brought with them to Tokyo a number of wrapped calendars, printed with their company's name, intended as gifts for their Japanese partners. On the evening before the crucial first meeting, in their hotel room in Tokyo, one of them did some reading on the art of gift giving in Japan, and it then dawned on them that offering such a 'cheap' item might be worse than giving nothing at all.

7.3 Dining, smoking and entertainment

There exists a vast variety of foodstuffs world-wide, ranging from caterpillars to marshmallows, over moldy cheese, bird's saliva or incubated eggs. While usually no-one will be literally forced to eat food one considers non edible, being open to new experiences in this field will be appreciated by the hosts in the country visited, and I believe that it is possible to train oneself to gradually become more open in this field as elsewhere.

Hospitality in Mauritania

When travelling with friends through the Sahara desert in Mauritania, we were invited by a family of nomads to have tea with them in their tent. Hospitality is a prime value in Bedouin culture, also in Mauritania. When we saw the tea being prepared, then served, it was clear that conditions of hygiene were nowhere near our own standards. People had very little water to spare, and washing the glasses in which the tea was served had clearly not been done for some time. In addition, we thought of a French friend we had met in Nouakchott, the capital of Mauritania, a few days earlier, who had contracted hepatitis recently, possibly by drinking contaminated water. But refusing the local people's offer for tea would be a terrible insult...

In the story above, we decided to drink the tea that was served to us; but this is the kind of decision where no textbook will be able to tell you what to do!

In many countries, business lunches and dinners are an essential element in the business relation. Above we described how in France the business lunch has the clear function of probing the other party's education and culture. In the Arab world as well, sharing meals (and socializing before the food is brought in) is an important element of a business relation (Nydell 1987: 62). Engholm (1991: 206) reports that in Japan, 1.5% of GDP is spent on business entertainment, as against 1% on defense.

In China, lavish banquets will be offered to visitors. These are not simply an occasion to feed oneself. Apart from the symbolism attached to various foodstuffs and their combination in Chinese culture, the way you eat your food will be carefully observed by the Chinese. A Chinese businessman tells Christopher Engholm (1991: 183) that "he decides whether he's going to do business with a foreigner simply by watching the foreigner eat": eating slowly means that you are a patient businessperson; happily trying food you have never had before indicates flexibility in business; politeness and formality mean that you will be careful to save face, etc. In China and some of the other less wealthy countries in Asia, a visit by foreign guests may be seen as an opportunity to enjoy the 'good life', because entertaining the foreign delegation will give access to luxuries one cannot afford otherwise (Engholm 1991: 260).

The Chinese are proud of their cuisine (with its many regional variants), considered to be one of the best in the world also by many non-Chinese. In Thailand too, the food is superb, but making extensive compliments about it is not usually done and sounds odd to the Thai. Engholm (1991: 204) confirms my own observations in this respect.

In Arab countries, if invited to someone's home for lunch or dinner, it is not appropriate to put too much stress on how good the food was, because this might convey the idea that the food in itself was more important than the hospitality and friendship (Condon & Yousef 1975: 37).

In many countries around the world, certain foodstuffs are taboo or not considered edible: pork (and alcohol) in Muslim countries, beef in India, non-kosher foods for orthodox Jews, etc. Many (though not all) Muslim countries tolerate that non-Muslims have different eating and drinking habits: a Westerner can have a glass of beer or wine in Morocco or in the Emirates, ethnic Chinese can raise pigs and eat pork in predominantly Muslim Malaysia or Indonesia.

Vegetarians (real ones, who eat neither fish nor meat), on the other hand, should be advised that they will have a hard time in many countries around the world, including continental Europe, particularly Southern Europe. Vegetarian restaurants in Paris, Madrid or Rome are few and far between, and those that exist are usually not places where you would go for a business lunch. Ordering a vegetarian meal in a regular upscale restaurant will probably result in getting the same dish as the others minus the meat or fish rather than in getting a vegetarian dish that was cooked as such. My American trainees or students often suggest getting a salad in such cases. But (apart from the frowns of the maître d'hôtel when ordering it) imagine having a mere salad, which you will finish in less than fifteen minutes, while others are having a three-course meal that will last over two hours... In Asia as well, it may prove impossible to be a vegetarian or to maintain a low-salt diet (Engholm 1991: 184). I stayed in Yokohama (Japan) once with a friend who is a vegetarian, and for whom our Japanese colleagues had made a little note in Japanese that he would show when we entered a café or restaurant. The note supposedly said something like 'I am a vegetarian, please take this into account when serving me food' – but my friend was still served anything from meat and poultry to fish and seafood.

Having lunch or dinner together with your hosts in a foreign country also involves table manners, such as seating arrangements, appropriate ways of helping oneself to food and drinks and bringing it to your mouth. We described the stratified nature of many Asian societies before. In such cultures, seating arrangements will most often be formally defined, depending on the social status of everyone. In many Asian countries, including China and Thailand, it is polite to serve other people with food and drinks: your neighbor will pour beer in your glass, put what he/she considers tasty morsels of food on your plate, etc.; doing the same may help in establishing a good working relationship (my own observations in Thailand in this respect are confirmed by Engholm (1991: 216) for Japan and possibly for other Asian countries).

Figure 20. 'No salad as a meal': an English phrase on an otherwise French restaurant menu in Brussels, meant to discourage American tourists from ordering salad only.

> China: serving others
>
> An American on assignment in China was one of the honoured guests of a lavish banquet where many Chinese delicacies were served. One item which arrived on her plate was a whole quail served with the head, beak and eye. As soon as she saw it, she knew she would never be able to eat it, and she was thinking of a way to get rid of it. She was aware of the habit, in China, of offering food to your neighbor at the table, and that is what she did. She put the quail on her neighbor's plate, saying something like 'This looks wonderful, let me offer it to you!'

In a face saving culture such as China, this was an appropriate way of getting rid of the quail. Her neighbor may well have understood that she did not want to eat it; but nothing was said about that openly, no disparaging remarks about the food were made.

In Hong Kong and China, oftentimes the head of the chicken is cooked and served with the rest of the meat. This is also a way of proving that a fresh chicken was used, as frozen chicken are not sold with their head. Yet this way of presentation (see F21) so horrified one off my Belgian colleagues (as it would, no doubt, have horrified many others including many Americans) that she was unable to taste the dish.

Figure 21. Hong Kong: the chicken's head on the plate proves it is fresh, not frozen.

Serving certain fish (such as trout) with the head is common in Europe, but not something Americans are typically used to.

In China, fish is fresh when it is still alive; you may have to choose your own fish in the restaurant fish tank, and then they will fish it out of the tank and cook it for you. On one of my visits to China, in the city of Xi'an the same treatment was reserved for snakes: they were held alive in little cages in the restaurant until a customer ordered one, and then they were killed and cooked to perfection.

Eating utensils also vary, and it is useful to train oneself in eating in different ways: with the fork in the left hand as in Europe, or in the right, as in the US; with chopsticks, or with your hands. Anyone who visits Asia should be able, where applicable, to eat with chopsticks in order to avoid embarrassment, both to him/herself and to the hosts. It does not take more than a couple of hours to learn, so just do it! Your Asian hosts may provide you with a fork if you request one, but they will look at you differently if you use chopsticks confidently.

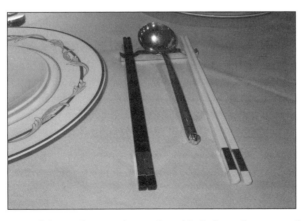

Figure 22. Two sets of chopsticks, one white and one black, for each guest at a luxury restaurant in Hong Kong: what might they be used for?

When the bill comes up in the restaurant, there is a simple rule that applies nearly everywhere outside the West: the inviter pays all. To my knowledge, this rule is valid throughout all of Asia and Africa, and probably in many other places as well. Insisting to pay the bill yourself if you were not the inviter is rude, and proposing to pay your share is even less acceptable. In poorer countries, insisting to pay because you feel you can afford it better than the locals who invited you is especially humiliating to them.

> **An African in Belgium: the inviter pays?**
>
> Soon after my brother in law arrived from Africa to study in Brussels, a Belgian fellow student invited him to go to the movies one night with the others and then have something to eat afterwards. He gladly accepted and joined the group with only some small change in his pocket, convinced as he was that the movie as well as the dinner would be paid for by the person who had invited him.
>
> He was wrong.

Drinking habits also vary widely. In most Asian countries, the standard drink with a meal in a restaurant is beer rather than wine, though this may be changing nowadays. It is quite acceptable, though, to decline drinking beer and ask for water or tea. In some cases, several drinks will be served (and drunk!) simultaneously: beer, wine, rice wine, tea...

Many Asian women drink very little or nothing, presumably because they think they will get drunk very quickly (there may be some truth in that, as the effect of alcohol is inversely related to body weight). Americans will find it strange that many Europeans, in particular in Southern Europe, drink wine during a business lunch, which takes place during the working day. In general, there is a much stronger pressure against drinking in the US than in Europe. Americans will be amazed to find out that beer and/or wine is being served at fast food hamburger restaurants such as McDonald's in Europe, where children might be present! In Central and Eastern Europe, on the other hand, drinking together is an integral part of the socializing process that precedes business discussions. Varner and Beamer (1995: 215) report that in Hungary, a non-drinker might very well be discarded as a potential business partner because of that.

> [F]riendships [in Eastern Europe] are best established over a dinner table and bonded with alcohol (Richmond 1995: 7).

> **Poland: How to Decline Drinks**
>
> A junior Belgian researcher who is a non-drinker was on assignment in Poland and she was constantly 'harassed' by well-meaning Polish colleagues in her company who wanted her to drink with them.

> Only after a few days did she find the one answer that definitively stopped the Poles from pressing on with the issue. She told them she was under medical treatment for drinking too heavily and could not touch one drop of alcohol because of that. The Poles could relate to that story and did not insist any further.

The acceptance of smoking may constitute a problem for non-smokers in many countries. In Central and Eastern Europe, smoking is still more common. According to Richmond (1995: 238), over half of the men are regular smokers in the Baltic states. In Arab countries also, the majority of adults smoke (women also, but seldom in public) and people may disregard 'No smoking' signs in waiting rooms. If you ask the Arab person to put out his cigarette, he may do so but light another one a few minutes later. Insisting will appear unreasonable (Nydell 1987: 66). Many Chinese and Japanese males are heavy smokers (Japanese males are among the heaviest smokers in the world, but the Japanese also have the highest longevity in the world, though there is no connection of course with smoking).

In several East and South-East Asian countries (Japan, Korea, the Philippines, Thailand) an evening out may end up at a karaoke bar. Whether you sing well or you have the worst voice possible does not matter that much, but refusing to participate will disappoint everyone. A Westerner is advised to learn a few well-knows song (the Beatles' *Yesterday* is a good one, or Sinatra's *Strangers in the Night*) before leaving for Asia. Engholm (1991: 213-4) rightly advises that the person who is invited to sing should decline once or twice before accepting; that holds for other invitations in Asia as well.

In several of the non-Muslim Asian countries, and in some others, if you are male and the locals get to know you better, a further stage in the getting acquainted process might consist of sexual entertainment, including being offered to spend the night with a prostitute. There are very few cases where it is not acceptable to politely decline, and in many cases your local business partners will respect you more if you refuse than if you accept, even if you forgo a chance of becoming part of the 'old boys club.' Remember that in a negotiation, any weak spot may be exploited by the other party. On the other hand, erotic entertainment does not necessarily imply sex in all cases; perhaps your hosts just want to take you for a drink to a bar with lightly clad dancing girls, or to a karaoke bar where you choose a girl to sing with you. For a description of the many regional variants of sexual entertainment, ranging from astronomically expensive in Japan to very cheap in Thailand, see Engholm (1991: 242-258).

7.4 Hands, feet, the head and other taboos

Etiquette consists of a set of conventions that regulate the behavior of people on social occasions in a given society. Most people are aware that foreigners will not master all the rules of local etiquette, and they may be quite forgiving when the foreigner blunders from time to time. Some types of behavior, however, are much more strongly inappropriate, and should be avoided at all cost by the foreign guest. In many instances, prohibitions find their origin in religion or go back to history.

As a child I was taught that using my left hand, for instance when handing something to someone, is impolite. Yet no-one thinks much of it anymore nowadays if you do use your left hand in Europe. In Arab countries (and in other Muslim countries as well), using the left hand in social interaction is strongly taboo, and must be avoided completely.

> Using the left hand
>
> - At Brussels airport, the boarding agent of an airline tore off all boarding passes with her left hand and gave the slip back to the passenger also with her left hand (she had a pen in her right hand, and the passengers were passing to the left of her anyway). It was a flight to Tokyo, and no-one seemed to be insulted by the employee's behavior. Yet if she does the same with a flight carrying Arab passengers, chances are that some of them would be very upset, or even feel insulted. The airline employee, when asked, appeared to be totally unaware of that.
> - I lived in India for a brief period of time some fifteen years ago. As I was still young and needed some money, I attempted to get hired as a tennis instructor at a local tennis club. I had been a tennis instructor at very two prominent tennis clubs in the USA just before I arrived in India. However, after an initial positive reaction I discovered to my dismay that my application had been rejected. Only after some insistence did the club management admit that they had rejected my application because I am a left-handed tennis player. They said that no-one would accept a left-handed person at the tennis club, let alone accept that their children be instructed by one and possibly become left-handed players themselves as a result of that (C. M., USA).

Showing the soles of one's shoes is to be avoided in the Arab world, as well as in large parts of Asia. The soles are the lowest, dirtiest part of the body, and should not be exposed to other people. Therefore, sitting with your feet on a chair or on the desk, as some Westerners might do, is totally inappropriate. Crossing your legs may expose the sole of your foot to someone; in addition, your foot might point toward someone and in Thailand that is equally bad, as mentioned above. Keep your feet preferably firmly on the ground! In one story a British university professor who received his Egyptian students with his feet on the table was never able to teach his class: the students felt insulted by him.

> Watch your Feet!
>
> - 'An American diplomat once deeply offended a visiting Chinese delegation to Washington by discussing feet at the banquet table – a grave faux pas in China, and not all that tasteful in the West, either' (Engholm 1991: 138).

- A store in Bangkok had ordered a complete one-hour photo developing installation in France. When the machines were shipped to Thailand, the French also sent an engineer to help install them in the store. As a final test, several prints were made of the same picture, in order to calibrate the color settings. Because there was not enough room for these prints elsewhere, they were placed on the floor, for comparison by the people present. As they were on the floor, the French engineer pointed to the different pictures with his foot. This caused serious consternation and dismay to the Thai who were in the room.

In Buddhist countries such as Thailand, while the feet are the lowest and dirtiest part of the body, the head (and the hair in particular) is the loftiest. Touching someone's head or hair must be avoided; one should not even rub a young child over the head in a gesture of affection.

Anthropology tells us that in many cultures, taboos rest on the female body. This may result in women not being allowed to touch certain objects or perform certain functions, lest those objects become 'impure.' In Thailand, as said before, monks[4] must not touch any part of the female body or dress at all, not even by accident. In a crowded bus, this creates a problem that is hard to solve – but is always solved successfully by the Thai people. At Bangkok airport, a special waiting area is reserved for 'monks only'; in reality, other men can also sit there, but women cannot, for by sitting next to a monk the woman might touch him inadvertently.

A special taboo sometimes rests upon women who are menstruating. This is the case, among others, with orthodox Jews, where men are not supposed to touch a woman who has her period. When the Jewish man checks in at the airport, however, he obviously does not know whether or not the female check-in agent in front of him has her period or not (in one exceptional case, at Brussels airport, the Jewish passenger *asked* the check-in agent about it). Therefore, to play it safe, the Jewish passenger will put or throw his travel documents on the counter rather than handing them directly to the agent, in order to avoid the risk of touching her hand.

Westerners should beware that in many cultures, admiring an object in someone's house may compel the host to give it to you. This is true from some Eastern European countries (Romania in my experience) all the way to China (Engholm 1991: 267). In Arab countries, expressions of admiration may be interpreted as envy even if you don't feel it that way: 'I wish I was as successful as you!'; 'I wish I had such a beautiful baby!' They attract the evil eye and are to be absolutely avoided (Nydell 1987: 106, 121). For similar reasons, Thais compliment mothers for having 'such an ugly baby', because beauty attracts evil spirits (Cooper & Cooper 1993: 160).

7.5 Belief systems and 'superstition'

In Arab culture, words have power in the sense that they can affect events. Curses and swearing feel much stronger for Arabs than for Westerners, because proffering a curse may have direct effects, just as repeated blessings contribute to keep things going well. Referring openly to bad events can make a bad situation even worse; referring to illness or death may attract precisely those dangers. Poor origins are similarly best left unmentioned in Arab countries. Insurance salespeople have a hard time in Arab countries, because openly referring to the potential occurrence of accidents in the future is unacceptable (Nydell 1987: 87, 105-7).

In many cultures, bad news should be either concealed, or else given with the utmost precautions, lest the person reporting it be held responsible for it, or lest the addressee's mood be too much affected by it. Throughout East and South-East Asia, bad news may be entirely concealed or else will be delivered only hesitatingly, possibly through a go-between (Engholm 1991: 110). Varner & Beamer (1995: 123) point out that in China, an unwelcome message (such as an additional request) should be delivered at the end, after a lot of praise and positive messages have been extended to the addressee. An Ethiopian student told me that in Ethiopia, breaking the news that someone has died will be done at the end of a long conversation containing a lot of joke-telling.

In many South-East Asian cultures, and more particularly with ethnic Chinese, words and numbers have a symbolic meaning that may influence reality. If, for instance, your own name or your company's name sounds like 'accident', 'unlucky' or the like when pronounced in Chinese,[5] it will be very difficult for the Chinese to accept doing business with someone who, in a way, carries bad luck with him/her all the time! When you have your bilingual English-Chinese business cards made, you may at the same time be given a different name if yours does not sound right. Chinese companies may include a word like 'lucky' in their company name in contexts where this may sound funny to Western ears *(Lucky Textile Company,* for instance). In Chinese restaurant, as the reader may have noticed, dishes may be called 'triple happiness chicken' and the like.

For similar reasons, peaches have a special place among fruits in China because the word for peach sounds like the word for 'happiness', 'prosperity'. Other foodstuffs may be given the shape and color of peaches so that they also carry that lucky meaning with them. Varner & Beamer (1995: 76-7) mention the case of a person in Hong Kong who has a jade bat in his office because the word for 'bat' sounds like the word for 'prosperity'.

In addition, in Chinese you should also worry about the way your name is written. Several different characters (ideograms) are usually available to transcribe the same word (sounds), and it is advisable to choose among those a 'good character', one with a positive meaning. Former British Prime Minister Margaret Thatcher's name is transcribed with a Chinese character that means 'distinguished' (Engholm 1991: 101). The brand name *Coca-Cola* was originally transcribed with Chinese characters that reflected its pronunciation as closely as possible; the trouble was that the meaning of the characters was absurd (something like 'a wax-flattened mare' or 'bite the wax tadpole'; Ricks 1993: 34). It is now transcribed with characters which reflect the pronunciation less accurately (they sound more like *Kekou Kele)* but which mean: 'tasty and enjoyable.'

> **A Gift of Bad Luck by President Bush**[6]
>
> On a visit to the People's Republic of China in 1989, US President George Bush (senior) presented to the Prime Minister of China a pair of Texas boots as a gift. This was not at all well received by the Chinese. Shoes are dirty and therefore not appropriate as a gift. In addition, the word for 'shoes' *(xié)*, sounds like the word for 'bad luck', 'evilness'.

Incidentally, the example above also shows once again that some of the most powerful institutions in the world (the presidency of the United States in this case), just like some of the largest multinational companies, continue to base decisions and actions of the Self Reference Criterion ('what is appropriate back home is appropriate everywhere') and remain woefully unaware of intercultural blunders that could be avoided easily; in this case, quite simply by asking a China expert, preferably Chinese, what would be an appropriate gift to bring under the circumstances.

Like words, numbers also carry a symbolic meaning in Chinese and some other South-East Asian cultures. The number four is the worst, because it sounds like 'death' in Cantonese. Wealthy Chinese entrepreneurs and businessmen are willing to pay thousands of US dollars in order to obtain a license plate for their car or a telephone number without fours but with many eights, sevens or threes. A television documentary about the Chinese community living in Belgium showed a predominantly Chinese street in Antwerp lined with cars with the 'right' license plate numbers. In Singapore and Hong Kong, sought-after telephone and license plate numbers are auctioned off by the authorities and awarded to the highest bidder. Varner & Beamer (1995: 77) quote a case where a person in Hong Kong paid over US$640,000 for a license plate with eights on it. Engholm (1991: 231) puts the figure at US$10,000 – substantially less (possibly because his book was published earlier), but still a lot of money. In 2003, Sichuan Airlines bought the 'ideal' telephone number 8888 8888 at a public auction in Sichuan province, China, for the equivalent of US$ 280,000 (BBC News website, 19 August 2003). There is also some evidence that Chinese and Japanese people, unlike Westerners where no such effect is observed, die more often on the 4th of the month (Phillips e.a. 2001).

The Alfa Romeo 164 could not be sold under that model name in Hong Kong or Singapore, because 1-6-4 could be read: 'on the road to death'. The name was changed to 168, which reads: 'on the road to prosperity'. One of Toyota's SUVs is sold under the name *Toyota 4Runner* in the USA; the equivalent car (they have now diversified) is Asia is called *Toyota Fortuner*, – a rather bizarre name in English, but one which contains the sound 'four' without using that number, and a name which in addition suggest good fortune, i.e. good luck.

Number and name symbolism also plays a role in other South-East Asian cultures, such as Thailand. In one example, a father calls his son *Thanakan*, i.e. 'bank' in Thai, because, he says, 'I want my son to have money and not be poor' (Odzer 1994: 49). Weddings are preferably celebrated during even-numbered (lunar) months such as the second, fourth, sixth or eighth month, or else in the ninth, 'because the number nine is associated in Thailand with progress and prosperity' (Segaller 1993: 25). In the same way, certain days of the week are propitious for certain activities, other days are not (Segaller 1993: 29).

This means that the foreign visitor cannot expect to make an appointment with his Asian counterpart on just any day of the week. Sometimes, the visitor will have to wait a couple of days until the right time for the appointment has arrived.

Nine as a Lucky Number in Thailand

In 1993 the Thai press reported that, when the new Prime Minister Barnard was installed as head of the government, he instructed his driver to drop him off at the main door of the building in Bangkok where the first cabinet meeting was to take place in such a way that he would be able to cross the door sill (but without stepping on it: that brings bad luck in Thailand, because the spirit of the house lives in the door sill!) at exactly 9: 09 a.m., believing that the double nine would bring good luck to the new government.

Similarly, "Cabinet ministers in Thailand yesterday approved a token 100-million-baht cut in the fiscal 2003 budget, bringing total spending to an auspicious figure of 999.9 billion". (*Bangkok Post*, 6 February 2002).

Notes

1. The *wai* is also used to convey other meanings, such as 'thank you' or 'I am sorry.'.
2. I am talking here only about *gifts*, not about bribes. The intercultural aspects of business ethics, including the issues of bribery and corruption, are extremely important, but go far beyond what I can treat in this volume.
3. We do not discuss here the intricacies of the Japanese and Chinese – and Dutch! – (but not Thai) custom of giving gifts to the appropriate people *inside* the company.
4. In Thailand most males become a monk for a certain period in their life (usually a number of months). Government officials get a special leave of absence for this purpose.
5. There are several variants of Chinese, which must in fact be considered different languages. The two most important ones for business purposes are Mandarin, the language spoken in Beijin (Peking) and considered to be standard Chinese, and Cantonese, the language spoken in Guangzhou (Canton) and Hong Kong. Most ethnic Chinese who emigrated to other South-East Asian countries (Singapore, Malaysia, Indonesia, the Philippines) were from the latter region, and as a result Cantonese is dominant among the Chinese in these countries. When doing business in South-East Asia, one is likely to be exposed more to Cantonese than to Mandarin (see also Kraar 1993). The two languages are etymologically related but not mutually intelligible. As the Chinese writing system is independent of pronunciation, however, Cantonese and Mandarin are written the same way (just like '7' is written the same in German and in French, but pronounced differently).
6. I owe this example, and some of the other information in this section, to Ms. Kexin Wang.

Chapter 8
Hierarchy

> A manager from Holland was running a metal construction plant near Malines, Belgium. Communication with his Belgian workers was not going well, and he wondered why. "I try to introduce participative decision making", he said, "I tell my workers: 'my door is always open, just come in and tell we how things can be improved'".
>
> His openness, however, received no response. None of the Flemish (Belgian) workers came to see him. Some even left the company. "How is this possible?" the Dutchman asked, "I mean it all so well".
>
> I tried to explain to him the psychology of the Flemish in a nutshell. "If you, the manager, ask your workers for advice, they become insecure. They don't say anything but they start thinking: 'Our boss does not know any more what to do, he has to ask us for advice. The company probably is not doing well, I'd better start searching for another job.'" (Eppink 2004: 68-9; my translation, I also shortened the text somewhat).

Undisputedly, cultures (and therefore also companies and organizations) differ with respect to the degree of hierarchy that exists in them. This difference influences all kinds of aspects of life: psychological distance between boss and subordinates and deferential behavior, decision making styles and worker participation, empowerment and supervision, and much more.

In what follows we start our discussion of hierarchy with Geert Hofstede's now classic account of what he calls 'Power Distance'. In this chapter and some of the following, we focus on the results obtained through Hofstede's survey and some others. For a discussion of the research methodologies, see chapter 12 below.

8.1 Power Distance in Hofstede's Work

8.1.1 What does Power Distance mean?

Power Distance is about inequality in society. In any group, be it human or animal, there exists a certain amount of inequality, a 'pecking order.' But this amount of inequality is relatively high in certain cultures, lower in others.

The questions in Hofstede's surveys which were used for determining the position of each country on the Power Distance Index (PDI) can be paraphrased as follows.

1. How frequently are employees afraid of expressing disagreement with their boss? In some countries, expressing disagreement with the boss appears to be difficult or nearly impossible; in some other countries, it is unproblematic.
2. Which decision-making style is closest to describing the actual behavior of your boss (the *objective* question), between a, b, c or d below.
3. Which decision-making style would you *prefer* your boss to adopt, between a, b, c and d? This latter is the *projective* question and expresses the 'value as the desired' rather than what actually happens in reality.
    a. *autocratic* decision-making (the boss *tells* you what to do, with little or no explanations)
    b. *persuasive* decision-making (the boss *sells* his/her decision, i.e. explains why he/she decided what he/she did, but he/she still makes the decision himself/herself, in a paternalistic fashion)
    c. *consultative* decision-making (the boss *consults* his/her subordinates before making up his/her mind, but he/she still makes the decision)
    d. *democratic* decision-making (the boss participates in the discussion, tries to reach a consensus with everyone involved, and *joins* the consensus which emerges).

In the survey, the answers to the three questions cluster together, and make up what Hofstede call the Power Distance dimension. In countries where employees are less afraid of expressing disagreement with their boss and where they have a less autocratic boss, they typically also *prefer* a consultative boss, one who does not make decisions in an autocratic way; in countries where employees are afraid of disagreeing with their boss and were they actually have a more autocratic boss, they also mostly express a preference, surprisingly maybe, for an autocratic or paternalistic boss. So, paradoxically perhaps, in countries where Power Distance is higher there is also a higher tendency to accept it as such: inequality is seen as part of a natural order of things. In low Power Distance countries, on the other hand, people by and large prefer even lower Power Distance than that which actually exists in the society.

Expressing disagreement with the boss

As a student, I worked for some time behind the bar of an Indian Members Club in London, together with an Indian guy called Ali. One day, the waitress transmitted a wrong order to us, with the result that the customer did not receive what he wanted. Just at the time when the customer was complaining about this, the manager of the club entered, and he started reprimanding Ali and me for the mistake that had been made.

I replied to the manager that he had better inform himself seriously instead of jumping to conclusions, and that it wasn't really our fault. But Ali did not say anything to support me.

> After the manager had left, Ali turned to me and said 'How could you talk like this to the boss?' In fact Ali seemed to be more mad with me than with the way the boss had treated us (D.B., Czech Republic).

Westerners may assume that throughout the world, equality is valued higher than inequality. This is not necessarily the case. In cultures influenced by Confucianism, unequal relationships may be felt to be more 'natural' than equal ones. The prototypical relationship between two human beings in Confucian philosophy is one of inequality: it is the relation from father to son. Both parties have obligations: the father owes support, help and protection to his son; the son owes respect and obedience to his father. This type of relationships also holds between superior and subordinate in the workplace, between older and younger (brothers for instance), and… between husband and wife.

In Thailand also, though the country's culture cannot be called Confucianist, inequality is the rule. Wyatt (2003: 173) claims that in the 1850s-60s no equal relationship existed in Thailand or in the Thai language. Cooper (1991: 168) confirms that still today social equality makes Thai people feel uncomfortable. In a hierarchical relation, every party knows how to behave: who should speak first, drink first, leave the room or enter the elevator first; in a relation of equality, all these certainties disappear and everyone's behavior may become unregulated and unpredictable.

PDI scores reflect the dependence relations between subordinates and bosses: in a high PD country, the subordinate depends on his/her boss. In a low PD country, on the other hand, there is mutual dependence or *inter*dependence: the subordinate depends on his/her boss, but the boss also depends on the subordinate for feedback and consultation.[1]

Perhaps two of Hofstede's own examples may illustrate the difference between a high PD culture and a low PD culture better than any theoretical explanation.

The first example is from India, a country with a high PDI score. It is about a senior Indian executive with a Ph.D. from a prestigious American university, who declares the following:

> What is most important for me and my department is not what I do or achieve for the company, but whether the Master's (i.e., an owner of the firm) favor is bestowed on me… This I have achieved by saying 'yes' to everything the Master says or does… [T]o contradict him is to look for another job… I left my freedom of thought in Boston (Negandhi and Prasad 1971: 128, in Hofstede 1980: 101).

Compare this with the following story that happened to the King of Sweden and was reported in the press in December 1988:

> Stockholm, December 23. The Swedish King Carl Gustav this week experienced considerable delay while shopping for Christmas presents for his children, when he wanted to pay by check but could not show his check card. The salesperson refused to accept the check without legitimation.

Only when helpful bystanders dug in their pockets for one-crown pieces showing the face of the King, the salesperson decided to accept this for legitimation, not, however, without testing the cheque thoroughly for authenticity and noting the name and address of the holder (Hofstede 1991: 47).

A story such as this will not occur in Sweden every day; otherwise, it would not be a newspaper item. But although exceptional, the story shows us an aspect of Swedish culture that is simply unthinkable in most places around the world. The King of Belgium does not go shopping himself, nor does he ever pay himself by cheque (or otherwise), certainly not at a cash register in a store. Imagine the reaction of my students in Thailand when I read this story to them: it sounded absolutely unbelievable. In Thailand, the King has a status which commands extreme respect and deference. In fact, when I attempted to discuss the implications of the story for Thailand, my Thai students had a worried look on their face, because they feared that in the course of the discussion, I might say something that could be a sign of disrespect toward the King; I could end up in prison if I did.

8.1.2 The Power Distance Index: country scores

A definition of Hofstede's five cultural dimensions can be found on Hofstede's website: http://www.geerthofstede.nl; the scores of individual countries are on the website of the training institute ITIM which he founded: http://www.geerthofstede.com.

These scores do not have any absolute, but only relative value. They can be used to compare one country with another, but a score of 10, say, on the Power Distance Index should not be taken to mean that there is only 10% inequality or almost no inequality at all in the country. Naturally, given the margin of error involved, differences of a few points on the PDI are not necessarily significant.

The overall reliability of Hofstede's PDI scores is highlighted by the fact that clusters of culturally close countries emerge. It is no accident that the following observations can be made.

- Despite large differences, most Asian and Latin American countries score at or above 60, i.e., towards the high PD side of the spectrum. There are some exceptions. Costa Rica scores very low, but this in itself corroborates what we know about that country, i.e. that it abolished its army in 1948, that the literacy rate, life expectancy and living conditions are exceptionally high by Latin American standards, etc. In fact national wealth is a good predictor of a country's PDI score: the richer the country, the higher its chances of having a low PDI score (Hofstede 1991: 44).
- Anglo-Saxon countries exhibit low PDI scores, ranging from 49 (South Africa) to 22 (New Zealand).
- Scandinavian countries score even lower, between 33 (Finland) and 18 (Denmark).

Among the many other interesting details, let us point out the following.
- The low score of Israel, which seems to correspond to accounts of people who know that country well. Pinker (2007: 387) confirms that deferential politeness does not seem to exist in Israel.
- The large difference between India and Pakistan, which after all were part of the same entity, the Raj, before independence. This may be linked to the difference between the more egalitarian Islam in Pakistan and the very stratified Hindu society with its caste system in India.
- The surprisingly low score of Austria, with the lowest PDI of all countries surveyed. Intuitively, one would expect the score for Austria to be closer to that of Germany. The PDI of Austria may, of course, not be a fair reflection of Austrian culture: perhaps the sample of respondents (IBM workers) was atypical.
- The high scores for France (68) and Belgium (65), with the highest PDI positions of all the Western nations, and way higher than the vast majority of those. We will get back to the position of France and Belgium later.

8.1.3 The origins of cultural dimensions

The question about the *origins* is commonly asked by many people: *why* are the PDI scores of, for example, Belgium and the Netherlands so different, when the countries are geographically so close, share in part a common language, etc.? In this book, we will not further explore such questions, intriguing as they are. The first reason for this decision is that hypotheses about the origins of differences in value systems and practices tend to be conjectural and controversial. Hofstede (1980: 124) traces differences in PDI scores back to differences in climate as well as to historical events. In moderate to cold climates, survival depends more on man's intervention with nature, therefore there is a higher need for technology; this technology implies a higher need for education of the lower strata in society, which in turn will lead to less dependence of the members of those lower strata upon the members of the higher strata, and thus to lower Power Distance (this is a simplification of Hofstede's more complex account). In effect, geographical latitude is the strongest predictor of the PDI position of a country (Hofstede 1980: 121-2). I strongly suspect however that, if the correlation between geographical latitude and Power Distance had been the other way around, an equally convincing or unconvincing explanation could have been put forward, something like: in a colder climate there is more need to master the adverse forces of nature, therefore there is a need for a strong leader, etc. In such a way, anything can be 'explained'.

More convincingly no doubt, differences in Power Distance between the Netherlands and Belgium can be traced back to the difference between Protestantism and Catholicism (the latter placing higher emphasis on central and unquestioned authority), which arose between the two areas some four centuries ago. In other words, while some of these explanatory hypotheses are reasonable, many of them are extremely tenuous and uncertain.

The second reason for not discussing the origin of present-day cultural features in this volume is that, quite simply, most of the time they are irrelevant from a contemporary point of view. It is intellectually challenging and historically relevant to try and determine why the PDI scores of the Netherlands and Belgium are so different, but what matters to a person who is communicating in an intercultural setting now, is knowing *that* they are, and that this will influence the way of doing business in the two countries. In fact, in the vast majority of cases the members of the cultures involved themselves are not aware of the origin of their culturally defined characteristics.

Below I limit myself to a discussion of those aspects of the Power Distance Dimension that seem to be most relevant in the business world.

8.1.4 Power Distance in business and organizations

Obviously, the dominant decision making style of managers will tend to be more autocratic in high PD cultures, more participative in low PD cultures, and managers themselves will tend to accept more participative behavior from their subordinates in low PD countries.

In high PD countries, the hierarchy is of an existential nature and a superior remains your superior regardless of whether you meet him/her in the factory or at the beach. If you meet your boss on Saturday in a shopping mall, he is still your superior and you owe him respect. In low PD countries, hierarchy is more an inequality of roles. For instance, there is no doubt that the King of Sweden will look and act like a King when performing official functions such as receiving a foreign head of state; that is his function. When he is standing in line at the cash register in a department store, however, he is not performing his function as a King and together with that role he also loses his special status and becomes (almost) an ordinary customer in a store.

In high PD countries, powerholders must try to look as powerful as possible, whereas in low PDI countries, powerholders tend to play down the difference between them and their subordinates. Hofstede reports the story of a Swedish university official who states that 'in order to exercise power, he tries not to look powerful' (1980: 121). Hofstede one day met the Dutch prime minister with his caravan (trailer) on a campsite in Portugal; the chances of meeting the French or Italian prime minister in a similar situation are close to zero. Similarly, the CEO of a large company in Norway declares that his office should be small, even though he would perhaps like a larger one, and that he will not fly first class if none of the other employees do (Moskowitz, quoted in Victor 1992: 94).

In high PD countries, powerholders tend to be more entitled to privileges. Privileges for powerholders can include for them to have their own parking lot, their own toilets or their own company restaurant; not having to legitimate what time they come in and go out, whereas the subordinates must use a time-clock; and so forth. In some cases, powerholders will be allowed to break company regulations, or even the law. We all know countries where powerholders are never brought to trial, regardless of what they may have done.

In a high PD country, organizations, including commercial companies, typically tend to be more hierarchical, with a taller organizational pyramid. The difference between the people in top positions and those on the shop floor will also be emphasized more, in terms of qualifications as well as in terms of wage differentials. Seelye & Seelye-James (1995: 83) consider that above a wage differential of 20 (in other words, the highest paid person in the company earns 20 times or more what the lowest paid person earns), an organization is 'high Power Distance' – but any cut-off point is of course to some extent arbitrary.

Organizations in high PD countries cannot be managed with the same methods as are used in low PD countries. Until recently, management theories were often exported wholesale from the United States (a country with a PDI in the mid to low range) and introduced without changes into countries with much higher PDI scores. Needless to say, this is bound to cause problems. For instance, a few years ago the fashion of the day in management theories was MBO, management by objectives. But in a high PD country, MBO will not work "because [it] presuppose[s] some form of negotiation between subordinate and superior which neither party will feel comfortable with" (Hofstede 1991: 36).

Similarly, team development exercises which require "face-to-face openness, frankness and feedback concerning the impact of [one's] own or other's behavior on the group" will not work well in high PD cultures (Rigby, quoted in Victor 1992: 177), and "French managers could not conceive of working in a matrix structure" and continue to report "budget anomalies exclusively to their immediate superior", not to lateral departments (Lane, DiStefano & Maznevski 2000: 37, based on research by Perret).

With respect to *empowerment,* Eylon & Au (1999) have argued recently that "individuals from high power distance cultures did not perform as well when empowered as when disempowered", whereas "participants from low power distance cultures performed similarly, regardless of the empowerment process." Littrell (2007) also questions whether empowerment can really be introduced in a country such as China. On the other hand, people from higher Power Distance cultures may exhibit higher *compliance* behavior even when the superior has low expertise (Schouten 2008).

8.1.5 Power Distance and professional class

The data on which Hofstede's country comparisons are based are from IBM sales and service personnel only (for a discussion of Hofstede's methodology, see chapter 12 below). In a few countries where IBM has fully fledged subsidiaries, it was possible to compare the positions on the PDI for different professional categories. Not surprisingly, Power Distance is the highest among unskilled and semiskilled workers (with a mean PDI score of 90), and lowest in the highest professional categories (mean score of 8). The difference between those two extreme professional categories is of 82 points. Recall that the difference between the highest country score (Malaysia, 104) and the lowest (Austria, 11) is of 93 points. We can therefore conclude that the PDI differences linked to culture are of the same order of magnitude as PDI differences linked to social/professional class. In other words, on this dimension class differences account for about the same amount of variation as cultural differences.

8.2 Hierarchy in the workplace

> **An American manager in Thailand**
>
> In 1993 one of the large hotels in Bangkok, part of an internationally renowned chain, just got a new managing director, freshly arrived from the United States. Although the hotel was not doing badly as far as business and profits were concerned, the new managing director thought that there was much room for improvement.
>
> In particular, he felt that middle management pretty much did things their way, with very little feedback from their subordinates. The American managing director therefore decided on his first move to change relations at work. He handed out an evaluation form to all workers, with which they were asked *to evaluate their boss*.
>
> To his surprise, this seemingly simple and reasonable measure created a huge uproar with the workers, and most of them did everything not to turn in the evaluation forms.

There is no doubt that understanding the cultural dimension of Power Distance is absolutely essential in any intercultural encounter in a business or organizational setting.

There are numerous stories of Western expatriates who neglect the external attributes of power in high PD countries and lose part of their prestige and authority because of that. In a high PD country such as Malaysia, it is not a good idea for an expatriate executive to be seen mowing the lawn or washing the dishes, or to push his/her caddie around in the local supermarket. In Arab countries also, "no upper-class person engages in manual labor in front of other people" (Nydell 1987: 70).

In high PD countries such as India, expatriates who, with the best of intentions, adopt a more consultative style of management and, for instance, ask their workers for their opinion before reaching a decision or issuing an order may suffer loss of authority and respect because of that. The workers' unstated reaction may be something like: this person gets a very high salary to be the boss, yet refuses to be in charge, asks *me* to do the decision-making in his/her place; that is not my role (see also Adler 1992: 166).

Within Europe, some of the more visible consequences of the higher Power Distance in France are a source of irritation (or worse) for other Europeans. French managers may seem 'arrogant' to, say, Northern Europeans, who do not understand that French managers need the external signs of power (their expensive clothes and shoes, their Rolex watch and Mont Blanc fountain pen, their large Mercedes, but also an authoritative tone of voice, etc.) to establish their authority in France.

French managers are usually also entitled to the 'privileges' Hofstede refers to, while their Dutch colleagues, for instance, are not. D'Iribarne (1989) tells the story of a Dutch CEO who is prevented by a worker from entering a certain area in the factory because the CEO is not wearing the required hard hat. In France as in many other cultures, the CEO would probably be allowed to break the hard hat rule without any of the workers daring to oppose him.

> **Exploit High PDI to Your Advantage if you Can!**
>
> When my African wife, who then held a passport from Zaire, was told by the French consulate in Brussels that she would have to wait for ten days before obtaining a visa for France (before, it had taken only one or two days), I applied my knowledge of cultural differences to the situation. In high PDI countries, you can appeal to your position to request certain privileges. I wrote a letter to the French consul (whom I do not know) in which I stated that I was a university professor and that I teach, among other things, business French. I presented myself as the representative of French culture in the city (and university) of Antwerp, and as an internationally renowned scholar. The consulate called us the next day and informed us that my wife could come by and pick up her visa immediately.
>
> Appealing to arguments based on your position to obtain certain privileges is likely to be counterproductive in lower PDI cultures. Imagine me writing a similar letter to the US or Dutch consulate than I did to the French: it would probably have had no effect (or worse).

In higher PD cultures, you can say: 'Do you know who I am?' If you say something similar in lower PD countries, the answer might well be: 'Who do you think you are?'

In lower PD cultures, where hierarchy is linked to role rather than to a form of existential inequality, roles can more easily be reversed. When I was teaching in the United States, one of my students was also my instructor for horseback riding lessons: our roles were reversed, she became the teacher and I became her student. Such a situation is unthinkable in many cultures around the world. Would a company executive accept that someone who works under him/her were his tennis instructor? Depending on the culture and its PD score, the answer is likely to be different.

> **USA: the boss becomes a repair worker**
>
> One of my American friends worked as an architect in a public institution (City Hall) in Washington D.C. for some years, and I had the opportunity to visit him and his family there.
>
> Although, at that moment, his house was being restored and some work being done, his wife and he were very pleased that I could spend the weekend with them. The first day they prepared a nice lunch so we were eating all together in the dining-room. As we started to eat, I saw a man working in the room next door. He was repairing some furniture, lying on the floor and completely covered with dust.
>
> The family just ignored him throughout the lunch, the father even jumped over him twice as the worker was in his way to the kitchen. After a while, the worker finished his work and came to the dining room to have a drink with us. Then he left, saying to my friend they would see each other on Monday. I asked my friend if the worker was coming back on Monday. He answered that this man was, in fact, his boss, so they would see each other at the office on Monday. His boss' hobby was woodwork, so he decided to help my friend with the house restoration against a symbolic payment.

> That really surprised me! Such a switch in hierarchy between boss and employee would not be usual in my country. It was difficult for me to understand his boss accepting to be for some hours just a manual worker, lying on the floor and getting himself dirty while his subordinate was having a nice meal in front of him.
> (D.B., from Turkey)

8.3 Beware of oversimplification!

In most of his charts, Hofstede describes a binary opposition between low PDI and high PDI cultures. From the PDI scores, however, it should be clear that there are not two clearly distinct groups of countries on this scale (nor are there on any other of Hofstede's dimensions), and that most countries range somewhere between the two extremes. Therefore, most countries will not neatly exhibit the characteristics Hofstede ascribes to low PD, or to high PD cultures, and it is in fact difficult or impossible to predict *how* the hierarchical structures really are set up in those cultures that score neither extremely high, nor extremely low on the Power Distance Index.

The following distinct logical possibilities come to mind.

1. Mid-range PDI countries might exhibit some characteristics of low PDI countries and some characteristics of high PDI countries. On the basis of the PDI score alone, it is then impossible to ascertain *which* characteristics of either category they will exhibit. For instance, in some mid-range PDI countries it might be difficult to express disagreement with your boss, in others it might be (almost) as easy as in low PDI countries.
2. Mid-range PDI countries, for all or most of the features that are in Hofstede's lists, might exhibit 'middle of the road characteristics'. For instance, in mid-range PDI countries it might be more difficult to express disagreement with your boss than in low PDI countries, but easier than in high PDI countries.

Which is correct, (1), (2), or sometimes (1), sometimes (2)? Only *qualitative* research will be able to answer that question. In other words, the PDI score, valuable as it is, does not in itself provide us with much information about the substance of power and hierarchy in various cultures (I have no reasons to believe that Hofstede would disagree with this statement; see also Usunier 1998: 65).

Consider a simple example. The PDI scores of Thailand (64) and Belgium (65) are nearly identical: both are mid-high. It would clearly be wrong to infer from there that the relation a subordinate has with his boss is bound to be similar in those two countries. In fact, my own research (Verluyten 1997, 1998c) gives me some reason to think that the mid-range PDI score of a country such as Thailand (and possibly also Japan, with a score of 54) is best explained by (1) above: Thailand exhibits some aspects of high PDI cultures, and some aspects of low PDI countries. More specifically, there is some tentative evidence that Thailand (and possibly Japan) exhibits the more formal aspects of high PDI countries (such as difficulty to express disagreement with your boss, need to pay respect to the boss, etc.), together with the more substantive aspects of exercising power that are commonly found in low PDI countries (feedback from subordinates in the decision-making process, for instance). Belgium, on the other hand, while its PDI score is nearly identical to that of Thailand, may be an example of (2) above. Belgians may have more difficulty in expressing disagreement with their boss than the Dutch, but less than Filipinos; Belgian subordinates are very probably less involved in their boss's decision-making than Dutch subordinates, but more than Filipino subordinates.

Note

1. Some subordinates in high PDI countries may reject the dependence relationship entirely, which is known as *counterdependence* in psychology (Hofstede 1991: 27).

Chapter 9
Individualism

9.1   Individualism: a Western and historically recent 'invention'

Two-thirds of Americans say it is important not to get too involved in the problems of others: you have to take care of yourself first and if you have any energy left, then help others (Zeldin 1998: 249).

In contemporary Western societies characterized by high individualism, people may overlook the fact that most societies around the world are much more group-oriented. A song such as Frank Sinatra's 'I did it my way' is a clear expression of how much Westerners (and especially Americans) value individualism: succeeding in life is important, but what is equally important is succeeding while 'doing it your way', presumably with minimum interference or help from others. People may pride themselves in being able to say; 'I made it, by myself, and I don't owe anything to anyone'. Such words must appear bizarre or even shocking to people from group-oriented cultures.

Individualism is a recent invention, including in the West (Vigarello 2005: 175-6). If we look back at the history of the West, we will notice that in the past group-orientation was dominant there also. Take the example of religious conversion. People in the West tend to think of religious conversion as a primarily individual decision. The right to individual religious conversion is inscribed in the United Nations' Universal Declaration of Human Rights (itself an instrument inspired by Western values and mainly concerned with individual human rights) under article 18. Yet historically, in Western countries like elsewhere, individual religious conversions are rare. When Clovis King of the Franks converted to Catholicism in 496 CE, all the Franks became Catholics with him. Was that because they each individually became simultaneously convinced that Catholicism was the right religion for them to embrace? Of course not. This case of religious conversion, as most examples of it around the world, is a group phenomenon and not a series of individual decisions (see also Hofstede 1980: 215). Today, while it is acceptable for someone in individualistic Western society, to convert individually, say, to Islam, it is much less acceptable for someone in a group-oriented Islamic country, from an Islamic family, to convert individually to Catholicism. In fact, the issue is not likely to arise frequently, because such an individual decision would not normally be considered by a group member in a group-oriented society.

The difference between individualistic values, where by and large every person is entitled to make his/her own decisions by himself/herself (and is responsible for those), on the one hand, and group-oriented values where a person is primarily a member of a group, is one of the main sources of incomprehension between the West and most other cultures. Malaysia is a multi-religious country with 35% or more of the population not belonging to the majority Muslim religion, but it is illegal for an individual Muslim to convert to another religion. Most Westerners will find this inacceptable; in less individualistically inclined societies, many may feel it to be normal.

What we said about religious conversion is also true for many other cultural practices. Marriage is another clear example of a practice which in the West is thought of primarily in individualistic terms[1] (as a contract between two people), whereas in many other cultures around the world marriage establishes a link between two groups (two families), and therefore the personal preference of the potential fiancés is only one element that is taken into consideration (or sometimes, not taken into consideration at all). I know more than one person from Africa who introduced a fiancé(e) to his/her parents, only to be told that the fiancé(e) was not the right choice, and that the family would oppose the marriage. In that case, the position of the family always prevailed in the cases I know, even when the son or daughter is well-educated and has a university degree. Similarly, in Thailand a marriage will not take place if the parents are against it (Klausner 1993: 295).

Having a *personal opinion* and being able to express it are considered natural and essential for freedom by a person in the West. In Scandinavia, there are several instances of married couples where both spouses have political mandates for different political parties. Such a situation is difficult to imagine in a group-oriented culture, and such a seemingly essential feature as having a personal opinion and expressing it is not highly valued in group-oriented cultures. It is therefore not always advisable to ask a worker for his/her 'personal opinion' in a group-oriented society; in fact, the question itself will not make much sense. Similarly, it is not advisable to give out individual rewards to workers in group-oriented cultures (including Japan). The individual involved as well as the group will feel awkward with that, because it singles out one person rather than considering the good performance by the group as such.

In group-oriented cultures, people are seldom by themselves, and personal privacy is not commonly valued. Hofstede (1991: 58) reports the case of

> [a]n African student who came to a Belgian university to study [and] told us that this was the first time in her life she had ever been alone in a room for any sizeable length of time.

I personally know several identical cases. Imagine the trauma it must be for such a student to come home every night and be alone in a room for evenings on end, with no-one else around and, presumably, television or radio as your only companion, when you have never experienced any such situation for the first twenty-five years of your life!

Similarly, in Thailand being alone is *mai sanuk*, 'no fun' (Welty 2004: 164).

As we have seen above, many languages do not even have a word to translate the concept of privacy, simply because the value does not exist in that culture.

It often comes as a surprise or shock to Westerners who travel to countries with group-oriented cultures that people may invade your room, sometimes uninvited, and even go through your personal belongings without asking. Varner & Beamer report (1995: 195) that at one Chinese university, a document marked 'confidential' (the professor's personal assessment of every student in her class) was published in the university periodical, with its heading 'confidential' duly translated into Chinese.

> **Keeping you company**
>
> Many Western visitors to Latin America (including myself) complain about the fact that it is very difficult to 'get some privacy'. As soon as you retire to your room, because you want to read a book for instance, or just because you want to be away from people for a while, people will start wondering where you are, and as soon as they find out that you are alone in your room, someone will show up 'to keep you company', – which is exactly what you don't want at that point in time. On one occasion, an American who was staying with a host family in Bolivia became so irritated with the impossibility of having the privacy she needed that she locked herself in her room; needless to say, the local people were extremely offended by her behavior.

According to Fernández-Armesto (2001: 25), most languages have no term for 'human being' universally: one is characterized as either a member of the in-group, or not. In several languages members of the in-group refer to themselves as 'the people' or 'human beings' (such as the Inuit), implying that members of the out-group are in a very different category. In Korea, a non-Korean is sometimes called *sangnom,* i.e., 'nonperson' (Engholm 1991: 55). The Welsh call themselves *Cymry,* i.e., 'the friends' and their country Cymru; the Anglo-Saxons called the same country Wales and the inhabitants Welsh, i.e., 'strangers, foreigners'.

Individualism may even extend into the nuclear family. As Hofstede points out (1991: 59), in high IDV countries such as the United States it is common for students to pay their own way through university, even if their parents can afford to pay for everything. On the one hand the parents want to raise their children to be independent, i.e., literally, not to depend on anyone, including the parents. On the other hand, the children will pride themselves in 'not owing anything to anyone' after they graduate (see also the discussion on indebtedness below).

9.2 Hofstede's Individualism Index values and their implications for work-related situations

The Individualism (IDV) scores for the countries included in Hofstede's study can be found on http://www.geert-hofstede.com. The opposite end of the Individualism dimension is called *Collectivism* by Hofstede, but because of the political meaning of that term, I will often use the term *Group Orientation* instead.

All the countries that score above 50, i.e. are in the upper half of the IDV scale, are Western countries, mostly from Europe or North America. Many of the highest scores go to Anglo-Saxon countries, with the United States on top. On the other hand, the eighteen countries at the opposite end of the dimension are either Asian or Latin American, plus the West African cluster.

We will discuss the reverse correlation between Power Distance and Individualism below. There is also a correlation between IDV scores and national wealth: the richer the country, generally speaking, the higher its score on the Individualism index.

Westerners may concentrate on what they see as negative consequences of group-orientation: the absence of personal opinion, of freedom of choice, of privacy, etc. However, group-orientation also carries with it many features that are undoubtedly positive. Within the group, there is a sense of protection and mutual help which leads to a feeling of belonging and security people in the West can only dream of in most cases.

In Africa, it is not uncommon for a person who has an income to provide for twenty or more others who have not (Hofstede 1991: 59; my own observations confirm this entirely). Family obligations may take precedence over work (especially in Africa), and a higher degree of absenteeism is therefore frequent (Hofstede 1991: 59).

What is considered moral behavior in a group-oriented culture may be considered unethical in a high IDV country, and vice-versa. A good case in point is *nepotism* (Hofstede 1991: 62). In a group oriented culture, preferring a person with better qualifications for a job when a family or clan member also applies will be considered immoral: how can you prefer a stranger to your own family? In Africa, giving a job to a relative or clan member is "both a duty and an obligation" (Richmond & Gestrin 1998: 150). In high IDV countries, on the other hand, when a case of nepotism is discovered, it will be morally (and sometimes also legally) sanctioned. In a group-oriented culture, the two key words are *loyalty* (which you owe to the group) and *protection* (that you get from the group).

As said above, one consequence of a strong group-orientation may be that the culture stresses the difference between in-groups and out groups. While loyalty and protection run very strong for the in-group, there may be little or no sense of obligation toward members of the out-group. Hofstede calls this value system *particularism*. The opposite is *universalism*, i.e., the idea that identical value standards are applied to all.

Compare my account of certain values in the Philippines:

> The Filipino values himself [...] and his family, friends and familiars, but does not extend this to the entire society or to mankind in general. There may be a striking difference in his treatment of a person, depending on whether or not that person belongs to one of the three categories mentioned. The goals and interests of the primary group also rank high above the good and interest of the country (Verluyten 1993).

In extreme cases, members of the out-group may be considered less than human, and it therefore matters little whether they live or die.

In high IDV cultures on the other hand, the prevailing idea is that identical value standards should apply to all human beings, regardless of whether they live next door or on the other side of the world.

> '(for Africans)... the very fact that we have a highly developed sense of responsibility towards our own kinsmen... has resulted in diluting our capacity to empathize with those that are much further from us.'
>
> In the West, news of a natural catastrophe in another part of the world brings forth floods of compassion and offers of assistance. The African, adds Mazrui, is much more moved by the day-to-day problems of a distant kinsman than a dramatic upheaval in a remote part of the world (Richmond & Gestrin 1998: 14; the first three lines are a quote from Mazrui).

Depending on the culture, the primary group can be the family, the tribe, the company, etc., or a combination of those. When the group is an organization such as a corporation, in a group-oriented culture the individual will expect that organization to take care of him/her. This can take different forms Western-trained managers may not be used to. An employee may ask the boss for money when he cannot make ends meet at the end of the month. Richmond & Gestrin (1998: 147) correctly report that in Africa a "loan request to the boss is considered by employees to be quite normal"; also asking for a leave of absence to visit relatives, etc. The employee may expect the company to guarantee life-time employment to him, such as offered by large companies in Japan. When a Western company does not extend such favors to its local employees in a group-oriented culture, the employees can become very alienated, as Hofstede rightly points out.

In individualistic cultures on the other hand, involvement of an individual with the company he/she works for is primarily calculative, and sense of loyalty is relatively low. When offered a more interesting or a higher paid job elsewhere, the employee will often quit the company without much hesitation. Every individual is expected to pursue his/her own best interest, even if that is detrimental to the company.

In group-oriented cultures your private life is invaded by the organizations and clans to which you belong. In many African countries (and to a large extent also among Africans who live in the West) a remote cousin who arrives in the city where you live may come to your house unannounced, in which case you are expected to take care of him, to provide him with food and lodgings, regardless of the time he will stay. Westerners will rapidly feel that they are taken advantage of; in African societies, people are more likely to consider this as a natural form of in-group solidarity.

9.3 Individualism – Group Orientation: discussion and further examples

The difference between Individualism and Group Orientation is, no doubt, one of the most crucial dimensions in understanding intercultural differences. Westerners should be aware, in this respect, that they represent one end of the spectrum, and that nearly all other cultures on earth tend to be less individualist than the West.

For instance, the relatively low IDV score of Japan (46) helps explaining a number of features of that country, such as the following.

- *Protection,* in the form of life-time employment and the impossibility to fire someone. Once you become a member of the 'family' (to which the Japanese company is often likened), the company will not fire you any more than a parent would send a son or daughter away from home for bad behavior.
- *Loyalty,* which makes it very difficult for Japanese to quit their present employer. In one example (Yoshimura & Anderson 1997: 211), only two out of more than twenty Japanese (i.e., less than 10%) left their company, – and then only to work for a foreign company.
- The importance for recently hired workers of having a *mentor* who will explain to them all the intricacies of the company. In one case, newly hired trainees were given a 70-page manual of business manners by their company (Yoshimura & Anderson 1997: 23). It is not uncommon for newly hired trainees to sleep together in a dorm, possibly with their mentors.
- The Japanese *reward system,* where rewards will go to groups rather than to individual workers.

Hendry (2003: 58) notes that in Japan, individualism is associated with selfishness and untrained behavior.

Collective rather than individual rewards are also the rule in most other group-oriented cultures. Lane, DiStefano & Maznevski (2000: 17) report that workers in a small sewing operation in Botswana went on strike after the introduction, by the expatriate manager, of an individual piece-rate incentive system. Western expatriates are generally prone on making the mistake of automatically rewarding individual workers – the Self-Reference Criterion once again ('what works back home works everywhere').

Conversely, firing someone who belongs to a group of friends and family may result in the whole family quitting the company, as Hall reports about Spanish-Americans in New Mexico (1976: 158), "with the result that disputes have a rather extraordinary interreticulated quality that is difficult for the linear-minded Anglo to sort out".

For management, 'groupism' may sometimes make quality control more difficult, if the quality check person comes from the same region, family or social group as the person who is being checked (Engholm 1991: 317). In group-oriented societies with a high degree of nepotism, people who work under a boss who is a relative, clan member, or the like, or who have been hired by him, may react in two opposite ways.

1. Their motivation and drive to work may increase because they are working for someone from their group. This may be the case, for instance, in the *maquiladoras* (Mexican subcontracting firms to large US companies) located across the US border in Mexico.
2. They may, on the contrary, feel that they are invulnerable and cannot be fired, so why would they work hard? This attitude, in my experience, dominates in Central Africa. In fact, employers in Congo (ex-Zaire) will often try to refrain from hiring relatives or members of the same group precisely because

of that. However, giving preference to a relative or group member remains a moral obligation; therefore, the employer may actually hide from his relatives or otherwise prevent them from seeking employment from him. He may, for instance, not disclose his telephone number to them. (For similar reasons, many Africans in Europe do not want their telephone number to be listed in the directory, for fear that too many 'cousins' might call on them with various requests.)

In many group-oriented cultures in Asia also, firing someone for incompetence is difficult or impossible (Engholm 1991: 318-9).

Many Westerners are so individualistic as to having almost completely lost the value of *sharing*. In many group-oriented cultures, on the other hand, sharing is highly valued. There is a moral obligation to share your resources, financial and otherwise, with those in your group who are less well off. As pointed out above, an African person who earns a living may well cater for twenty or more group members who are unemployed. Children from less well-off relatives or group members will be raised by those that can afford it better. People will share their meals with any group member who happens to come by at that moment. The food that is available will simply be divided into smaller portions if need be. Nydell (1987: 65) reports the adverse reaction of an Egyptian who describes that, in an American dinner, everything is counted, not only the steaks, but even the potatoes (one baked potato per person).

Sharing what you have

A Filipino woman was staying with a Belgian family on a visit to Europe. One day, unexpected visitors arrived at the Belgian family's home just before lunchtime; they were welcomed and served drinks. Half an hour or so later, the Filipino was absolutely shocked when she heard both the hosts and the guests agreeing that it was time for the visitors to leave now, as the family was going to have lunch and there would not be enough food for everyone otherwise.

The moral obligation to share resources with those in need constitutes the very fabric of African (and many other) societies. It is what holds them together and it helps explaining why, in extremely poor countries, destitute people go less hungry than one might expect. On the other hand, it makes investing in business ventures more difficult. As soon as a person's business starts making a profit, there will be a large number of relatives and group members who put in requests for financial help (often with good reason). Similarly, Pinxten (1994: 104) reports that it is nearly impossible for a Navajo to own a business, because all clan members would point out to the owner that it is his duty to help other group members, and he would be under a moral obligation to extend endless credit to them. Under such circumstances, the business would rapidly go under.

As said above, the concept of *privacy* may not exist in certain group-oriented cultures. In China, unmarried university teachers live in dormitories, just as the newly hired Japanese trainees in the example we gave above. For people who are used to being in the company of others almost constantly, being on your own for long periods of time may be traumatizing. Bassett & Vasey (1996: 179) report that

> [i]t is [...] difficult for [Chinese] students to get used to the solitude involved in having a room of their own, probably for the first time in their lives, after living in a crowded family home and then a student dormitory.

This is also the case for many African students, as we reported above.

Chinese students like crowds

A Czech student writes the following story about his stay in England.

Last semester I spent studying in Stoke-on-Trent, England. I lived in a dormitory with many Chinese students. Each inhabitant of our dormitory had a similar, small room. From my point of view, if you were alone in the room, it was all right, but two people really was the limit; whenever there were more than two of us, we used to meet in the kitchen. As to the Chinese, their attitude was simply the opposite: the more people in the room, the better.

Once I asked them about this explicitly and they revealed to me that in order to feel at home, there would need to be many more people not only in the rooms, but also on the streets (to me, the streets were crowded enough as they were).

I saw them a bit more satisfied shortly before Christmas. They finally could squeeze their way through the crowds in the streets, bump into other pedestrians – they finally felt like home.

Conversely, the extreme loneliness of so many people is one of the most striking characteristics of Western countries to many people from more group-oriented regions of the world. Fifty percent of the inhabitants of Paris live by themselves, i.e. in a situation which is the epitome of unhappiness for people from most group-oriented cultures. Studies show that homeless people in the large cities of Europe and North America often have close relatives living in the same city. The homeless are either too 'proud' to ask their relatives for shelter and help, or they are convinced they would not be helped by them anyway. This is incomprehensible to my African friends.

Get some company!

One day my African wife happened to be by herself in the centre of Brussels with a few hours to spare before an evening class she was taking, and she decided to go to the movies.

When leaving the movie theatre she met some African friends of hers who were very surprised to discover that she had been to the movies by herself. They said to her: 'We live so close, you could have come and fetched one of our daughters to accompany you to the movie!'

To people from group-oriented cultures, being on your own does not convey a message of independence, but one of misery. Therefore, when travelling to a group-oriented culture for business purposes also, it is often advisable not to go it alone.

9.4 Related and correlated concepts

Several concepts that originate from other authors are identical to Hofstede's Individualism dimension. We will come back to the relationship between all of Hofstede's dimensions and those put forward by other authors in chapter 12, where we discuss methodological issues in general.

Here we (re)consider only those concepts that are correlated to Individualism, but not directly inspired by that dimension.

9.4.1 High vs. low context communication, vagueness and tolerance of silence

In a group-oriented culture, there is typically less need for explicit, low context communication, because people most often know each other well and also know each other's feelings and needs. For the same reason, a higher degree of vagueness and silence will be accepted in such cultures. Hofstede (1991: 60) reports that when an Indonesian family on Java visit relatives (always unannounced), they sit together but nobody speaks, and nobody is embarrassed by the silence that reigns; the same may happen in Native (North) American cultures.

Conversational indirectness is correlated with a person's self-construal as interdependent (i.e., lower individualism) and directness with a person's self-construal as independent (higher individualism) (Schouten 2007): in more group-oriented cultures, there is a higher fear of causing loss of face and hurting the other person's feelings, therefore, more indirect, high context communication is likely to be used.

9.4.2 Shame vs. guilt cultures

In an individualistic culture, the primary ethical norm which prevents a person from performing certain actions which he/she considers immoral is a feeling of guilt. Guilt establishes a link between the person as an individual and his/her own, private conscience (itself possibly linked to the idea of a God); other people are not primarily involved in this.

When on the contrary a person is prevented by *shame* from doing certain things, as is the case in group-oriented cultures, the primary norm is: what will other people think of me (Hofstede 1991: 60)? A strong reason for refraining from immoral behavior then is that such behavior might shame the family, the tribe, etc. Arab culture is often described as giving priority to shame over guilt. Nydell (1987: 82) reports that an Arab child is conditioned to feel ashamed because others see him as behaving badly, not because he inwardly regrets having done wrong. Social pressure dominates; the capacity for self-criticism on the other hand is less developed. Given that many Arabs claim to have over a hundred 'fairly close' relatives (Nydell 1987: 75) who may be watching, needless to say this social pressure is strong.[2] Nydell adds that Arab parents, and mothers especially, welcome their children's *dependence*, not independence, and "try to keep their children tied to them emotionally" (1987: 84) – exactly the opposite of the American children who are raised to be independent of their parents.

9.4.3 Face saving and harmony

People from individualistic cultures are sometimes under the impression that in group-oriented cultures, everyone is playing a role rather than 'being himself/herself'. This impression arises from the fact that in group-oriented cultures, the opinion of the group as such prevails over personal opinions of individuals. Group harmony is crucial and everything should be done to preserve it. This is often interpreted by people from the West as submissiveness, an unwillingness to stand up for your personal opinion. But people from group-oriented cultures do not see it as such. I argued elsewhere (Verluyten 1993) that a Western interpretation of the Filipino value of *pakikisama* is erroneous:

> [...] *pakikisama* does not 'emphasize the Filipino attitude of submission', as MCD[3] states. It is more an indication of the Filipino's sense of belonging, of being part of a peer group with which he identifies himself. Related to this is the crucial concept of maintaining *smooth interpersonal relationships (SIR),* to which GI[4] and also MCD refer. The Filipino will concede with the decisions of the majority rather than strongly stand up for his own personal opinion. But to the Filipino, this does not imply submission any more than, for a Westerner, going along with a group of friends to a movie which he or she would not have chosen by himself/herself.

9.4.4 Indebtedness

As we have seen above, mutual help and favors within the group (what Westerners in certain cases would call nepotism) run strong in group-oriented cultures. The bonds within the group are strengthened by feelings of indebtedness: there are most often a number of people within the group who helped you in the past, and therefore you owe them a favor in return (and vice versa). The Filipino value of *utang na loob* is an illustration of this:

> *Utang na loob* is a very important trait [...]. Literally it means 'debt of the inside.' A Filipino remains indebted for a favor someone else has granted him. This indebtedness may span several generations. Thus, if my grandfather has helped your grandfather, you would still be indebted to me, on the basis of *utang na loob,* two generations later. If I come up to you applying for a job and thereby refer to the help granted to your grandfather

by my grandfather, you are bound to give me the job, regardless of whether I am the best qualified applicant or not (Verluyten 1993).

Similarly, Thai *bunkhun* or indebtedness may also be returned after many years (Klausner 1993: 275). In fact, paying off such a moral debt too quickly may be considered as refusing to enter into a relationship with the other party. Engholm calls Westerners 'instant reciprocators' – while the ideal, in Asia, is rather to have a ledger of reciprocal debts that never gets balanced (Engholm 1991: 68-9), for that is what forges an ongoing relationship.

Hendry (2003: 251) notes that people in Japan keep track of value of gifts received in order to be able to reciprocate properly at a later time.

In nearly all non-western cultures, networks based on mutual indebtedness and favors are widespread,[5] from Africa (Richmond & Gestrin 1998: 66) over Latin-America to Asia. The Chinese *guanxi* or networks were already mentioned above. Abramson & Ai (1999), on the basis of a survey of 138 Canadian companies operating in China, found that the single most important success factor is the ability to build guanxi relationships: on-going, mutually beneficial and trusting relationships between colleagues.

In individualistic cultures, people pride themselves in 'not owing anything to anyone.' 'Being successful without any help seems to be almost as important as success in itself. Westerners are frequently embarrassed when requesting help even of a close friend ('I really hate to ask you, but...'), while in more group-oriented cultures where indebtedness networks run high, one does not hesitate at all to request a favor of a friend (Varner & Beamer 1995: 93). In Africa, wealthier group members receive requests from less well-off members constantly, and it is sure sign of high social status to receive (and be able to honor) many such requests.

In group-oriented cultures the idea of not relying on help when needed, of not being indebted to many people, is not at all valued positively. It is more or less taken to mean that you are all alone on earth, that you have no-one to support you; it is the epitome of being miserable.

As explained before, in many poorer countries (which also happen to be the more group-oriented), when the locals take you to a restaurant, it is a matter of course that those who invite also pay for the dinner. Westerners may feel awkward because of this, particularly when you know that the person who invites you relies on an income that is perhaps one fifth or one tenth of what you are earning.

The Philippines: the inviter pays it all

A Belgian academic embarrassed and shocked our local colleagues in Manila more than once by his insistence to pay for his share when we were taken out to dinner by them. To the Filipinos, it must have been as though he refused to become part of that network of mutual indebtedness: he did not want to 'owe anything to anyone'. It is like refusing a gift, a token of someone's friendship. In addition, they must have been under the impression that in the West (a) all debts have to be settled immediately, and (b) help, hospitality and friendship are expressed in *money:* it was with money he wanted to pay them, not in any other, perhaps more indirect and tactful way.

9.4.5 Getting acquainted and being part of the in-group

As we saw above, in group-oriented cultures you need to become acquainted with a person before that person accepts to do business with you: you do business with people you know and trust. If the other person belongs to your in-group, you are normally already acquainted with him/her. But if the person does not belong to your in-group, a process of getting acquainted needs to take place before you will consider doing business with him/her, and that process will often seem lengthy in Western eyes.

> We give [the Vietnamese] a presentation of our company, who we are, our references. References are essential, businesses as well as persons. Such a presentation may last several hours, and they ask a lot of questions. Then the Vietnamese present their company. After that, a relationship starts to build up and evolve, but it takes a few months before concrete business talks will start [...]. Sometimes it takes over a year before you finally get a contract (G.L., Belgian banker, in Trinh (2004); my translation).

Hofstede (1991: 49) tells the story of a Swedish engineer who went to Saudi Arabia to try and obtain a contract for his Swedish firm. For a long time, to the Swede's annoyance, all the meetings he has with his Saudi counterparts are held in the presence of the Swedish businessman who had established the first contact (because this is the person the Saudis know and trust). Only after two years and six visits, just when the Swedish company started to doubt whether it was useful to pursue this connection any further, the Swedish engineer got word that a contract worth several million dollars was ready to be signed in Riyadh. Unfortunately, precisely because of that success the engineer was promoted to a management position where he was no longer in charge of the Saudi account. He was replaced by someone else, but his successor never managed to get the deal with the Saudis signed: there appeared to be some detail that was not acceptable. Only when the engineer the Saudis had been doing business with before reappeared for the negotiations, the issue was quickly resolved and the contract was signed.

The tendency to do business with partners from the in-group even when the deal is less advantageous financially is also likely to be higher in group-oriented cultures. Penetrating such a market may be very difficult, unless you have something to offer that members of the in-group cannot provide for.

Chinese prefer doing business with the Chinese

Mr. John Doe of Fox Machineries Inc., USA, was asked to negotiate a deal with Lucky-Tex Co. in the Philippines. He expects to close sales for two different kinds of items, A and B, since he is confident that his company makes the highest quality items at very competitive prices. However, even while negotiations are going on, the Chinese owner of Lucky-Tex closes a deal with another Chinese-owned, Philippine-based company, Solid Mill Inc., to supply them with item A.

> Mr. Doe does not like what happened since he believes that Lucky-Tex could have gotten a better deal for item A with his company. He feels furious and betrayed. Mr. Doe is now contemplating if he should still continue negotiations in view of closing a deal involving item B. He is starting to feel that further talks would only prove futile, what with the unpredictable and irrational attitude of the owners of Lucky-Tex.
>
> Obviously, Mr. Doe has not studied the business culture of the Chinese well enough. Chinese have a tendency to keep wealth within their group. Translated into business practice, this means that they will give first priority to Chinese buyers and sellers whenever possible, even if a deal with a stranger would seem more advantageous. This is especially true in places where the Chinese community is a minority in the population. They tend to help each other out against the 'strangers' and thus create a form of extended nepotistic network. What happened to Mr. Doe is a very normal thing. He need not worry about negotiating further for item B, especially because there are no other companies, specifically Chinese ones, who could produce item B (reported to me by a Filipino of Chinese descent).

Engholm (1991: 8) confirms that the Chinese like to do business with each other: they feel more comfortable doing so because they can *trust* the other party more easily.

In fact, in group-oriented cultures in Asia a company A may in certain cases jeopardize its own profitability in order to 'help out' a partner company B by providing it with an order, even if company A could have found a better deal with another supplier. In one example, a Japanese bank makes illegal payments to help clients in need (Yoshimura & Anderson 1997: 38).

9.4.6 Dependency relations

> **Dependence vs. Independence**
>
> - A development[6] worker in Africa with the best of intentions decided to cook his own meals, wash his own dishes and his clothes, etc., rather than hiring one or more servants for those jobs. He considered that he wasn't any better than the locals and therefore he could do this himself, and also he felt it demeaning for a servant to wait on him and execute his orders.
> - A Belgian researcher who was working at a university in Bangkok was told that there was a 'coffee-lady' she could call anytime she needed coffee or another drink to be brought to her office, and also that it was customary to give this woman a small tip at the end of each month. The Belgian replied that she did not have any need for this service and that she would go to the secretariat and get the drinks there herself when necessary.

People from high IDV cultures feel that they can and should do things by themselves as much as possible, without asking others; in addition, these people are also from low PDI countries, and they tend to have difficulty issuing orders and coping with submissive behavior. In low IDV, high PDI cultures, however, dependency relations are common. Therefore, the behavior of the two Europeans shocked the local people, who surely felt that they were egoists, too stingy to share some of their wealth with others.

9.5 The correlation between Hofstede's Power Distance and Individualism

In most cases, cultures combine either high Power Distance and low Individualism, or low Power Distance and high Individualism. Both Power Distance and Individualism are also correlated with the national wealth of the country, as expressed in its GNP per capita: the richer the country, the higher its IDV score and the lower its PDI score tend to be, and vice-versa.

Hofstede's (1991: 54) graph (F23), where IDV is plotted against PDI, expresses the reverse correlation very clearly. As one can see, there are many countries in the upper right hand quadrant (high PDI, low IDV) and also in the lower left hand quadrant (low PDI, high IDV). The two other quadrants are virtually empty. Only Costa Rica (COS) combines group-orientation with a lower degree of Power Distance than most group-oriented cultures; we already discussed the special position of Costa Rica in this respect above

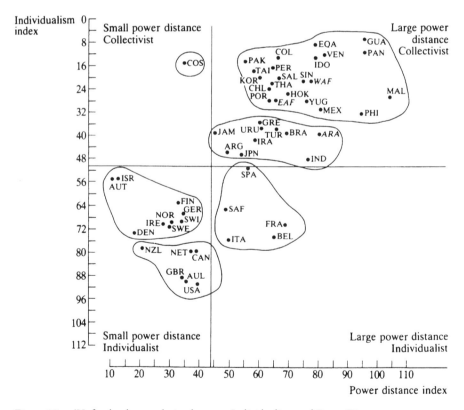

Figure 23. 'Hofstede: the correlation between Individualism and Power Distance.

In the lower right hand quadrant, apart from three borderline cases (Spain, South Africa, Italy), there are only two countries which clearly combine a high degree of Individualism with high Power Distance: France and Belgium. Hofstede appeals to two French scholars for an explanation of this peculiar phenomenon, at least as far as France is concerned: Michel Crozier and Philippe d'Iribarne.

> Face-to-face dependence relationships are... perceived as difficult to bear in the French cultural setting. Yet the prevailing view of authority is still that of... absolutism... The two attitudes are contradictory. However, they can be reconciled within a bureaucratic system since impersonal rules and centralization make it possible to reconcile an absolutist conception of authority and the elimination of most direct dependence relationships (Crozier 1964, in Hofstede 1991: 55).

Crozier's compatriot Philippe d'Iribarne, in his comparative study of a French, a US and a Dutch organization describes the French principle of organizing as 'the rationale of honor' *(la logique de l'honneur)*. This principle, which he finds already present in the French kingdom prior to Napoleon, means that everybody has a rank (large power distance), but that the implications of belonging to one's rank are less imposed by the group than determined by traditions. It is "not so much what one owes to others as what one owes to oneself" (d'Iribarne 1989: 59). It is a stratified form of individualism (Hofstede 1991: 56), or 'Vertical Individualism' (Chirkov, Lynch & Niwa 2005). We will discuss d'Iribarne's work in more detail below.

Notes

1. At least nowadays, that is. In Europe, also, marriages were arranged by a 'professional mediator' until the middle on the 17th century in England, early 18th in France, and late 18th in Italy; and affective individualism is recent in Europe (Vigarello 2005: 176).
2. The size of the family may in itself be an indication of group-orientation. The Kikuyu (Kenya) are 'able to recite exactly how they are related (step by step) to a network of hundreds of kinspeople' (Ferraro 1994: 20). My African wife knew a (to me) bewildering number of aunts and uncles, cousins, nieces and nephews. I am personally unable to recite the names of all my cousins (13 total, I think, but I am not even sure of the number), let alone my nephews, most of whom I have never seen. This is incomprehensible to my African friends.
3. MCD = Harris and Moran, *Managing Cultural Differences*, 1987.
4. GI = Copeland and Griggs, *Going International*, 1985.
5. We keep stressing that the reader should adopt a *relative* interpretation of statements such as these, not an absolute one. We are obviously not claiming that such networks play no role in the West, only that they are less dominant in many Western countries, where it is more conceivable to get things done, or to make a career, without relying on them.
6. I use this well-known terminology, which refers to economic and technological development, but it should be clear that there are many other forms of development (with respect to arts, friendship, happiness, to name just a few) that are not necessarily correlated to 'development' as it is commonly used.

Chapter 10
Work, ambition, career-orientation vs. leisure, family and vacation

One of Hofstede's cultural dimensions is called Masculinity, and its opposite pole Femininity. It is important to understand that these concepts should not exclusively be understood in terms of *male* vs. *female,* even though there is a connection with this opposition. Masculinity refers to a set of values and practices that are associated with the (traditional) male gender role; conversely, Femininity refers to concepts associated with the female gender role.

A list of qualities that are associated with both ends of the spectrum may clarify the meaning of both terms:

Masculinity	*Femininity*
assertive	modest
hard	soft
tough	tender
achievement	care
work	leisure
performance	service

Hofstede uses both concepts to describe cultures where, as a whole, either Masculine or Feminine characteristics are more prevalent, and not to refer to males vs. females.

Individual females may very well exhibit values and practices that are associated with the Masculinity side of the dimension. But generally, males will tend to exhibit more Masculinity traits and females more Femininity traits. There is an additional complication. In low MAS countries, it appears to be the case that the MAS scores for males and females tend to very similar. In high MAS cultures, on the contrary, gender roles are more differentiated, with males exhibiting more of the values and practices associated with Masculinity, and females those associated with Femininity. In Japan, the socially expected gender roles are for the husband to work and provide income for the family, and for the wife to take care of the household (including its finances!) and the children. Studies show that Japanese men have less contact with their children than those in other countries.

According to Hendry (2003: 205), Japanese men may qualify their vacation as 'family duty'. Full-time work for women, on the other hand, is disapproved of (Finkelstein, Imamura & Tobin 1991: 54).

Masculinity is the only one of Hofstede's four dimensions where men and women score consistently differently, except in extreme feminine countries.

Japan, and to a lesser extent the United States, are prime examples of high MAS cultures. Here also, the scores for various countries can be found at http://www.geert-hofstede.com.

Competition, achievement and work have high value, in particular for males. Competition starts at school, at a young age, and everyone is trained at aiming to be 'the best.' I once saw a six or eight year old boy in the United States who was wearing a T-shirt that said: *Second place is the first loser*. My European friends were horrified. Failure at school (in particular in Japan) or at work (in the USA) is traumatizing. Every year, a number of Japanese children commit suicide when they learn that they have failed at school. In the Netherlands, on the other hand, a country with a very low Masculinity score, such competition is nearly non-existent (Blom 2008: 155-6), and American exchange students are very surprised when they discover how little the Dutch students care about their grades.

In the United States, there is little sympathy for people who fail in life. Or perhaps more accurately, failing may be acceptable, but only if you try again and never give up until you succeed. Calling someone a 'loser' is clearly an insult. American heroes embody an ideal of being tough and aggressive, such as Rambo, Superman, and many others. In low MAS societies, people express more sympathy for the unfortunate, whereas in high MAS cultures, sympathy goes mainly to the successful achiever (Hofstede 1980: 294).

Lane, DiStefano & Maznevski (2000: 330) describe an American woman who always competes with the other workers even when this is not asked for: 'I always had to do something to keep myself challenged.' Even during their leisure time (riding a bike, travelling on a holiday), Americans may appear to Europeans as being in a competition.

Competition vs. solidarity

A European MBA student in the US heard all the other (mostly American) students in his accounting class complain that they did not understand the subject matter of the class well, because it was too technical for them. The European student, who already had a degree in accounting, offered to tutor the other students to help them pass their exams in accounting. The other students gladly accepted. Afterwards however, though grateful, some of the American students expressed surprise at his offer. In their very competitive graduate schools, most students wish to stand out as much as possible above the others, and the help he provided reduced the difference in level between him and the other students.

In low MAS countries such as Scandinavia and the Netherlands, someone who tries to be much better than the others, be it at school or at work, may be frowned upon. There is a tendency towards *leveling*, i.e. towards behaving like everyone else rather than trying to stand out and be the best. In Thailand, another country with a low MAS score (34), ostensibly outperforming others is to be avoided. Cooper (1991: 36-8) quotes the example of a sports competition between two villages where things go terribly wrong because, under a new coach, one of the villages *really* tries to win against the other village, contrary to what had happened in the previous years.

Gender roles are more differentiated in Japan and, to a lesser extent, in the USA than in Scandinavia or the Netherlands. In Sweden, when a baby is born, the father can get paternity leave as well as the mother can get maternity leave: the parents may divide the total number of weeks of leave of absence between them as suits them best.

In Sweden it is accepted by society that, in case the wife has a successful career, she may wish to pursue her career after giving birth, and that her husband will stay home and take care of the baby and the household. This is unthinkable in Japan, but also in the United States as well as in many other countries, where career aspirations are one possible option for women, but are socially compulsory for men (see also Hofstede 1991: 93).

Obviously, the balance between work and leisure is different in high MAS and in low MAS cultures. Because of the performance oriented, 'live to work' attitude in high MAS countries, it is quite common for companies to expect their workers to finish a task after hours or over the week-end. When walking through the business district of an American city, one will frequently see people working in their offices on Saturday or Sunday, or late at night. The Japanese are also willing to work overtime quite easily. In low MAS countries, this is much more exceptional. People may work hard, but they want to strike a different balance between work and leisure, being with their family, etc. Therefore, they will be less willing to give up evenings, weekends, holidays and vacation when a job needs to be done. In high MAS countries such as Japan and to a lesser extent the US, it is not uncommon for workers not to take up the full number of days of vacation they are entitled to. A US manager might say: 'I haven't been able to take a vacation for several years!' – thus illustrating how important her work is to the company. Many Europeans will think that this is crazy: you work in order to be able to go on vacation, while Americans perhaps tend to see their vacation as a period of rest which enables them to perform better at work afterwards.

Business or Vacation?

An American (US) student in Maastricht saw a beautiful Delft vase in a store and she wanted to offer it as a gift for her mother. She decided to come back to the store the next week to buy it. Unfortunately, when she returned there was a sign saying that the store was closed for three week's vacation: it would not reopen before the student had left the country. The student was really upset as well as puzzled by this. She wrote in one of her papers for my course that she could not understand how a store could close down and 'lose out on profitable business' during that time.

The Dutch owners would probably have answered that they would not want to lose out on their valuable summer vacation…

Figure 24. Work vs. Leisure: the hair salon in Bangkok decided to extend its opening hours until midnight; the shop in Ravenna, Italy, is normally open for two hours in the morning (10: 30-12: 30 and three in the afternoon (16: 30-19: 30), but today will open only at 17: 30; it is also closed Tuesday afternoon (and Sunday, that goes without saying).

There is a story (it is probably just a joke, but it illustrates the low MAS value system well) about a Norwegian executive who was having a telephone conversation with a partner in the United States on a Friday afternoon. In the middle of the conversation, the Norwegian looks at his watch and says 'Oh, it's five o'clock!' He interrupts the conversation in the middle of a sentence and puts down the telephone.

More seriously, several accounts (for example Adler 1992: 55) confirm that Swedish businesspeople expect the work week to end at 5 p.m. on Friday and that they want to reserve the week-end for their families, which may be misinterpreted as 'inadequate commitment to work' by some of their colleagues from higher MAS cultures such as Americans (US). In high MAS cultures, people tend to accept a higher degree of interference of the organization they work for in their private lives than in low MAS countries (Hofstede 1980: 296). A good example is the story 'What Eurodisney demands of its workers' under 12.2.2 below.

Americans (such as my American students in Maastricht) frequently express surprise at the fact that Europeans seem to have so much leisure time, spend their time having drinks in outdoor cafés, indulge in long lunch breaks, etc.

In one of my large classes with a mix of American and European students, I submitted the following question to them. Suppose a student sends an e-mail on Friday afternoon to one of her professors, with a question she needs answered. When would it be reasonable for her to expect the professor's answer? Europeans felt that the student should not expect an answer before Monday; Americans felt that this is too late, the professor should check her professional e-mail also over the week-end, and respond to those messages.

High MAS countries also tend to have more industrial conflict. In high MAS countries such as the United States, 'there is a feeling that conflicts should be resolved by a good fight' (Hofstede 1991: 92). In the Netherlands, on the other hand, industrial conflict is rare. This prediction, however, is not borne out by the facts with respect to Japan, where industrial conflict is rare even if the country has the highest MAS score of all the countries surveyed.

Not all predictions one could make on the basis of the country MAS scores will be borne out by observed behavior, of course. For instance, service orientation is predicted to be lower in high MAS cultures. However, both Japan and the United States exhibit a customer and service orientation that is clearly above that of European countries.

Chapter 11
Uncertainty Avoidance: stress, anxiety and fear of the unknown

Hofstede's dimension of Uncertainty Avoidance reflects the level of anxiety about the future which is present in a culture.[1] In high Uncertainty Avoidance cultures, people will tend to have a higher degree of stress and they will tend to pursue to a higher degree strategies that provide them with a form of certainty for the future, such as *employment stability, saving money* and *rule orientation.*

Rules may take away part of the stress involved in coping with uncertainty. If there are rules and procedures for almost everything, you feel that you know in advance what the course of events will be, and you don't have to negotiate on a case-by-case basis every time a new issue arises. Good rules can allow people to perform better because they can set energies free for other things. But on the other hand, too strong a rule orientation may destroy a person's autonomous judgment completely (Hofstede 1980: 158).

Obviously, employment stability is an essential element in avoiding uncertainty about the future. In high Uncertainty Avoidance cultures, people tend to prefer a stable, possibly even lifetime job, to a more challenging but temporary position. This is clearly the case in Belgium (a country with one of the highest Uncertainty Avoidance scores in the world), for instance: many people will prefer a job as a civil servant, which guarantees lifetime employment, to a job in the private sector which normally pays much more for the same qualifications, but does not guarantee job security. Similarly, Yoshimura & Anderson (1997: 193) state that in Japan, jobs in government ministries are more prestigious than jobs with corporations. Uncertainty Avoidance is negatively correlated with the need for achievement.[2]

The savings quote also tends to be higher in high Uncertainty Avoidance cultures. It is, for instance, notoriously high in Belgium and Japan, two countries with high Uncertainty Avoidance scores. Savings money is one way to partly absorb the uncertainty which is inherent in the future.

11.1 Country scores on the Uncertainty Avoidance Index (UAI)

The scores of the different countries in Hofstede's survey on the Uncertainty Avoidance Index (UAI) can be found at http://www.geert-hofstede.com. Again, clusters of countries clearly emerge. Anglo-Saxon and Scandinavian countries have low UAI scores. In fact, the vast majority of countries with UAI scores in the lower half of the scale belong to one of those two groups. Many Latin-American countries have high UAI scores, as do European countries of the Romance (Latin) group: Portugal, France, Spain, Italy and also Belgium exhibit high to very high UAI scores. Asian countries, on the other hand, do not score particularly high (except Japan), and some are even in the lower range of the spectrum.

There is a strong relationship between Uncertainty Avoidance and age: older people tend to have higher Uncertainty Avoidance. This means that there is a possibility that the UAI scores of the countries listed could be due to the age difference of respondents to Hofstede's survey in various countries. Therefore, Hofstede (1980) also lists UAI scores that are controlled for age. If we control for age, however,

> [t]he various country clusters remain essentially the same, but some countries shift somewhat [...]. The country differences in UAI certainly cannot be accounted for by an average age artifact. We cannot claim either, that the age-correlated UAI scores are more 'correct' than the uncorrelated ones. The average age of HERMES[3] employees in a country is partly a *consequence* of a high UAI norm. A higher UAI implies, among other things, a hesitation to change jobs; therefore, the average seniority in such a country will be higher and, with it, the average age, which reinforces the tendency to stay. I shall therefore continue to use the 'raw' UAI values in order to characterize countries, not the values corrected for age (Hofstede 1980: 167).

11.2 The UAI Scores in the workplace

In organizations, there are certain *rituals* whose primary function is that they *absorb uncertainty,* i.e. "they do not make the future more predictable, but they relieve some of the stress of uncertainty by creating a pseudo-certainty within which organization members can continue functioning" (Hofstede 1980: 159). Such rituals include the following.

- *Memos and reports.* Some memos and reports are needed, but many others will never be read, or "contain no information that anyone will act upon"; they are a device to 'stop time' for a moment (Hofstede 1980: 159). When a Belgian academic like me receives a travel grant from the Belgian National Science Fund to attend an international scientific conference, after his/her return the academic has to send a report about that conference to the NSF. No-one reads that report, and absolutely no action will be taken on the basis of it. Its function seems to be that it absorbs the uncertainty which is inherent in giving money to someone and not being able to check how the person spent that money in another country.

- *Certain parts of the accounting system.* In some cases, the accounting system may be so detailed that "it absorbs uncertainty to such an extent that it absorbs all usable information as well" (Hofstede 1980: 159). Accounting information is often after-the-fact justification of decisions that were taken for non-logical reasons in the first place (Cleverley, quoted in Hofstede 1980: 159-60).
- *A considerable part of the planning system.* No-one is able to predict the future, yet organizations, like people, exhibit a tendency to make rather detailed plans for the future. In actual fact, when the unforeseen happens, plans will often be bypassed. Having a planning system, however, allows managers to sleep more peacefully, even if it does not really work. It may also help members of an organization to believe in what they are doing, which is an essential element of success in overcoming crisis (Hofstede 1980: 160).
- *A considerable part of the control system,* such as "the minute checking of the figures of travel accounts where there is no possibility to judge the necessity of the trip". 'Control overkill' can lead to a situation where "those whose activities are controlled receive the message that correct figures are more important than correct facts" (Hofstede 1980: 160).
- *The nomination of experts.* "Outside consultants are often used when various persons within the organization cannot reach consensus, to absorb this inside uncertainty" (Hofstede 1980: 161). In lower Uncertainty Avoidance countries there may be a point where one feels it is useless to hire professional planners, and one prefers to live with the uncertainty ('wait and see'); this attitude will be less common in high Uncertainty Avoidance countries.

Many forms of *registration,* with the authorities and elsewhere, can also be considered uncertainty avoidance rituals. One of my first intercultural experiences with the United States happened to me when I arrived there as a graduate student in 1976. I inquired with the other students 'Where I need to go to register?' It came as a surprise to me that in the United States, you do not need to tell the authorities where you are living. In the same vein, high Uncertainty Avoidance countries will have a higher tendency to introduce identity cards for their citizens (Hofstede 1991: 127-8). In Belgium, when told that there are quite a few countries where identity cards do not exist, many people cannot believe that a society can function without them. How can the state allow its citizens to roam free in the streets without an official piece of paper that shows their name, address, national registration number, etc.?

Claes & Gerritsen (2002) point out the striking correlation that exists between countries' UAI scores and obligatory identity cards (since 2002, the situation has changed in some countries as a result of terrorist attacks or threats):

	UAI	Obligatory	Voluntary	None
Greece	112	X		
Portugal	104	X		
Belgium	94	X		
France	86	X		
Spain	86	X		
Turkey	85	X		
Italy	75	X		

	UAI	Obligatory	Voluntary	None
Austria	70		X	
Germany	65	X		
Finland	59		X	
Switzerland	58		X	
Netherlands	53			X
Norway	50			X
Great Britain	35			X
Ireland	35			X
Sweden	29			X
Denmark	23			X

Figure 25. Obligatory identity cards in Europe.

As unknown people carry with them a higher degree of uncertainty and ambiguity, there may be more reluctance to accept someone who comes from another company as a manager in high UIA countries; and even more so, to accept someone from another culture. Hofstede predicts that in high Uncertainty Avoidance countries there will tend to be more racism ('what is different, is dangerous' – Hofstede 1991), intolerance and political totalitarianism (totalitarianism is a radical way to eliminate uncertainty/ambiguity). Lower Uncertainty Avoidance may lead to more strongly favoring multiculturalism (van de Vijver, Breugelmans, Schalk-Soekar 2008: 101). People from low UAI cultures may also be prepared to expatriate themselves more easily than people from high UAI cultures (Hofstede 1980: 177).

The search for certainty will lead high Uncertainty Avoidance cultures to prefer experts as managers rather than generalists, and, concomitantly, in high Uncertainty Avoidance cultures expert careers will be more valued that generalist careers. In Belgium or Germany, a civil engineer (who is an expert in a rather narrow field, such as electronics or mining) will be held in higher esteem than a graduate from a business school; in the United States or the UK, it tends to be the other way around. In high Uncertainty Avoidance cultures, even managers will tend to be specialists (experts) rather than generalists. In low Uncertainty Avoidance, managers will tend to be involved in strategy, and leave the details to be worked out by others. "French and German top managers want to be better informed about the details of their business than do British top managers" (Hofstede 1980: 188, reporting a study of Horowitz; see also Laurent 1983).

A higher degree of empowerment of subordinates will be accepted in low UAI countries, whereas in high UAI countries, initiative of subordinates should be kept more under control (Hofstede 1980: 177). Subordinates themselves will tend to prefer clear requirements and instructions in higher UAI cultures, broad guidelines only in lower UAI countries (Hofstede 1980: 176).

In low Uncertainty Avoidance cultures, managers will also be more willing to take risky decisions, whereas in high Uncertainty Avoidance countries, managers will be more afraid of treading unknown territory and stick to the certainty of what is known. Because job security is valued more in high Uncertainty Avoidance countries, and because entering a new job inevitably entails a higher degree of uncertainty, labor turnover tends to be lower in high Uncertainty Avoidance countries. In low Uncertainty Avoidance countries, as we saw before, career advancement tends to have priority over job security. Therefore, employees tend to be more ambitious in low Uncertainty Avoidance countries.

Typically, low Uncertainty Avoidance cultures may be more innovative and creative and accept transformational leadership (as against purely transactional leadership) more easily (Ergeneli, Gohar & Termirbekova 2007).

Rule-orientation also tends to be higher in high Uncertainty Avoidance cultures, as we saw before. In low Uncertainty Avoidance countries people prefer fewer rules and they also are more willing to break the rules or to change them if need be.

In low Uncertainty Avoidance countries, dissent will be accepted more easily, whereas in high Uncertainty Avoidance countries, dissent is seen as a threat.

11.3 Uncertainty Avoidance: discussion

A number of features Hofstede mentions have to do with the fact that high Uncertainty Avoidance goes together with high anxiety and stress. In low Uncertainty Avoidance countries, people will tend to be more relaxed and exhibit a lower tendency to work hard. When we look at the UAI scores for various countries however, we may not see any clear correlation with lower stress: do people in Greece or Portugal exhibit high job stress, and do people in the United States have lower job stress and a lower tendency to work hard? Do people in Asian countries in general exhibit lower job stress and do they value hard work less than people in Latin America? Of course, we should not forget that other parameters inevitably intervene (including the Masculinity dimension we discussed above), and that these may blur the picture as we see it. But many of the predictions are counterintuitive, to say the least. There are few countries where rule orientation is as high as in the US, yet that country has a rather low UA score (46).

Other features are related to the idea that in high Uncertainty Avoidance cultures, which are also high anxiety cultures, people exhibit a higher tendency to express emotions. This seems to be generally accurate when we look at some of the country scores on the UA scale. In Latin cultures people no doubt express emotions more easily than in Asian, Scandinavian or Anglo-Saxon countries. Japan must then be considered as an exception, as it scores very high on the UAI, yet the Japanese normally do keep the expression of emotions strongly under control. When faced with uncertainty, people from cultures with higher Uncertainty Avoidance may respond with hostility and even aggresion (Merkin 2006).

Notes

1. Contrary to *fear*, which has an object, *anxiety* refers to a vague feeling without any precise object.
2. This may be counterbalanced, in Japan, by the country's high Masculinity score.
3. The pseudonym HERMES is used for IBM in Hofstede's 1980 book.

Chapter 12
Research methodologies

This book is primarily meant to be a guide for practitioners: managers, diplomats, students, anyone who has contacts with people from others cultures, i.e., in fact, almost anyone in our global world. The aim of the book is to turn readers into better 'intercultural communicators', not into intercultural researchers; the latter would take another approach altogether.

A very hasty reader who is only interested in acquiring intercultural skills may skip this chapter and move on to the next one. But most of us surely want to gain some insight into the various research methodologies that are being used in the field we are studying. This brief overview may enable the reader to critically assess the reliability and importance of the empirical studies our understanding is based on.

There are several domains in the social sciences which contributed to the birth and development of the scientific field that is now called 'intercultural communication':[1] sociology, cultural anthropology, psychology, linguistics and communication theory, possibly more. Each of these brought its own methodology to the new field, and they complete each other rather than competing with each other. In a field as complex as intercultural studies, one research methodology only cannot yield sufficient insight and understanding, and purely quantitative research exclusively even less so; a kind of "messy research" (Usunier 1998: 85, 147, 151) is the best approach. Hofstede himself accepts the need for methodologies other than his own sociological approach to this field (Magala 2005: 77).

12.1 Sociology

12.1.1 Geert Hofstede

From the chapters above, the reader will have gathered that Geert Hofstede is a pivotal figure in cross-cultural research. Even though the data on which it is based are old by now, Hofstede's large-scale study (1980) called *Culture's Consequences. International differences in work-related values*[2] is still a major reference at present, for its methodology as well as for its findings. At the time, it was innovative also because it was by no means an established fact in the 1970s that culture did influence management style, organizational behavior and work-related values; on the contrary, many were convinced that there exists one optimal management style which can be applied everywhere in the world. American-style management was being introduced to various countries in the 1950s and 1960s, and there was a period were Japanese management was fashionable in the 1970s. Nowadays, most intercultural scholars deny the existence of a 'global manager' (see Bartnett 1997), though the idea is still alive in some circles (see also Bartlett & Ghoshal's 1992 article in the *Harvard Business Review*).

Hofstede's study is without any doubt the most widely quoted, reviewed and replicated research project in the field. Less than fifteen years after its publication, Sondergaard (1994) counted thirty-six reviews of Hofstede's 1980 book, 1036 quotations and sixty-one replications (many of which remain unpublished, however).

Let us take a look at the set-up of the study. At the time when the survey was carried out, Hofstede was working for IBM Corporation in the United States.[3] It was then that he carried out a large-scale survey into the work-related value systems of employees in IBM subsidiaries throughout the world. Because IBM does not have development or manufacturing operations in all the countries where it is present, the country comparison is based on data from the marketing and service divisions of the company (Hofstede 1980: 73).

The data bank which resulted from different surveys carried out between 1967 and 1973 contains data from approximately 117,000 questionnaires and more than 65 countries. A list of the countries surveyed, with the languages used for the questionnaire, can be found in Hofstede (1980: 62).

In those cases where the data for some countries were limited, Hofstede does not include then in his 1980 book. However, some of them return in a subsequent book in 1991, either separately (Malaysia) or grouped into clusters: Arab countries (data from Egypt, Iraq, Kuwait, Lebanon, Libya, Saudi Arabia, United Arab Emirates), East Africa (Ethiopia, Kenya, Tanzania, Zambia), West Africa (Ghana, Nigeria, Sierra Leone).

Although Hofstede's study encompasses a large part of the world, Africa is underrepresented; and, unsurprisingly, a major blank spot on the map are the then socialist countries (Central and Eastern Europe, the Soviet Union, the People's Republic of China), where there were no IBM subsidiaries, and where Hofstede would not have had access anyway under the communist regime. In (the former) Yugoslavia, a survey was carried out in the same type of industry, but not IBM.

On www.geert-hofstede.com , one now finds scores for many further countries, including many of the former socialist republics: China, Russia, Poland, etc. However, as these figures are based on replications of the original study in different companies, or sometimes purely on estimates, they do not have the same reliability as the figures stemming from the original IBM study.

A look at the impressive list of countries and languages, and the number of questionnaires from which data are gathered, may give the reader an idea of the sheer size of the whole enterprise. No-one has carried out a similar operation on the same scale (or found the funding for it) since then. Simply consider the translation problems. In some cases, the wording in the original English version of the questionnaire had to be changed because a word appeared to be difficult to translate into other languages. Such was the case, for instance, with the English word 'achievement.' Back-translation was sometimes used to check the accuracy of the translated questionnaires.[4]

Mishap inevitably occurred more than once: questions were left out when the local people administered the questionnaire, packages with questionnaires got lost in the mail or stolen, etc.: "A painful process of correcting, recoding, and discounting suspect information is necessary to arrive at results that make sense" (Hofstede 1980: 64).

Eventually, after factor analysis, about 50% of the variation observed in the answers of respondents to the questionnaire was explained through four theoretical 'dimensions', as we have seen above:
- Power Distance
- Individualism
- Uncertainty Avoidance
- Masculinity

These four dimensions are theoretical, explanatory constructs. It is therefore a mistake to write, as some do, that Hofstede 'discovered' these four dimensions in the world of cultural differences. Rather, he constructed them in order to explain some of his research findings.

A fifth dimension was added later, and is various called 'the Confucian dimension' or 'Long-term vs. short-term orientation'.

12.1.2 'Dimensions', 'value types', values: terminological and conceptual issues

In Hofstede's view (2001: 29), his five dimensions (and any valid cultural dimensions really) exhibit the following characteristics:
- Each dimension is rooted in a basic problem with which all societies have to cope
- The dimensions are independent (statistically distinct)
- They occur in all possible combinations (though some more frequent than others)
- They are empirically found and validated

One side of a cultural dimension represents what Hofstede calls a 'typology' and Schwartz (see below) a 'value type' (I prefer to call it a 'value cluster'): a number of values that usually go together. Thus, a culture characterized by high Power Distance (hierarchy) will typically exhibit a number of values which are usually correlated: respect for superiors, centralized decision making with little feedback from subordinates, powerholders being entitled to privileges, paternalism (superior helping and protecting subordinate), etc. Notice that if the values which belong to the same value type are *usually* found together, this also implies that in some cases they will not. Thus, in Japan perhaps we discover a culture which is high on 'respect for superiors', but at the same time does not exhibit 'decision making with little feedback from subordinates'.

Schwartz (1999) lists 45 values (without claiming that these are the only ones that matter), grouped together into 7 'value types', which in turn make up three 'polar dimensions':
- Conservatism vs. Autonomy (related to Hofstede's Individualism)
- Hierarchy vs. Egalitarianism (Hofstede's Power Distance)
- Mastery vs. Harmony (this dimension is related to one of Kluckhohn and Strodtbeck's 'value orientations', – yet another term!)

As Autonomy is split up between 'Intellectual autonomy' and 'Affective autonomy', the three dimensions actually yield seven value types rather than six.

Even if Schwartz's methodology is different from Hofstede in that it attempts to measure values directly (by asking respondents how important this value is for them) rather than indirectly (by probing the behavioral outcomes of a particular value, as Hofstede did), the reader will immediately notice that the framework of cultural dimensions Schwartz proposes is rather similar to some of the dimensions put forward by Hofstede.

In both cases however, it is by no means clear what qualifies as a 'value type' and what as a 'value'. According to Schwartz (1999), values are 'conceptions of the desirable' that guide social actors or 'trans-situational criteria or goals'. For him, 'egalitarianism' is a value type; 'freedom' however is a value, as is 'reciprocating favors'. But isn't 'freedom' closer, in its level of abstraction, to 'egalitarianism' than it is to a behavioral rule such as 'reciprocating favors'?

I would also like to warn once more against the naïve idea, which most scholars seem to share, that all behavior is the surface manifestation of underlying values. In reality, cultures carry with them remnants from a remote past: a behavioral trait may subsist a long time, possibly centuries or millennia, after the value which gave rise to it has been lost (such as the handshake). In addition some behavior may have arisen in a totally arbitrary way, without ever having been the expression of an underlying value (such as the number of kisses in various regions of France, see F8 above).

In an attempt to sort things out, and at the risk of introducing yet further terminology, I would propose the following concepts:
1. *Dimensions:* axes on which the position of a given culture represents a set of values that are typically correlated and thus form a value cluster. Example: Strong vs. weak Hierarchy.
2. *Value clusters* (similar to Schwartz' 'value types' and to Hofstede's 'typology'): a group of values that are often correlated with each other. Example: Strong hierarchy
3. *Values:* abstract mental principles guiding a person's behavior in varied circumstances. Example: respect for superiors.
4. *Rules of behavior* (sometimes called 'attitudes'). Example: Being afraid of disagreeing with the boss.
5. *Behavior* (practices).
    a. *Behavior as a result of a rule of behavior.* Example: Not voicing disagreement with the boss.
    b. *Conventional behavior.* Example: shaking hands.

Levels 1-4 are hierarchically related. Observed behavior (4) may be the outcome of a rule of behavior (3), which is itself the expression of a value (2) that belongs to a specific value cluster (1). Dimensions are a convenient way of grouping together two (or possibly more) value clusters that are opposites of each other.

Only level 5, behavior, is directly visible. The higher levels can only be tested through their influence on behavior, such as observing or surveying.

Conventional behavior (5b) is by no means less important to learn about than behavior which is the expression of an underlying rule and value. In fact an important part of our everyday behavior falls under that category, such as (most of) greetings, table manners, dress code, etc.

12.1.3 Authors inspired by Hofstede

Hofstede's seminal work has been a source of inspiration for many researchers. There are, on the one hand, pure replications of Hofstede's survey, using the same questionnaire and methods. These are extremely valuable as they are a means of confirming or disconfirming the results originally obtained. As mentioned before, Sondergaard in 1994 already counted sixty-one replications of Hofstede; we are not going to discuss these here. Overall, "the analysis of the replications showed that the differences predicted by Hofstede's dimensions were largely confirmed" (Sondergaard 1994: 451).

On the other hand there are those scholars who use a different methodology, but whose work is still clearly inspired by Hofstede, even if they may disagree with his approach.

The most well-know of these is probably Fons Trompenaars. Trompenaars' results are based on surveys carried out in various companies, with the questions typically representing a behavioral dilemma the respondent must choose between. One of the most well-known is the following (Trompenaars even devoted an entire book to it in 2003, with the title *Did the Pedestrian Die?*):

> You are the passenger in a car driven by a close friend. He hits a pedestrian. You know that his speed was at least 35 miles per hour in an area of the city where the maximum speed allowed is 20 miles per hour. There are no witnesses. His lawyer says that if you are prepared to testify under oath that he was only driving at 20 miles per hour it may save him from serious consequences.
>
> What right has your friend to expect you to protect him?
> a. My friend has a DEFINITE right to expect me to testify to the lower figure.
> b. He has SOME right to expect me to testify to the lower figure.
> c. He has NO right to expect me to testify to the lower figure.

On the basis of responses to this dilemma, Trompenaars construes his Universalism-Particularism dimension. In a culture which is higher on Particularism, members of the in-group (such as your friend in the dilemma) are entitled to a higher degree of protection, and this may include a false testimony. In cultures with higher Universalism, everyone is treated in the same way, regardless of whether or not he is a member of your in-group. Interestingly, in cultures with strong Particularism the willingness to give a false testimony goes up when the accident is more serious, e.g. when the pedestrian dies: the tougher the situation, the more your friend is entitled to your absolute loyalty and protection. In cultures with weaker Particularism, it goes down under the same circumstances: perhaps I can protect my friend with a minor lie, but I am not going to cover up a criminal act he committed.

Trompenaars eventually identifies seven value dimensions:
1. Universalism vs. particularism
2. Communitarianism vs. individualism
3. Neutral vs. emotional
4. Diffuse vs. specific
5. Achievement vs. ascription
6. Relationship with time
7. Relationship with nature.

Of these, most are either identical to one of Hofstede's dimensions (such as 2, identical to Hofstede's Individualism-Collectivism) or they represent one aspect of them. Thus, Universalism-Particularism refers to the in-group/out-group distinction which is itself strongly correlated with Collectivism-Individualism. Diffuse-Specific refers to a distinction similar to the 'getting acquainted' aspect referred to above, and is thus also closely related to Individualism-Collectivism. In a more individualist culture, I can concentrate on one specific aspect of the person I am communicating with: he is my partner in business, for instance, and I do not need to get to know him personally very much (specific). In a group-oriented culture, I like to do business with someone I trust, and I therefore need much more background information about the other person (diffuse). Neutral-emotional obviously refers to a distinction between cultures where members express their emotions more openly or refrain from doing so: it may represent a behavioral aspect of Hofstede's Uncertainty Avoidance. Achievement-Ascription refers to cultures where a person's status is mainly based on her own achievement, or ascribed on the basis of family background and the like: it is related to Hofstede's Power Distance dimension, and perhaps also to a certain extent to his Individualism-Collectivism (Power Distance and Individualism are themselves usually correlated; see 9.5 above).

Trompenaars' 'relationship with time' draws heavily on older work by Edward Hall (including the polychrony-monochrony distinction we discussed in chapter 3), and 'relationship with nature' on Kluckhohn and Strodbeck's value orientations (1961).

Methodologically, Trompenaars study raises questions. It is not altogether clear why some of the dimensions are kept separate rather than subsumed under one heading, as we have seen.

Some of Trompenaars' charts with figures resulting from his survey leave the reader perplexed. As the list of countries included differs from one chart to the next, comparison is sometimes impossible: in the chapter on individualism for instance, Belgium is included in chart 5.2 (1993: 52), but not in 5.1 (1993: 48). Also, quite a few countries score very erratically with respect to one and the same dimension. Spain, for instance, scores very high when respondents are asked whether they opt for individual freedom (rather than taking care of others even if it obstructs individual freedom; chart 5.1); the same country scores very low when respondents are asked if they believe in individual decisions (rather than group decisions; chart 5.2). While it cannot be expected that all results are consistent, such inconsistencies are so frequent in Trompenaars' date that they cast some doubt on the explanatory power of the dimensions he distinguishes. Inconsistent scores are never discussed throughout the book, and even more curiously the figures in the charts are seldom referred to in the text.

Trompenaars frequently refers to concepts introduced by other scholars: low and high context cultures, doing vs. being, and all the concepts he 'borrowed' from Parsons 1951 (see for instance Gudykunst & Kim 1992), etc., without properly acknowledging the source. Needless to say, this goes against all established practices of intellectual honesty, in particular if it happens frequently and, no doubt, consciously.

Hofstede (and others) profoundly dislikes Trompenaars' work, which he once (1996: 189-98) called "a fast food approach to intercultural diversity and communication", in an article with the title 'Riding the Waves of Commerce', a pun on Trompenaar's book *Riding the Waves of Culture* (for Trompenaars' reply, see Hampden-Turner & Trompenaars, 'Response to Geert Hofstede', 1997). As Hofstede is primarily a researcher, he emphasizes the complexities of the intercultural field of study. In the business world, however, some would like to learn, in the shortest possible time, hard and fast rules that guarantee success. I personally once got an invitation from a company for a 20 minute intercultural training seminar; I declined. Even if it is easy to argue that such an approach is illusory, some may opt for an intercultural trainer who claims to be able to achieve just that: turning a trainee into a skilled 'intercultural communicator' in less than half a day. The front cover of Trompenaars' 2003 book *Did the Pedestrian Die?* states that he is 'the world's greatest culture guru'; but gurus are usually not the best scholars...

Looking at the various cultural dimensions being put forward by Trompenaars and others, the conclusion appears to be that there is not that much new under the sun since Hofstede' research. Many of the subsequent surveys represent variants of the same. I could make this point with respect to many other research projects, such as the *Globe* study focusing on leadership in 62 societies or the *World Values Survey* carried out every five years in almost 100 countries. Thus, the *Globe* study identifies nine cultural dimensions, including Uncertainty Avoidance, Power Distance, Collectivism (subdivided into Institutional Collectivism and In-group Collectivism), etc.

Subdividing the large cultural dimensions into subcomponents may be useful when needed. Thus, Hofstede's Collectivism refers to the loyalty one owns to his in-group and the protection one gets from it. But it does not specify in itself which is the primary in-group in a given culture. In some cases it might be your tribe (perhaps in Africa), in others your company (Japan). Magala (2005) uses the term 'unzipping' a cultural dimension for the operation of subdividing it into subcomponents. At one level, there is Collectivism; at a more detailed level, there may well be Tribal collectivism, Company collectivism, etc.

12.2 Anthropological approach

12.2.1 Qualitative vs. quantitative research

As Hofstede's work has shown, a sociology-type approach, based on surveys and yielding qualitative results, offers valuable insights into the value systems and the behavior of people from different cultures. In fact the vast majority of studies carried out in the intercultural field use this methodology. A glance at the leading research journals in the field, such as the authoritative *International Journal of Intercultural Relations*, shows that almost all the studies are survey-based. Perhaps this is due to Hofstede's overwhelming scientific influence[5]; in fact, many published articles rely on his cultural dimensions mainly. It may also be due to the fact that researchers find it easier to carry out a survey and statistically process the results of it, than to endeavor using one of the other methodologies as described below. If the researcher is also an instructor at a university of school, he may have a captive audience of students at his disposal: you draw up a questionnaire based on dimensions that have been extensively described, you administer a survey in one of your larger classes, and you process the results through SPSS. You have a potential publication in an A-journal in a few weeks or months, and the pressure to publish is such that this is an understandable option. Whether the plethora of small-scale surveys, carried out with students, is the best way to further our understanding of cultural differences and intercultural communication is another issue.

> ...attempting to generalize from a college student sample to a nation looks silly and damages... credibility (Visser e.a. 2000, quoted in Chirkov, Lynch & Nirwa 2005: 472)

In any case, the quantitative approach does not give us the 'flesh and blood' feeling of a real intercultural encounter; its needs to be complemented by a more qualitative approach, and a good candidate for this may be a methodology which is inspired by cultural anthropology.

The traditional distinction between sociology and cultural anthropology, where the former was the study of Western society, and anthropology was the study of the societies of so-called 'primitive' peoples, is no longer tenable today. The difference between the two disciplines nowadays no longer lies in the object they study, but rather in the dominant methodology they use. In simple terms, one could say that sociology studies a culture from the outside and compares it with others (the 'etic' approach, as it is sometimes called), anthropology studies it from the inside (the 'emic' approach)[6]; anthropology is also called 'participant observation'.

According to the anthropologist Kilani (1992: 94), sociology starts from hypotheses that have already been elaborated and searches to refine or verify them through surveys. An anthropologist distances itself from institutions and builds its own problem-setting progressively, as he discovers the organizational principles of the society he studies.

In what follows, we present a prime example of a qualitative approach to intercultural research: the work of Philippe d'Iribarne and some of his followers (as in the 1998 *Cultures et mondialisation. Gérer par-delà les frontières*, with Alain Henry, Jean-Pierre Segal, Sylvie Chevrier, Tatjana Globokar).

12.2.2 An example: Philippe d'Iribarne, The Logic of Honor

Introduction

D'Iribarne's approach is similar to the anthropologist's, even if to my knowledge he does not refer to his own work with this term. For his seminal book *La Logique de l'Honneur* (1989) 'the logic of honor'[7], d'Iribarne selected a company with three subsidiaries, one in France, one in the US and one in the Netherlands. He then spent a fair amount of time with the workers in each of these subsidiaries, observing what went on around him: the way workers relate to each other and to management, the way work is organized, etc. The three subsidiaries are involved in exactly the same production process: the results they try to achieve are identical. Yet the way they go about achieving these results are vastly different. As the production process and overall corporate culture are the same, the differences d'Iribarne observed are likely to be due for the best part to the *culture* of the three countries involved.

D'Iribarne's book does not include figures or charts with quantitative data, and this makes it more difficult to summarize, perhaps more elusive. However, it does not make it any less valuable or less scientific. His research will give 'flesh and bones' to the bare data which sociologists provide us with. I argued above that quantitative data in themselves are insufficient in helping us to understand cultural differences, say in hierarchical relations, between countries.

Below I mention some salient features of French, American and Dutch culture as d'Iribarne describes them on the basis of his observations in the three subsidiaries he visited for his 1989 book.

France

D'Iribarne's book is called *La logique de l'honneur* ('the logic of honor') because, in his opinion, the main motivating force for the French workers is honor, personal pride in a job well done, often according to time-honored traditions of the profession. This also means that the first priority, for the French workers, lies not with what the boss might think, or whether customers are satisfied. Financial rewards are not a strong motivating factor either: it is impossible to get things done through money alone.

Other authors have observed the fact that service-orientation and customer satisfaction are not very high in France. Until recently, the (mainly French) sales delegation for Airbus airplanes was practically exclusively made up of engineers; sales and marketing specialists were not felt to be important in selling the airplanes. When customers ask for a product to be modified in order to suit their wishes, one likely reaction in France might be that the engineers who developed the product feel hurt in their personal pride and will attempt to counter the customer's wishes. The engineers also tend to prepare and deliver to the customer a machine or a piece of equipment that is technically superior rather than the one the customer ordered (but hence also more expensive). The engineers' attitude is that they know best what is good for the customer: after all, they are the specialists of the equipment you ordered!

The priority that is given to personal pride and responsibility also means that control of performance by the management will be resisted. When management attempts to get precise production figures, workers may well boycott the entire scheme and not provide the figures as requested. Attempts to introduce performance pay schemes are resisted equally strongly, because giving a financial bonus to the best performing workers is only possible, obviously, when the performance figures for each individual worker are known to the management. In brief, what is going on on the shop floor has a high degree of opacity for the management: they have no detailed information about the workers' activities and performance. The workers do not want their boss to be looking over their shoulder, and the French bosses may not want to come down and wander around on the shop floor.

Firing someone for poor performance, for being late, or for any other reason is virtually impossible; workers themselves describe it as 'unthinkable.'

The honor of the worker is based on the traditions of the profession he belongs to and the rank he holds. Every profession forms a closed group of workers, each with their own traditions and privileges. Newcomers are often made to go through some kind of initiation rite before they can become members of such a group. The importance of rank leads to an elaborate hierarchy with many strata within the company.

Belonging to such a professional group is highly valued by the workers, and they will resist attempts to introduce changes in this field. D'Iribarne describes a simple rationalization scheme with which management attempted to merge two professional groups in the plant, the crane drivers and the lorry (truck) drivers. Sometimes there is a temporary shortage of crane drivers, while some lorry drivers go idle; and sometimes it is the other way round. Doesn't it make sense, then, to train the lorry drivers to operate cranes, and vice versa, and to form one professional group of crane-and-lorry drivers? This may seem rational, but workers in both groups opposed the proposal very strongly: crane drivers would feel degraded driving lorries, and lorry drivers would feel equally degraded driving cranes. Their professional honor is at stake.

The rights and privileges of every worker find their origin not so much in what the contract stipulates, but rather, once more, in the traditions of the profession. There is little respect for official rules and regulations anyway. For gathering information as well as for getting things done, relying on the official channels will not get you very far. Much more important are the unofficial networks everyone develops with his co-workers. If the worker who requests help to get something done is a trusted and respected member of such an unofficial network, the person whose help is requested will go out of his way to help him, even beyond the limits of his task description. If the person who requests help does not command such respect and relies purely on company regulations when requesting help, there is not much he will get done at all. To get a person's or a group's co-operation, you need to be on good terms with them.

The atmosphere in the plant is nearly always confrontational, in particular between the management and the workers. Conflicts are very open, and people may yell and shout at each other when they disagree. However, when there is an emergency in the company, feuds will be moderated and in a move of solidarity everyone will work together to redress the situation.

The United States

In the US subsidiary, the key value which describes worker-employer relations might be *fairness*. D'Iribarne notes that there is no good translation of the English word *fairness* in French; nor is there in Dutch. The relation between a worker and his/her employer can be likened to the relation between a supplier and a customer: the workers sells his labor, the company buys it from him/her. A contractual link between the two parties describes the extent and the limits of this transaction. Loyalty to the company does not play a major role in the relation between the worker and his/her employer.

> **What Eurodisney demands of its workers**
>
> When Eurodisney (now *Disneyland Paris*) opened, some of the stipulations in the contract Eurodisney makes its workers sign seemed totally outrageous to Europeans; in fact, several have since been thrown out by French courts. For instance, workers had to stay on the premises and pay rent for their room (stay and pay policy), yet were not allowed to have overnight guests; various aspects of their physical appearance were regulated by the contract, including the maximum size of earrings to be worn, the prohibition to wear make-up or perfume for women, the maximum size of sideburns and the prohibition to wear a moustache for the men, etc.
>
> When I discuss these stipulations with European audiences, most people are outraged, as the Eurodisney workers themselves were. When I confront American audiences with the same facts, however, most do not see what the fuss is all about. Their typical reaction is: no-one is forced to sign such a contract; any worker is free to enter into this type of contractual relationship with its obligations or, if these do not suit him/her, to look for a job elsewhere.
>
> In the same vein, companies in the US often prohibit love affairs and sexual relations between co-workers, a stipulation that would be unacceptable (as well as probably illegal) in Europe.

While the French worker might feel that he cannot submit to authority without being servile, i.e., without losing his pride and honor, the contractual link between the American worker and the employer allows one to accept the boss's authority without any feeling of servility or degrading submission.

In the US subsidiary, there is always someone 'who runs the show'. The boss is 'in charge', but (in contrast to the French boss) he/she is also very accessible: any worker can walk up to the boss whenever there is a problem to be solved. Because of the direct responsibility the boss has for a task and for the workers who report to him/her, horizontal co-ordination between different units may be difficult to realize.

Control mechanisms are readily accepted by the workers. There is little or no resistance against performance appraisals (they are carried out annually in the company d'Iribarne describes), and firing a worker whose performance is below a certain minimum level is felt to be entirely acceptable.

Clear objectives and detailed rules and procedures are drawn up in order to ensure that everyone's performance is assessed in the fairest possible way. Because of this concern for fairness and objectivity, there is a tendency to rely purely on quantifiable data; non-quantifiable or more subjective factors which may be equally important are often overlooked. Also, short-term financial results prevail over long-term considerations.

More generally, and in line with the low-context nature of communication in the US as we described it before, written rules and procedures are extremely explicit and detailed. In the American subsidiary, for instance, a written procedure regulates the assignment of extra hours to workers. As the demand to work overtime is higher than the number of hours available, workers compete for them, and a number of factors are taken into account in deciding who gets the extra hours and who does not. The procedure lists ten base situations and nine categories of personnel, includes twenty-five articles and clauses plus three additional memoranda. It even stipulates what to do in case the worker has no telephone or the company has the wrong telephone number, it specifies that when two workers come out ex-aequo on the basis of the listed criteria alphabetical order will prevail, and so forth.

Conflicts may occur, but these remain within the bounds of the rules. Grievance procedures are laid out with a high concern for fairness and consistency also.

In the American subsidiary, frequent reference is made to ethics, to moral principles, which are surrounded by an aura of sacredness. Honesty and integrity are highly valued, cheating is universally condemned.

Many examples could be quoted which corroborate the fact that references to morality and respect for the law permeate American culture to a much higher degree than most European societies.

Moral principles and breaking the law

- When Bill Clinton was a candidate for the presidency of the United States, a discussion raged in the press as to whether or not he had, years before when studying in England, smoked a few marihuana cigarettes, i.e., broken the law. There was a distinct feeling that if he had done so, he was morally less well suited to become the next president, and it might seriously harm his chances of winning the race.
- During an election campaign, the press revealed that the wife of one candidate for the Senate had employed, years before, a maid who was an illegal alien. California senator Diane Feinstein may well owe her re-election in part to the fact that this candidate was her opponent in the 1994 elections for the US Senate.
- *Petrified Forest National Park* in Arizona is renowned for its beautiful fossilized trees of all shapes and sizes. It is tempting, as a visitor, to pick up a piece of this colorful rock and take it home as a souvenir, but of course taking away even the smallest piece is prohibited by park regulations. The visitors' centre of the park has a glass display cabinet with the letters of conscience-stricken Americans who sent back the stones they took from the park. In one case, stones that were taken from the park in 1947 were sent back with an accompanying letter in 1987 by a son at the request of his mother, shortly before her death.

- In Belgium, some years ago, the Minister of Transport, sitting at the steering wheel of his large BMW, was asked by journalists if he never violated traffic laws. The Minister admitted smilingly, on television, that whenever he felt no police was present, he was happy to go well over the speed limit on the freeways. The next day, not one article in the press reported, let alone discussed the fact that the very person who bears the ultimate responsibility for upholding the law (and traffic rules in particular) admitted violating it himself.

Not every European country shares the low rule-orientation of, for example, France and Belgium. When the German Minister of Health was asked on television (in the late 1990s; the situation has changed since) why Germany did not have non-smoking laws that are as stringent as the French, he replied sarcastically: "If we applied our laws in the way the French do, we could have introduced a strong non-smoking law a long time ago."

The Netherlands

D'Iribarne's description of relations within the Dutch subsidiary of the company corroborates some of Hofstede's findings, in particular with respect to the combination of low Power Distance and low Masculinity in Dutch culture.

It is impossible for the Dutch boss to issue orders. If the boss were to issue an order and a worker would not carry it out, there is very little the boss could do anyway: sanctions are virtually unheard of. The boss is an organizer more than anything else. His/her role is to create a consensus among everyone involved about the decision to be made. This is done through numerous meetings where things are discussed and explained, and where a compromise that suits everyone will be elaborated.

This procedure sometimes makes it difficult to introduce changes. On the other hand, once the consensus is reached almost everyone will stand behind the decision that was made: (apparent) harmony prevails. Open conflicts are almost non-existent. Strikes are extremely rare. Sometimes, Dutch trade unions actually refuse an offer by the management for a pay raise, because they feel it is against the general interest. Often a 'collective convention' is signed between the management and the unions. In this consensual setting, on the other hand, when a worker is dissatisfied with the way things are going it will be difficult for him/her to bring the problem out in the open. A frequent result is *withdrawal,* i.e., the worker performs his/her task minimally but does not feel otherwise implicated in the company any more. Absenteeism runs high in the Dutch subsidiary. Workers may not show up, for instance, when there is a football (soccer) game they want to watch.

Checks and controls are less common than in the US, but more than in France. The Dutch workers value openness and accept control mechanisms which measure their performance (unlike the French), but they do not accept that sanctions be taken against poor performers (unlike the Americans). When the management attempted to introduce a performance bonus scheme, the workers only accepted this when it was agreed that the performance bonus would be the same for every worker of the same level and would be written into the workers' contract – making, in fact, the entire scheme rather meaningless.

Social hierarchy is weak, protocol and ceremony are absent. One worker refuses his boss access to a certain area in the plant because the boss is not wearing the required hard hat; the boss readily accepts the fact that his subordinate denies entry to him.

Planning is long-term more than in France or the US. At one point, the French and the Dutch subsidiaries collaborate on the creation of a new plant, and the French are surprised that their Dutch colleagues make plans for up to two years in the future.

Conclusion

La logique de l'honneur illustrates that a non-quantitative approach to cross-cultural differences can be very enlightening: it makes us *understand* how an organization works in a particular country. Of course, we should exercise due care when extrapolating from the three organizations d'Iribarne describes to other, possibly very different, organizations who operate in the same countries; but that is equally true when we extrapolate from IBM, in Hofstede's survey, to other companies.

Several points that Hofstede established in his survey are confirmed by d'Iribarne, using a very different methodology. That is in itself an indication of the reliability of both studies. For example, the high Power Distance of France and the low Power Distance of the Netherlands leave clear traces in the behavior of workers and their relations to each other, as described above. The lower drive to performance in the Netherlands, related to low Masculinity, is also clearly observed.

D'Iribarne points out that, with very different organizational systems, the three industrial plants he studied achieve similar results: their productivity is about the same. There is an important lesson to be learned here, as it illustrates that one should avoid premature value judgments as to the suitability of certain culturally defined traits for economic success or for industrial production. An American who is confronted with of certain aspects of the French organization (impossibility to rely on official information channels and rules, lack of dialogue between bosses and subordinates, conflictual atmosphere...) is likely to react: 'This can never work!' In fact, that is exactly the reaction of many Anglo-Saxon expatriates (and others) when arriving in France to take up their new position. Nevertheless, the French industrial plant *does* perform well, and more generally France's economy is successful on a world scale.

12.3 Cross-cultural psychology

Some knowledge cannot be gathered through surveys (as in sociology) nor through 'participant observation' (as in anthropology). For instance, as we mentioned in chapter 6 above, scientist have discovered that human beings universally recognize six (or perhaps more) facial expressions; and moreover, that Asians focus more on the eyes, Westerners more on the whole face. The only way to discover this is to submit subjects to experiments: place them in a properly equipped room and measure their response to a stimulus or record their behavior. In other words, to use a methodology which is typical of psychology (for a detailed study of eye contact, see for instance Winkel & Vrij 1990).

Cross-cultural psychology has a long history, but is relatively neglected as a fruitful field of study. M. Cole (1998) wrote a book about it which he tellingly calls: *Cultural psychology: A once and future discipline...*

Some of the knowledge mentioned throughout this book could not have been established without this methodology. Measuring eye contact between interlocutors accurately (6.2 above) is only possible with sophisticated *eye tracking hardware* used in a laboratory room.

Fascinating insights as to how thought patterns differ between 'East' and 'West' are studied in Nisbett's *The Geography of Thought* (2005). *Field dependence* (the degree to which perception of object is influenced by its background) is different for both groups; *holistic thinking* (everything is related; Nisbett 2005: 129; see also Zhang 2008) is more typically Asian. Van Oudenhoven (2002: 49) mentions an experiment showing that Mexican farmers have a very hard time interpreting perspective in drawings. Etc.

We will not study the methodology of psychology in this book, as it is quite specialized and technical; but the reader should be aware that its experimental method is an important complement to the other methodologies mentioned here.

12.4 Linguistics: discourse analysis and conversational analysis

There exists a well-established practice of studying intercultural communication in the field of linguistics, usually called 'conversational analysis' (some good examples of it can be found in Blommaert & Verschueren 1991, a book entirely devoted to intercultural communication), and the knowledgeable reader may be surprised that I refer to it rarely in the present work (though there are some instances). The main reason is that I often feel there are methodological flaws in conversational analysis as it is practiced today. This book is not the right place to explain my arguments in detail, nor can I do justice to an entire field of study in one or two pages. Bu as it is an established field of study, and as the reader should not take my word for what I am saying, I do, however, want to list my main objections briefly in order to justify the fact that I do not refer to this approach too often in this book. The reader who does not feel concerned by this academic controversy may safely skip the following pages and proceed directly to the next section.

Conversational analysis is almost purely descriptive-inductive. Its main practice (also its main purpose?) is the analysis of 'raw' data, in the form of a literal transcription, as detailed as possible, of real conversations. Many conversational analysts spend several pages, in their articles, simply paraphrasing the dialogue as it is transcribed. As an example, Gumperz & Roberts 1991: 58-9 (Gumperz, professor at Berkeley, is one of the main figures in the field of conversational analysis) spend over two pages paraphrasing a dialogue that is in itself a page and a half long in its transcription (1991: 84-6). In my view, formulating hypotheses and theories and testing them against the available evidence (quantitative, but also qualitative) is a better way of furthering our understanding of the world than 'describing what you observe'. You don't need to blindly follow all of Popper's ideas to accept Popper's basic point that pre-theoretical observation and description is a naïve, illusory practice in science (and elsewhere).

Paradoxically, the literal transcriptions of conversations that are analyzed often leave out the all-important non-verbal aspects of the communication process, such as gestures and eye contact, entirely: these are not transcribed at all, or else in an extremely rudimentary form. Several examples of this can be found in various articles in Blommaert & Verschueren (1991). Gumperz transcribes non-verbal aspects a bit more, but still limits himself to indications such as '*briefly* looks up', '*slight arc-like* movements', etc., that are hardly precise.

I argued above that a large part of conversational analysis is not even inductive as such, but purely descriptive. In those cases, on the other hand, where inductions are made (in the sense that the analysis of the examples leads to a general conclusion), the generalizations at which the authors arrive are sometimes extraordinary. Gumperz (1991: 67, 68-72) formulates generalizations about 'Asian clients' and 'British clients', 'British counselors', 'Asian and British definitions of what activities are involved in interviewing', and so forth, on the basis of the analysis of some ten short 'fragments' of conversations at neighborhood centers in Britain. And these are the same scholars who may criticize Hofstede for overgeneralizing...

Very often the 'analyses' of conversational analysts are idiosyncratic (cannot be reproduced by another person, and are therefore unscientific) and/or biased by the political and social ideology of the author. For example, in a dialogue between a housing officer and Mr. O., an 'ethnic' customer, Gumperz (1991: 74-6) detects an unsympathetic attitude on the part of the housing officer that I cannot read in the dialogue itself. Gumperz contrasts this with a more co-operative response from the part of the housing officer in a conversation with a white, middle class, native English speaker (1991: 76, fragment 9). But fragment 9 is so short that I find it very hard to read into it any clear signal of co-operation or lack of it. Moreover, fragment 9 is about a woman who simply comes in to turn in an application form she filled in, whereas the Mr. O. comes in to enquire about the status of his application after having waited in vain for five-six months. It is therefore hardly surprising that the tone may be tenser in this case, regardless of the ethnic background of the customer. Ascribing the difference in the attitude of the housing officer to the ethnicity of the customer rather than to the situation is the result of an ideological bias on the part of the author, not the result of any objective differences between two conversations with different customers about comparable topics; it is an attribution error. In the same vein, Blommaert & Verschueren (1993) describe a conversation between a trainer and a group of police officers in Belgium where the trainer starts the training program with the classical question about the estimated numbers of migrant workers in the city; typically, the number is overestimated by most. The authors interpret the fact that this question is being asked as the indication of an underlying xenophobic assumption: that there is, indeed, a problem with those migrant workers. But here also, there are other, much simpler and more straightforward explanations as to why such a question is commonly asked at the start of a multicultural training program, for instance as an illustration that participants should question their own assumptions (about the number of migrants, and therefore also about the problems they supposedly create).

A recent example of conversational analysis is Poncini's *Discursive Strategies in Multicultural Business Settings* (2004). While Poncini correctly criticizes some of the current research in the field of intercultural communication as putting too much emphasis on the problems rather than on what facilitates communication (2004: 18-23) and as neglecting individual variation, her analyses of recorded business conversations are again most often purely descriptive and some of her conclusions seem trivial: 'there is a range of ambiguous referents for *we*' and 'markets can be seen as networks of relationships, both direct and connected' (2004: 143-5). Interested readers can also consult various publications by Helen Spencer-Oatey, some in collaboration with others scholars, to understand the contribution of linguistics to the study of intercultural communication.

12.5 Cases and examples

It is hard to imagine a book or a course in intercultural communication without examples, critical incidents and case studies. They are invaluable both as illustrations and as a pedagogical means. At the same time, such examples should ideally satisfy a number of conditions, as follows.

Reliability
Many stories about (people from) other cultures go around in our world, and not all of them are reliable.

Some stories have to be relegated to the domain of urban legend. Europeans often quote the example of the American woman who attempted to dry her cat (or was it her dog?) in the microwave oven. Americans usually have never heard this story, and it is very likely false. Similarly, the often quoted story of the Chevrolet Nova not being successful in Latin America, because in Spanish 'no va' means 'doesn't run', is very probably false:

- The various versions of the story mention totally different countries (Puerto Rico, Mexico, 'Spanish speaking', South America...) but never refer to sales figures or published sources.
- Spanish does not really use the expression 'el coche no va' to refer to a car that does not run.
- Nova (in one word, as in the cars' name) refers to a supernova star, which may have positive connotations.
- One of the most widespread brands of gasoline sold in Mexico is called Nova. Etc.

As any other piece of information used in science, be it the physical or the social sciences, these stories should be thoroughly checked for accurateness and

authenticity before being used. The anecdotes and intercultural incidents we use in this book come from three basic sources:
- stories based on our own observations
- stories from witnesses such as students in our classes and people from business and international organizations we meet, when there seems to be no reason to doubt their reliability; in case of doubt, the story will not be used or its authenticity will be qualified
- stories from published sources (books, articles, the press) where the overall reliability of that source is established.

Representativity
A story or anecdote is representative only if there are good reasons to think that it is typical of the culture described. It is essential to make a distinction between two kinds of examples:
- examples which are illustrative of the *average* values and practices of the culture described;
- examples which illustrate *extreme* values and practices which exist in the culture described.

Sometimes, 'extreme' stories may have a better illustrative value than those representing average practices. This is because the latter could, conceivably, also have happened in the other culture, even if their chances of occurring there are smaller. The 'extreme' stories, on the other hand, could normally not happen in the other culture, and therefore they may help clarifying what consequences some of the values and practices in a given culture may lead to. In the Eurodisney example we described above, the fact that the company asks its workers to always smile to the customers may be close to what an average American company requests from its employees, but it could conceivably also happen in France. The fact that an employee is fired for wearing a woven bracelet is rather unthinkable in France, so it may open our mind to some aspects of American culture that we would not have thought of otherwise.

Representativity also means that examples and anecdotes should illustrate *current* features of the culture described. That is not so easy to achieve, as cultures obviously evolve over time, and something that was true a generation ago may not be applicable any more today. In one account of the Philippines (Harris & Moran 1987; see also Verluyten 1993), the authors write that women may use their fans to convey non-verbal messages to the males they feel attracted to. When I checked the accuracy of this story with many people in Manila in 1992, no-one had ever seen or heard such a thing, and most Filipinos just started laughing at the thought of it. Women may have exhibited this behavior in the Philippines (as in Spain) around the turn of the 20th century or somewhat later, but the practice has disappeared a long time ago.

A final word of warning with respect to examples and anecdotes. Apart from publications where representative, reliable and carefully selected examples are used to illustrate cultural traits, the market is flooded nowadays with superficial, anecdotal accounts of cultural differences which are mainly based on old stereotypes and very little on serious research or current knowledge. They may be fun to read (and they are actually sold by the thousands), they may occasionally yield some insight into local habits, but they are unreliable and also dangerous, because they tend to reinforce deeply ingrained prejudice. They do little to create better understanding and communication between cultures. In the worst case, some of those publications are not only superficial and unreliable, but also very hastily written and full of factual errors.

Well-known examples of books which (some may feel) are fun to read, and occasionally insightful, but can hardly be qualified as seriously researched, are John Mole's *Mind your Manners,* about cultural differences between European Union countries, and Richard Hill's *EuroManagers and Martians.* "The Belgians are salespeople by instinct and, if anything, manufacturers by accident", writes Hill (1994: 121). Does this *mean* anything? Aren't they, perhaps, manufacturers by instinct and salespeople by accident?

Robert T. Moran's Cultural Guide to Doing Business in Europe, by Johnson and Moran (1992) is an example among others of a book that adds insult to injury by accumulating numerous factual errors on top of being superficial. In the section on Belgium, that country is said to have "highly productive natural gas fields [which] made the country Europe's leader in gas output and exports." In actual fact there is no natural gas in Belgium; the authors mix up Belgium and the Netherlands. It may be difficult to differentiate such small countries when looked at from an American perspective, but it hardly illustrates the right attitude for doing business in Europe...

12.6 Cultural clusters

Even though associating cultures with countries is in itself debatable (as most countries exhibit cultural variety, and people belong to several cultural groups at once), keeping track of some 200 different countries, each unique in its own right, is difficult. Therefore, many authors attempt to group cultures together into cultural clusters which exhibit common or similar characteristics. Surely Austria has more in common with Germany than with China!

One of the most well-known attempts at grouping similar cultures together was proposed by Hofstede on the basis of his Uncertainty Avoidance and Power Distance dimensions. Considering that the score of a country on each of these two dimensions can be either high or low, Hofstede arrives at a quadrant with four possible combinations.

In each of the four quadrants a company will exhibit features of, respectively, the following implicit organizational models.
- *Low PD, weak UA: 'the village market'.* This includes most Anglo-Saxon countries, as well as some Scandinavian countries and the Netherlands. In a village market there are no set prices or strict procedures for buying and selling, nor is there a clear hierarchical relationship between buyers and sellers. Similarly, in a company of this type, there will be few pre-set rules and procedures, and many problems will be settled pragmatically, on a case-by-case basis, through discussion, on an equal footing, between those who have a conflict or disagree.

- *Large PD, weak UA: 'the family'.* This is the prototype of many companies in various Asian countries. In a (traditional) family just like in a company of this type, there is a clear hierarchy and one person (the oldest male, the head of the family or the head of the company) has the final say in any decision that needs to be made; but there are few or no written rules or predefined procedures for settling disagreements or conflicts, most of which will be decided upon after discussion and on a case-by-case basis.
- *Low PD, strong UA: 'the well-oiled machine'.* This is a metaphor for companies in some German speaking countries: Germany, Austria, Switzerland. Rules, regulations and detailed procedures are there to ensure that everything runs smoothly and to prevent unforeseen events from occurring and discussions from arising.
- *Large PD, strong UA: 'the pyramid of people'.* This typifies organizations in France, Belgium and in many Mediterranean and Latin-American countries, where there is a clear hierarchical (pyramidal) structure and where, in case of conflict, there is a procedure to refer decisions up to the person who is higher in the hierarchy, and up to the CEO if necessary.

Hofstede (1991: 139-143) reports the story of Owen James Peters, an American professor at the INSEAD business school near Paris, who submitted to the students in his class a case study that involves a dispute between the sales manager of a company (who wishes to satisfy all his customers speedily) and the production manager (who feels that small, unprofitable orders should wait). Upon studying the answers of some 200 students to this managerial problem, Peters was struck by the fact that the majority of the French, the German and the British students come up with a different diagnosis and solution.

The majority of the French students suggest referring the decision up to the general manager anytime there is a dispute. In the pyramidal organization model, the person at a higher level in the hierarchy must settle disputes that arise at the lower level.

The majority of the German students diagnose the case as a lack of structures and of clearly defined competencies. They suggest establishing procedures, by a consultant or a task force, which will provide an unambiguous answer to most potential conflicts that might arise. In that way, everything will run smoothly and without unforeseen events.

The majority of the British students diagnose the case as a human relations problem. The two department heads should develop their negotiating skills in order to be able to discuss conflicts together and arrive at a mutually acceptable solution. There are no predefined answers; disputes are to be settled on a case-by-case basis through negotiation.

Clearly, the typical answer that was given by the three groups of students was determined by their respective cultural backgrounds with respect to the combination of Power Distance and Uncertainty Avoidance as shown in the chart above.

When I asked a group of 48 American (US) students I was teaching in Maastricht which solution they would prefer, about two thirds of them chose the 'British' solution, and one third the 'German' solution; none of them suggested that the conflicts be referred to the general manager, as most French students presumably would suggest. The students' preferences are in agreement with the position of the USA on both dimensions: small PD and weak UA, like Britain, but with somewhat higher UA than that country, which may explain the higher preference for the 'rules and regulations' solution in the USA.

Many other proposals have been made for grouping cultures with similar characteristics together. When the grouping is made on the basis of a single dimension or value cluster, the groups are obviously large. Thus, Pinto (1990) distinguished what he calls fine-mazed cultures (with tight social control) from coarse-mazed cultures (with higher acceptance of individual freedom).

The *World Values Survey* contains an 'Inglehart-Welzel cultural map of the world' (the map can be found on http://www.worldvaluessurvey.org) which distinguishes some eight cultural clusters on the basis of two dimensions, Secular-Rational vs. Traditional Values and Survival vs. Self-Expression Values:
1. Catholic Europe (France, Belgium, Italy, Spain, etc.; also includes Uruguay)
2. Protestant Europe (Germany, Switzerland, Netherlands, Scandinavian countries)
3. English speaking (USA, UK, Canada, Australia, etc.)
4. Latin America (plus Portugal)
5. Africa
6. South Asia (India, Bangla Desh, Pakistan, but also Turkey, Indonesia, Iran...)
7. Confucian (China, Taiwan, South Korea, Japan)
8. East Europe (Russia, Romania, and some of the former states of the USSR and Yugoslavia)

Clearly, Western culture is rather finely subdivided (encompassing clusters 1 to 4, and also 8), and Africa much less so (in fact, not at all). This may be due to cultural bias, and also to the fact that less data are available for Africa. The Middle East is missing, and some Arabic-Muslim countries in North Africa (Egypt, Algeria, Morocco) are grouped together with 'black' African countries such as Nigeria, Ghana, Uganda, Tanzania and Zimbabwe, which seems to me highly debatable.

Such groupings may be useful for understanding and pedagogy, but any clustering is based on only a few selected cultural characteristics and thus to a certain extent arbitrary.

12.7 Stereotypes and how to deal with them

Stereotypes have bad press. Webster's New World Dictionary defines them as a "fixed [...] notion or conception, as of a person, group, [...] allowing for no individuality, critical judgment, etc." On the other hand, it is undeniable that we all carry stereotypes about other groups and cultures around in our minds. In a global environment, it is impossible to gather scientifically proven knowledge about all cultures or groups of people we work with. The mental picture we have of a certain group is often the only information we can rely on to try and make our initial communication and co-operation with a member of that group as non-problematic and smooth as possible. Therefore, it does not make much sense to require people to get rid of stereotypes; in many cases, we have nothing to replace them with. There are, however, a number of operations we can perform to improve the accuracy and depth of our mental picture of others.

Let us consider an example. The European stereotype of 'Americans' (from the US) will probably include adjectives like the following (based on Kohls (1981) and on what my European students usually tell me):

- overweight
- tastelessly dressed
- informal
- loud
- boastful
- immature
- superficial
- friendly
- hard working
- racially prejudiced
- know little about other countries
- in a hurry.

> "American students are so friendly and so nice. They are so open about wanting to get together, but they never take my phone number and they never contact me again. When I see a woman I met two days ago, she does not seem to know me or remember my name."
>
> "One German student commented. There are some surface things about American friendliness. Like 'How are you?' A girls asked me that one day when I was feeling sick, and I answered that I wasn't too good but she just went on like I had never said that" (Nathan 2005: 68-69).

When we consider the terms that are used, we notice that many of them are not neutral, but imply a value judgment; in addition, this judgment is often negative. For instance, when Europeans qualify Americans as 'loud', they are not simply saying that on the average, when conversing, Americans speak at a higher number of decibels than they themselves do; it is also implied that the Americans speak *too loud*. In reality, of course, speaking louder or softer is culture-specific: Arabs probably speak even louder than Americans, (some) Europeans less loudly, and South-East Asians even less so:

> *Average loudness of voice*
>
> | Arab. | US | Europe | S.E. Asia |
> |---|---|---|---|
> | loud ——————————————————————————— soft |

One position on this scale is obviously not intrinsically better than any other position: any given culture simply 'chooses' its own average. This brings us to the first (mental) action we can take to improve our stereotypical vision of other people and cultures:

(1) Avoid value judgments
By doing that, we can turn (often negative) value judgments into factual information which may be to some extent correct, and which we can use to combat the risk of mistaken attribution. Rather than jumping to the conclusion that Americans are boastful and overbearing because they are so loud (thus attributing an incorrect meaning to the Americans' behavior, based on a discrepancy with the loudness of voice we are used to), we can then understand that average loudness differs from one culture to the other, and we know that Americans are on the louder side of the spectrum than most Europeans are, for instance. Notice also that some additional negative value judgments which are themselves based on our primary value judgment will disappear with it. When Americans are felt to be 'boastful', this judgment is based on a number of characteristics they typically exhibit,[8] and one of them is being 'loud.' When it is understood that speaking at a higher number of decibels does not imply any arrogance, but is simply a culture-specific feature, the (negative) judgment of boastfulness will disappear with it.

Secondly, the information the stereotype provides us with, while not entirely incorrect, will frequently be incomplete and one-sided. Consider the idea expressed above that Americans are 'fat' and 'tastelessly[9] dressed.' A recent trip to the United States brought me, among other places, to Disneyworld, Florida and to Midtown Manhattan, New York. In Disneyworld my wife and I were indeed struck by the number of overweight people which was undoubtedly much higher than in any comparable location in Europe, and to a lesser extent also by the careless and tasteless way (to a European) in which many were dressed. In Manhattan, however, things were more or less the other way round: most people are more 'dressed up', in a way Europeans would qualify as tasteful, than in the centre of Paris or Brussels, and the number of overweight people is not particularly high in the streets of New York either.

This brings me to the second action I recommend in order to make (what is originally) a stereotype more accurate and more useful:

(2) Enrich and qualify the information you have
In this case, it is probably accurate to say that *some* groups of Americans (perhaps geographically or socially defined groups) count many overweight people who are poorly dressed (in European eyes), but these properties cannot be ascribed to other groups of Americans. Similarly, many Americans may be 'wealthy' when compared with Europeans (per capita GNP is higher in the US than in most European countries), particularly those who can afford to travel to Europe; but at the same time, the United States has a higher percentage of people below the poverty line than most European nations; and so forth.

Finally, let us consider the idea that Americans are 'friendly' but 'immature' and 'superficial;' see box above. The last two adjectives again imply a negative value judgment. When you come to think of it critically, ascribing 'immaturity' or 'superficiality' to an entire nation of over two hundred million people is of course rather absurd in itself.

But then where do those ideas come from? According to the many stories Europeans have told me about their experience with Americans, one of the main causes is the following. When introduced to someone, Americans will rather quickly and easily get 'intimate' (in European eyes) with the other person. When meeting someone for the first time, the American might talk about his/her unhappy divorce and career aspirations, invite you to his/her house, etc. In addition, starting a conversation with a stranger is done easily: it may happen at a bus stop, in the supermarket, and so forth.

> **Meeting with a stranger in the US: an acquaintance or a friend?**
>
> In the Summer of 1980 I was living in a campus dorm at the University of New Mexico in Albuquerque, when I met a young woman at a bus stop on campus: she simply started talking to me, and we ended up having a conversation together while we were waiting, and then on the bus. Her career had brought her to Albuquerque recently, and she had just bought a house there; she expected her husband to join her a few months later. When she learned that I would be staying on campus for over one month, she invited me over to her house and she suggested I bring my laundry with me: it would be much easier to put it in her washing machine than to look for a laundromat somewhere.
>
> So, on my first visit to the house of someone I had seen only once before and spoken with for less than fifteen minutes, I brought a plastic bag full of dirty linen with me and put it in her washing machine while we cooked dinner together. Over the next few weeks, we did the same thing perhaps two or three more times.
>
> After I left Albuquerque, I never had any more contact with this 'friend' or 'friendly person.'

In Western Europe, you normally do not start a conversation with a stranger in the street, let alone invite him into your house and suggest he bring his laundry with him. Inviting someone to your house, and even more allowing that person to put his linen into your washing machine, can only mean, Europeans will think, that the two persons are *friends*, or at least that the person who invites you wants to be your friend. At first, many Europeans will therefore conclude that in America, it is very easy to make friends. However, when the person they had an intimate conversation with does not recognize them anymore two days later, or when the American who invited them for dinner to her house does not reply to the letter or the Christmas card they sent from home, they will then conclude that all this was 'superficial': like (immature) children, Americans are quick to establish friendships, but equally quick to forget about it afterwards.

The real cause for this cultural misunderstanding is that the structure of a person's public and private sphere is different in the US and in Europe.[10] Simplifying, one might say that like Europeans, Americans may have a small circle of close friends (and as elsewhere close friends are not made overnight), but they have a large circle of 'acquaintances' into which it is easy to enter. Europeans have no clear equivalent of the American's second circle, i.e. those people you meet one day and talk with, invite to your house perhaps, but who are nothing more than casual and temporary acquaintances. Because of the fact that this category has no clear equivalent in Europe, and because of the fact that in that type of relationship Americans will exhibit behavior that is reserved for real friends in Europe (such as cooking dinner for that person or letting him do his laundry in your house), Europeans will confuse the Americans' second circle ('acquaintances') with their own first circle ('friends').

Once you know this, you will understand (some of) the reasons why Europeans (mistakenly) attribute 'superficiality' or 'immaturity' to Americans, and see that these adjectives are totally inappropriate, even if they hint at a cultural difference between the US and Europe, related to the structure of the private and public sphere in both parts of the world.

Therefore, we need to work constantly toward the following:

(3) Understand the underlying causes of what you observe or know about other cultures
Obviously, the three recommendations I issue for turning stereotypes into more accurate, workable information about other people and cultures go together: enriching and qualifying the information you have, and studying its underlying causes, will lead toward an ever deeper understanding of the other person's culture, and one from which value judgment will be more and more absent.

> **Superficial observation vs. deeper understanding: Manhattan dress code**
>
> One of my trainees who had recently visited New York ridiculed the elegantly dressed professional women she had observed in Manhattan wearing sports shoes: how tasteless to combine an expensive suit, possibly bought at Chanel's, with a pair of Nikes! No European woman would ever do that!
>
> Her interpretation of what she had seen changed drastically when another student pointed out to her that these women only wear Nikes to protect their expensive designer shoes from getting ruined by the frequent rain and snow in the streets of Manhattan, and that they change to their high-heeled shoes as soon as they enter the building or the office where they work.

The reader can apply the same mechanisms in order to 'deconstruct' the following stereotype about the French, or about 'Parisians', expressed by a Flemish female flight attendant:

> We can single out the real Parisians easily: smug, demanding, and rude. The Flemish on the other hand are real darlings; Walloons, in fact, also. Sometime I come home and I say to myself: "a good flight with all nice Belgians" (Dolores D.W., in the Flemish magazine *Knack* 1996 n°7: my translation)

Objective reasons that may give rise to this stereotype of 'arrogance' have been analyzed throughout our book:
1. The French may have a higher interrupting frequency in a conversation, leading to the attribution that they know better or don't want to listen (3.1.2)

2. Social acceptability of open conflicts, including yelling and shouting, is higher in France (5.3.3)
3. Power distance is high in France, as a result of which powerholders have a higher need to look important to be respected (chapter 8).

Notice, also, that the stereotype quoted above is immunized against possible refutation: 'real Parisians' implies that those who do not correspond to the stereotype are not real Parisians.

12.8 Change and evolution of cultural values over time

A fascinating question is how rapidly, or how slowly, culturally defined value systems change over time. Not surprisingly, opinions differ. Some scholars are convinced that fairly rapid changes in value systems may occur, for instance when the political situation changes, as was the case in Central and Eastern European countries after 1989. Most scholars, however, including Hofstede, contend that value systems change only very slowly over time (corroborated by a recent study of Barkema & Vermeulen 1997). If we trace the differences in value systems between the Netherlands and Belgium back to the difference between Protestantism (in the Netherlands) and Catholicism (in what is now Belgium), we trace a present-day cultural feature back to the 16th-17th century! If certain values of some Asian countries go back to Confucius, that means that we trace some culturally defined values back to approximately 2,500 years ago.

If that is so, then the way the communist system was implemented in the various Central and Eastern European countries might also be, to a large extent, *pre*determined by culturally defined values that were already there before.

The future evolution of Central and Eastern European countries may provide us with an interesting test case with respect to the evolution of cultural values and practices.[11] Unlike other developed countries, most Central and Eastern European countries were subjected to two major breaking points dividing, in effect, their 20th century history into three clearly distinct periods:
1. The pre-socialist era (before World War II; before World War I for Russia)
2. A 40-45 year long socialist period (approximately 70 years in the case of Russia)
3. The post-socialist era (from approximately 1989 onwards).

Central and Eastern European countries all have a long and well-documented cultural history going back many centuries. By studying their present-day cultural features, it is therefore in theory possible to determine whether present-day cultural values and practices
a. date back to the pre-socialist era
b. are mainly due to the mark that was left upon society by the socialist period
c. cannot be traced back either to (a) or to (b) and are therefore of recent origin.

Naturally, it is equally possible that the present-day cultural set-up of Central and Eastern European countries is a mixture of (a), (b) and (c). To give this some initial plausibility, let me develop a possible example of each.

There is some agreement that Power Distance is higher, relatively speaking, in Eastern European countries, such as Russia, and lower in Central European countries, such as Poland (see, for instance, Kruzela 1995). Now there can be no doubt that Marxist doctrine is egalitarian in itself, implying low Power Distance. How, then, could such a doctrine be turned into an extremely un-egalitarian reality in Russia – but not to the same extent in Poland? The most plausible explanation seems to be to trace such culturally defined differences on the Power Distance scale back to the pre-socialist period. There is little doubt that throughout the modern era Polish society was less hierarchically structured (relatively speaking, of course) than czarist Russia (see, for instance, Davies 1997). In other words, a prominent cultural difference between countries, and one that has a direct bearing on relations in the workplace, goes back several centuries and still leaves a clearly detectable trace nowadays (a similar hypothesis is made by Kruzela 1995 about Czech egalitarianism vs. Russian Power Distance, and traced back to historical differences linked to religion).

There is agreement that Uncertainty Avoidance is high or very high in both Central and East European countries. If that is so, it is not unreasonable to hypothesize that this is mainly due to the mark left on the Central and Eastern European countries by decades of a socialist regime which provided a very high level of certainty to the citizens in many domains: jobs, health care, education, retirement, and so forth. If this explanation is substantiated, then in this case a cultural feature of Central and Eastern European countries is traced back to the influence of the socialist period (for a very different analysis, where *un*certainty is thought to be inherent to the communist rule in Czechoslovakia, see Nehring 1995).

Finally, there is little doubt that (perhaps more superficial) practices in the field of consumer behavior and its evolution can be traced back neither to the socialist, nor to the pre-socialist period, and must therefore be of recent origin. In studies about marketing and consumer behavior, not surprisingly, the stress lies on recent changes in the Central and Eastern European countries (see, for instance, ESOMAR 1993). There is some evidence that more superficial practices (such as consumer behavior) may change relatively rapidly, while underlying values remain intact or evolve only very slowly over time.

Of course only time will tell to what extent the hypothesis of slow cultural change will be confirmed or not by the future evolution of these countries.

In his dissertation (2008), my graduate student Zhang Hao made an important contribution to the study concerning the evolution over time of culturally defined communication patterns.

Recall that the scores of various countries on Hofstede's dimensions do not necessarily change over time even if, say, Power Distance goes down or Individualism goes up. Hofstede's scores reflect the relative positions of countries with respect to one another and do not express absolute values; therefore, if all countries evolve over time at more or less the same rate, the scores do not change. On the other hand, the country's wealth (as expressed, for instance, in its per capita GDP) is a strong predictor of its position on the Power Distance and Individualism scales. Therefore, if a country experiences exceptionally rapid economic growth over a period of time (as is the case for China), its position on the Power Distance and Individualism scales may shift relative to that of other countries.

Researching the change in Chinese business negotiating behavior over the last twenty years, this is exactly what Zhang found.

> Chinese negotiating behaviors based on collectivist values have shifted toward a less collectivist direction. [...] Chinese negotiating behaviors based on hierarchical values have changed to less hierarchical orientation (Zhang 2008: 146).

Interestingly, however,

> Chinese negotiating behaviors based on holistic thinking have remained unchanged (Zhang 2008: 146).

The tentative conclusion might be that cultural values may change over time, though only slowly and gradually; but deep-seated culturally defined cognitive mechanisms (such as holistic thinking) are more likely to remain unchanged over long periods of time.

Notes

1. A difference is sometimes made between the terms *intercultural* and *cross-cultural*. In that case, *cross-cultural* refers to a comparison of different cultures, which does not necessarily imply that they are in contact with each another, and *intercultural* refers to the interaction between cultures.
2. A revised edition was published in 2001 under the title *Culture's Consequences. Comparing Values, Behaviors, Institutions and Organizations across Nations.*
3. In the original full account of the study, the 1980 book *Culture's Consequences*, Hofstede uses the pseudonym HERMES for IBM Corporation. In his less arduous 1991 work *Cultures and Organizations. Software of the Mind,* IBM is mentioned under its own name.
4. Back-translation consists in having a second translator translate the translated version back into English. If the backtranslated English version is close to the original English version, chances are that the version in the target language is also reasonably accurate. Evidently, this technique more than doubles the translation costs.
5. In the social science citation index, Hofstede is one of the most widely quoted social scientists in the world.
6. Not everyone necessarily attaches the same meaning to the terms *etic* and *emic* (derived from the terms *phonetics* and *phonemics* respectively), and we will not use them in this book. See also Usunier (1998: 34).
7. Geert Hofstede wrote the introduction to the English translation of *La logique de l'honneur,* thus illustrating that his own quantitative approach and d'Iribarne's qualitative work complement each other rather than competing with each other.
8. Other culturally defined characteristics that contribute to the mistaken attribution of boastfulness have been mentioned before, such as the use of superlatives (5.3.1).
9. Bourdieu (1979) will tell us that judgment about what is *good taste* is itself specific to a certain group (social class, but also culture) and that good taste cannot be defined in absolute terms. But let us assume for the sake of the argument that what my Belgian students would call 'good taste' prevails here.
10. For the sake of simplicity, I shall not discuss variants *between* European countries here. See also Trompenaars 1993: 73-5.
11. This section is based on Verluyten 1998b.

Chapter 13
Attitudinal issues and ethics

A book about intercultural communication would be incomplete without a discussion of social, political and ethical issues related to interculturalism. The reader will understand that in this chapter (and to some extent also in the following ones), I inevitably defend my own position on certain issues, with which, of course, not everyone will agree.

13.1 Ethnocentrism

> At the conference in Valladolid, 1550-1551, the Spanish rulers examined the question if the Indians are barbarians who must be civilized. Las Cases argued in favor of the *right to be different*, the right for every people to practice the religion its history has handed down to them. Does a people who believes itself superior have the right to impose its rule, even temporarily, upon a people deemed inferior? And *who decides* about the superiority or inferiority of peoples? (Soissons 2000: 231; my translation, I also modified the text somewhat and added italics).[1]

Ethnocentrism is the idea that one's own culture is superior to others. It was the prevailing attitude in Western Europe[2] throughout the 19th century, and it constituted one of the foundations of colonialism. In Africa in particular, the autochthonous populations were described as 'savages' who needed to be 'civilized', inasmuch as possible, by Europeans:

> The Negro, in mass, will not improve beyond a certain point, and that not respectable (Richard Burton, British consul in Dahomey, 1863, quoted in Fage 1988: 353)

> If the European should ever come [to Africa], he should come as a master (Binger, French explorer in Volta, 1888, quoted in Fage 1988: 353)

> [We were] sure that we were bringing with us civilisation and progress, certain that we would help these people from their backward state (the French General André Beaufre about Morocco in the 1920s, quoted in Thomas 1980: 601)

Keay (2000: 429) cites further extreme examples of ethnocentrism: William Wilberforce, anti-slavery champion declares missionary access to India "the greatest of all causes". It was so important, he told the House of Commons in 1813, because "our religion is sublime, pure and beneficent [while] theirs is mean, licentious and cruel." Hindu deities are "absolute monsters of lust, injustice, wickedness and cruelty." Emancipating Hindus from "this grand abomination" (i.e., Hinduism) was as much the sacred duty of every Christian as emancipating Africans from slavery.

The quotes above are moderate in comparison to some other 19th century accounts where black Africans as well as some other peoples in the world are considered to be closer to apes than they are to 'civilized' human beings.

Such an extreme form of ethnocentrism has all but disappeared today, except in some limited circles. In a more moderate form, however, Western ethnocentrism still permeates many aspects of relations between Western countries and the rest of the world, and in particular relations with so-called 'developing' countries. It sometimes seems that when Westerners consider a non-western country, only economic success is felt to be a sufficient reason to drop the idea of their own superiority, at least to a certain extent. Few Westerners would contend today that they are 'superior' to the Japanese, for instance, and there have been attempts in the 1970s to introduce Japanese-style management techniques into Europe and North America – even if at the same time many Westerners would qualify their admiration for Japan with a number of reservations about the quality of life in that country, and the like.

But as soon as economically poorer countries are concerned, the prevailing attitude remains an attitude of 'us' going over there to help 'them', and helping them virtually always means getting them to assimilate *our* technology, *our* management styles, *our* products, in brief, *our* values and *our* practices, i.e., *our* culture. The idea that Western cultures might be changed for the better by assimilating some features of Africa, for instance, is practically non-existent. We will come back to this below.

13.2 Universalism and cultural relativism

It would be nice if all cultures shared some basic values: this would give a universal base to ethics. However, virtually all anthropologists agree that there exist no substantial human values that are universal.

> There are formal universals that exist in all cultures such as *truth, morality, beauty*, but if mankind as a whole reveres the truth, enjoys beauty, and behaves morally, it does so in ways so diverse that an objective set of absolute values appears impossible of achievement (Beals & Hoijer, 1971: 587)

> [The question is] whether the dualism between empirically universal aspects of culture rooted in subcultural realities and empirically variable aspects not so rooted can be established and sustained. And this, in turn, demands (1) that the universals proposed be substantial ones and not empty categories; (2) that they be specifically grounded in particular biological,

psychological or sociological processes, not just vaguely associated with "underlying realities"; and (3) that they can convincingly be defended as core elements in a definition of humanity in comparison with which the much more numerous cultural particularities are of clearly secondary importance. On all three of these counts it seems to be that the *consensus gentium* approach fails; rather than moving toward the essentials of the human situation it moves away from them (Geertz 1973: 39).

The alternative, then, is cultural relativism:

> [E]ach culture may be evaluated only in its own terms, and [...] it is objectively impossible to distinguish world-wide levels of cultural progress (Beals & Hoijer 1971: 587)

Cultural relativism is the position shared by the author of this book. However, many do not feel comfortable with it. Cultural relativism entails that it is inadmissible for someone from one culture to emit criticism against some of the values or practices of another culture. Hence, some will feel, it leads to each culture being like an island, and prevents intercultural dialogue (Evanoff 2004). In addition, some scholars add that refraining from criticism is in any case impossible:

> It is [...] impossible for individuals who have been exposed to these differences to simply accept them all on equal terms. Inevitably, distinctions will be made between what is considered 'good' and 'bad' in any given culture (Evanoff 2004).

Colonialism and other forms of cultural imperialism should make us suspicious, of course, of criticizing another culture and wanting to 'change it for the better'. However, Evanoff argues, there is an alternative to that, which he calls 'constructivism'. While there are no universal cultural values at the outset, humans can create these together through an intercultural 'dialogue between equals'.

But does Evanoff's view really express a dialogue between equals? Consider the following quotes from his articles (2004, 2006):

> Asians as a whole, not just leaders and intellectuals, should be given the opportunity to decide if they prefer to stick to Asian values – or perhaps to embrace Western human rights or selectively combine the two.

> Competing constructions can be evaluated according to the pragmatic criterion of how well they enable us to get along in the world.

So Asians should be entitled, on the basis of fair exposure to different value systems such as their own and that of the West, to decide which one they prefer to embrace. Curiously, Evanoff does not mention that Westerners should also be given the opportunity to decide if they prefer a more 'Asian' value system (family, long term orientation, respect) or the more individualistic, short-term oriented Western system. Is it just coincidence that in Evanoff's quote Asians might consider changing their values, not Westerners? I don't think so.

As to the criterion of 'how well [these competing constructions] enable us to get along in the world', this seems to me to be similar to the formal universals

without substance, mentioned above by Beals & Hoijer. Consider the following ways of getting along in the world:
- a Wall Street stock broker seeking to make as many millions as possible in the shortest possible time
- a Catholic (or Buddhist) monk living in total seclusion and having made the vow never to use his voice.

Both may be feel that their life's fulfillment has been reached, but they do so in ways so different as to make a substantial definition of 'getting along in the world' and its use as a criterion, impossible.

Fine authors fall into the trap of applying their own standards to judge aspects of other cultures. Typically, they never consider the reverse, i.e. acknowledging that other cultures might wish to criticize features of Western society; the underlying and implicit idea is still that 'we' are superior to them, and a model for them to follow.

> There is nothing inherent in the theory of relativism which prevents relativists from criticising activities and beliefs in other cultures. But relativists will acknowledge that the criticism is based on their own ethnocentric standards and realise also that the condemnation may be a form of cultural imperialism. Under extreme circumstances, meaning that an action in another culture violates one of the relativists' most deeply held beliefs, the relativists may decide that criticism and even intervention are lesser evils than either ethnocentrism or cultural imperialism (Bidney 1953: 698).

The above quote has at least the merit of being explicit: if a characteristic of *your* culture violates *my* deepest beliefs, then I am entitled to intervene in your culture, if need be by force. This is not relativism, however; it is a strong form of ethnocentrism. As Las Cases asked in the 16th century, *who decides* which aspects are worth intervening against? Those with the gun, i.e. with the strongest military?

> Certainly the moral criticism loses some of its force if it no longer stems from universal standards. Nevertheless, relativists are not prevented from offering criticism, and the force of their argument against a practice may not be uninfluential. In an interdependent world, if culture A objects strenuously enough to a practice in culture B, culture B may fear a loss of foreign aid and other privileges. Thus, it is not obvious that acknowledging that a criticism is ethnocentric renders it impotent. It is better to be honest about the local source of the criticism than to pretend that it is universal (Dundes Renteln 1990: 77).

In this passage Dundes Renteln refers to withdrawing foreign aid. It is therefore clear again that the author is thinking of wealthy and powerful, mainly Western countries criticizing, and interfering in, the affairs of a 'developing' country, and not the other way round. Would Westerners accept that representatives from other cultures came in and attempted to change some of 'our' ways of thinking and acting because these ways are utterly shocking to them, as exemplified in the following quote?

> On recent or current showing, people in Western civilization are doing badly by the standards of the rest of the world, despite – or, perhaps, because of – enviable levels of material prosperity [...]. Families are foundering

as divorce rates increase and people opt out of marriage. The numbers of the homeless and the alienated are increasing. Individual anomie takes a sinister turn when the pursuit of individual self-fulfillment makes people forsake loyalty to traditional communities, associations, civic responsibilities and fraternities of mutual support. These trends are all grounds for indictment of Western civilization. To those of us on the inside, they are things-to-improve. In the eyes of the advocates of the superiority of value systems rooted elsewhere in the world, such as Islam or "the Asian way", they are must-avoids (Fernández-Armesto 2001: 445-6).

Only radical cultural relativism can help us avoid the asymmetry and the dominance relations between cultures described above, and lead us to a sympathetic understanding, acceptance and enjoying of the world's cultural diversity.

Values and values systems are incommensurable, and therefore cultural relativism is the only non-ethnocentric position available.

> A scholar can hardly be better employed than in destroying a fear. The one I want to go after is cultural relativism. Not the thing itself, which I think merely there, like Transylvania, but the dread of it, which I think unfounded. It is unfounded because the moral and intellectual consequences that are commonly supposed to flow from relativism – subjectivism, nihilism, incoherence, Machiavellianism, ethical idiocy, esthetic blindness, and so on – do not in fact do so and the promised rewards of escaping its clutches, mostly having to do with pasteurized knowledge, are illusory (Geertz 2000: 42).

> The trouble with ethnocentrism is not that it commits us to our own commitments. We are, by definition, so committed, as we are to having our own headaches. The trouble with ethnocentrism is that it impedes us from discovering at what sort of angle (...) we stand to the world; what sort of bat we really are (Geertz 2000: 75).

In addition, the values and norms of Western culture constitute in most cases an exception on a world-wide scale. Westerners tend to think that monogamy is the rule; in fact it is the exception, as over 80% of human societies are polygamous (Dawkins 2004: 17). Westerners believe that the best course of action is the most 'rational' and/or the most 'moral' one; but in other cultures, it might be the most aesthetically pleasing one:

> The mannered cast of Balinese interpersonal relations, the fusion of rite, craft, and courtesy, thus leads into a recognition of the most fundamental and most distinctive quality of their particular brand of sociality: its radical aestheticism. Social acts, all social acts, are first and foremost designed to please – to please the gods, to please the audience, to please the other, to please the self; but to please as beauty pleases, not as virtue pleases. Like temple offerings or gamelan concerts, acts of courtesy are works of art, and are meant to demonstrate, not rectitude (or what we would call rectitude) but sensibility (Geertz 1973: 400).

We might think that *gender,* at least, is stable cross-culturally. But in fact gender (unlike sex, which is biologically determined) is also a cultural construct.

In Thailand, transsexuals arguably constitute a third gender, alongside men and women. When the police takes someone's identity in Thailand, there are three possibilities as to the gender of the person arrested, not two. In India, the *hijra* (transsexuals; often wrongly translated as 'eunuchs') are struggling to win the right of being recognized as a third gender. According to Watson (2005: 451), certain tribes of native Americans (American Indians) recognized six types of gender: hyper-men (warriors), men, *berdaches* (androgynous), amazons, women, and hyper-women (who excelled at, say, female crafts).

Cultural relativism may possibly go beyond what is described above. Even the perception of the most basic, seemingly universal categories such as simple *objects* may not stable cross-culturally. The object may of course be associated with a function, and this function may differ depending on the culture. After World War II ended, people in poor, 'remote' regions of Southern Italy used the flush toilets that were installed in their houses under reconstruction programs to rinse the olive harvest: they assigned to this object a function which was new and different, but still perfectly 'rational'.

A more radical form of relativism consists in saying that the category of 'object' itself may not be culturally neutral, or that an object may actually be perceived in one culture while it is literally not seen, not perceived, in another: the very basis of human perception would then not be universally the same, it would be culturally defined. Many readers will find this hard to accept: if I see a tree or a rock, doesn't everyone in the world see a tree or a rock where I see it? We believe that the answer to this question may be 'no' in certain cases. Firstly, what qualifies as an object? Several descriptions confirm that the Navajo do not categorize objects as Westerners (and many others, no doubt) categorize them. To the Navajo, a tree (as any other 'object' as Westerners may see it) is a *process*. It is referred to by a verb; there is no clear category of nouns in the Navajo language (see, for instance, Pinxten 1994: 39). The reader might object that I myself argued against across-the-board application of the Sapir-Whorf hypothesis above, and that the fact that the Navajo do not recognize objects as a category in their language does not necessarily mean that they do not perceive them as such: surely when a Navajo is driving his truck, he will avoid running it against a tree as much as any Westerner would!

But consider the following quote from Bronislaw Malinowski in his classic *Argonauts of the Western Pacific:*

> The most remarkable of these beliefs is that there are big, live stones which lie in wait for sailing canoes, run after them, jump out and smash then to pieces. [...] Sometimes, they can be seen, at a distance, jumping out of the sea or moving on the water. In fact I have had them pointed to me, sailing off Koyabatu, and although I could see nothing, the natives, obviously, genuinely believed they saw them (Malinowski 1978 [1922]: 235).

There is, of course, no objective way of determining who is 'right' in this case: the natives, who can see the stones, or the anthropologist, who does not. In other words, the cultural origin of the observer may, in certain cases, determine whether an object is actually perceived or not. Examples like the one I quote above are hard to come by, but this may be due more to the fact that Western anthropologists tend to discard them, and not record them, than to the rarity of the phenomenon of differential perception in itself.

If relativism permeates the very perception of objects, the question arises if there remains anything that is cross-culturally stable in our perceptual environment. In fact I believe there is a reasonable *stable core* in human's perception of reality. The position that there is a relativistic *aspect* to every perception does not entail that *everything* is relativistic. In many or most cases, the stable core will carry much more weight than the relativistic fringes.[3] To develop an example I mentioned before: if you put members of different cultures in a car and let them drive through a territory that is cluttered with rocks and trees, I have little doubt that everyone will avoid those obstacles, regardless of their cultural background.[4]

Sokal & Bricmont (1997: 285-7) rightly say that a (Western) anthropologist who is describing an American Indian myth about the origin of the Indian people (which says, for example, that they originated in America) should do so within the philosophical framework of the culture involved without commenting on it from his/her own perspective (and say that it is contradicted by evidence that shows that present-day American Indians originated from Asia). But I am more of a relativist than Sokal & Bricmont who go on to claim that on the level of *knowledge,* both theories (the American vs. the Asian origin of American Indians) are incompatible and that therefore only one of them can be 'true'. My position is that they may be incompatible, but that does not preclude that one can be true within the framework of traditional American Indian cosmogony, the other within the (equally traditional) framework of modern science. The 'either... or' way of thinking where the logical truth of A by necessity entails the absolute logical falsehood of non-A may in itself be typically Western, or at least not universally shared. Above I have argued on different occasions that in some East and South-East Asians cultures (among which the Japanese), the same thing may be true or false depending on the perspective and the context.

(I hasten to add that I fully agree with the other point Sokal & Bricmont make in their book *Intellectual Impostures:* many postmodernists write pure nonsense about topics they do not even have the most basic knowledge of. Relativism does not count as an excuse for incompetence and imposture!).

> Understanding a people's culture expose their normalness without reducing their particularity (Geertz 1973: 14).

13.3 Minimizing and normalizing differences

Many well-meaning proponents of a multicultural society (in Western Europe, for example) also happen to be strong defendants of human rights (as they are defined in the Universal Declaration of Human Rights, for instance). The trouble is, many of the cultures which they would want to accept in a multicultural society exhibit clear features that do not conform to the Western standards with respect to human rights, and our 'Western multiculturalists' may be torn between their desire to accept cultural differences in value systems and practices without judging them on the one hand (cultural relativism), and their desire to defend what they see as universal human values and rights on the other hand (which may lead to intervention, i.e. ethnocentrism).

A common reaction of Western intellectuals to this dilemma is to deny that such deep-seated, possibly incompatible cultural differences actually exist. Shocking features of non-western cultures are minimized or their existence is denied. Below I examine some instances of this attitude.

The group-orientation of many non-western cultures, in which group opinions prevail over individual opinions, runs counter the ideal of *individual* human rights as they are defined in the Universal Declaration of Human Rights (itself an emanation of Western culture, as it was established by the United Nations in 1948, at a time where the vast majority of its member states were Western nations). For example, the right to individual religious conversion is inscribed in the UDHR. However, in a group-oriented culture the whole concept of individual conversion is either unacceptable or absurd. A common reaction of Western intellectuals is to deny or minimize the relevance of the group, and to stress that the individual must prevail in all cases. In their book *Antiracism* (1994: 50), Blommaert & Verschueren contend that [my translation] "[d]iversity must be taken seriously. Central in this is the individual, not the group." In several passages of their book, the same authors argue that groups are 'constructed' on the basis of "arbitrary, non-objective criteria" (also in Blommaert & Verschueren 1991: 1) and they endorse a claim made by Dov Ronen (ibid.) that "we ought to take for granted only two basic human entities: individuals and all humanity". Non-Western, group-oriented cultures are hereby kindly requested to conform to the Western world view! They are literally *westernized*, and their non-western cultural specificity (that the group prevails over the individual, in this case) is denied.

In reality, the 'individual' is a Western concept that is by no means universal:

> The Western conception of a person as a bounded, unique, more or less integrated, motivational and cognitive universe, a dynamic centre of awareness, emotions, judgment and action, organized in a distinctive whole... is, however incorrigible it may seem, a rather peculiar idea, within the context of world cultures (Clifford Geertz, quoted in Usunier 1998: 106).

> [Native American] people took their identity from the various subgroups in society and had no separate status (Watson 2005: 451).

According to Hall (1976: 231), for the Pueblo Indians the basic unit is *the group*, not the individual. The latter has no significance independent and distinct from the group, and competition between men, as in the Western school system, "is like having different parts of the psyche in competition".

If the mere existence of a culturally defined underlying value system such as group-orientation can be denied, this is impossible for well-documented practices that also run counter to Western cultural standards. One well-known example of a practice that is particularly shocking to many Westerners is *female circumcision*, where the clitoris of girls (or part of it, or a larger part of their sexual organs) is removed. While Blommaert & Verschueren cannot deny that the practice exists, they minimize its relevance to the discussion around refugees. In their words, "in the present context the problem is entirely fictitious" (1994: 121, my translation) and the possibility that members of groups who practice female circumcision would arrive in the country (Belgium, in this case) and thus raise a real issue is presented as pure speculation.

In reality, there have been several cases of female circumcision in European countries as diverse as France, the UK or Norway, so the possibility that it could happen (or does happen) in Belgium is real, not imaginary. On March 3, 2004, the BBC news website reported that

> Experts believe 74,000 first-generation African immigrant women in the UK have undergone female circumcision.

In France, several cases have been brought to court, and the old women who had practiced the circumcision were sentenced after court hearings which are tragic examples of the total absence of any communication or understanding between the accused West African woman and the French judge; see, for instance, Lefeuvre-Déotte (1997).

Denying the existence of an issue or minimizing it is definitely *not* the right way to further intercultural communication and understanding.

Blommaert & Verschueren perform the same mental operation of minimization or denial with respect to the issue of Muslim women wearing, or having to wear a veil:

> Concretely speaking, there exists no danger whatsoever that women in our regions will ever be forced to wear the veil (1994: 120; my translation).

This is, quite simply, false. There are thousands of Muslim girls and women who are forced by their parents or their husbands to wear the veil in Belgium, in France and in other European countries where there is a large Muslim population (as there also are cases, of whom I know one personally, of girls wearing the veil *against* the wishes of their parents). Notice also that, when pushed to their limits, most 'parlor multiculturalists' are likely to give higher priority to their Western cultural ideals than to their professed acceptance of multiculturalism. Blommaert & Verschueren qualify the forced wearing of the veil as a 'danger' in the quote above, and with respect to female circumcision they point out that, if ever a case would arise in Belgium, it could "perfectly be countered within the existing legal framework which protects the physical integrity of the individual" (1994: 122, my translation). In neither case do they even take into consideration that a cultural practice which runs counter to Western standards might, quite simply, be *acceptable* in the multicultural setting they supposedly defend.

A special case of minimizing the existence of culturally defined features Westerners may find unacceptable consists of contending that these features were not historically present in the culture described, but were actually the result of Western influence. We are getting even closer here to a modern version of *le mythe du bon sauvage*, where non-Western cultures are presented as originally pure and subsequently corrupted by Western influence (I am not denying, of course, that Western colonization resulted in widespread destruction of non-western cultures; I am questioning the way in which some describe the primeval state of those cultures). For example, in a booklet called *Understanding Asian Values* published by the respected European Institute for Asian Studies in Brussels, it is said about Thailand and the Philippines that "sexual exposure and prostitution is alien to the domestic culture of these countries" (1996: 26) and is "an imported phenomen[on], caused by foreign soldiers and tourists." This is blatantly false at least for prostitution in Thailand:

> One must, of course, accept the fact that prostitution is traditional in Thailand and not the product of western or US military influence. In every up-country town, one or more houses of prostitution can be found. Traditionally, one of the accepted perks of a government official on a visit up-country is the services of one of the town's most favored ladies of the night.
>
> Very often, a trip to the brothel is in the nature of a Saturday night on the town; it might be a movie just as well. [...]
>
> It was only in the late fifties that prostitution was declared illegal [...] in response to international pressures, particularly by the UN [...]. However, as one might expect, prostitution continued under different guises. Medical control lapsed, and venereal disease increased (Klausner 1993: 224-5; this text was originally published in 1977).

The quote from Klausner also illustrates the role the United Nations plays in 'normalizing away' practices that Western nations deem unacceptable, and the damage (in cultural, but also in human terms) that may result from such attempts at normalization.

The intricate example of Westernization that can be found in Pinxten (1994) is the last one I will discuss here; but I could multiply the examples at leisure. Pinxten raises the interesting question as to how cultural groups with seemingly incompatible values, practices and priorities might establish a fruitful dialogue with one another. Clearly, this cannot be done on the basis of the value system of either one of those cultures. Pinxten therefore suggests that we establish an 'intercultural meta-referential framework' or IMR (1994: 126) in which an objective description of commonalities and differences between two cultural groups (in his example, host Europeans and migrants) is the basis for identifying those areas where discussion and negotiation between the two groups is likely to be easiest as well as those where they are probably going to be most difficult. The idea of establishing a framework for dialogue which *transcends* both cultural groups seems to be exactly the opposite of an attempt at Westernization (forcing the others into 'our' framework), and maybe it is. Yet only a few pages further (1994: 131, my translation), Pinxten posits "a strict separation between religion and politics" as a "non-negotiable base for negotiations" and thereby betrays that ultimately his own, Western view must prevail in the dialogue, against possible alternatives and/or the establishment of a real meta-cultural framework: Westernization once again!

In my view, we cannot even begin to address the difficult issues of intercultural understanding, communication and co-operation if we do not admit that there are bound to be many areas where members of one culture will be shocked by the values and practices of the other culture. A fruitful dialogue can only be based on acknowledging differences, not on denying or minimizing them.[5]

13.4 Cultural bias

13.4.1 Cultural bias in publications

The question is if it is at all possible to eliminate all forms of ethnocentrism, including milder ones which might be qualified as 'cultural bias'.

Some examples of cultural bias are naïve and easy to pinpoint. Thus Peterson (2004: 4) claims that Americans have invented the automobile; this is indisputably false.

But given that our cultural background defines virtually all our values and practices, cultural bias is difficult to avoid. In fact, publications in the field of intercultural communication are themselves culturally biased.[6] As most publications are American (US), it is not surprising that issues are constantly referred back to the American context. When Nancy Adler, in a very good introduction to intercultural issues in business, writes in the Preface to her book that "much of our understanding of management came from the American experience", and when she challenges us "to go beyond our parochialism" (Adler 1992: ix), she obviously means *American* when she uses the word 'our' in both instances.

Not surprisingly, American publications are not ideally suited for a European, let alone an Asian, or African reader. This is true not only because of some (perhaps trivial) cases of word usage such as in the example given above, but also because, quite simply, practices and values in the United States are not identical to practices and values elsewhere. In a presentation at a conference in 1995, I showed that the computer software *WordPerfect Presentations,* a graphic presentations program that was then sold all over the world, exhibits a strong cultural bias, sometimes Western, most often American, in its figure library. Its section on the theme of *Religion* contains approximately 14 pictures related to Christianity, against 4 to Judaism, 1 to Islam, 1 to Buddhism, 1 to Hinduism. It goes without saying that these proportions would have been different if the program had been designed in a non-western part of the world (or adapted locally). More subtly, the section on *Transport* contains pictures of individual means of transportation mainly (cars, motorcycles; no bicycle) and does not contain any picture of community transport systems such as trains, buses, etc. If the program had been designed in Europe, again, things would very probably have been different.[7]

To the extent that the present book is written by a European, it is likely to present a European cultural bias, even if I attempted to eliminate the most obvious and blatant examples of it.

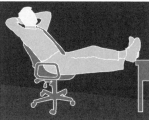

Figure 26. 'Feet on desk' in Microsoft Word clipart: unthinkable in many cultures.

At a less superficial level, however, cultural bias is even harder to eliminate. Consider the following example, from Ferraro's book *The Cultural Dimension of International Business*. Ferraro is anthropologically trained, his book shows deep sympathy for non-Western cultures and a critical attitude towards Western or American values and practices; in brief, he is certainly less subject to cultural bias than most. Yet at one point, Ferraro writes:

> Middle-class North Americans have worked out one set of cultural patterns, whereas the Indonesians may have developed a radically different solution. In most cases, one solution is probably not more inherently rational than another (1994: 152).

This is a passage which is meant to argue *against* ethnocentrism and which stresses cultural relativism, yet cultural bias appears even here, in particular with the use of the word *rational*. Rationality is used here as a common value standard, and this allows Ferraro to argue that Indonesian cultural traits are not any less *rational* than American cultural traits. But who says that Indonesian culture is looking for *rational* solutions to the issues involved? Priding oneself on being rational is in itself a Western value, not necessarily shared or valued as highly in other cultures, as we have argued above.

At an underlying level, given that nearly everything a person thinks and does is linked to his or her culture, it may be difficult to avoid cultural bias entirely. One possible solution could be to develop intercultural communication manuals cross-culturally, i.e. through co-operation of different co-authors from different cultures. Apart from the fact that even then the number of co-authors can never be large enough to accommodate most, or even many, cultures, it is not even sure that such a book would be readable. In fact, a certain amount of cultural bias may be necessary in order to adapt a publication optimally to the public it is meant for. This being said, blatant examples of cultural bias must and can be avoided, and the author did his utmost to eliminate them in this book.

13.4.2 Hofstede's survey and the Chinese Values Survey (CVS)

Hofstede himself admits a form of cultural bias in his own IBM survey. Even if a Western researcher like him and his team go through great lengths to ensure that a questionnaire's wording is free from cultural bias, the questions themselves he and his collaborators chose to include in the survey are likely to exhibit a Western cultural bias, as all members of the team who compose the questionnaire are either European or American.

Non-Western respondents may be able to answer the questions that are asked, but we cannot be sure that these questions, and the values they were probing to discover, are particularly relevant for respondents from non-Western cultures. In addition, other dimensions of non-Western value systems possibly remain undiscovered because no questions which would lead up to their discovery were included in the survey.

In Hong Kong a Canadian researcher, Michael Bond, had asked a number of Chinese social scientists from Hong Kong and Taiwan to draw up a list of ten basic values which they felt were relevant for Chinese people. On the basis of their input, Bond composed a questionnaire of 40 items which he called the *Chinese Value Survey (CVS)*. Not surprisingly, some of the items in the CVS may appear strange to a Western mind, such as *filial piety:* "honoring of ancestors and obedience to, respect for, and financial support of parents" (Hofstede 1991: 162; see also Eliseef 2003: 51). The Confucian concept of filial piety expresses a set of values that is important for the Chinese people, whereas it is less relevant in the West.

Bond's CVS was administered to 100 students in 23 countries around the world. Although the questions asked were very different from those that are included in Hofstede's surveys, the dimensions that come out of the CVS are significantly correlated with three of the Hofstede dimensions: Power Distance, Individualism-Collectivism and Masculinity. This does not mean, of course, that the interpretation of every dimension and the virtues that are associated with each pole of it are similar in both surveys; in fact, they are quite different. It is revealing to mention some of the values that are used in the CVS: they will sound rather 'exotic' to Western ears, and some may be hard for Westerners to understand.

The dimension which is most closely correlated with Hofstede's Power Distance is the CVS factor *moral discipline*. It stresses less the 'power' aspect as such, and expresses more

> that inequalities in power go together with different virtues in one's personal life. The person in a large power distance culture should balance power with restraint; the person in a small power distance culture should move around with care (Hofstede 1991: 162-3).

Hofstede's Individualism-Collectivism dimension is correlated with a CVS dimension called *integration*, with collectivist values such as *filial piety, chastity in women and patriotism* on one pole, and *tolerance of others, harmony with others, having a close, intimate friend and contentedness with one's position in life* at the other end.

Hofstede's Masculinity corresponds to the CVS factor *human heartedness*. Here again, the CVS stresses different aspects of the dimension, with *patience, courtesy and kindness (forgiveness, compassion)* on the masculine end, and *patriotism, a sense of righteousness* on the feminine end.

Hofstede's Uncertainty Avoidance cannot be correlated with any factor in the CVS (more generally, Uncertainty Avoidance is the least robust of Hofstede's dimensions; Sondergaard 1994, Usunier 1998: 36). On the other hand, a fourth dimension which came out of the CVS is unrelated to any of Hofstede's dimensions. Bond calls this dimension 'Confucian dynamism'. As it refers essentially to a long-term vs. a short term orientation, that is the name many scholars including Hofstede use for it; but this captures only one aspect of this non-Western dimension.

Using a Chinese-based questionnaire in this case clearly contributed to eliminate cultural bias that was present in Hofstede's original work.

13.5 Tolerance

13.5.1 Religious (in)tolerance and syncretism

Historically, religious *in*tolerance may have arisen only with the advent of Judaism and Christianity, as they were the only religions which refused syncretism with others (Mordillat & Prieur 1999: 71-2).

Examples abound of high degrees of tolerance, religious and otherwise, throughout history. One of the most widely quoted is the 'convivencia' (literally, living together) of Jews and Christians with Muslims in al-Andalus: Spanish Andalusia under the Muslim sultanates (Lewis 2008: xxiv).

More generally, Islam has always been much more tolerant towards its minorities, Christians and Jews, than Christianity (in the West, not including the Byzantine Empire) has been to its minorities, Muslims and Jews (Van den Broeck 1995, Armstrong 1999, and many others; for a partly dissenting voice, see Hourani 1991: 47).

Under the Ummayads (7th-8th c. CE), the Saint John basilica in Damascus was divided into two sections, one for the Muslims and another for the Christians. For a long time, followers of the two religions were praying side by side in contiguous locations. At Homs also, the major church hosted ceremonies of the two religions during four centuries. This situation only changed with the arrival of the Crusaders (Courbage & Fargues 2005: 8).

Similarly,

> The ambassador [of Louis IX, 13th c. CE] reported, interestingly enough, that among the Mongols there was absolutely no religious discrimination: the Great Khan – Jenhiz's son Kublai – though in theory shamanist, regularly attended Christian, Muslim and Buddhist ceremonies (Norwich 2007).

Religious tolerance was higher in Eastern Christianity than in the West. In Constantinople itself there was a Moslem quarter and a mosque – something that provoked the contempt and anger of the Crusaders (Bradford 1972: 20).

Many East and South-East Asian cultures are characterized by a high degree of religious syncretism: they combine elements of different religions rather effortlessly. Ashkenazy & Jacob (2000: 144) point out that 170 million Japanese are registered to one of the official religions – out of a population of 120 million: in other words, many Japanese define themselves as belonging to more than one religion, usually Buddhism and Shintoism. Christianity is a problem, because it is exclusive; still, Christian weddings are common among the Buddhist-and-Shintoist Japanese (Hendry 2003: 130). Notice that neither Buddhism nor Shintoism implies the existence of an all-powerful god (Gruzinski 2004: 188), and this makes religion in Japan as in other East and South-East Asian countries very different from the monotheistic traditions people are familiar with in the West.

Similarly, in Thailand most people are nominally Buddhists, but they worship Hindu gods. In fact the distinction between Buddhism and Hinduism may have been invented by 18th-19th century European orientalists (Watson 2005: 676). On certain occasions a Buddhist monk will be brought in to perform certain rites, on others it will be a Brahmin priest, sometimes both. Segaller (1993: 31) describes the ceremonies with which a new house is blessed in Thailand:

> [Buddhist] Monks or a Brahmin priest may perform the ceremony, it is up to the owner.

Entering (Buddhist!) monkhood starts out with a Brahmin ceremony...

> ... then the Brahmin ceremony suddenly ends and the Buddhist part just as suddenly takes over as the young man enters the chapel (Segaller 1993: 57).

A Thai scholar, Suntaree Komin (1990), has shown that in addition, Thai Buddhists may occasionally decide to worship in places associated with yet other religions, such as a Catholic church (for Thai religious syncretism, see also Klausner 1993: 173).

Thailand: religious eclecticism

The King of Thailand is the guardian of Buddhism in the country, and when the Queen Mother died in 1995 the ceremonies were Buddhist. But two royal princesses not only attended a Catholic mass, but *led the service* at it in Bangkok's Assumption cathedral (reported in *The Nation*, Bangkok, July 24, 1995).

I have difficulty imagining an analogous situation involving one of the European royal families...

In addition, Buddhism, and certainly the Theravada Buddhism practiced in Thailand, may well be considered an *atheist religion,* as we have said above. The Buddha is an example to follow, but he is no god and he has no divine powers: there is no petitionary prayer in Theravada Buddhism (Welty 2004: 93, Celli 2006: 274); the gods are Brahmanic (Klausner 1993: 173).

Figure 27. A Buddhist and a Hindu shrine side by side in a suburb of Bangkok.

In China also, syncretism is common, and temples are devoted to 'religions' that involve no god, such as Confucianism and Daoism:

> Civil temples reflect Confucian rationalism and an awareness that Confucius was a man and not a deity (Shaughnessy 2005: 88).

In traditional Chinese cosmogony, there is no creation myth, no creator-lawgiver, and no supernatural deity who ordained the order in the universe (Watson 2005: 193)

This naturally leads to tolerance. According to Boorstin (1983: 193) "[t]olerance is too weak a word for their complaisant pluralism." He refers to a stone inscribed in tree languages – Chinese, Tamil and Persian – in Galle, on the South West coast of Ceylon, 1409, in honor of the Chinese emperor: praise to Lord Buddha in Chinese, to Hindu deities such as Vishnu in Tamil, and to Allah and Muslim saints in Persian...

Non-Christians praying in a Catholic church

I once received two Chinese scholars whom I had met before in Xi'an, China. While visiting one of the gothic churches in Brussels, the two ladies started praying. I said "Oh, I did not know you are Christians". They replied "No, we are not, but..." [now that we are in a church anyway]

It has been noted by many scholars that in some Asian societies, people's religion cannot be defined primarily in terms of 'beliefs', but is better described in terms of a search for a virtuous life. Whereas Western monotheistic religions (including Islam) can be associated with a man's search for Truth, the Confucian dimension is more geared towards a search for Virtue.

Celli (2006: 52) writes that schisms within Buddhism did not happen because of differences in doctrine (as in Christianity), but because of different views concerning the appropriate code of conduct. Hofstede (1991: 159) quotes the example of a Nepalese scholar in the Netherlands to whom questions about his 'beliefs' make little sense.

Western questions as to which religion is 'right' or 'true' (and, a Westerner would think, all the other ones must then logically be considered 'false' or 'untrue') make little sense in many Asian cultures. This type of question appears to be relevant for the three religions of 'the Book' (Judaism, Christianity and Islam), but many Asian cultures approach different systems and doctrines in terms of integration and synthesis rather than in terms of mutual exclusion.

A beautiful illustration of the underlying idea is the yin-yang symbol (F28). When asked, my Western students (European and American) describe the relation between the colors *black* and *white* as absolute opposites: something is *either* black *or* white; it cannot be both at the same time. But the yin-yang symbol symbolizes that

a. you need both (black and white, male and female, etc.) to make the world (the circle in many cultures symbolizes the whole, completeness, perfection)
b. the borderline between the opposites is wavy, not straight: white intrudes into black territory, and vice versa
c. inside all black, there is some white (a white dot in the symbol), and inside all white, there is some black.

Figure 28. The yin-yang symbol.

Similarly, Varner & Beamer (1995: 71) describe Chinese thought as the establishment of *linkages,* with hot implying cold, etc. In such a framework, a meeting or toast between two negotiating parties at present is related to encounters between representatives of those two nations in the past. This helps explaining the importance of historical references in toasts and introductory speeches, as mentioned above.

In Japan as elsewhere in East and South-East Asia, people can accept two interpretations of one event as reality, by adopting different perspectives (Yoshimura

& Anderson 1997: 8). People think in term of *and... and* rather than in terms of *either... or*. Shadid (1998: 72) also mentions the fact that the Japanese accept inconsistencies. Lane, DiStefano & Maznevski (2000: 125) link Japanese tolerance of ambiguity to Zen Buddhism – but this feature is not limited to Japan only.

13.5.2 Tolerance and openness today

Well-meaning people in the West will often declare that they are 'tolerant' towards other cultures. But as has rightly been pointed out by various scholars (for example Blommaert and Verschueren 1994: 63) tolerance is not a very positive attitude. While *to tolerate* may mean "to recognize and respect (others' beliefs, practices, etc.) without sharing them", the same term also means "to bear, to put up with (someone or something not especially liked)"; both definitions are in Webster's dictionary. Tolerance is a minimalist attitude where one refrains from acting against someone else's practices, but no attempt is made to share them or even to understand them from the inside.

Openness has more positive connotations. Being open to what is new or unknown entails that one will look at features from other cultures with sympathy and understanding, and be willing to share in the practices that go with them whenever possible and appropriate, even if it means stepping into unknown territory. In order to become a better 'intercultural communicator', one should train oneself in developing a higher degree of openness, because it is one of the prime assets in dealing with people from other cultures.

While many people will *claim* to be open, in reality such openness does not come about that easily and naturally. You can test your openness as far as food is concerned by asking yourself whether you would be willing to eat
- *sushi* and *sashimi* (Japanese dishes with raw fish)
- monkey meat (in Africa)
- caterpillar stew (also in Africa)
- roasted grasshoppers (sold by street vendors in Bangkok)
- incubated duck's eggs, with the chick's embryo inside *(balud,* a local delicacy in the Philippines).

The categories of what we find edible and inedible are arbitrarily defined in a given culture rather than based on objectively definable limits. Europeans watch with disgust a television documentary where the Masai are shown to drink their cow's blood, but many of these same Europeans are happy to eat blood sausage: liquid cow's blood is not edible, coagulated pig's blood is. Most Europeans would probably have no qualms eating duck's eggs as well as duck – but not the *balud* which represents an intermediate stage in the development from egg to duck.

If you are willing to try all or most of the above foodstuffs, you probably possess a high degree of openness – at least as far as food is concerned. But many people I meet are reluctant to try any of the above foodstuffs, and quite a few outright refuse to do so. If you think you fall in this latter category, please ask yourself: *why* do I accept to eat shrimp (which look like insects, complete with legs and antennae), and refuse the grasshoppers that look fairly similar? Why do I (probably) eat raw meat (steak tartare, carpaccio), but possibly refuse to eat raw

fish? The answer to that question will almost invariably be: because the one is labeled 'edible' in the culture I grew up in, and the other is not.
A similar mechanism is at work in the following story:

> I once knew a trader's wife in Arizona who took a somewhat devilish interest in producing a cultural reaction. Guests who came her way were often served delicious sandwiches filled with a meat that seemed to be neither chicken nor tuna fish yet was reminiscent of both. To queries she gave no reply until each had eaten his fill. She then explained that what they had eaten was not chicken, not tuna fish, but the rich, white flesh of freshly killed rattlesnakes. The response was instantaneous – vomiting, often violent vomiting. A biological process is caught into a cultural web (Kluckhohn 1968: 25-6, quoted in Ferraro 1994: 20-1).

In other words, the violent rejection is caused not by the food as such, but by the *label* which is attached to it. People start to vomit not when they are eating their sandwiches, but when they hear the word 'rattlesnake'; a beautiful example of culture as 'mental programming'…

The examples involving food are not as trivial as they may seem. If we cannot bring ourselves to be open with respect to a rather superficial and harmless practice such as eating different kinds of food, how likely are we to be open when deep-seated values from other cultures are concerned?

The moral of all this is that, firstly, openness does not come naturally to most of us. Secondly, a higher degree of openness *can* be acquired if there is a willingness to do so; the author of this book personally tried all the foodstuffs mentioned above. Such training is part of a long-lasting, in fact a never ending process towards becoming a true intercultural communicator. The beauty of it is that with every step in the process, you will feel more at ease in different parts of the world, and people from other cultures will most often respect and appreciate your attitude of not only not looking down upon their practices and values, but genuinely wanting to experience them for yourself. This does not mean that you need to assimilate all practices from another culture. There is no need for imitation, nor is it *always* appropriate to share practices from other cultures with the people involved. But it is hard to overestimate the positive impact true openness will have upon your interlocutors and business partners from other parts of the world.

This brings me to the third point I want to make. The more you open yourself to practices and values from other cultures, the more you will often feel that they are, quite simply, pleasant and enjoyable, and that they are enrichment for your own life. After all, they have been tried and refined by other peoples, and be found enjoyable by them. Of the foodstuffs I described above, I liked all but one, and many I enjoy now so much that I positively look forward to having them again when I happen to be in a location where they are available. On a completely different level, assimilating some elements of African culture (with which I am often in contact), in particular with respect to time, makes me go through life less hurriedly, and enjoying it more than before.

Finally, it must be acknowledged that for everyone there will be a point where openness stops, and there is no need to hide this. Openness will stop at the caterpillar stew for some of us, for others it will be at some other point. Only then, when one feels unable or unwilling to share certain practices and values, should the minimalist attitude of *tolerance* come in, i.e., the attitude of at least accepting and respecting that other people behave and think differently.

Of course, if you feel that your own openness is *very* limited and will probably remain that way, then you may want to draw the conclusion from there that other people are better equipped to interact with foreigners, and that you will feel most at ease in a job where your contacts with other cultures are rare or altogether absent.

Openness may lead to a positive appreciation of 'foreign' practices or values: you may actually start to like this outlandish thing so much that you decide to take it over. After all, many Europeans nowadays do go to Japanese restaurants and eat sushi and sashimi, just like many Japanese enjoy Beethoven, and Americans start enjoying soccer alongside American football.

It would be erroneous to believe that this is a recent phenomenon. In the past also, Europeans as well as others have taken over values and practices that were imported from elsewhere (often after a period of initial rejection), and integrated them into their own culture(s). An impressive number of the foodstuffs Europeans (and many others) eat and drink as well as the materials they use in their clothes originated elsewhere: oranges and tomatoes, chicken and lamb, coffee and tea, cotton and silk, none of those are of European origin. Our alphabet is based on an ancient Phoenician invention; the paper we write on is produced with a process invented in China. Our present-day religion and the moral system that goes with it (even for those of us who are not religious any more) originated in Palestine and completely wiped out the autochthonous religion of our European ancestors. Etc.

13.6 Nationalism vs. multiculturalism

13.6.1 A homogeneous society?

Many extreme right-wing[8] political parties in Europe defend the vision of a culturally homogeneous society, where the autochthonous culture has to be shielded from outside contamination by other cultures (be it American television series or the Islamic religion) and where more often than not members of those other cultures (Muslims, Jews, etc.) are not welcome in the country, unless, maybe, if they completely adapt to the 'local' culture, i.e. if they totally lose their own cultural identity.

Perhaps because of the association with the extreme right and/or with what happened under the Nazi regime, declaring a preference for a homogeneous society in general is often equated with racism, and therefore ethically wrong in all cases (this is particularly clear in Blommaert and Verschueren 1994, for instance).

I am not convinced that being in favor of cultural homogeneity within a certain territory is in itself and always morally wrong. Any group of people may decide that they wish to be left alone and have nothing to do with the outside world. Japan closed itself virtually completely off from the outside world for nearly two centuries (1639-1853), until it was forced to open itself up to international (read: Western) trade by commodore Perry's American gunboats. Was Perry right, and the Japanese wrong? I find nothing intrinsically immoral in the Japanese attitude.

In fact, many of the same people who declare cultural homogeneism to be a form of racism, and therefore morally wrong, would probably be the first to defend (and rightly so in my opinion) the right of Indian peoples who live in the Amazon forest and other indigenous peoples to remain free of outside interference if they so desire. In other words, I do not consider that "homogeneism is intrinsically racist" as Blommaert & Verschueren put it (1994: 73, my translation).[9]

But while I feel that cultural homogeneism is not morally wrong in itself, that is a far cry from applying the concept to modern nation states. In the case of most modern nation states, the ideal of cultural homogeneism is unrealistic, harmful, and ethically very questionable.

It is *unrealistic* because in our age of global communications networks, no nation state is capable of shielding itself off from outside influences. No state would be capable of deporting enormous groups of peoples to their country of origin (if there is such a country), nor can a democratic state force those people to assimilate completely, for this would mean, among many other things, forcing them to abandon their language, their religion, and so forth, all of which is against internationally agreed standards for the protection of human rights.

It is *harmful* economically, because no modern economy can afford to work for the domestic market only and to close itself off from the rest of the world. Operating economically on the global market is impossible without allowing foreign capital and foreign companies into your country, and with them come foreign expatriates, foreign delegations, etc., and conversely it also entails being present yourself in foreign countries.

It is *ethically very questionable* to support a position where vast numbers of people are expected either to leave, or to lose their cultural identity completely, when these same people were invited to the country not so long ago and contributed fully to its economic development with hard work, courage and perseverance.

13.6.2 Nationalism

One particular and perhaps deemed more respectable form of ethnocentrism and/or homogeneism is nationalism.

Scholarly opinion differs as to the origin of nationalism. Ernest Gellner *(Nations and Nationalism,* 1983) remains famous for claiming that nationalism only really appears in the modern world, due to sociological changes in our society. Others may claim its roots are much older.

Nationalistic feelings may crystallize around anything a group has in common, which distinguishes it from its surroundings. In Belgium, it crystallized around language[10] (the Flemish, speakers of Dutch, against the French-speaking); in Northern Ireland, around religion, Catholic vs. Protestant; in Rwanda, around the elusive concept of 'ethnicity', Hutu vs. Tutsi.

There is no doubt that nationalism is constructed, and therefore to a large extent arbitrary.

Maalouf (1998) rightly points out that the same individual may well have proudly claimed to be (a) Yugoslavian in 1980, (b) Muslim around 1992, and (c) Bosnian and European today.

In the 19th century, nationalism was 'Belgian'; now it is becoming predominantly 'Flemish' in the North of the country. The same historic event, such as the Battle of the Golden Spurs (1302), where Flemish cities but also the Duchy of Brabant opposed the King of France can be construed as a symbol of Belgian nationalism (against France) or of Flemish nationalism (against French speakers).

Even if in theory nationalism may refer simply to a feeling of belonging to a nation, it is hard to dissociate it from the feeling that 'our' nation is superior to all others, and/or should be protected against 'foreign' influence to retain its integrity. It almost inevitably leads to a form of ethnocentrism.

Present-day readers may easily forget how recent nationalism is, and how multicultural (i.e., non-nationalistic) historic states were.

The Ottoman Empire, particularly in its heyday (16th century) is a good case in point,

> [...] in no sense a national but a dynastic and multiracial empire, whose varied populations, whether Turkish or otherwise, Moslem or Christian or Jewish, were above all else Ottomans, members of a single body politic which transcends such conceptions as nationhood, religion, and race (Kinross 1977: 614).

Only in the late 19th century does European style nationalism completely override 'Ottomanism' (Kinross 1977: 585).

The (then very small) city of Athens, in the early 19th c., had a population made up of at least 50% Albanians, with Greeks and Turks together making up the rest. Now is has become the capital of a national, Greek State, after Greece's independence from the Ottomans (Norwich 2007).

On the island of Cyprus, for centuries Greeks and Turks lived together in reasonable harmony, with Greek villages, Greek villages with a Turkish minority, Turkish villages and Turkish villages with a Greek minority. After political turmoil, a situation emerged with two national states, one Greek and one Turkish (this is the factual situation, even if only Greek Cyprus is recognized internationally), and a UN controlled zone separating them (F29).

The Austro-Hungarian Empire might also be characterized, during one period, as a multicultural entity. Francis-Joseph I (r. 1848-1916), who described himself as 'the last monarch of the old style', ruled over a truly multinational state, where the imperial hymn could be sung in any one of seventeen official languages, including Yiddish (Davies 1997: 829). This empire too is now split up into 'national' states: Austria, Hungary, the Czech Republic, and parts of several other surrounding countries.

So most modern-day European states, nationalism-based, are recent.

> Of the sovereign states on the map of Europe in 1993, four had been formed in the 16th century, four in the 17th, two in the 18th, seven in the 19th and no fewer than 36 in the 20th (Davies 1997: 456).

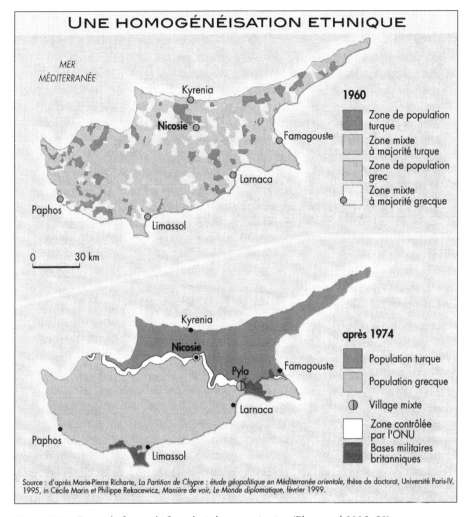

Figure 29. Cyprus before and after ethnic homogenization (Plasseraud 2005: 59).

In Asia also, various countries including Thailand went from multicultural to nationalistic: in the first half of the 19th century Siam was very multicultural, with plenty of non-Thai people (Dutch, Persian, Greek) even in government positions (Wyatt 2003: 98 and 136-7); later a multi-ethnic country was turned into a unified 'Thai state' (Phongpaichit & Baker 1997: 14 and 233).

'Le nationalisme, c'est la guerre' (nationalism means war) once said President François Mitterrand of France; Amin Maalouf (1998) uses the term *identités meurtrières,* 'deadly identities'. The idea that the ideal situation would be one in which every country's borders coincide with one language, one ethnic group and one culture is an illusion. There are virtually no examples of that, neither in history, nor in the present, nor, presumably, will there be in the future.

It is illusory to think that modern nation states could revert to a situation of cultural homogeneity. In fact, 'revert' is not the right term, for as we have seen many of the large states that existed before the advent (the invention?) of nationalism in the 19th century were multicultural to a much larger extent than many of us might imagine today, as we have just above.

13.6.3 A multicultural society

> King Stephan of Hungary said, around 1030: «Guests come from various lands and they all bring with them their languages, customs, instruments, various arms, and all this diversity is an ornament for our kingdom, a jewel for our court, an object of fear for our enemies from outside. For a kingdom which has only one language and one custom is weak and fragile.» (Le Goff 1982: 256; my translation).

Even though many well-meaning Europeans, including politicians, claim to be in favor of a multicultural state, in reality they seem to have difficulty accepting true multiculturalism, which implies that various cultural groups within the boundaries of one state may have and preserve their own cultural features. If, applied to Muslims for instance, that means not eating pork and abstaining from alcohol, this will not be much of a problem. But what about including Muslim holidays in the calendar? Allowing Muslim women to wear a headscarf whenever *they* choose to do so? Accepting polygamy? In fact, *why* would that be a problem, and *why* is even the headscarf now being turned into a problem?[11] Some might say that allowing such differences might lead to a breakdown of society as we know it. The same has been said (and is still being said by some) about accepting homosexuality, abortion or birth control, – which have all been accepted to a large degree in many European countries. It seems that many have more difficulty accepting differences in 'others' than in accepting those in people we define (rather arbitrarily) as part of 'us'.

> The sort of idea that, say, Shi'is, being other, present a problem, but, say, soccer fans, being part of us, do not, or at least not of the same sort, is merely wrong (Geertz 2000: 76).

In the Ottoman Empire, Turks could marry more than one wife, as they were Muslims; Greeks could marry only one, as they were Christians. As the Ottoman Empire lasted for centuries as a fairly stable political entity (much longer than any modern national state has survived until now), we can hardly invoke the risk of societal breakdown to argue against having different judicial systems for different cultural groups. Under Muslim rule, in many cases in the past, each religious group had its own tribunals and judges, applying their own judicial code, both civil and penal. In self-proclaimed multicultural Europe, on the other hand, Muslims have to appear before non-sharia[12] courts (Van den Broeck 1995: 115).

In various well-known publications (e.g. Berry 2005, 2008), Berry describes four acculturation strategies an immigrant may have when trying to cope with his life in a new country. They depend on two variables: how much of your original country you preserve, and how much you take on of the new culture you are in.

	Maintenance of heritage culture and identity high	Maintenance of heritage culture and identity low
Relationships sought among groups high	Integration	Assimilation
Relationships sought among groups low	Separation	Marginalization

Of course, the possibility of embracing one of these strategies also depends on the reaction of the host population to the newcomers:

	Maintenance of heritage culture and identity high	Maintenance of heritage culture and identity low
Relationships sought among groups high	Multiculturalism	Melting pot
Relationships sought among groups low	Segregation	Exclusion

It may seem that the best choice would be the integration-multiculturalism option. However, surveys show that this is not always the preferred option by either hosts or newcomers.

Many Europeans (unlike, perhaps, Canadians) prefer assimilation and the 'melting pot' option, i.e., homogeneism (Van Oudenhoven 2002: 192; van de Vijver, Breugelmans & Schalk-Soekar 2008): you are welcome here provided you completely adapt and become 'one of us', – even if becoming one of us is in reality made difficult or impossible through discrimination. The real number of people who prefer assimilation is probably even higher than surveys may show, as there is a strong social desirability effect in favor of saying that newcomers should be allowed to preserve their own culture.

The same study by Van Oudenhoven (2002: 189-192) in the Netherlands also shows that a sizeable number of newcomers opt for the separation strategy. A study with the Dutch military by Bosman, Richardson & Soeters (2007) also concludes that respondents prefer assimilation in a public context and separation in a private context.

Notice that separation (by the newcomers) does not necessarily correspond to Berry's segregation (by the hosts): segregation is imposed by the majority group, separation may be a deliberate choice made by newcomers. Claiming that "separation is equivalent to segregation" (as in van de Vijver, Breugelmans, Schalk-Soekar 2008: 94) is erroneous.

In any case, Berry's concept of integration-multiculturalism as the preferred acculturation strategy cannot be properly evaluated unless one clearly defines what it entails. In reality, integration has never been properly defined and it is quite possible that marginality (Bennett's 'constructive marginalization') is a form of integration in certain cases (Boski 2008). Supposedly, integration means that minorities and newcomers can maintain their own cultural heritage and identity, while at the same time having close contacts with the majority or the host population, and the latter making allowances to accommodate the newcomers. But what if the positions of the two groups are incompatible? And *how much* accommodation and preservation of cultural heritage will be possible?

Above we considered a few issues, related to Muslims:
1. Eating and drinking habits, such as abstaining from pork and alcohol (therefore, having alternative dishes without pork in schools, hospitals, company restaurants, etc.)
2. Introducing Muslim holidays into the calendar (and possibly scrapping some Christian ones if the total number becomes too high)
3. Allowing differences in dress code, such as a headscarf for women (also those working as teachers, civil servants, nurses, in the police, etc.)
4. Introducing legal differentiation, with Muslims being subject to a legal system that is partly different from that applied to the majority population.

This little list, incomplete as it is, illustrates how poorly European countries score on the 'multiculturalism scale', as most of the points mentioned above seem to be either unacceptable or at least problematic.

Within Europe, official government policies differ widely. In most of continental Europe, assimilation seems to be the government's preferred choice, as is particularly clear in France, even if it is debatable how much influence this government policy has on the real situation (Barrette e.a. 2004). In Great Britain, allowances for cultural diversity, including in public life, are much greater. Sikhs can enter the police force in Britain and wear their turban (in black and with the police insignia) with the police uniform; there is no doubt that if the request to do that was ever made in France, or Belgium, or many other continental European countries, it would be denied.[13] At the same time it illustrates how simple it really is for some multicultural allowances to be made: *nothing terrible really happens* when the authorities allow some police to wear a uniform which in some aspect deviates from the norm; and it may make minorities feel really at home in the country where they are living now.

North Americans (including Canadians) probably accept to accommodate cultural differences more than continental Europeans, even if they are still a far cry from true multiculturalism. When Muslims from Somalia who were working as cashiers in local supermarkets in Minneapolis decided that they would refuse to handle pork products, the management's reaction was one of understanding, and they proposed that customers with pork products scan that product themselves, or use another cash register. Similarly, when some Muslim taxi drivers refused to take passengers who are carrying alcoholic beverages in their luggage, the municipality proposed having color-coded lights on the taxis to indicate whether drivers accept alcohol in their cars, or not (source: various news websites). All this is unthinkable in Europe today.

The differing reactions towards such issues may well be related to Hofstede's Uncertainty Avoidance Index. One aspect of high Uncertainty Avoidance, as we have seen above, is that 'what is different, is dangerous'. Therefore, allowing for cultural variation may be harder to accept in cultures with higher Uncertainty Avoidance scores.

Among Berry's accommodation strategies, separation is supposedly not a preferred option. However, there are interesting examples of strong separation where this situation seems to be fairly unproblematic and stable.

The Hassidic (ultra-orthodox) Jews in Antwerp are the one of the largest such communities outside Israel. They have their own schools, shops (mainly for food), language (many speak Yiddish, some may speak another language, but usually not Flemish/Dutch, the language spoken by the majority population in Antwerp) and more generally their customs are totally different from the rest of the population. In fact, human-to-human contact between the two groups is limited, even if of course they share the same streets, sidewalks, and the Jews may buy their car or bicycle in the same store as the others. There are no signs that this situation of strong separation leads to instability or conflict.

The Parsi in Mumbai (Bombay) are another good case in point. Originally from Persia (now Iran), they are Zoroastrians, and are supposed to marry only inside their own group. Their houses of worship are off-limits to other Indians. Their funeral rites will seem abhorrent to most Hindus, Muslims or Sikhs: they leave the body of the deceased person on top of a tower to be scavenged on by birds of prey (this is becoming a problem in a big city like Mumbai where birds of prey are rare, but that is not the issue here).

Figure 30. A Zoroastrian temple in Mumbai: 'For Parsis only'.

This example also illustrates that, in a multicultural society, the majority must accept that other groups engage in practices which may seem shocking or horrifying to them. Lest we fall in the trap of ethnocentrism again, cultural relativism should warn us against judging such practices from the outside.[14]

Multicultural states may be harder to govern (are they, really?), but, if properly managed, they can be very successful, and peaceful as well. Singapore may perhaps count as a present-day example, even if it is not a Western-style democracy. Extending facilities to cultural minorities is a cornerstone of multiculturalism. In Singapore, Tamils make up less than 10 percent of the population, but Tamil is an official language of the country, Tamils have their own educational system, religion, etc. The official signs in Singapore always include the Tamil language, along with Chinese, Malay and English. Then why don't Europeans extend the same facilities to their own minorities, and include Turkish, Arabic or other minority languages in their official communication channels, include those languages in school curriculums for those who want it, and more?

Figure 31. Singapore: a sign in four languages.

It may also be argued that multicultural states are more resilient:

> In modern times, a few generations ago – when racial explanations were fashionable – it was maintained that Rome fell because its ethnic purity suffered pollution. The opposite is rather the case. Despite intermixtures with many peoples over the course of the centuries, the tough character of the Romans had not changed – as their continuing achievements testify. Indeed, the trouble was rather that, psychologically, they had not changed enough: if only they had been able to adapt themselves to getting on with the Germans, the western empire might have been preserved (Grant 1979: 344).

Will the future will bring us a 'clash of civilizations' (Huntington 1993) or, on the opposite end, a global generalization of liberal democracy and economic liberalism (Fukuyama 1992), possibly leading to a 'globalization of nothing' (Ritzer 2004) where everyone eats the same hamburgers (Ritzer, *The MacDonaldization of Society*, 1993)[15] and spends his days in the same non-places such as shopping malls or Las Vegas?

If we wish to avoid war, and if we value cultural diversity as much as biological diversity of species, then multiculturalism is our only option for the future.

13.6.4 Diversity

This is only a brief note on the complex issues involved in working in an environment that is culturally (or sexually, or age-wise...) diverse. There is a whole body of literature on this topic, to which we cannot do justice here.

According to the well-know similarity-attraction hypothesis (Byrne 1971), the more similar people are, the more they will be attracted to each other. Using a different terminology, the concepts of Cultural Distance and Cultural Fit similarly predict that, the greater the cultural distance, the more difficult the Cultural Fit will be the (Chirkov, Lynch & Niwa 2005). On the basis of that, we may predict that it will be more difficult to work together with people who are from another culture, and therefore less familiar, than with people form one's own cultural group.

Nancy Adler argues that multicultural teams more often than not are indeed less effective than single culture teams.

> Multicultural teams have the potential to become the most effective and productive teams in an organization. Unfortunately they frequently become the least productive. [...] Culturally heterogeneous teams tended to be the most or least effective, whereas the homogeneous teams tended to be average [...]. What differentiates the most from the least effective teams? Why are culturally diverse teams either more or less effective than homogeneous teams but rarely equally effective?
>
> Highly productive and less productive teams differ in how they manage their diversity, not, as is commonly believed, in the presence or absence of diversity. When well managed, diversity becomes a productive resource to the team. When ignored, diversity causes process problems that diminish the team's productivity. Since diversity is more frequently ignored than managed [...], culturally diverse teams often perform below expectations and below the organization's norm (Adler 1992: 134-5, based on research by Carol Kovach).

So diversity may be an asset if properly managed, but even then multicultural teams encounter problems that homogeneous teams do not have to deal with. In the initial and final stages of the work, diversity makes the process more difficult. Initially, building trust and developing group cohesion will be more difficult in a multicultural team. In the final stage, reaching a consensus about the decisions to be made, and implementing these decisions (taking action), will also be more problematic. Between those two stages, however, there is a stage where ideas have to be put forward, solutions to problems have to be devised, and there the multicultural team exhibits a higher degree of creativity, facilitated by the divergence which is inherent in a multicultural group of people (Adler 1992: 137). A study by Ng & Tung (1998) also finds that culturally heterogeneous branches of a Canadian bank exhibit positive features (lower absenteeism, higher productivity and profitability) as well as negative ones (lower job satisfaction, lower organizational commitment and workplace coherence, higher turnover rates) when compared with homogeneous branches.

In brief, working in a multicultural environment is not always easy, and it may not be everyone's piece of cake. Diversity in the workplace is economically neither always more efficient, nor less efficient: that depends on the process involved, and it may vary depending on the different stages in the process also. In some cases, the cost of having a culturally diverse workforce may well be greater than the benefits, because of the higher difficulty with co-ordination and decision making (Palich & Gomez-Mejia 1999).

Having multicultural contacts should not be an aim in itself, an objective that should be equally applicable to all people who work in the company or the organization. Working in a multicultural environment may be a question of necessity in many cases (when you are working in an export-oriented company or in an international organization, you won't be able to do without), a question of choice for those among us (such as the author of this book) who positively enjoy the diversity, unpredictability and challenge of a multicultural environment and consider it an enrichment of their own life.

Notes

1. The school of Salamanca on the other hand, with theologians including Francisco Vitoria and Luis de Molina, argued that American Indians were a third species of animal between man and monkey, "created by God for the better service of man" (Watson 2005: 446).
2. This is not to say that ethnocentrism as a prevailing attitude is limited to Western cultures. In fact, quite a few cultures in the world tend to see themselves as being superior to all others.
3. Just as Einstein's relativity theory or quantum mechanics does not prevent us from applying Newtonian physics in almost all cases in everyday life, and beyond.
4. If there is a perceptual core that remains fairly stable cross-culturally, this perceptual core is even more stable within a given culture. I am in clear disagreement here with Western post-modernists who would contend that 'anything goes', that, any text for instance, can be interpreted as being about anything you like. The *Divina Commedia* is not a text about motorbike repair! (Though some postmodernists no doubt might maintain that it could be construed as being just that).
5. As I criticize various positions and ideas of Blommaert and Verschueren here and elsewhere in this book, maybe I should emphasize, to avoid all misunderstanding, that there are also numerous positions of those two authors with which I agree; the same is true for Pinxten.
6. See Verluyten 1999 for a fuller treatment of the issue of cultural bias in publications by specialists in intercultural communication.
7. Many other, often hidden cases of cultural bias can be found in the program, and sometimes they can be correlated to cultural characteristics of the United States as these are described elsewhere, for instance to the position of the USA with respect to Hofstede's dimensions. I gave a full account of this at the ENCODE conference in Saint Gallen, Switzerland, 1995.
8. But also others, in a less explicit way, as Blommaert & Verschueren (1992) have shown.
9. Blommaert and Verschueren's denial of cultural differences is itself an example of a homogenization attempt.
10. Equating one language with one 'nation' is a farily recent, mainly 19th century phenomenon. Throughout European history, language has never been a strong ethnic marker (Wickham 2009: 100).
11. Blommaert & Verschueren rightly talk about *problematization,* i.e., turning something rather unproblematic into a problem, or creating a problem where there was none before.
12. Sharia is a complete and complex judicial system, on a par with the Napoleonic code or civil law. I cannot do justice to it here, but let me just say that it is *not* about cutting off the hand of every thief.
13. A the time the first women entered the police force, vestimentary allowances were made for them: they wer allowed to wear skirts rather than the until then obligatory pants. Why then is it so difficult to extend a similar measure to other groups?
14. I disagree with Evanoff (2004) who claims that cultural relativism also prevents criticism and change from the inside. If I am a member of a club, and in particularly of a club with democratic rules, I am entitled to argue in favor of changing some of the rules of that club, in a way an outsider is not.
15. Some French intellectuals and artists such as the Goncourt brothers and the painter Eugène Delacroix expressed concern about the 'Americanization' of France in the 19th century, with 'industry taking precedence over art', 'everything being up for sale' and a private firm erecting a building for the *Exposition Universelle* (Higonnet 2002: 356).

Chapter 14
Adaptation strategies: who should adapt to whom?[1]

Figure 32. The *Thai Orchid* restaurant in Tehran, with the Thai statue wearing a headscarf (the *Bangkok Post*, 24 March 2008).

14.1 An often ignored issue

There exists a substantial body of literature on *acculturation*, i.e., the adaptation process of migrants and sojourners who move to a new country and culture. But curiously, the more punctual, short-term adaptation strategies of businesspeople are seldom addressed in a systematic manner in most of the standard textbooks and manuals in intercultural communication.

The item *adaptation* does not even figure in the index of widely adopted texts such as Adler (1992), Varner & Beamer (1995) or Victor (1992); nor does *acculturation*. In 2006, for a presentation at a conference, I examined twenty-nine standard books on intercultural communication; in none of these, the issue of who should adapt to whom was addressed.

Consider the research as we described it in this book: most of it is *cross-cultural* rather than *intercultural*. Hofstede, d'Iribarne and the like describe different cultures comparatively; but their main focus is not on questions such as:
- If I meet someone from a different culture, how do I cope with that?
- What is my best strategy in an intercultural negotiation process: should I adapt to them, expect them to adapt to me, or do nothing out of the ordinary?

> [This is] one of the most important, but rarely addressed aspects of leadership: the question of how to best manage the interaction between leaders and managers who are culturally different. Very little research exists to address this question, which is a very salient issue for managers faced with a culturally diverse workforce (Thomas 2002).

The reasons for this gap in our research have to do with methodology. It is relatively straightforward to, say, organize a survey involving respondents from different cultures. But how do I study whether, in a negotiation for instance, adapting to the other party enhances my chances of success, or just the opposite? Which empirical set-up will allow me to answer this question scientifically?

The similarity-attraction hypothesis we mentioned above (Byrne 1971) suggests that two negotiating parties which are (culturally) similar to each other may be more successful than two parties that are more dissimilar. Thus, Brett & Okumura (1998) found that US-Japanese intercultural negotiations achieved lower gains than US-US intracultural and Japanese-Japanese intracultural negotiations. However, there is conflicting evidence concerning this hypothesis. In some cases, monocultural joint ventures or joint ventures between similar cultures are found to be more sucessful than more multicultural ones; but in some other studies, the opposite conclusions are reached (for an overview, see for instance Kealey e.a. 2005).

On the basis of purely theoretical arguments we might think that, if I try to become more similar to the other party (i.e., if I try to adapt to them), this will improve my chances of success. But there is little, if any, empirical research to substantiate this claim.

> Adapting to the behavioral style of the other culture should be done with some caution. Prescriptions for effective negotiation that suggest adapting one's behavior to that of the other participant's culture are common. For example, Weiss (1994) suggests that negotiators have several options as to what behavioral style to use depending on the cultural knowledge of the parties involved. In general, the model suggests adapting to the party with the least cultural knowledge of the other, or in cases of low knowledge by both, employing a mediator. *Although adaptation may have a positive effect based on similarity-attraction, there is substantial evidence that high levels of both linguistic and stylistic adaptation lead to less positive responses.* That is, there might be some optimal level of cultural adaptation, which is difficult to recognize until it has passed (Thomas 2002; my italics).

The few studies about optimal adaptation strategies I am aware of are based in a methodology that is so shaky as to be very unreliable. For instance, Francis (1991) studies the response of Americans to the behavior of 'Japanese and Korean business people' in three scenarios: the Asians substantially adapt to a presumably American negotiating style, or moderately adapt, or do not adapt at all. The problem is, the Korean and Japanese businesspeople are her American students, simulating the Korean and Japanese behavior in the three scenarios, and then the response of other American students to this is described.

14.2 Some preliminaries and a research program

For a better understanding of adaptation strategies businesspeople may use in intercultural encounters, we would need (at least) the following modules:
- A *typology* of adaptation strategies
- A list of *predictive factors* which determine the likely outcome of the adaptation process
- An *evaluation module* which assessed the outcome of the adaptation process in terms of its *appropriateness for success* in business encounters.
- In this final chapter I sketch a preliminary outline of each of these three modules.

14.2.1 A typology of adaptation strategies

As a first typology of adaptation strategies, I propose the following major types, which I shall briefly develop in turn.
1. No communication ('quit')
2. Communication without adaptation (for various reasons)
3. Bilateral adaptation (compromise)
4. Unilateral adaptation.

14.2.2 No Communication

'Quitting', or refusing the intercultural encounter itself and the communication process it entails, may at first seem inappropriate in all cases. There is no a priori reason, however, that the intercultural communication process is always possible or advisable. Suppose a European company is considering one of its female executives for an assignment as head of a negotiating team they will send to a country where gender roles are not what they are, at least in theory, supposed to be in most Western cultures, and where sending a female head of a delegation will undoubtedly cause some problems. The business woman, and her company, are faced with two basic options, after assessing the financial risk to the company and the emotional risk to the person involved:
a. sending the female person anyway
b. abandoning the idea of sending a female head of delegation to that country.

Who is going to blame them if they decide that, all things considered, the first option risks being too costly both in human and in business terms? When asked, most of my European and American students and other audiences in fact prefer option *b* in the case at hand.

It is not difficult to think of other cases where the values and/or practices of two cultures are incompatible to the extent that the best course of action is to steer clear of intercultural encounters. I see nothing morally wrong with this option. Of course nowadays many countries are in themselves multicultural to an extent that sealing oneself off from most contacts with other cultures may be impossible as well as outright absurd; but the 'quitting' option may still be the preferred alternative in certain specific cases.

14.2.3 Communication without adaptation

No need

Contrary to what many might think, there are numerous instances where smooth intercultural communication is possible without any (mutual or unilateral) adaptation. A Western businessman who travels to Saudi-Arabia is unlikely to adopt the Saudi dress code; in fact, it would seem quite bizarre, and certainly be inappropriate, if he did; and perhaps it is even illegal.[2] The Western suit he wears may cause some minor discomfort (it may be too hot, uncomfortable to sit in certain positions, etc.), but it does not hamper the communication process between the differently dressed interlocutors in any major way.

As high a degree of awareness as possible of intercultural differences is needed anyway in all cases (and, therefore, previous intercultural training) in order to avoid attribution mistakes; in many instances, this may be sufficient. A loud voice (such as that of many Westerners, or Africans even more) will be interpreted in several South-East Asian countries (Japan, Thailand) as a sign of aggressiveness and vulgarity; conversely, Westerners may attribute shyness, vagueness or lack of determination to the soft voice of a Thai or Japanese person. With the necessary intercultural training, both parties will become aware that their original interpretation (attribution) is mistaken. Adaptation is then not really needed, and both parties may continue to communicate with the loudness of voice they are accustomed to.

No willingness

In certain cases where a unilateral adaptation strategy might be the most advantageous for doing business, the party or person may be unwilling to adapt and take over foreign practices or values. A Western businessperson may certainly be at an advantage for doing business in some Muslim countries if he/she converts to Islam; yet instances of religious conversion as an adaptation strategy in business are rare or non-existent (at least nowadays; this has not always been so in the past). In the case of deep-seated cultural values, the willingness to adapt will be low. At the level of practices also, a person may, for instance, be unwilling to try new kinds of food, even if he/she is well aware that the refusal will make an unfavorable impression upon his host.

Impossibility

In many instances, a person will be, quite simply, incapable of adapting to the other's culture, even if he/she would be quite willing to do so. If I travel to China,

I would love to express myself in Chinese; the only thing is, I never learned to speak it, and that makes any attempts to do so futile. Automatic, subconscious behavioral features may also prove nearly impossible to change, particularly in the case of the businessperson we are considering here, who travels to the foreign country for a relatively brief period of time. Such features include the amount of eye contact one establishes during a conversation, backchannelling frequency and style, and many more. Again, awareness of these intercultural differences is crucial in order to avoid attribution mistakes. The need for adaptation may or may not be felt, but even if it is, changing one's behavior (or values) may prove impossible. Can I really turn my average eye contact in a conversation back from 35% to 15% when I get off the plane in Japan?

14.2.4 Bilateral adaptation: compromise

Bilateral adaptation, in the form of a compromise solution, may be the most natural outcome of the intercultural encounter for certain points. Suppose the culturally defined interpersonal distance between two interlocutors is clearly different: your Thai partner may feel most comfortable standing at approximately 80 cm from you, while you would tend to stand at about 60 cm from him. In that case, a compromise solution (which may or may not centre around the mathematical average, 70 cm) may impose itself. Here also, awareness of what is going on will be needed in order to avoid attribution mistakes (ascribing an erroneous interpretation to the other person's behavior). Similarly, if the French businessperson expects an extended, two-hour lunch before the actual negotiation, and his Dutch counterpart would favor having a cheese sandwich on a paper plate and some coffee in a plastic cup at a corner of the desk in the office, a compromise may be to take the French person out for a light lunch in a nearby restaurant (Merk 1986).

14.2.5 Unilateral adaptation

Unilateral adaptation is perhaps the adaptation strategy most people think of first when the issue is raised: who will adapt to whom, and why. Of course, examples of (voluntary or forced) unilateral adaptation abound in real life: non-native speakers expressing themselves in English, Japanese shaking hands for greetings, Africans adapting to the oppressing time constraints of the Western world, devout Muslims trying to function normally in secular states where women (as well as men, in fact) appear to be dressed in the most indecent ways, and so forth.

It seems to me, however, that unilateral adaptation must by no means always be the most common or the most frequent outcome of intercultural encounters. In reality we are likely to witness a complex mix of the four strategies described above, but I would stress in particular that, contrary to what many of us might think at first, there are numerous instances where intercultural communication can proceed smoothly without adaptation, provided the awareness of intercultural differences has been built up sufficiently to avoid attribution mistakes.

14.3 Predictive factors

As said above, a lot more research needs to be carried out in order to understand what determines the actual outcome, in terms of adaptation, of an intercultural encounter. The literature on acculturation may help business communication scholars in defining some of the factors that clearly play a role; others are specific to business encounters. We only mention a small number of basic determining factors here.

- *Numerical majority – minority.* Other things being equal, the minority will tend to adapt to the majority more than the other way around. When attending a multilateral meeting where the vast majority of the participants are able to express themselves in English, even if they are not native speakers, it will be hard for an Argentinean to insist on carrying on the meetings in Spanish. In fact, this may well be impossible, and it can be predicted that adapting to the majority is the only viable option in many cases.
- *Dominant – dominated relations.* The numerical factor we just described is only one instance of a situation where one group dominates the other. A dominance relation may be established on the basis of historical, cultural or other factors regardless of numbers. During the colonial period, sometimes extremely small groups of Europeans dominated the local population in colonized countries: the colonial administration of Nyasaland (Malawi) employed ten European civilians and two military officers, plus seventy Sikh soldiers, to rule over a territory of 1-2 million inhabitants (Reader 1998: 573). Needless to say, adaptation went nearly exclusively in one direction. The dominant mode of doing business today remains Western (or Anglo-Saxon, or American), and the way an international meeting or encounter that involves participants from different cultures is carried out nowadays is likely to resemble more a monocultural American meeting than a monocultural Vietnamese or Bolivian meeting. Even those non-Western cultures that are most successful in the global economy accept to a large extent that in international encounters, the prevailing style will be American. Nothing guarantees, of course, that this will remain so forever.
- *Physical location.* A lone person or a small delegation arriving in a foreign country is more likely to adapt, to varying degrees, to the local culture than the locals are likely to adapt to the visitors. Here again, this is only true all other things being equal, and other factors may interfere with this one, as the example from colonization above illustrates.
- *Buyer – seller relation.* All else being equal a seller is more likely to adapt to his potential customer than vice-versa, for obvious reasons. The degree to which a seller is willing to 'go out of his way' in order to satisfy the buyer is probably in itself culturally defined: it is, presumably, substantially higher in Japan than in most European countries, for instance.
- *Perceived need or possibility.* The perceived need or possibility to adapt may not coincide with the real need or possibility; yet it is the former that will determine the likelihood of adaptation taking place. A person may believe, mistakenly, that there is no need to learn Chinese for a given assignment, and therefore not start learning that language. He or she may also believe, mistakenly or not, that Chinese is nearly impossible to learn within a reasonable time, and not make a start learning it because of that.

- *Perceived cultural distance.* This admittedly vaguely defined factor needs further exploration (the same can of course be said of all the other factors I mentioned). It seems to me, however, that there are clear cases where this factor plays a role. There was a good deal of acceptance, and little or no aversion that I am aware of, when ostrich and antelope steaks started appearing in Belgian supermarkets in the 1990s. Crocodile meat was also attempted, but it vanished rather quickly from the shelves of the supermarkets I go to. And I can hardly imagine that caterpillars and grasshoppers, also widespread and delectable foodstuffs, could have made their way into my supermarket with the same ease. Presumably, the reason is that ostrich or antelope fall into, or are closer to, alimentary categories Europeans are familiar with (birds, four-legged grazing animals, red meat, ...), while the categories of edible reptiles (unlike amphibians: frog legs are widely sold) and insects has no members for Belgians, and is perceived as much more remote from any familiar, previously accepted foodstuffs than the ostrich or antelope.

14.4 Evaluating adaptation strategies

The fact that a given adaptation strategy is perhaps the most common does not, of course, make it necessarily the most appropriate or felicitous. Any account of adaptation processes is therefore in need of an *evaluation module* that is capable of assessing to what extent a given course of action will lead to a desired, appropriate or felicitous outcome. The primary criterion of the evaluation process is different in a business setting from what it is in society at large. In the literature on acculturation of humans and groups, the main criterion for assessing success or failure of the acculturation process is the psychological and social well-being of the individual(s) involved. An acculturation process where most migrants end up feeling miserable and forcibly isolated from the social texture of their host country will be considered a failure; one where both the migrants and the hosts end up with a feeling of psychological and social well-being will be considered a success.

In a business setting, however, the success or failure of the intercultural encounter that took place is most likely to be assessed primarily in terms of business itself. An intercultural negotiation that leads to the signing of a contract that is beneficial for the corporations involved will be considered a success, even if the parties involved felt miserable and frustrated most of the time because of the food, the habits, the communicative style or the values of the others. Conversely, a negotiating process where each party felt psychologically at ease with the others' cultural idiosyncrasies, and possibly even enriched by the experience, but where no deal was ever reached or no contract ever signed, will be considered a failure.

As said above, a vast amount of research needs to be carried out before we can even think of arriving at an adequate evaluation module for intercultural adaptation strategies. However, in my experience some types of inappropriate adaptation strategies are clearly attested and need to be included in any classification.
- *Unnecessary or unwanted adaptation.* As said above, adaptation is not always needed, nor is it always advisable to try and adapt. As a greeting, it may be better to shake hands with your Thai or Japanese counterpart, rather than trying

to master the intricate social stratification reflected in the *wai* or the bow, and still make a fool of yourself by doing it wrong (as many tourists do in Thailand). In most cases, Thai or Japanese people do not expect Westerners to wai or bow at all. The Japanese, in particular, do not necessarily appreciate that a *gaijin* (foreigner) attempts to act Japanese; they may call that person a *henna gaijin*, 'strange foreigner'.

- *Reciprocal adaptation, leading to reverse inadaptation.* This is the case where A adapts to B and B to A, the result being that both end up exhibiting the behavior of the other's culture, and possibly confronting the same incompatibility that was there at the outset, only reversed. It is the story of the Asian immediately opening the gift he just received from his American colleague (because he was told that this is the appropriate thing to do with Americans), while at the same time the American puts the gift *she* received from the Asian away without opening it (because she learned this is appropriate in most Asian cultures).
- *Overadaptation and hypercorrection.* In this case, persons make a fair attempt at adapting to the foreign culture, but they overshoot their target (overadaptation) or correct errors that were not really there in the first place (hypercorrection; I borrow the term 'hypercorrection' from linguistics, where it has a similar, though not necessarily identical or uniform meaning: see Crystal 1980: 176, Dubois et alii 1973: 246). The following is a typical example of a hypercorrection error. In 1993 a sign in my Bangkok hotel room read, rather meaninglessly: HAVE A PRESENT STAY (in 1995 it was corrected to the intended 'Have a pleasant stay').

Figure 33. A welcoming sign on the desk of a hotel room in Bangkok.

- The mistake Thai people normally make is to replace r with *l*: rice becomes *lice*, etc.; but here, the mistake went the other way: the *l* of *pleasant* was turned into an *r*. The most likely explanation is that the author of the incorrect sentence knew that Thai people often mistakenly replace *r* by *l* in English, and that, therefore, he assumed that the pronunciation *pleasant* must be an error of his for *present* (moreover, the latter word may be more familiar than the former).

He therefore decided to replace *pleasant* by *present,* thus creating an error that was not really there in the first place.

As intercultural training programs become more common, inappropriate attempts at adaptation may also become more common. A few years ago I did a consulting job for the European headquarters of a Japanese firm, where approximately 70% of the office workers are Europeans of various nationalities, and approximately 30% are Japanese. Not surprisingly perhaps, there were communication problems between the two groups. Also expected was our finding that the vast majority of the complaints the Europeans had about the Japanese could be explained by the indirect, implicit, high context communicative style of the latter, as it has been described so often now in many publications. The Europeans felt that the Japanese were vague, never spoke out or expressed a clear opinion about anything, that it was impossible to know what they were really thinking, etc. To our surprise, however, some 20% of the complaints were exactly the opposite of what one would expect: Europeans felt the Japanese could be particularly impolite, rude and brutal. The most likely origin of this unexpected phenomenon appeared to lie in the intercultural training program the Japanese received before coming over to Europe. There they were told that, while in Europe, they needed to be much more direct, assertive, outspoken than they would ever be in Japan. The trouble is, they do not necessarily know where to stop, and they overshoot their target, becoming direct and outspoken to a degree that is unacceptable even in Europe.

Intercultural trainers are themselves partially responsible for this kind of inappropriate attempt at adaptation. All too often, intercultural differences are put in absolute terms ('the Japanese are indirect, high context; Westerners are direct, low context') rather than relative terms ('the Japanese *tend more* towards this, Westerners more toward that end of the spectrum'). Inappropriate, simplistic and damaging intercultural training programs do exist, and they may have a tendency to spread because they seem to offer what managers would like to believe is possible: the acquisition of intercultural competency in a short time, with no pains and minimal effort. It is what Hofstede (1996) calls the "fast food approach to intercultural diversity and communication", and it is the duty of academics to warn against this danger, while at the same time being willing to transform academic research findings into training programs that are appropriate for the business community (see also Verluyten 1997).

Needless to say, the road is still long before we arrive at a satisfactory account of intercultural adaptation strategies applied to business settings.

Notes

1. This chapter is based on Verluyten 1998a.
2. At many Indian universities on the other hand, Western female faculty member are expected to wear the sari.

Chapter 15
Globalization?

15.1 Convergence[1]

Theodore Levitt (1983) may have been the first author to have argued that, at least in the industrialized world, countries and cultures are growing closer together, and soon there will only be one global market, where people live similar lives and where the same products will be sold everywhere.

After all, is it not true that Americans, Europeans, Chinese and many others drink the same Coca-Cola, eat the same McDonald's hamburgers, wear Benetton sweaters and Nike shoes, drive their Toyota Corolla to work, use a similar personal computer equipped with Microsoft software in the office, and so forth?

But while it is true that there are some products that can be considered global, such as Coca-Cola, one very quickly runs into cultural differences.

Firstly, the conditioning of the product may differ depending on the environment in which it is sold. As Japanese refrigerators are smaller than European ones, and American refrigerators larger than both, the size of Coca-Cola bottles will need to be adapted to the local situation.

Sometimes the advertising campaign will need to be adapted to local customs and preferences. Kentucky Fried Chicken's main slogan in the United States is *It's finger-licking good!* This slogan only makes sense when you eat the fried chicken using your fingers, as is the case in most places where you will find KFC fast-food restaurants. In Thailand, however, it is not proper to use your hands when eating, and the Bangkok KFC restaurant offers knives and forks with the meal, which nearly everyone uses. But because of that, the slogan *It's finger-licking good* does not make sense either, and is not used in that country.[2] (Also, the company does not use its full name *Kentucky Fried Chicken* any longer but only *KFC*, because Americans, in particular, may associate the word *fried* with fat and cholesterol, and *Kentucky* with backwardness).

Figure 34. In Europe (left), this Roland McDonald is sitting in a position (with the sole of his shoe showing) that would be totally inacceptable in Thailand (right), where he is performing a *wai*.

There may be a need to adapt the product itself to local markets because of legal constraints. The amount of coloring that is permissible in soft drinks is limited in some countries to the extent that it makes Coca-Cola look grayish rather than brow.

The same product may also be positioned differently in the market depending on the country. A McDonald's hamburger is a cheap, everyday kind of food in the United States; it is slightly more expensive and probably not eaten with the same frequency, in Europe; and it may be a luxury item in certain other countries. In Manila, I saw a poor family having a wedding dinner in full wedding gown in a fast-food hamburger restaurant; for them that may have been the only occasion in a long time to visit a restaurant. The marketing strategy and advertising campaign for the same product may be different depending on the position of the product in the market. BMW builds (nearly) identical car models for the various European markets, but BMW acknowledges that the attitude of the owner toward the car is different in different European countries and that therefore, 'local marketing is necessary' (Kustin 1994).

A good example of a case where globalization of the position of a product was decided for ideological rather than for pragmatic reasons is to be found in Usunier 1996: 193-6. At one point the new management of the Parker Pen Company decides to globalize the marketing strategy for their products. While Parker pens had had a very different image in different countries, ranging from luxury fountain pens to inexpensive writing instruments, from now on the same advertisements were to be used all over the world, often against the advice and the wishes of local management in the different countries. Parker Pen's globalization strategy resulted in disastrous sales figures. The management was replaced, and a more pragmatic, flexible approach to marketing the product internationally was reintroduced. Meanwhile, Parker Pen has been taken over by Gillette, and it is now accepted in the company that tapping the power of global brands often requires acknowledging country differences and respecting local norms – thus strengthening, rather than weakening, the local country unit (Kanter & Dretler 1998).

The best mix between global and local can only be decided on a case-by-case basis. McDonald's is a good example of combining a global brand with recognizable, global products (the big Mac, the logo) and local adaptations: serving beer in Belgium, providing forks in Thailand, having lamb burgers in India, calling its hamburger 'beefburger' in Malaysia (in order to avoid the association with 'ham', i.e., pork), etc. (Magala 2005: 68-9, Smet 2002).

A product which was explicitly announced by its manufacturer as being global is the original Ford Mondeo/Contour.[3] The Ford Motor company spent US$ 6 billion to create a 'global car', one which can be sold successfully in markets around the world. In order to achieve that, the product was also designed on a global level. The design originated from four design centers (one in Italy, one in Germany, and two in the United States), and a Cray supercomputer was purchased to allow engineers on either side of the Atlantic to work on drawings simultaneously. The car's V6 engine, its automatic transmission, gear box and the air-conditioning system were engineered in the US, with most of the others parts and their overall integration originating from Ford Europe. The car was to be sold in 59 countries around the world. Even so, experts express criticism about (a) the high price of the product (Chrysler spent US$ 1.6 billion developing a popular new car for the US market, as against US$ 6 billion for the new Ford) and (b) the time it took to develop (6 years, as against 2-4 years normally). What is of interest from the intercultural side is that, while most of the 'invisible' components of the car (underbody, suspension, powertrain) are common to the US and the European versions, significant changes were made to the visible parts in order to adapt these to differences in taste between Europeans and Americans. The name of the car itself was changed: it is called Ford Mondeo in Europe and was Ford Contour (discontinued in 2000) in the USA. In fact, eventually the only external items the Mondeo shared with the Contour were the windscreen, front windows, front mirrors and door handles (Wikipedia, article 'Ford Contour').

15.2 Divergence

There are clear signs that globalization itself triggers a reaction in the opposite direction.

Research by André Laurent (reported in Adler 1992: 59) shows that working together in one multinational company *magnifies* cultural differences rather than reducing them. Berry (2008) also present evidence that intercultural contact leads to increased identification with one's own cultural community, and that therefore cultural convergence can no longer be assumed.

> The globalization of culture is likely to b a self-defeating phenomenon. Whenever people get involved in big entities, they reach for the comforting familiarity of their local, regional or national roots. [...] If peoples of the

whole world ever do come to think of themselves as sharing a single global civilization, it will be a civilization of a very heterogeneous kind, dappled with differences from place to place (Fernández-Armesto 2001: 465).

In product development also, companies feel compelled to modify their product to local needs and tastes when they fear that launching a standard, global product would cost them market share.

As we have seen, Ford's attempt to launch the Mondeo as the first global car was not carried out in its entirety, nor was it particularly successful, as the model was discontinued in the US in 2000.

Honda went from having one Honda Accord and one Honda Civic model which was sold all over the world, to having at least two very different models for different markets, in particular the USA and Europe. This is costly in terms of loss of economies of scale; still, Honda felt it was necessary because of the differing tastes of customers in different countries concerning cars.

Figure 35a.   The Honda Accord 2008 in the USA (left) and in Europe (right).

Figure 35b.   The Honda Civic 2010 in the USA (left) and Europe (right).

Adaptations to different markets abound, whether slight or far-reaching. The grille and the back of the late 1990s Asian Toyota Corona were different from the Toyota Carina, its equivalent in Europe. The 1994 Toyota Carina added the letter 'E' to its name and was presented as the first genuinely European Toyota, developed in Britain, whereas in fact, it looks almost identical to the Asian Toyota Corona. (Meanwhile, the name has been changed from 'Carina' to 'Avensis' because of another cultural consideration: 'Carina' means something like 'little darling' in Italian, and this was considered too effeminate for the name of the car).

Whether the marketing strategy stresses the cultural specificity or the global character of the product is not necessarily related to the global or local character of the product itself.

Even with the most global products on earth, cultural considerations are essential in their development, their adaptation and their marketing because "widespread diversity in consumer preferences and tastes exists within and across national boundaries" (Akaah, quoted in Kustin 1994). For bed linen, a product that may seem fairly easy to standardize in order to achieve economies of scale, the majority of the major UK manufacturers "engage in some form of product modification" (size, packaging and labeling, design, color – not including legal constraints) even for export to EU countries and Norway (Kustin 1994).

Moreover, along with these more or less global products, there are many other products which are even more culturally bound: many foodstuffs and drinks, cosmetics, clothes, interior decoration items, household appliances, etc., stand absolutely no chance of being sold if they are not adapted to the local markets whenever need be.

In Asia, cosmetics typically search for association with *whiteness:* white skin, purity, etc. This marketing strategy would be certain to fail in Europe, where people value suntanned skin.

Figure 36. Cosmetics in Asia: 'white' products and brands (La Neige, i.e. 'snow'), unknown in Europe.

In the field of communicative styles (negotiation style, non-verbal communication, etc.), there is even less of any discernible trend toward globalization than in the field of products. Intercultural considerations are not close to being wiped off the face of the earth through the supposed progress toward globalization (see also Hofstede 1998).

In fact the whole globalization movement may itself trigger an opposite movement, towards 'fragmentation and singularization, especially in the area of consumption' (Usunier 1998: 22).

The more sophisticated a market becomes, the more likely people are to insist on having products that are specifically adapted to their needs. When the first refrigerators were commercialized in the 1930s, they represented such a wonderful innovation (keeping your food products cooled in the middle of the summer, without ice!) that everyone who could afford it would want one. The manufacturers could get away with selling one model worldwide, and this lasted until the 1950s at least. Some of those familiar-looking 1950s refrigerators are still in use today.

Figure 37.   1950s: the last 'global' refrigerator.

Nowadays, refrigerators have diversified into at least three distinct types of models, as F38 illustrates.

Figure 38.   Divergence: typical refrigerators today in the USA (side by side, with ice dispenser), Europe (freezer on top) and Asia (same model available in different colors).

In addition, many Koreans have a second, *kimchi* refrigerator in their home for their preserved pickled vegetables, a product that is not sold elsewhere.

To sum up, phenomena of convergence and divergence happen simultaneously in our present-day world; cultural differences in general show no signs of disappearing from the face of the earth in the foreseeable future.

15.3 Cultural features and economic growth

One question is often asked after people learn about cultural differences, such as those expressed in Hofstede's dimensions or otherwise: which position is better? Is it better to have high Power Distance, or low Power Distance? High or low individualism? Etc.

The simple answer to this question is: there is no simple answer, or even, perhaps no answer at all. Better for what, in any case? The discussion below will center on economic success, but of course this is by no means the only criterion one could use, nor is it even the most important one in my eyes.

To Hofstede, a culture's specific position on one of his dimensions may be an asset for certain types of economic activity, a liability for others. Thus large Power Distance may be an asset for activities where discipline is more important than personal responsibility (such as an army, perhaps), and small Power Distance for activities where it is the other way round. Similarly, low Individualism will go together with qualities such as a high degree of corporate loyalty and employee commitment, but, on the other hand, high Individualism will be an asset when mobility is more important. Low Uncertainty Avoidance is an asset when research and innovation prevail (they entail a high degree of unpredictability), high Uncertainty Avoidance may be an asset for activities where precision is most important. Higher Femininity may lead to better customer-orientation and personal service; Masculinity, with its emphasis on performance, competition and growth may be an asset for efficient mass production, heavy industry and bulk production, where producing the most at the lowest possible cost is more important than tailoring the product to customer needs (Hofstede 1991: 240).

Hofstede usually refrains from formulating judgments about culturally defined values, but in some cases he does, and in my view his line of reasoning is unconvincing and spurious.

On the basis of his Uncertainty Avoidance dimension, Hofstede draws the conclusion that

> ...people from some cultures will cooperate more easily with foreigners than others. The most problematic are nations and groups within nations which score very high on uncertainty avoidance, and thus feel that 'What is different, is dangerous.' (Hofstede 1991: 237).

If this were true, international co-operation across cultural barriers would be a very serious problem in high Uncertainty Avoidance countries such as Portugal, Belgium, France or Spain, and we would have to detect a marked difference, a far as intercultural understanding and co-operation goes, between these and low Uncertainty Avoidance countries such as India, Great Britain or Ireland. I can see no trace of such a marked difference.

In the same vein, Hofstede states that

> [a]lso problematic is the co-operation with nations and groups scoring very high on power distance, because such co-operation depends on the whims of powerful individuals. In a world kept together by intercultural co-operation, such cultural groups will certainly not be forerunners. They may have to be left alone for some time until they discover they have no other choice but to join (1991: 238).

Is intercultural co-operation with Brazil (PDI score 69) really much more difficult than with Argentina (PDI score 49)? Or is there such an obvious difference in this respect between France (68) and Belgium (65) on the one hand, and Switzerland (34), Finland (33) or Austria (11) on the other? Again I cannot even detect a vague trend in that direction.

The discussion is particularly interesting in the light of attempts to explain the recent economic success of so many Asian countries, as against Africa for instance. In terms of GDP per capita, in 1960 Senegal or Ghana (and most other African countries) were substantially wealthier than South Korea, Thailand or India. In 2006 on the other hand, GDP per capita in South Korea is some 25 times higher than in Senegal and Ghana, in Thailand some 5-6 times, and even India went from having a GDP per capita in 1960 that was less than half that of the two African countries, to a figure in 2006 that is substantially higher than theirs (see also Reader 1998: 658).

Hofstede explicitly states that Long Term Orientation, his 'Confucian dimension', helps explaining the present economic success of certain Asian nations.

> The correlation between *certain* Confucian values and economic growth over the past decade is a surprising, even sensational finding (Hofstede 1991).

Not everyone agrees that Long-term Orientation in East and South-East Asia is a value system that finds its origins in the remote past. Yoshimura & Anderson (1997: 149) contend that the association between Japan and Long-Term Orientation is only fifteen years old, and that Japanese R&D is in fact more applied and less long-term. D. G. E. Hall (1995: 912), in his classic *History of South-East Asia*, mentions the low domestic savings rate, and the fact that

> [l]ong-term investment was alien to most South-East Asians, and the high expenditure on clearly short-term things such as ornaments and festivities which characterize the newly-independent states of the region [in the 1960s].

Yeh & Lawrence (1995) criticize the link, as Hofstede establishes it, between national culture and economic growth in Asia. Amartya Sen (2003) rightly points out that such arguments are only put forward *post hoc,* after the facts. In the year

1000 CE, no-one could have guessed that a few centuries later, Europe would start to dominate the world. In fact, the most developed and most powerful areas at that time were probably China and the Islamic world. It is only *after* Europe became dominant that attempts were made to explain this success (military and economic success, that is) in terms of 'European values' (or protestant values?) such as a drive to explore, innovate and re-invest. And it is only *after* Japan became the first non-Western country to achieve economic success on a par with (or above) that of Western countries that explanations were put forward which referred to the *bushido*, the code of honor of the samurai where the individual sacrifices everything for the good of the country. Now, with the more recent economic success of countries such as Singapore, Hong Kong, South Korea and more recently China, 'Confucian values' (thrift, order, ...) are the explanation; again post hoc. Besides, why then was Korea so poor until the last few decades? The Confucian values were already there! And what about Malaysia? Or the more recent success story of India? The bottom line is, no single set of cultural values can explain success, including economic success, which is the result of a complex set of factors including, perhaps, some cultural features, but also historical events, international and national politics, social issues, international finance, and much much more.

It is unfortunate that a thorough and objective study of cross-cultural differences in value systems such as that of Hofstede ends with a number of sweeping generalizations, only some of which I mentioned above. Some of Hofstede's 'speculations on political developments' (1991: 242-5) are equally spurious in my opinion, even if I will not discuss them here.

Notes

1. The theory of *convergence* includes the idea that the values and practices of two distinct cultural groups who are exposed to each other will converge over time at a rate that is dependent on a number of specified factors and in a proportion that also depends on certain factors, such as the respective size of both groups. Convergence theory is applied more often to large cultural groups, such host populations and and groups of migrants. For a short introduction, see Kincaid 1996; also Van Oudenhoven 2002: 159).
2. Unless stated otherwise, examples from Thailand, the Philippines, the USA, Africa and several others without references are based on my personal observations in the countries involved.
3. My account of this story is based on an article which appeared in the *Financial Times,* March 29, 1994, p.22.

Chapter 16
Further explorations

This book is meant to be a practical introduction to intercultural communication. If the reader now commits fewer intercultural mistakes than before, makes fewer misinterpretations and understands 'the other' a little bit better, I will have achieved the book's modest goals.

Of course, much more awareness, knowledge and skills should be acquired at a later stage. We have considered intercultural encounters in general, but particular fields should be studied depending on the person's needs. Below, we very briefly consider a few: intercultural negotiations, expatriation, cross-cultural management and marketing, and the need to study more extensively the specific countries and cultures one is going to have most contacts with (area studies). These short sections are only meant as an introduction to further study, and they contain some useful references to that end.

16.1 Intercultural negotiations

One of the most common as well as one of the most difficult intercultural communicative activities a businessperson is likely to enter into are international negotiations. Negotiation theory as such is beyond the scope of this book. Ever since the outcomes of the Harvard Negotiation Project started to be published, our views on successful negotiations have changed; see, in particular, Fisher & Ury's *Getting to Yes* (1981); also Fisher & Brown (1988), Ury (1991). We can now oppose 'traditional' negotiating style and 'new' negotiating style, which exhibit the following main characteristics respectively.

a. *Traditional negotiating style:* starts with defining positions (your asking price is one million, I offer you six hundred thousand), then bargaining occurs in an attempt to bring the opening positions closer together until an agreement is reached; is often confrontational and based on the idea of 'winning', even at the expense of the other party 'losing' the negotiation.

b. *New negotiating style:* no opening positions, focus on interests rather than on positions, a common search for objective criteria (that will help determine a fair price, etc.); higher emphasis on co-operation.

Note that the authors favor the new style over the traditional style, and co-operation over conflict, not because they want to make the world a better place, but because the objective evidence is that this usually leads to a better outcome of the negotiation for *you* (also in the long term).

The authors argue (convincingly, in my opinion) that contrary to what one might think at first glance, the co-operative attitude can be used even with difficult or uncooperative negotiating partners. If the sales representative who is trying to sell her machinery to you puts the asking price at US$ 250,000, rather than countering with a lower offer you will react with something like 'Please explain to me, Madam, how you arrived at this figure? Which criteria did you use to determine the price?' It is then difficult or impossible for the seller to refuse any explanation or dialogue.

The question remains whether this very rational, possibly very 'Western' approach to negotiations is applicable in different cultural settings or in international negotiations between cultures. Some contend it is not:

> The problems inherent in assuming a single, universally valid model of negotiation were demonstrated before the 1990-91 Gulf War, which followed the unprovoked Iraqi invasion of Kuwait. Roger Fisher, founder of the Harvard Program on Negotiation, whose Getting to Yes (written with William Ury) is a classic account of 'win-win' negotiating,[1] called in a series of newspaper articles for fair and sympathetic consideration of Saddam Hussein's reasonable needs and concerns. President Bush had to 'make clear to Saddam the ways in which Iraq will be better off withdrawing from Kuwait.' Iraq had 'legitimate' concerns that had to be addressed [...], and right to a 'fair process for dealing with its concerns.' Both Iraq and the United States, Fisher argued, had 'to try to convince the other of what ought to be done in the light of precedent, international law, or some other objective criterion. If agreement is reached, neither has given in to the arbitrary position of the other. Each can explain to his constituents why the result is fair.' Fisher's recommendations are strikingly incongruous and, indeed, culture-bound. His projection of Western concepts of fair play, negotiation by reasoned persuasion, due process, and equity onto the Iraqi dictator are inappropriate to the point of naïveté. 'Win-win,' designed for a domestic American market, was totally unsuited to the requirements of compelling the brutal Iraqi leader to withdraw his army of occupation from Kuwait. It merely repeated the initial, erroneous assumption underlying the policy of conciliation that had tempted Saddam into the invasion in the first place: the belief he was a reasonable statesman who would prefer a peaceful, compromise outcome to war (Cohen 1991: 216).

Of course the fact that a particular non-Western leader may not be open to a reasoned agreement cannot be taken as evidence that reasoned negotiations are necessarily inappropriate in international or non-Western settings. After all, Saddam Hussein can hardly be considered as representative of most non-Western political leaders any more than Hitler would be typical of Western leaders. Moreover, Fisher & Ury also argue in their publications that a negotiated agreement between two parties may not always be the best outcome, and that alternatives to a negotiated agreement must be considered at all times (develop what they call your BATNA, 'best alternative to a negotiated agreement'). That does not prevent the *attempts* to arrive at a negotiated agreement that is acceptable to both parties to proceed; and under threat of war, any such attempt is surely worthwhile. The question is not whether the new approach is always successful or not, the question is whether the traditional approach *or* the new approach is more likely to be successful in international settings. I see no argument in Cohen's text that convinces me to reject the new approach offhand in intercultural situations; the question remains open.

Up to now, however, most approaches to international/intercultural negotiations stick to the traditional style (for example, Kremenyuk 1991). The synthesis between the new view on negotiations put forward by Fisher & Ury on the one hand and intercultural settings on the other remains to be made.

16.2 Expatriation

16.2.1 The failure rate of expatriates

Expatriate managers are facing a variety of stressful challenges, from (lack of) language proficiency and the need to understand subtle, non-verbal cues to ethical dilemmas (Cassiday 2005). Understandably, some of them cannot cope with all this and decide to return to their home country prematurely. The rate of expatriate premature return varies widely, but estimates are most often between 10-20% and 40% (figures based on a review of the literature in Deshpande & Viswesvaran 1992: 395-6). In addition, about half of those who did not return early may function below their normal capacities (ibid.; see also Kealey & Protheroe 1996: 143). The direct cost of one failed expatriate adjustment was estimated at approximately US$150,000 twenty-five years ago by Copeland and Griggs (1985). A more recent study by Selection Research International that was reported in the Belgian press *(Vacature,* 15 September 1996) also puts the failure rate of expatriates at between 10% and 40%, and the cost of one failed expatriation at between US$ 200,000 and 400,000 – figures that are consistent with Copeland & Griggs' earlier estimates.

These figures are no exaggeration, on the contrary. In Singapore, for instance, in the early 2000s, the rental for a house with a swimming pool was around 6,000-14,000 US$ a month, and a mid-sized car such as a Honda Accord cost 75,000 US$, plus some 17,500 US$ for the 'certificate of entitlement' (auctioned off by the government), the permit you need to buy before you are allowed to purchase a car. Add to that the cost of sending the children to an international school, having adequate health insurance for the family, and more. In a recent survey with 750 US, European and Japanese companies by Black & Gregersen, the failure rates are slightly lower (possibly because more European and Japanese companies were included) but still alarming: premature return rates are between 10% and 20%; one third of the expatriates who stay on do not perform up to expectations; one quarter of returning expatriates leave the company for a competitor, twice the turnover rate of those who did not go abroad (Black & Gregersen 1999: 53). Black & Gregersen put the cost of a fully loaded expatriate package at between US$ 300,000 and US$ one million a year.

European expatriates seem to fare better than their American counterparts (Lane, DiStefano & Maznevski 2000: 49), but for them also failure rates are high. The problem is not limited to commercial companies. The fastest growing category of expatriates nowadays are UN peacekeepers, numbering about 70,000 from some 70 providing countries, and operating in 17 host countries (1994 figures, quoted in Kealy & Protheroe 1996: 143); they also face serious intercultural misunderstandings and failures.

Clearly one failed expatriation costs the company or international organization much more than a fully-fledged training program would, or even than hiring full-time staff for intercultural training purposes. If such a training program manages to avoid *only one* failed expatriation, the company gets its investment in training back a manifold. Lack of intercultural awareness is of course not the only factor that explains expatriate failure, but there is widespread agreement that it is one of its principal causes. The problem is compounded by the fact that many major companies continue to select future expatriates primarily on the basis of technical competence, not on the basis of intercultural awareness and skills. Several companies still fail to offer adequate pre-departure training, either because they remain unaware of intercultural issues altogether, or because they believe training is not very efficient or cost-effective (Black & Mendenhall 1990, Kealy & Protheroe 1996). Deshpande & Veswesvaran, on the basis of a meta-analysis of the literature, conclude that their results

> provide support for the thesis that cross-cultural training has a strong and positive impact on cross-cultural skills development, cross-cultural adjustability, and job performance of individuals. This study provides the evidence that academicians need to support their belief that cross-cultural training is effective, and it should remove any doubts that corporate leaders have about the effects of cross-cultural training [of expatriate managers] (1992: 306).

The effectiveness of pre-departure intercultural training is also demonstrated by Black & Mendenhall (1990), Osman-Gani & Rockstuhl (2009), and many more.

16.2.2 Selection of appropriate candidates for expatriation

The first stage ought to be the selection of appropriate candidates for expatriation. As said above, all too often expatriates are selected on the basis of technical skills only, and their intercultural fluency is not taken into account. Inherent to this attitude is the SRC again: "many executives assume that the rules of good business are the same everywhere" (Black & Gregersen 1999: 53). This book has convinced the reader, I hope, that this is not so.

> [T]echnical skill is frequently the main reason that people are selected for open posts. But managers often send people who lack the ability to adjust to different customs, perspectives, and business practices. In other words, they send people who are capable but culturally illiterate.
>
> Companies that have a strong track record with expats put a candidate's openness to new cultures on an equal footing with the person's technical know-how (Black & Gregersen 1999: 56-8).

Black & Gregersen's research shows that companies who manage expatriation most successfully seek the following characteristics in their expatriates:
- A drive to communicate: extrovert, not afraid to speak a foreign language
- Broad-based sociability: not sticking to a small circle of other expats
- Cultural flexibility: openness to new food, etc.
- Cosmopolitan orientation: respect diverse viewpoints, live and let live
- Collaborative negotiation style.

There exist several tests which purport to assess the intercultural skills of future expatriates, usually based on the candidate filling out a questionnaire and then having the answers rated on a given scale. Some of them are so simple-minded that I have serious doubts about their validity. An alternative is to observe the candidates in real-life settings. Take them with you on a foreign assignment and observe their behavior:

> Do they approach the strange and unusual sights, sounds, smells, and tastes with curiosity or do they look for the nearest Pizza Hut? Do they try to communicate with local shopkeepers or do they hustle back to the Hilton? (Black & Gregersen 1999: 58).

Even at home, one can observe the behavior of potential expatriates when receiving foreign visitors, for example. For a good description of the complexities of the selection process, see Tung 1981; for the issue of female expatriates, see various articles by Nancy Adler, and also Lowe, Downes & Kroeck (1999).

16.2.3 Pre-departure training and repatriation training

Pre-departure training for future expatriates is available and cost-effective, and companies should make use of it. We cannot offer a description of such a program here, but below are a few points that should receive attention in all cases (see also Harvey 1997b, Selmer, Torbiörn & de Leon 1998).

All too often, training programs are limited to offering factual information about the country or region: climate, population size, politics, etc. While this is useful and necessary (as we will argue below), equally important is the kind of awareness-building that has been the focus of this book. People can and should be trained to develop a more open, flexible and appreciative attitude with respect to cultural differences, and learn how to avoid ethnocentric reactions, attribution errors and reliance on the SRC.

It is essential that the *spouse* (and children, if applicable) of the future expatriate be included in the training program. While abroad, the spouse will often feel even more isolated that the expatriate, because the spouse usually does not even have an occupation and responsibilities that may compensate for feelings of isolation and frustration. The problems of expatriation are even more intricate in dual-career couples (Harvey 1997a).

The adjustment processes and problems the expatriate faces once abroad have been studied extensively. Ward and others (1998) present an overview of the literature and argue against the popular view which represents adjustment as a U-curve process, with an initial period of enthusiasm and elation followed by a period of depression and frustration and ending with a period of stabilization at a given level of satisfaction and adjustment.

Upon returning from their assignment abroad, many expatriates experience 'reverse culture shock': they have difficulty re-adjusting to their home country. This problem is compounded by at least two factors. Firstly, returning expatriates may see their social status debased because they often lose some of the privileges they were entitled to in the foreign country: a large house, a car with a driver, maids and servants, etc.

More crucially, the skills they have acquired while abroad are often not properly appreciated in the company. Black & Gregersen quote the case of a senior engineer from a European electronics company who was sent to Saudi-Arabia on a four-year assignment, at a cost to his employers of about US$ four million.

> During those four years, he learned fluent Arabic, gained new technical skills, and made friends with important businesspeople in the Saudi community (1999: 60).

Yet upon his return none of this is appreciated, let alone put to use, by the company.

> Not surprisingly, the engineer left to join a direct competitor and ended up using the knowledge and skills he had acquired in Saudi Arabia against his former employer (ibid.).

In one case I am familiar with, a Belgian executive who returned from an overseas assignment did not even have a chair to sit on when he returned to the head office: everyone had forgotten that he was coming back!

16.3 International management

International management requires a number of competencies and skills of which intercultural communication is just one. International organizational behavior, international human resources management, international strategy, and more, are all beyond the scope of this book.

The best we can do is to refer the reader to the many introductions to this complex field, such as:
- Nancy Adler (4th edition, 2001), *International Dimensions of Organizational Behavior*
- Helen Deresky (7th edition, 2010), *International Management. Managing Across Borders and Cultures*
- Nigel Holden (2002). *Cross-Cultural Management*
- Henry Lane, Joseph DiStefano & Martha Maznevski (2000), *International Management Behavior*
- Richard Mead & Tim Andrews (2009), *International Management. Cross Cultural Dimensions*

- Susan Schneider & Jean-Louis Barsoux (2nd edition, 2002), *Managing Across Cultures*
- David Thomas (2002). *Essentials of International Management. A cross-Cultural Perspective.*

16.4 Cross-cultural marketing

The reader should be convinced by now that, when marketing a product internationally, all aspects of it should be re-examined and an assessment should be made of whether they are acceptable in the target culture(s), or not. This involves the product itself, but also its packaging (colors, size) and the way it is advertised.

16.4.1 Pictures and names

> An airline from the USA made a beautiful poster they wanted to use in an advertising campaign in Japan. It showed an attractive Japanese woman dressed in a silk kimono, reclining in a first class seat, and looking the photographer straight into the eyes. What the Americans saw is what I just described; in the Japanese perception, however, this woman could only be a prostitute.
>
> Fortis Bank, then the biggest banking company in Belgium, decided to stop giving piggy banks to children for fear of offending Muslims; they also dropped Knorbert the Piglet as a mascot for the bank.

In some cases, the product's name itself may be inappropriate.

> **Poland: a leather briefcase called 'Plastyk'**
>
> On a visit to Gdansk, Poland, I purchased a beautiful full leather briefcase of the highest quality at a fraction of what it would cost in Western Europe. The brand name, however, is *Plastyk*. That word means 'artist' in Polish, but most tourists will not know that. Fortunately, the name does not appear on the outside of the product. Who would want to carry a leather briefcase called 'plastic' around?
>
> **Japan: a White Elephant**
>
> A Japanese company manufactures batteries under the name *White Elephant*. They attempted to export these under the same name to South-East Asian and other countries, but to their surprise the name proved to be a serious handicap.

16.4.2 Colors, sounds and smells

The color spectrum is physically identical everywhere, but the 'same' color will be perceived differently depending on the culture. Doctor F. Rémy, who later became head of UNICEF, tells of an incident that happened while he was a medical doctor in Morocco (Rémy 1983). In the hospital run by French medical staff, as soon as patients checked in they were asked to undress and to wear a white hospital gown. It became clear that many patients hated this profoundly. The reason is that in Muslim countries, the body of the deceased is undressed completely and placed in a new, white piece of cloth. Where the French doctors saw a patient dressed in a white gown, the Moroccan patients saw themselves undergoing the rites reserved for the dead – hardly reassuring in a hospital setting.

> ### Thailand: white cement?
>
> A cement plant in Thailand is run almost entirely by Thai staff, including the general manager; the production manager, however, is American. One of the products the plant manufactures is a kind of cement used to cover the external walls of houses and buildings in Thailand. To this effect, powder is added to the cement to make it look white. In order to save money, the production manager's concern is to put in the least amount of powder necessary to make the cement look white. The company, however, gets several complaints from customers who feel that the cement they purchased is not white, but grey. When confronted with the issue, the management of the company decide to inspect a sample of the product together. All the Thai managers agree that the cement is not white but grayish; the American keeps insisting that it is white.

An American company committed a blunder by offering green company hats to a visiting Chinese delegation (Engholm 1991: 295): in China, a green hat is the symbol of adultery or cuckoldry.

According to Ferraro (1994: 31),

> before a laundry detergent – normally packed in a green box in the United States – would be accepted in certain parts of West Africa, the color of the packaging would need to be changed because the color green is associated with death in certain West African cultures.

> ### A Czech Bringing Colorful Gifts to China
>
> One of my Czech students shared the following story with me.
>
> During my stay in China I was invited many times by a Chinese family of three ladies living in two small rooms: an 85-year old mother and her two daughters aged 50 and 53. Once the old lady told me that I could be her 'son' which means that she and her family will help me anytime I would need anything.
>
> Before I left Beijing I decided to offer them presents that I had brought with me from Prague: colorful belts, which are being worn especially in Western Bohemia on costumes for special occasions such as festivals. I chose three belts, a blue one, a yellow one and a white one, and I did not care about which color I gave to whom.

> When I presented a belt to each of the three ladies, I could read in their eyes that something was wrong, but they did not say anything clearly. Only the 53-year old daughter asked me reproachingly: 'Why did I receive the yellow one?'
>
> Later, I asked a professor at the University in Beijing what had happened. Now I know I should have given the yellow belt to the mother and a red, pink, purple or blue belt to both daughters...

An extensive survey of the symbolic meaning of colors in a number of cultures has been carried out by Adams & Osgood (1973); see also Berlin & Kay's 1969 article, and Kay & Berlin's *World Color Survey* (2009). For instance, the color *red* elicits strong feelings in all cultures, because it is the color of human blood. But from there, its symbolic meaning may evolve to 'strength, vigor, life', or else to nearly the opposite, 'danger, death' – or sometimes both. Similarly, *blue* may have connotations of 'royalty', or 'cold', or perhaps both.

Perception of sounds is equally culture specific. Western refrigerators that seemed silent enough could not be sold in Japan because the Japanese perceived them as too noisy (presumably because the walls are thinner in Japanese houses; Ricks 1993: 22). Many Europeans like their car's engines to emit some sporty roar, while Americans prefer more silent cars.

Smells also may be perceived differently in different cultures. A smell that is perceived as 'fresh' in one culture, and might be used for a kitchen detergent, may well be associated with 'illness' in another culture.[2] David Ricks' *Blunders in International Business* (1993) lists many cases where marketing blunders result from assuming that people in a target culture will perceive things the same way as people in your home culture.

For further study on the topic of cross-cultural marketing the reader may wish to consult Usunier's *Marketing across Cultures* or some of Marieke de Mooij's publications; also the *Journal of International Marketing* and the *Journal of Global Marketing*.

16.5 Intercultural communication in general

The knowledgeable reader might point out that some well-known intercultural scholars have not been referred to in this book. There are, of course, various reasons for this, including ignorance by the author of this book; nowadays, it is absolutely impossible to know about everything that is being published, let alone read and study it.

As the focus of this book is on intercultural communication in business and international relations, publications may also have been left out because they do not directly relate to this field.

In any case, if some major publications and scholars have not been quoted here, the reader should by no means infer from there that they are unimportant or that I do not appreciate them.

Study of this field is incomplete without reading Gudykunst's work about cultural adjustment, Ting-Toomey's about conflict resolution, without knowing Bennett's models, and so much more that has not been touched upon here.

A classic reader (with articles) which will introduce the interested reader to the field of intercultural communication in general is Samovar & Porter (1997).

16.6 Area studies

While studying sometimes deep-seated intercultural differences, we should not lose sight that there is also a need to acquire factual knowledge about the country or region one is going to visit. I often present to my students the story of a European who made an appointment with his Indonesian sales representative in Jakarta on a Friday afternoon. To his surprise, when he arrives the Indonesian is not in the office and it seems that he is not coming back that day. Most students, after going through my course, rightly point out that perhaps the European suggested a date for the appointment over the telephone, to which the Indonesian is likely to respond positively even if he cannot make it on that date: above, we discussed the notions of face saving and saying 'yes' in detail. On the other hand, fewer students point out that Indonesia is a Muslim country (it has, in fact, the largest Muslim population in the world), and that therefore businesses are likely to close down (partially or entirely) on Friday afternoon: that is when the men go to the mosque to say their prayers. I went to my university's library and in less than fifteen minutes I found a book with the telling title: *Doing Business in Asia: the Complete Guide*. In the chapter on Indonesia, there is a section called *Work Schedule* where I read:

> Some businesses close at midday on Fridays in observance of Muslim worship (Dunung 1995: 223).

If it is so easy to find the factual information which could have avoided a costly mistake, involving the re-scheduling of an appointment in Jakarta, then why did the European businessman not bother to look it up before leaving? The answer is the same again: he relied on two instances of the SRC, in assuming that
a. to make an appointment, I suggest a possible date and the other party will answer 'yes' or 'no' depending on their availability
b. business days are the same all over the world: Monday through Friday.

The first error can be avoided through training in intercultural communication. In order to avoid the second error, I need as much information as I can get about the countries I am going to visit.

Sources for quick reference are books such as the one I quoted above; there are many of those. A few examples:
- Copeland & Griggs' *Going International* (1985)
- Harris & Moran's *Managing Cultural Differences* (1996)
- Dun & Bradstreet (1997)
- *Doing Business Internationally* (1997)

They all contain short descriptions of various countries, each being a couple of pages long. Brigham Young University in Utah publishes *Culturgrams,* four-page descriptions of salient cultural features of a given country. True, such descriptions are superficial and sometimes hastily written, as the authors attempt to cover many countries they do not have in-depth knowledge about (I criticized some of them myself, in Verluyten 1993). But reading four pages about the country you are going to is better than reading nothing at all, and it may allow you to avoid some errors you might otherwise make. Some websites, such as the *World Factbook* on the CIA website (www.cia.gov) may also be consulted.

If you have more time, document yourself more seriously. This applies in particular to expatriates or to others who intend on spending prolonged periods of time in a country. In-depth information about a country should include the points in the following list, which can be used as a checklist for the reader (partially based on Martin & Chaney 1992).

1. *History:* main historic periods, salient events, heroes people are proud of, monuments and statues, wars with neighbors or others, internal conflicts, violence
2. *Geography:* regions and cities, uneven economic development, cultural differences, scenic landscapes and tourist attractions
3. *Politics and economics:* political regime, main ideological tendencies, freedoms and human rights, economic policy and development, strengths and weaknesses; trade unions and lobbying groups
4. *Social structure:* social classes, social stratification or equality, power and prestige, poverty-wealth extremes, income distribution, age groups, minorities; housing
5. *Religion:* role of religion in business, major religion(s), religious minorities
6. *Languages:* official and regional languages, power and prestige of various languages, writing systems, use of English, Spanish or other transnational languages (Cantonese, Swahili, …), Creole and pidgin
7. *Art and literature, leisure, etc.:* outdoor and indoor sports, exercising, travel and recreation
8. *Legal system:* business and social law, holidays and working hours, driving laws; nonwritten laws
9. *Communication:* telephone and fax systems (do they work?), access to e-mail and internet, roads (are they practicable?) and railroads, airline connections; radio and television, press
10. *Education:* schools and universities, contents of programs and teaching methods, degrees (the value and the prestige attached to them), academic titles; scientific research
11. *Family:* children, marriage and sex, old people, gender roles, relation parents-children
12. *Etiquette:* introduction and greetings, protocol; food and drink, restaurants, parties and entertainment; smoking habits, consumption of alcohol, drugs; dress codes for various occasions
13. *Work-related values:* position on Hofstede's dimensions, ethics
14. *Time and space*
15. *Communication patterns:* high/low context, negotiating style, silence, etc.
16. *Non-verbal communication:* eye contact, touching/non-touching, gestures, body posture
17. *Perception:* sounds and smells, colors and shapes

Unsurprisingly, you will find plenty of information about some countries, very little or next to nothing about some others. Japan was the object of numerous studies and books, for Western audiences, mainly in the 1970s and 1980s. Nowadays, the number of books being published purely about cultural aspects of doing business in China beats all the records.

A small selection of them, all published in the last 15 years or so:
- Tim Ambler & Morgen Witzel (2004), *Doing Business in China*
- Carolyn Blackman (1997), *Negotiating China. The whos and whys of successfully negotiating with the Chinese*
- Kevin Bucknall (2002), *Chinese Business Etiquette and Culture*
- Tony Fang (1999), *Chinese Business Negotiating Style*
- Ge Gao & Stella Ting-Toomey (1998), *Communicating Effectively with the Chinese*
- Huang Quanya e.a. (1997), *Business Decision Making in China* Scott Seligman (1999), *Chinese Business Etiquette*
- Mary Wang e.a. (2000), *Turning Bricks into Jade. Critical Incidents for Mutual Understanding among Chinese and Americans*
- Hu Wenzhong & Cornelius Grove (1999) , *Encountering the Chinese*
- Andrew Williamson (2003), *The Chinese Business Puzzle. How to Work More Effectively with Chinese Cultures*
- Y.H. Wong & Thomas Leung (2001), *Guanxi. Relationship Marketing in a Chinese Context*

The amount of information available seems directly related to the economic importance of a country in the contemporary world. Regrettably, information about certain countries and cultures will therefore be scarce or unavailable.

Notes

1. It is incorrect to associate the Fisher & Ury approach with 'win-win' negotiations. The 'win-win' approach is one variant of the 'traditional style', along with 'win-lose'. Both are based on principles that are very different from the innovative approach as it is proposed by the Harvard Negotiation Project [my footnote].
2. It has been described that Filipinos associate lemon smell with illness and therefore would dislike a detergent with lemon smell. In 1992 in Manila, however, none of the Filipinos I surveyed made this association between lemon and illness, which has possibly disappeared after people ceased trying to cure illnesses with lemon juice (as I recall they still did in Belgium in the 1950s).

Exercises

Chapter 1. Open your mind

In order to understand other cultures, you will have to drop some basic assumptions which are implicit in your way of reasoning and which may, unconsciously, seem unquestionable to you. That is the case in the following examples.

1.1 Connect the dots

Using four lines, connect the dots of this 3 x 3 grid. You must use a continuous series of *straight* lines, and may not lift your pencil off the paper as you connect the dots.

Got it? Now do the same thing using *three* lines, under the same conditions as above. You will have to drop an additional implicit assumption to do so.

● ● ●

● ● ●

● ● ●

1.2 Coca Cola

"Coca Cola" in the Thai language. Identify the thai characters *k (=c)*, *o*, *l* and *a*.

Coca Cola
โคคา โคล่า

1.3 "Amar no Miramar"

Where are we? Identify the language first! What is this billboard poster advertising for?

1.4 **Fancy dresses**

Open air market clothing stalls in a town in Thailand. But who are the fancy dresses in the righthand picture for?

1.5 Wooden sculptures in Ghana

What is the function of these man-size objects?

http://news.bbc.co.uk/2/hi/in_pictures/4215923.stm

1.6 **Water bags**

Bangkok, Thailand: plastic bags filled with water, at the windows of a student cafeteria at NIDA, a major university. What might the function of these plastic bags be?

Chapter 2   Know the World: Test your Knowledge

Coping with other cultures and becoming a better 'intercultural communicator' is impossible without knowledge about the geography, the history, the social and political structure of the various countries that make up our world.

Test yourself on the basis of the following 20 questions. Your score will give you an idea of the extent of your basic geographical and cultural knowledge. If it is below 10, you may have serious gaps in the knowledge you need to perform internationally.

"Test your knowledge" score sheet

Question	Your answer	Correct answer	Points: 1 or 0
1. Staple food			
2. Country			
3. Country			
4. Arrow			
5. Religion			
6. Country			
7. Country			
8. Country			
9. Brushes			
10. Country			
11. City			
12. Country			
13. Country			
14. Area in city			
15. City/region			
16. Country			
17. Message			
18. Country			
19. Country			
20. Country			
		TOTAL SCORE:	**/20**

2.1 A staple food in many countries

Identify this root. Find a couple of the different names is it known by.

2.2 Churches

In which country are we, and why?

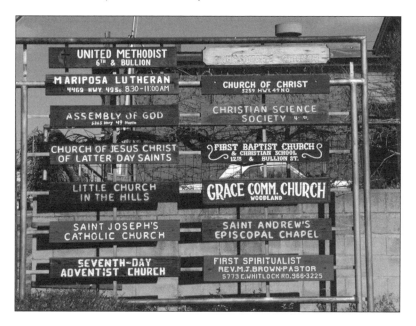

2.3 Orange and yellow

In which country are we, and why? There may be more than one reasonable answer.

2.4 A hotel room in Kuala Lumpur

Why is there an arrow painted on the ceiling, labeled "kiblat"?

Photograph Anne De Cort

2.5 Which religion is this a temple of?

2.6 In which country are we?

2.7 KFC (1)

The picture on the first page of the KFC website in two countries (2005): identify these countries

2.8 KFC (2)

2.9 Xi'an, China

What are all these brushes for?

2.10 **A reclining Buddha**

In which country are we?

2.11 **Architecture from 1960s**

Identify the country *and the city*. This is a tough one. You may assume that this type of architecture is typical of nearly the entire city you are trying to identify.

2.12 A cemetery in Essaouira, Morocco

The tomb of the bottom picture is inside the pavilion. What kind of cemetery is this?

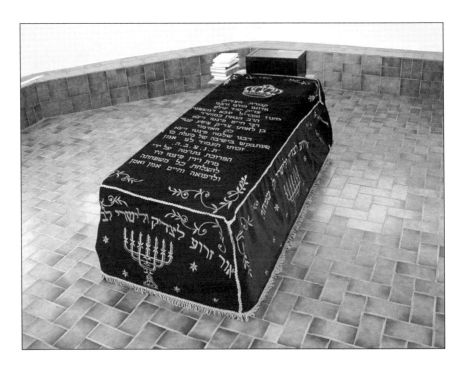

2.13 **Parkson department store**

In which country are we?

2.14 **A gateway**

Which area or neighborhood of the city does this gateway lead to? Subsidiarily, can you also identify the city?

2.15 **German-style architecture...**

... and a restaurant called *Abelshoffer;* but another one named *Au Pied de Cochon.* Where are we? Identify the city or the region.

2.16 Two languages: German and...

A bilingual sign explaining when the historic church is open to tourists. In which country are we?

2.17 Which message does this poster try to convey?

2.18 A house and a car

In which country are we?

Note: This country is wealthy: it has a GDP of US$ 35,750 (Sweden US$ 26,050, Japan US$ 26,940) (with PPP: what is that?). But the same country has a Gini index (what is that?) of 40.8 against Sweden 25.0, Japan 24.9 (2002-3 data).

2.19 The window display of a candy store

In which country are we?

2.20 **A shop called named 1453**

In which country are we?

Chapter 3 Observe and Analyze

Before attempting to understand cultural differences, one has first to see them. Obvious enough, but sometimes our SRC (self-reference criterion), i.e. our conviction that our own assumptions are 'normal', is so strong that we *fail to notice* differences. Once you have noticed that things are different, ask yourself: why?

3.1 **Two cities in Europe**

Compare these two pictures, both taken in Europe. What is so different between them? Can you identify the countries?

3.2 Two food stalls

A question similar to the previous one. Compare these two food stalls and comment on their differences. Identifying the countries may be harder.

Photograph Anne De Cort

3.3 **A living room**

Where are we? What kind of lifestyle does this picture suggest?

3.4 A hardware store in Bangkok: brooms, buckets, paint, ...

Identify the three languages or writing systems. What is the middle one? Explain! What else can we learn about Thai society from this picture?

3.5 Large jeeps used for public transportation

In which country are we? Why?

3.6 A showerhead...

The three positions of the switch are labeled *morna, fria, quente*: which language is this, and what do these words mean?

Water is heated by electricity as it runs through the showerhead: you can see the electrical wiring. Would you use this shower? Why (not)?

3.7 A hotel lobby and a wall-mounted remote control

Where are we? What is the remote control on the wall for?

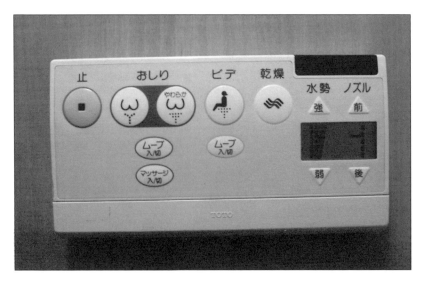

3.8 **A butcher's shop in Morocco**

Comment on this picture.

3.9 **Two toilets**

Two similar toilets: in which function do they differ? Why? Formulate some hypotheses.

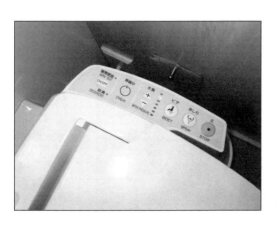

283

3.10 **A hair dryer in a hotel room**

Comment on what you observe. One of the labels says: "Do not remove this tag – N'enlevez pas cette étiquette."

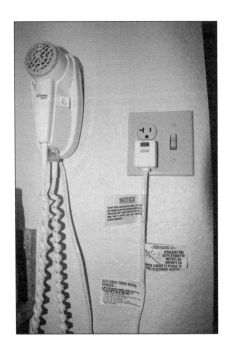

3.11 **Fish in China**

Xi'an, China: what kind of place are we in?

3.12 China: people sitting on stairs in the street...

Xi'an, China: describe what you observe and formulate possible explanatory hypotheses.

3.13 A sign in three languages: English, Chinese, Spanish

In which country and in which city has this picture been taken?

3.14 Cars on the street

What is peculiar about this scene? Where might the picture have been taken?

Chapter 4 Apply Concepts That Help You Understand

Applying the theoretical concepts that have been elaborated by interculturalists will help you in understanding how things may work differently in different cultures.

4.1 Two similar buildings

Timișoara and New York City: different cities, same type of building... What kind of building?

4.2 A pier in California and its warning sign...

... and a very similar pier in Sopot (near Gdańsk), Poland. There is no warning sign about the wooden surface.

Does that suggest that the Polish authorities care less about the risk of people getting hurt than those in California?

4.3 «Please sit down»

Where are we? The sign in English reads *Please sit down taking photos in the hall*: why? Why is it the only sign in English?

4.4 **Washington, DC**

Which words are you likely to find on the board this man is wearing?

4.5 **"We are closed"**

Which of Hofstede's dimensions might explain why some people find this sign more 'outrageous' than others?

Translation: "For the Christmas and New Year's holidays, the store will be closed from Friday December 24th until January 5th 2005. This will be followed by vacation from January 5th to January 29th. Reopening on Monday January 31th."

4.6 Japan: Samperegurino

What *is* Samperegurino?

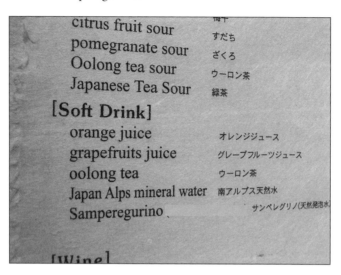

4.7 Public transportation in Bangkok

Four buses. Comment on what you observe and formulate explanatory hypotheses.

1

2

3

4

4.8 A bus stop sign in Bangkok

A bus stop sign blocking the sidewalk of a busy thoroughfare in Bangkok. Comment and formulate explanatory hypotheses.

4.9 Takuma Sato

The Japanese Formula 1 driver Takuma Sato is one of the few Asian drivers in this competition. He has not been very successful: he is never among the first to cross the finishing line. A the Belgian Grand Prix in Spa-Francorchamps 2005, his Honda crashed into Michael Schumacher's Ferrari. At the China GP in October 2006, he finished 14th, one of his better performances; but then he was excluded by the stewards for ignoring the blue flags near the finish and holding up another pilot. In November 2006, he occupied rank 23 out of 27 drivers.

Many Japanese, and other Asians, blame this on a specific characteristic of his car, which is visible in the picture (www.takumasato.org)

4.10 **The train station in Bamako, Mali: train delayed**

Which concept might explain why such a delay of more than 10 hours is more common and 'normal' in some countries than in others?

Photograph Ann De Schryver

Translation: "Day 30-7-2006. The departure of the Autorail train B[ama]ko-Kayes, initially scheduled for 9: 15am, is delayed until 7: 30pm. Thank you."

4.11 **The number one ranked cardiac surgeon**

Which of Hofstede's dimensions might explain that such rankings are more likely to be found in the USA than, say, in Europe?

Chapter 5 Cultural identity and intercultural ethics

5.1 A Sikh boy at a school in Quebec, Canada

In the following story from the BBC News website, do you agree with the school authorities who banned the dagger, or with the Quebec courts which upheld the boy's right to wear the (blunt) dagger?

You are in: World: **Americas**
Saturday, 18 May, 2002, 03:36 GMT 04:36 UK

Sikh wins right to wear dagger

Devout Sikhs must wear the dagger at all times

By Mike Fox
BBC correspondent in Montreal

A Quebec court has ruled that a 12-year old Sikh boy should be allowed to wear his ceremonial dagger - known as a kirpan - while he is at school.

The decision overturns one made by his school and school-board which banned him from carrying the small blunt metal dagger because they regarded it as an offensive weapon.

The issue has created stark divisions between many other parents at the school and the Sikh community, which feels that the majority community in Quebec has failed to understand the importance of the kirpan to their beliefs.

Gurbal Singh: At centre of dagger fight

The controversy started last November when Gurbaj Singh fell over in the playground and the kirpan dropped out of its wrappings under his clothes.

The authorities at Ste Catherine Laboure school in LaSalle near Montreal decided it was dangerous and banned him from wearing it.

5.2 Another Sikh case...

And what about this case? Should the New York Police Department let Mr. Amric Singh Ratour wear his turban and keep his beard while on the police force, or request him to shave off his beard and wear the regular police hat?

BBC NEWS WORLD EDITION

Last Updated: Thursday, 6 March, 2003, 14:15 GMT

✉ Email this to a friend   🖶 Printable version

Sikh sues New York police

By Emma Simpson
BBC correspondent in New York

A Sikh man is suing the New York Police Department after he was dismissed from the force for refusing to remove his turban or shave off his beard.

Amric Singh Ratour from Queens is accusing his bosses of discrimination on religious grounds.

Sikh men wear turbans to cover hair they cannot cut

He had applied for a job as a traffic policeman two years ago.

He passed all the required tests and was eventually sworn in as a new officer.

But two months into the job, he said he was fired because he wouldn't shave or wear a police hat instead of his turban.

Mr Ratour was born and raised in New York and said that he felt betrayed because he had been denied an important expression of his religious faith.

5.3 Shark fin soup at Hong Kong Disney

If you were the General Manager of the Hong Kong Disney theme park, how would you handle this issue?

Last Updated: Thursday, 9 June, 2005, 10:31 GMT 11:31 UK

E-mail this to a friend   Printable version

HK Disney answers soup critics
By Chris Hogg
BBC, Hong Kong

Disneyland Hong Kong has responded to criticism from environmentalists of its plans to serve shark's fin soup at a new theme park opening later this year.

Disney said it would hand out leaflets to people booking banquets, explaining the cruelty of shark fishing.

Hong Kong and China are the biggest markets for shark's fins

Disney has resisted calls to drop the luxury dish from its menus because of the damage done to shark populations by intensive farming methods.

It has now also pledged to buy shark's fins from responsible suppliers.

Environmentalists across the world have been lobbying Disney to drop shark's fin soup from the menu for banquets and weddings at its new theme-park in Hong Kong.

The company has defended its decision, insisting it is appropriate to serve the dish in a part of the world where it is considered a delicacy and a sign of affluence.

5.4 The opening ceremony of the Olympic games in Athens 2004

As part of the opening ceremony of the 2004 Olympics in Athens, a gigantic replica of a Cycladic head (3rd millennium BC) broke open to reveal a replica of a Kouros sculpture (6th century BC).

A few American viewers found the display of "male genitalia" offensive and complained to the US broadcasting company NBC for showing it on television.

Should the Greek organizers of the opening ceremony have been more careful not to offend some viewers in the USA?

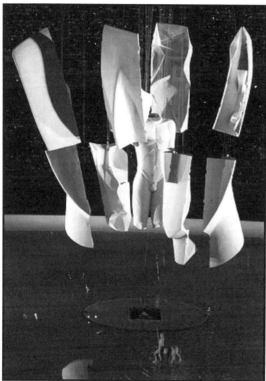

The display at the opening ceremony   *An original Kouros figure*

Some of the complains written by American viewers of the event (*The Washington Post*, 22 December 2004):
- "Not only is this a display of bad sportsmanship, it is also a blatant obscenity on national TV"
- "How could NBC be allowed to show the male genitalia on national television"
- "... a [...] gratuitous display of pornography and indecency during what was supposed to be [a] family viewing event"

5.5 An advertisement for underwear

The BBC News website offers the following story about an advertisement for women's underwear that was placed near mosques in Leeds and Manchester. How should Triumph International, the company that owns the Sloggi brand, react to the complaints that were made?

Last Updated: Tuesday, 8 June, 2004, 23:57 GMT 00:57 UK

✉ E-mail this to a friend   🖶 Printable version

Underwear ad's placing criticised

An advert for women's underwear has been criticised after it was put up on billboards near two mosques.

The poster, for Wiltshire-based company Sloggi, shows four women wearing only G-strings and high heels, alongside the slogan "It's string time".

Sloggi say the advert was not meant to cause offence

But complaints were made after the image was put up next to mosques in Leeds and Bury, Greater Manchester.

A similar poster in Brussels, November 2006

5.6 **Jef Lambeaux**

Near the main mosque and Islamic center in Brussels, there is a small temple-like building called *Le Pavillon des Passions humaines* ("the pavilion of human passion"), devoted to a single work of art: a large erotic haut relief sculpture by the Belgian artist Jef Lambeaux (1852-1908). For many years the building was closed because it was in bad shape; it was still closed when the mosque was opened, in the 1960s. Then it remained closed because the proximity of this kind of artwork to the mosque, it was felt, would be offensive if visible. The building was restored and re-opened recently.

Were the city authorities of Brussels right in keeping it closed, or in reopening it?

5.7 **Beach screens for Muslim women in Italy**

This is an article from the American newspaper *USA* Today, August 2006, about the Italian city of Riccione on the Adriatic coast near Rimini.

Do you agree with the decision taken by the Riccione city authorities?

> **Muslim women get beach screens in Italy**
>
> The Italian resort city of Riccione voted to allow hotels to screen off sections of beach for Muslim women to shed their headscarves and long robes to enjoy the sun in privacy. Only female waitresses and lifeguards would serve the beaches. "If we wanted to, we could create a beach section reserved for nudists; it would be the same thing," said Loretta Villa, Riccione's councilwoman for urban planning. "We live on tourism and we can't survive if we don't satisfy the requests of our customers," she said.
>
> USA Today Aug.4-6, 2006

5.8 Pitcairn

The story of the island of Pitcairn is truly amazing. In 1790 mutineers from the British ship the *Bounty* settled on the tiny island, together with some women they had taken with them from a previous stay on the island of Tahiti. All of the current inhabitants of the island, approximately 50 total, are descendants of the 1790 mutineers. The island of Pitcairn, technically a British colony, remains one of the most isolated inhabited places in the world. Needless to say, there is no judiciary system in place on the island.

In 2004 seven men from Pitcairn (about half the adult male population) were brought to court before judges from New Zealand, for allegedly abusing young, underage girls for sex. The locals however, including local women, have argued that this practice is an island tradition and is consensual.

Should the seven men be tried by judges from another country (New Zealand in this case), or be left alone?

(For a fascinating narrative of the mutiny and its aftermath, read *The Bounty: the True Story of the Mutiny on the Bounty*, by Caroline Alexander (Viking Penguin, 2004).)

5.9 US aid in the fight against Aids

Under pressure from the 'religious right', US aid to developing countries intended to assist them in their fight against HIV/Aids seems to become more and more conditional:
- The money cannot be used to treat prostitutes, because this is seen as promoting prostitution
- Abstinence should be promoted over the use of condoms.

Brazil decided to reject US funds because of these conditions. In Uganda, some feel the conditions are threatening the fairly successful anti-HIV/Aids campaign of the country.

Is it acceptable for the US government to make financial assistance conditional upon criteria which are inspired by the morality that prevails in the US?

"The message has shifted towards abstinence, especially for young people" (Will Ross, BBC correspondent in Uganda)

"Uganda is gradually removing condoms fro m its HIV/Aids strategy and the consequences could be fatal" (Tony Tate, Human Rights Watch)

Chapter 6   Intercultural Incidents and Vignettes

6.1 Middle East

6.1.1 *Smoking on the street in Turkey*

This Summer I spent two weeks in the south of Turkey together with a friend of mine.

We had a wonderful time and people were extremely friendly. Almost instantly upon arrival to Turkey we started to develop a friendship with Özkan, the manager of the hotel and some friends of his.

One evening Özkan and I were walking towards a restaurant where we were going to meet some people. I notice that Özkan picks up a cigarette. I sort of feel like smoking myself, and so, as I do not have a lighter, I ask Özkan for one. He looks at me with extremely worried eyes and says "no". I remember how puzzled I got.

Of course, he said, I could smoke if I wanted to. However, as he seemed so upset about this, I decided not to light my cigarette until we were seated at the restaurant (Jenny N., Norway)

Why was Özkan so upset at the idea of Jenny lighting a cigarette, while at the same time he himself was smoking?

6.1.2 Will we be late for the movie?

When I was in Izmir, some six years ago, being on holiday and having not much to do of our evenings, my cousin and I decided that it would be a fair idea to go to the movies. However, given the high temperature of the season, we decided to go to a local open air one. The movies were scheduled to start at 8:00pm.

We needed some 20 minutes by foot to get to the place. At 7:45, my cousin went in the bathroom to get himself ready. I was quite panicked, thinking that we obviously would be late. My cousin came out of the bathroom at 8:00 and I asked him if it was still worthwhile to walk there only to see that the movie had started (Mete S., German, of Turkish descent)

What is Mete's cousin likely to reply?

6.1.3 A failed invitation in Lebanon

My father is Lebanese and my mother is French. Last year we were in Lebanon and we met some friends of my father's family in their home. My parents decided to invite them, to thank them for their hospitality.

My father invited them twice to come to our house. The first time they refused but the second, they accepted.

So we set a date and an hour. But at the crucial date, nobody came, we waited all the day for nothing. My father called them to know why they did not come and they replied that they were not expected to come (Melanie C., France).

Why did the invited guests not show up for the dinner party?

6.1.4 Moving to a different city in Gaza

The majority of my relatives live in one neighborhood, the Araifa neighborhood. I decided to go and live in a separate apartment in a different city, not so far away. Rumors spread that I had a dispute with my parents, and several of my relatives came up to me asking why I could not get along with my parents any more. (Firas A., Palestine)

Which of Hofstede's dimensions explains best the reaction of Firas's relatives?

6.1.5 Empowerment of subordinates in Gaza

In my previous job in Gaza, I initially gave my supervisees the possibility to set their own timetables through common agreement. However, they never managed to organize this properly among themselves and worse, they blamed me for the unfairness and imbalance of the schedule they had arrived at.

I ended up making the timetable myself without consultation, and though the result was equally unfair to some workers, none of them argued or came up to me to voice dissatisfaction. (Firas A., Palestine)

Which of Hofstede's dimensions helps explaining what went on here?

6.1.6 Offering a bottle of wine to a Palestinian

At my home university for the first two years of my studies I was in one group with a Palestinian boy, Ahmed. He was granted a scholarship by the Polish government to study economics. Although he had had a year-course of the Polish language, he quickly discovered that it wasn't enough to understand lectures, at least at the beginning. He asked me and a few other people for help with particular subjects.

After passing his exams, Ahmed invited me and other people who had helped him for a dinner prepared by himself, to thank us. We bought a couple of bottles of wine and brought them to Ahmed's dinner party. (Izabela P., Poland)

Why is this gift likely to be inappropriate?

6.1.7 At a university in Israel

In 1997 I was studying economics at the Hebrew University of Jerusalem, Israel for a year. As a person who grew up in Antwerp, Belgium, the informal way in which the interaction between professors and students took place was striking.

During the first lesson all professors gave us their office as well as their private telephone number. We were told that we could phone them whenever we wished.

Most of the professors could be addressed by their first name, regardless of their seniority. The contact with the students was very informal, in a way which would probably be considered disrespectful in Belgium.

Another striking aspect was their clothing. Ties and suits were rarely seen. Most professors dress just like students in jeans, sometimes even shorts and T-shirts. I cannot imagine such a situation at the University of Antwerp. (Amiel Z., Belgium)

Which of Hofstede's dimensions may explain the differences as described between the universities in Jerusalem and in Antwerp?

6.1.8 *Lobster*

When the Israeli ambassador was leaving his post in Brussels, the German embassy organized a farewell dinner. The first course on the menu was lobster. (Marc F., Belgium)

Why is this dish totally inappropriate in the given context?

6.1.9 *The sign of the cross in Saudi Arabia*

Fifteen years ago my father worked in Saudi Arabia for some time, and our whole family moved there with him. When applying for a visa, we all had to show our certificates of baptism in order to prove we are not Jewish. And what if we had not been baptized, we were wondering?

My father was working for M+R International. At one time there was a conflict between the mainly Western expatriate management and the workers, not all of them Saudis, but Muslims in any case. They insisted that the "+" sign be removed from the company's name, because it looked like a cross and christian symbols are completely forbidden in Saudi Arabia. (Yannick M., Belgium)

What would have happened if the family were, say, atheists and had never been baptized?

How do you react when the Muslims insist that the "+" sign be removed from the company name?

6.2 East Asia: China, Japan, Korea

6.2.1 *Greeting etiquette in China*

An American business delegation consisting of some young fashion designers and models was taking part in the Dalian International Fashion Festival in China. The general director of the Dalian foreign trade office, a very serious and aged person, was in charge of receiving the foreign delegation. When they met for the first time, these young Americans greeted their young Chinese counterparts first, and then the older director.

After I discreetly reminded them that this was not proper behavior, they went up to the director and showed their regrets and their esteem for him by hugging him and tapping him on the back and shoulders. (Zhang Y., China)

Why is the reaction of the young Americans inappropriate?

6.2.2 *Dress code in China*

When I was working at Dalian Machinery Import and Export Co Ltd. as the assistant of the manager, I had a chance to meet the manager of a French trading company in the lobby of the hotel where he was staying. After greetings and introductions, a young lady came in and sat down next to the French manager.

"This is my wife, Sofia", he said. Sofia smiled and shook hands with everyone present. She was wearing a bikini-style top and a very short skirt, I guess she was just returning from a work-out at the hotel gym. My boss, a middle-aged man, terminated the encounter in a hurry and left the hotel with me. On the way out, he turned to me and said, "That foreign lady is so impolite!" (Zhang Y., China)

Why does Mr. Zhang's boss consider the behavior of the French woman impolite?

6.2.3 A first visit to do business in China

When I was sales manager with a European tire manufacturer my company send me on a visit to Northern China where we hoped to meet new business partners.

During my two-day visit to the Chinese tire manufacturing plant the only thing we did is eating and drinking. I did not find it easy at all to start drinking whisky or cognac as an apéritif at 11: 00am, but the Chinese toasted "to our Belgian friends" and it was virtually impossible not to participate.

The second day I asked when we could start talking business, as I was leaving soon now. The Chinese replied that this would happen on my second visit, later on. Dismayed I returned to Belgium and reported negatively on my Chinese experience to my Belgian boss. (Ivy P., Belgium)

Is Ivy right in having a negative impression of her business trip to Northern China?

6.2.4 A Chinese dinner: when do you have enough?

A few years ago my brother Steve became friends with Danny G., an ambitious young Belgian of Chinese origin. Danny's company sent him as an expatriate to China on an assignment that was to last several years, mainly because of Danny's knowledge of the Chinese language.

A few days before his departure, Danny invited my brother to a farewell dinner. In the past Steve had been to a number of Chinese restaurants of course, but this time he would attend a real Chinese family dinner.

After finishing the truly wonderful Chinese food, Steve told everyone around him how marvelous the dinner was. Suddenly Danny's mother appeared with an additional helping which she put on Steve's plate. Steve was reluctant to be impolite and say no, even if his stomach was already very full, so he made an effort to eat everything the mother had put on his plate. Subsequently, however, each time Steve's plate was empty, Danny's mother filled it again, and this repeated itself many times. Steve was really desperate and of course any enjoyment of the dinner was completely gone.

The next day Danny informed Steve that his parents were horrified that they had failed in their role of hosts. (Hedwig V.R., Belgium)

What is the reason for this unfortunate mutual misinterpretation?

6.2.5 *Chinese trainees in the USA*

Last Summer I worked as a Thailand and China correspondent for an international refrigeration and air conditioner business in Sidney, Ohio; the company has subsidiaries in these two countries.

The China plant was beginning its first stages of operations so they sent two representatives to Ohio to learn how to order parts in time for production deadlines. I was fortunate enough to be one of their instructors on how much to order and when. As I was explaining how many gallons of oil to order per month, the two Chinese representatives, both women, continued to nod their heads incessantly throughout my explanation.

It gets rather complicated because the oil order is divided into three parts, for less is needed of one component than the others, so this component has to be ordered only four times a year rather than once a month.

So I asked over and over if they understood, and they always said yes with a nod of the head. I had them put together a simulated practice order, and all went fine except for an excessive order for oil. After they ordered too much, I explained the process again. The women had no questions and again nodded in affirmation that they understood.

They then returned to China to manage the orders themselves. When the supply of oil arrived in China, it contained three times too much of one component, and on top of this it had all been ordered in liters instead of gallons! (Dan H., USA)

What went wrong in the communication process between the American and the two Chinese?

6.2.6 *"It's up to you" said the Chinese*

In April of last year I accompanied a delegation of the Xian Economics and Trade Institute to Bradford, England as an interpreter. Bradford University's vice-chancellor one day invited us for dinner at a Greek restaurant near the university campus. While we were all looking at the menu, the vice-chancellor asked us what we would like to order. Four of the five Chinese answered "Sui bian", which I could only translate as "it's up to you". This left the vice-chancellor very uncertain about what to do. (Zhang B., China)

Why did the Chinese give such a vague answer to the vice-chancellor?

6.2.7 *My Chinese grandmother was laughing*

My father's mother emigrated from China approximately thirty years ago. She speaks broken English so sometimes it is difficult to communicate with her. For years, I can remember her laughing very frequently while talking to people.

Recently as she has developed health problems, I noticed that she laughed whenever a member of my family or I talked to her about them. I thought it was strange that she would be laughing about something that caused her so much worry. It seemed so out of place and contradictory. (M. Tjan, USA)

Why was Tjan's Chinese grandmother laughing when she was addressing the topic of her illnesses?

6.2.8 The Chinese student began to laugh (1)

As discussion leader for the problem-based learning discussion group of my International Business class in Maastricht, the Netherlands, it was my responsibility to present the learning goals and to develop a group discussion on the proposed topic.

To begin the discussion, I called on Lin, a Chinese student. I asked her to define 'Diaspora', but instead of answering my question she began laughing. Before asking the question, I was a bit unsure of the pronunciation of the word 'Diaspora', so I took this to mean that I had mispronounced the word, and apologized. However, Lin informed me that I had pronounced the word correctly, but that she did not know the answer. (Jamie P., USA)

Why does Lin start to laugh rather than admitting that she does not know the answer to the question?

6.2.9 The Chinese student began to laugh (2)

In my class there is a student named Liu Kang from Singapore. Whenever the tutor asks Liu Kang a question, Liu looks away and giggles. Upon seeing this, the tutor asks Liu Kang what it is that he finds so funny. This causes Liu Kang to smile and laugh even harder. The tutor becomes frustrated and berates Liu Kang for not taking the course seriously. (Keith R., USA)

Why does Lui laugh even more as the teacher lets him know that he shouldn't?

6.2.10 Not a lucky day for shopping

After graduating I had the opportunity of spending three weeks at my uncle's house in Hong Kong. During my stay there, I noticed that my uncle had this kind of calendar that he consulted every day. It looked like a thick pad of papers, one sheet for every day, and it was written in Chinese. I wondered what these writings were about, perhaps they were a list of saints and religious holidays as in the Philippines.

One day I asked my uncle permission to go shopping in the city. He consulted the calendar again and I was astonished to hear him reply that no, this was not a lucky day for me to go out, so he refused me permission to go shopping. (Dennis Y., the Philippines)

How do you explain Dennis's surprise, and how should he react now?

6.2.11 *The power of numbers*

When I first visited Australia in 1995, the head of a university in Shaanxi province one day was with me in a department store in Melbourne, buying souvenirs for his family and friends. When he took all the gifts to the cash register, it so happened that the total price of everything he bought added up to AU$ 250. The cashier was astonished when the Chinese man requested to pay AU$ 251. (Zhang B., China)

Give a couple more examples of word and number symbolism in China.

6.2.12 *Pronouncing foreign names in China*

When I was working for a trading company, I was introduced to an American whose business card showed that this name was *Tyrone O'Haughnessy*. I felt a twinge of panic: I did not have any idea how to pronounce that name (Zhang Y., China)

How do you think Ms. Zhang will cope with her worries about the correct pronunciation of the American's name?

6.2.13 *A business card in Japan*

About ten years ago Mr. B., a Belgian executive from a firm called Hansen International, had participated in a trade fair in Tokyo, where he had a conversation with a number of Japanese businessmen with whom he exchanged business cards. After his return, however, no further contact was ever made between him and these Japanese.

Last year, Mr. B. was in Tokyo again and he ran into some of the Japanese he had met ten years before. The Japanese did not recognize him, but as soon as they heard his name they all produced the businesscard they had received from him ten years before (Lesley P., Belgium).

Which cultural feature of Japan made this small miracle possible?

6.2.14 *Gift giving in Japan*

My father had an extensive tour of East and Southeast Asia, visiting companies that did business with his company. Unlike his business trips around the US or Europe, he and his team were given many gifts from these companies. The most significant gift was received from the president of a Japanese company during a dinner. Each person on the team (all were male), received an electric razor worth at least US$ 250.

While the gifts seemed excessive, my father could not refuse because it would have been disrespectful to the president of the company. He also presented gifts to the president. The president, and other high officials, received high quality golf accessories with his company's logo on them; the value of these gifts was approximately US$75. (Matt R., USA)

Were the golf accessories an appropriate return gift under the cinrcumstances?

6.2.15 The Japanese students began to laugh

Dr. W., a business professor at Pennsylvania State University, teaches an introductory class about international business operations. He enjoys including various students in his lecture to create a discussion. He does this by pointing out random students and asking their opinion on the topic.

On three separate occasions, he called on two Japanese girls. On all three occasions, the two girls would giggle wildly but not say anything. Dr. W. would clearly become frustrated with this behavior. On one of the occasions, he told them to stop laughing, but this made them laugh even harder. (Karen R., USA)

Why were the Japanese girls laughing more and more? Is Dr. W.'s reaction appropriate here?

6.2.16 The Japanese student did not speak

I am teaching Dutch to non-native speakers in Antwerp, and my students are of the most varied cultural origins. One of my students is Japanese, and although I try to make my classes as interactive as possible, it appeared nearly impossible to get one word out of her. When asked a direct question, she just smiled, but did not say anything at all. Curiously, her reactions sometimes showed me that she understood better than most, but she just would not open her mouth.

And then, after a few weeks, she suddenly started speaking, and it was nearly flawless. Everyone was astonished, including the other students. (Greet W., Belgium)

Why did the Japanese student virtually refuse to speak for several weeks?

6.2.17 "Rabb san" in Japan

Donald Rabb, an American executive working for an American company went to Japan to close a merger deal with Kometsiu Industries, a rival in the global market. The meeting began with lunch between Donald, his interpreter and some Japanese Executives. After Donald's introduction to the Japanese, they began to call him "Rabb San". After a long informal meeting at lunch the meeting moved locations to the corporation's Board Room. When Donald walked into the room there were many new faces. Donald then introduced himself as "Donald Rabb San". His interpreter interrupted him immediately, and then asked Donald to apologize for his arrogance. The mood had changed, and the deal was not made that afternoon. (Robert S., USA)

What went wrong here?

6.2.18 An accompanying wife in Japan

My father went on a business trip to Japan with my mother. During their stay, a Japanese business associate of my father, Mr. Hiroko, sent them an invitation to his son's wedding. The invitation was addressed: Mr. Eugenio Laddaran (my father). (Christine L., the Philippines)

Is it appropriate for Mr. Laddaran to bring his wife with him to the wedding?

6.2.19 On bowing, or a comical incident turns tragic

An American, I will call him Larry Biggs, was a senior executive of CityBank in New York City. One day, he was scheduled to meet a very important new client for a lunch, whom I will call Mr. Hashimura. Mr. Hashimura was to be City-Bank's first major Japanese account, and CityBank was doing everything to curry their potential client's favor: they paid for his stay in the Waldorf-Astoria. On the phone the previous day, Mr. Biggs had told Mr. Hashimura that he would pick him up at the Waldorf to take him out to lunch. To be extra polite, Mr. Biggs decided to wait for Mr. Hashimura by the elevator banks, to avoid any confusion trying to find each other in the lobby. The elevator doors opened before Mr. Biggs and there stood Mr. Hashimura. Mr. Biggs said hello and immediately Mr. Hashimura bowed.

Mr. Biggs followed suit, to which Mr. Hashimura bowed again. This went on for about a minute until finally the elevator doors shut. Mr. Hashimura had been so busy bowing that he had forgotten to step out of the elevator. Mr. Hashimura never returned to the lobby again, and CityBank never got his account. (Kim D., USA)

Why are Mr. Biggs and Mr. Hashimura caught in an endless loop of bowing to each other? Why did Mr. Hashimura not return to the hotel lobby?

6.2.20 Giving a presentation in Japan

A French company develops CAD/CAM systems. The systems they develop have found applications mainly with textile and shoe-manufacturing businesses. In the past they have developed major systems which are used for the production of interior upholstery for a French car manufacturer. Now they attempt to sell a similar system to the Japanese car manufacturer Mitsubishi.

Establishing the first contacts with Mitsubishi goes on smoothly, and a delegation of the French firm are invited to come to Japan and explain the advantages of the system they have developed. However, conversations with the 12 Japanese who attend the presentations by the French appear to be stalling. One after another, they fall asleep while the French are speaking. All the time, some of them are listening but some others are taking a nap.

How should the French react after this has been going on for a few days with no apparent progress being made?

6.2.21 A young general manager in Japan

A European has been appointed head of the Japanese branch of his (French) company. He will supervise about 20 Japanese employees, who work at the branch office. However, he is only 24 years old, and in Japan a leading managerial function is normally not attributed to someone who is that young.

What can he do in order to ensure that his workers will respect him and accept to take orders from him?

6.2.22 Japanese are invited to a birthday party in Holland

It was two months after I came to Maastricht. A 39-year old Dutch man, who often takes care of us Japanese told us to keep the next Saturday open for him. He was a very kind person, and since we arrived here, he often took us to many interesting places to enjoy our stay.

So I thought that he had some more sightseeing plans. But in fact, next Saturday was his birthday, and it turned out that he was going to give his birthday party. How surprised we were!

We were embarrassed because we didn't know how to get prepared for a birthday the Dutch way. But in fact, he did not expect us to do anything. Eventually, he himself prepared a birthday cake, many foods, and wine, and he paid for all of them. At the party, we were just eating his food and drinking wine which he had bought.

The party started at 8: 00pm. He served two kinds of cakes at first. I expected that the main dinner would be served just after finishing those cakes. However an hour later, I was still drinking Sangria, which I was tasting for the first time, always wondering when the real dinner would arrive.

I was nearly exhausted by such a long time of conversation only, when a mount of cheese and bread were served more than an hour later. I started to eat and chat again though I felt both to be a torture. The party finished after midnight. (Akiko S. and Yuko F., Japan)

Why are Akiko and Yuko so surprised by the way this birthday party is put together?

Why do they feel that the dinner is real torture? How are they likely to react when the bread and cheese are served?

6.2.23 The Koreans are slurping

Since I cannot eat out all the time I cook my meals in the kitchen of the dorms. All the students on my floor share this kitchen and sometimes we eat dinner at the same time. Recently I was sitting at the table eating when the students from South Korea came in with their dinners. They seem to eat together every night. So they sat down around the table with me and began to eat. I could not believe at the way they ate. They just shoved the food in their mouths and were slurping and chewing very loud. I looked around and it didn't seem to bother them like it did me. (Jaclyn C., USA)

If you were in Jaclyn's place, how would you react?

6.2.24 Brigitte Bardot and Korean food

Before the 2002 World soccer cup which was to take place jointly in Korea and Japan, the French former movie actress and defender of animal rights Brigitte Bardot called on the Koreans to give up eating dog meat, saying that to Europeans this habit would strongly damage their image as a co-organizer of the World cup. (Le Soir newspaper, 9 December 2001)

How should the Koreans react to this suggestions?

6.3 South-East Asia

6.3.1 Touching my hair

Adison Teesusat is a Thai studying at Ateneo de Manila University. He has been staying at my dorm for two years, and he gets along well with everyone. But on one occasion, when Adison entered the room, his Filipino roommates noticed that he had just had a haircut. They started making fun of his new hairstyle. Adison did not seem to mind the joke, until one of them touched his hair in an attempt to mess it up. Suddenly, Adison exploded in anger. (Michael F., the Philippines)

Why does Adison react so strongly when his roommates attempt to touch his hair?

6.3.2 Playing tennis and signing a contract

My boss plays tennis frequently after work, and this also allows him to meet many people. I was a sales executive with his company, which specializes in express courier service in Vietnam. One day I had a meeting with a very important potential customer, and I explained to him in detail all the advantages of working with our company. He seemed hard to convince, asking me many questions about our quality standards, wondering explicitly if he could not get a better price elsewhere, and more. The meeting ended without him seeming even close to signing a contract with us soon.

The next day I was walking with my boss in the direction of the tennis court where my boss usually plays, when we ran into this same potential customer. He happened to play tennis with my boss frequently, and was surprised to discover that I was working for the same company. He turned to me and invited me to come to his office the next day for the signing of the contract. (L.H.T., Vietnam)

What made the potential customer change his mind so suddenly?

6.3.3 Asking for directions in Vietnam

I went to Vietnam last Summer to travel for two months. One of the first days I was there, I wanted to eat dinner at this Vietnamese restaurant my dad had recommended when visiting on one of his business trips. Since it was supposed to be fairly well-known, I decided some of the locals could give me directions. I followed the directions from the first man I asked, but they did not help at all. I asked a second person and the woman proceeded to tell me another way, one that was definitely different from the first. This pattern kept occurring several times after. My "helpers" kept sending me in wrong directions. (Sarah G., USA)

Why did the Vietnamese keep sending Sarah in the wrong directions?

6.3.4 Invited for dinner in Vietnam

I was living in Vietnam with my parents. I became friends with a young Vietnamese girl who was in my class, and she invited me for dinner one night at her parents' home.

She told me several times she had four members in her family. I could not figure out why she said this to me repeatedly, so I asked some local people why she gave me this information.

When dinner was served I was given the best meat and everything was well. But when I started to talk about music this seemed to spark a conflict in the conversation. The girl I was having dinner with said she liked one type of music and I said I liked another; but once the father stated what he liked, the discussion stopped completely. This happened several times as the night carried on and I wondered why this was so. The mother always said she had no opinion. (Derek V., USA)

Why does the Vietnamese girl find it important to specify the number of family members?

Why does the discussion stop when the father says which music he likes, and why does the mother not have any opinion to express?

6.3.5 The Vietnamese started to laugh

I was having a cup of coffee at the house of a Belgian businessman living in Ho Chi Min City, Vietnam. Suddenly my cup fell off the saucer and the coffee was spilled on the pale beige sofa of my host's living room. My immediate reaction was to smile and even giggle, but I noticed that this did not go down well with the Belgian. (B.T.H., Vietnam)

Why did B.T.H. start to laugh when he spilled coffee on the sofa, and how was this laughing interpreted by the Belgian?

6.3.6 Completing a deal in Vietnam

In 2003 I witnessed the signing of a deal by a Belgian businessman in Vietnam. After all the necessary signatures had been apposed on the contract, the Belgian's entire demeanor manifested how elated he was that a deal had finally be reached, after laborious and lengthy negotiations. His entire body, from his bright smile to his raised arms, reflected his intense happiness.

It was clear to me that this behavior was not well received by the Vietnamese. (Jean-Marc G.R., Belgium)

Why do the Vietnamese not appreciate the way in which the Belgian businessman displayed his joy?

6.3.7 Raising eyebrows

In my company in Manila, a Western executive who had a Filipino secretary once caused a big commotion. In the course of their daily routines the executive called his secretary into his office and told her a number of things he wanted done by tomorrow morning. The secretary, while listening to him, kept on raising both of her eyebrows. Suddenly the Westerner gets up, grasps the secretary's hands and starts trying to kiss her. (Dexter N., the Philippines)

What is the cause of the misunderstanding in this incident?

6.3.8 A Filipina woman

When my sister was traveling to the USA two years ago, she was seated beside a Japanese man in the airplane. The man started a conversation with her, and he became particularly interested when he learned that she was Filipina. However, after a while he really started to harass her and my sister had to complain to the stewardess and ask for another seat. (Lee S., the Philippines)

What went wrong in this encounter?

6.3.9 Helping a poor man in Indonesia

My brother and I were in Indonesia one summer. We stopped to stay in a little village for a week. The area was rather poor, and we could clearly feel the contrast between the Indonesians of this village and ourselves: our nice clothes, my brother's expensive camera equipment, etc.

When we were out walking in the street many people bent their head when we passed.

One day a man on a bike, with a box of vegetables on it, lost control over his bike and fell. There were vegetables all over the street. My brother and I immediately started helping to pick up the vegetables for him, but people got very upset, the expressions on their faces and their gesticulations with their arms obviously meaning that we should not be doing this. The man gave us a little smile, but looked extremely embarrassed. (Silva M., Sweden)

Why did the help that Silva and her brother provided not go down well with the locals, including the man they were trying to help?

6.3.10 *An appointment in Indonesia*

A foreign businessman made an appointment with his prospective sales representative in Jakarta for a meeting which was to take place Friday afternoon at the representative's office. However, when the foreign businessman arrives for the meeting, the representative is not there, and it appears that he will not be back for the rest of the day. The foreigner is rather perplexed by this. The secretary who receives him speaks very little English and can only point to the little memo she received from her boss, apparently proposing a new date for the meeting.

Was it possible for the foreign businessman to foresee this course of events?

6.4 South Asia

6.4.1 *A traffic accident involving a Mercedes in India*

While traveling in India one Summer, the traffic on the road happened to be rather heavily congested with cars, scooters, bikes, people etc. There were no traffic signals, and a friend I was driving with got into a relatively minor collision with the car in front of him. It was instantly clear to both of us that my friend was at fault in the accident.

No one was hurt, but a police officer was nearby and was beckoned by the other driver.

My friend and I happened to be driving in a large Mercedes, while the other driver was in a relatively cheap vehicle, a Maurati, worth less than US$ 5000.

The other driver explained what happened, but the police officer responded by scolding the driver, telling him not to waste his time over such trivial matters. The officer returned and apologized to my friend for the delay and the confusion over the incident.

While my friend was certainly at fault, the officer chose not to acknowledge the incident, passing it off as if nothing had happened. (Raj R., India)

Why did the police officer react in such a seemingly unfair way?

6.4.2 *Fifteen seconds of silence*

One of my very good Dutch friends had a long argument with someone and looked pretty upset afterwards. I asked him what was wrong and he told me a long story which contained some unbelievable events. I was completely shocked by what I heard and could barely say a word when he finished. At the end he said: "Tell me what you think, I want to hear your thoughts." I wouldn't say anything, so I blankly shook my head. After about 15 or 20 seconds of silence, my friend said, "Say something, I don't like this silence." I told him I was surprised by what he told me and I needed time to think. So, I stood silent for a few minutes more. I noticed that the longer I stayed quiet, the more impatient he got. (Parool S., India)

Why does the Dutch person get impatient while the Indian feels his behavior is quite normal?

6.5 West Asia, i.e. Europe

6.5.1 *Nudity in Sweden: who adapts to whom?*

I was staying with a Swedish family in their large house and after a few days they invited me to have a sauna together with them, the sauna being in their own house. I gladly accepted and went up to my room to put on a bathing suit. When I came down the stairs, the whole Swedish family, from young to old, were standing stark naked before my astonished eyes, ready to get to the sauna. (Kristine A., Belgium)

How would you react if you were in Kristine's place?

6.5.2 *A German chain of gas stations in Poland*

A German chain of gas and service stations opens a subsidiary in nearby Poland. A German is in charge of quality control for the Polish operations. Although he sends the Polish managers time and time again written reports complaining about the unacceptable state of their gas stations, the Polish stations remain as they were, unclean, stained with oil and grease, and the goods in the convenience stores that are attached to them also remain as chaotically displayed as they always had been. (Rainer H., Germany)

For what reasons might the Polish managers choose to ignore the German supervisor's reports?

6.5.3 *Drinking vodka during negotiations*

My father and I went on a trip to Italy and decided to visit a friend of us, an Italian man whom we have met in Russia some months before. My father had spent some time with him in Moscow discussing business matters.

The Italian told us that when he was in Moscow, he was shocked by the way the negotiations take place. Although he had been aware of the famous "drinking reputation" of the Russians, he was still surprised to see that alcohol can be consumed continuously through the negotiations.

Particularly one episode at the end of the deal had struck him. After more than two hours of negotiations with the Russians, and finishing over two bottles of vodka, one of the Russians said: "Well, it's great we have reached a compromise, now I invite everybody to celebrate it". Then they went to the company's sauna, where they spent more than four hours and drank some additional bottles of vodka. (Dimitri T., Russia)

If you are not a heavy drinker, what would be an appropriate reaction in this situation?

6.5.4 Pouring coffee in Russia

Although my grandmother is of Russian origin my father was born in Belgium and he is only vaguely acquainted with Russian culture.

Still, because of his origins he was sent by his company to Moscow to assist in opening their subsidiary there, and our entire family actually spent seven years in Russia before returning to Belgium.

One of the earliest incidents I remember is that we were invited by one of our aunts who lived in Moscow, and upon arrival she proceeded to serve us cake and coffee. I decided to put in a helping hand, and while she was cutting the cake I poured in the coffee, filling each cup approximately for two thirds, as I would do in Belgium, so that people who so desire can pour milk in their coffee.

As soon as she sees this happening, my aunt gets really mad at me and starts yelling at me in Russian. She said "Why don't you wish me a full and happy life?" (Ine V.H., Belgium)

What might have caused Ine's aunt to be so upset?

6.5.5 Have you been invited for dinner?

About a week ago, I was at a Dutch person's house watching a movie, around 2: 00pm. When the movie ended he and his parents started preparing dinner. Since I was rather far away from my dormitory I expected that I would stay for dinner and go home later that evening. However, I noticed that as time went by, I had not yet been asked to stay for the meal. Around 6: 00pm, the table was set and I was still sitting on the coach, waiting for the invitation to stay for dinner. (David W., USA)

What is likely to happen next?

6.5.6 A doner kebab for lunch in Holland

In Holland and the rest of Europe, Middle Eastern food seems to be the equivalent to American fast food. The stores where one buys this food are small and mostly consist of a counter where the food is to be taken away. One day I was late for a class and had not yet eaten any lunch. I stopped at a Middle Eastern restaurant in the hope of getting something quickly and eating it on my way to class. I ordered a Doner Kebab, which I knew was a sandwich that could be prepared quickly.

The sandwich was indeed prepared fairly quickly, but before I could pay for it, the man working behind the counter had already started preparing something else for another customer. Before I was finally able to pay, he was actually handling two or three other customers. He even took someone else's money while he still had mine in his hand, allowing the two of us to pay at once.

The entire transaction took longer than expected and left me confused as to why the staff at this restaurant was so disorganized. (Dave S., USA)

Were the staff "disorganized"? Which cultural concept helps explaining what went on here?

6.5.7 **An unexpected visitor at lunchtime**

My family and I were having lunch at the residence of a Belgian family near Ghent, Belgium. Suddenly the doorbell rang and the host excused himself to attend the unexpected visitor at the door. He did not let him in, though, and even more surprising, I heard him say to the visitor "We are just having lunch." When the host arrived back at the table he made a disparaging remark about the visitor's manners. I was horrified. (Elisabeth D., the Philippines)

Why is Elisabeth horrified by the Belgian's attitude?

6.5.8 *Japanese at a dinner in Belgium*

I have been in Belgium now for almost a year and I have been invited several times for dinner in Belgium as well as in some other European countries. I still don't understand very well, however, how to behave when food is served that I do not like at all. I hear some Europeans comment on the food their hosts are serving, and sometimes they might say "I don't care for this, I'll just skip it". Is that really appropriate? (Masaya J., Japan)

Why is Masaya so puzzled with table manners in Europe?

6.5.9 *Being on time in Germany*

Last Summer I accompanied my father on a business trip to Germany. My family exports artificial plants to Europe and the United States, and my father was considering entering the German market.

Our contact in Bonn was a man by the name of Joseph Wagner, a retired army colonel. A meeting was set up with Mr. Wagner for 3: 00pm. Because of the fact that lunch took longer than we had expected, we missed the 2: 30 shuttle and we arrived 7 minutes late. My father said, "Hello Mr. Wagner, how are you doing", but throughout the meeting, the German man seemed visibly upset. (Paolo P., the Philippines)

In fact Paolo and his father made two cultural errors that might have upset their German contact: which ones?

6.5.10 *Being on time for a lunch engagement*

Upon arrival in Maastricht, the Netherlands, I had met a French girl, Monique and a Polish girl, Doroty. One day we decided to meet each other for lunch at the main market square at 1: 00pm. Doroty arrived at the restaurant on time; however, Monique arrived almost 45 minutes late. Doroty and I were so frustrated and annoyed that we had ordered our food and drinks before she arrived. When Monique finally showed up we were practically finishing our meals. We were very embarrassed that we had eaten lunch without her. Monique was also upset and angry because we had invited her to lunch and proceeded to eat without her. She was unable to understand our reasoning and looked at us like we were a couple of rude, impatient human beings. (Genevieve S., USA)

What caused the misunderstanding in this incident?

6.5.11   *A vegetarian negotiator*

The best negotiator in an American company also happens to speak very fluent French. He is a vegetarian and never drinks alcohol, wine or beer.

Would you recommend sending him to France to negotiate a contract for his American firm?

6.5.12   *A heated discussion in France*

A Filipino businessman traveled to France to conduct a business transaction with a French company. The following day he met with the French representative in the morning and they decided to continue their discussion over lunch. Everything was going fine, and they were both enjoying the food and the wine, – until the discussion hit an argument. The Frenchman started making disparaging remarks about the Filipino government. At first the Filipino let it go, not wanting to offend the Frenchman for fear of jeopardizing the business deal. But the Frenchman insisted and finally the Filipino decided he could not let this pass anymore so he expressed his strong disagreement with the Frenchman, upon which the latter seemed to become ever more excited, angry and upset.

After the dinner was finished, the Filipino was really convinced that the Frenchman would never want to see him again, but while they were leaving, the Frenchman said "Well, I enjoyed our discussion, John. See you tomorrow at my office, hopefully we can work out the last few details and sign the contract." (Sylvia E., the Philippines)

Which cultural feature might help explaining why the Frenchman did not react as the Filipino had feared?

6.5.13   *"Sticking to a tight schedule" in Southern France*

My brother in law is an executive at a construction firm in Zaventem near Brussels, Belgium. For a major construction project, large equipment and machinery needed to be purchased that proved impossible to find in Belgium. After an extensive search operation involving several foreign suppliers, the best offer seemed to lie with a well-known firm located in Southern France.

Therefore the task force of the Belgian construction firm which was in charge of the purchase of large-scale equipment traveled to this city in Southern France, after arrangements had been made to meet with the top-level management of the French company.

It was to be a one-day visit, so the Belgians insisted they would be on a tight schedule. The French nominally agreed to this, but without discussing the agenda for the visit more specifically.

Upon arrival in the morning the Belgians were offered a tour of the French company's production units which seemed to be only marginally relevant to the purchase of equipment they wished to arrange. Then the Belgians and their French hosts were driven to one of the top restaurants in town for lunch, which lasted well into the afternoon. Attempts by the Belgians to start discussing business issues such as price, delivery dates and payment terms over lunch seemed to lead simply nowhere. By the time dessert arrived, the Belgians were completely frustrated and their French hosts seemed to be equally irritated. The day ended with a hurried drive to the airport, lest the Belgians miss their return flight to Brussels.

Afterwards the representative of the French firm in Belgium who had made the initial arrangements for the visit tried to smoothen things out and said that it had all been a simple misunderstanding. (Kurt B., Belgium)

What is the main cause of the mutual frustration in this story?

6.5.14 *Aircraft identification delayed at Airbus headquarters*

On November 12, 2001 an American Airlines Airbus A300 lost its vertical tail fin and crashed in New York, killing 260 people on the plane and five in a residential New York neighborhood.

Years before, in 1987, one of two American Airlines Airbus A300 planes, while still being assembled in Toulouse, France, had been blown back onto its tail by storm winds because its engines had not yet been mounted, which made it tail-heavy.

After the 2001 fatal accident American investigators wanted to known whether the plane that had crashed was the same one that had been blown onto its tail in 1987 (this proved not to be the case).

In the second half of December 2001, the Americans sent a formal request for identification to Airbus headquarters in Toulouse. Exact aircraft identification, however, suffered delays because it proved difficult to locate Airbus officials who could check the records in Toulouse. (International Herald Tribune, January 7, 2002)

Why was it so difficult to have a speedy identification process in this story?

6.5.15 *"Oo dos"*

When I was studying in Spain as an exchange student, the Spanish students just could not believe that I had never heard of *Oo dos* (that is how they pronounced it). Similarly, I had difficulties at first in the computer class, because the teacher talked about operations such as *day-lay-tay* or *low-ad*. (Michael P., Belgium)

What are "oo dos", "day-lay-tay" and "low-ad"?

6.5.16 *The floor of the bar was covered with trash*

We were in Northern Spain when we came upon a small town. My family and I wished to stay there for the night, and so we rented a room, showered, and prepared to go out for dinner. In halting Spanish, I asked the owner of the hotel if there was a place that he could recommend for dinner. He said that there was a nice place right down the street, a local tapas bar. So off we went, excited with the possibility of a local meal, with local atmosphere.

When we arrived, we were appalled by the condition of the bar. There were napkins and food thrown on the floor! It was everywhere, completely covering the walkways in trash up to a few centimeters thick. (Gregory H., USA)

How should Gregory react in this situation?

6.5.17 Making an appointment in Spain

At the end of my stay in Spain as an Erasmus student, I was very keen on having the necessary formalities for credit transfer completed before I left, for fear that otherwise it would be difficult to obtain the documents that are needed.

This did not prove so easy. I insisted on several occasions with the local Erasmus-coordinator asking him to complete the necessary documents, but every time he put it off until later, saying there was no urgency.

Finally I had an appointment with him on the very day I was leaving, a few hours before my flight was due to depart, and even then he arrived 25 minutes later than the stated time of the appointment, seemingly unhurried. (Michael P., Belgium)

Was there anything Michael could have done to avoid the unpleasantness and stress of the events as described?

6.5.18 An arm gesture in Italy

My aunt had found work in Italy and traveled there from New York with two big pieces of luggage. This proved problematic in a very busy Milan airport. She struggled and stumbled through the airport straining her body and energy. After she had finally gotten out and settled in her new home that day, she decided to walk around town. Her heavy bags had strained her elbow and arm muscles, and in order to soothe this pain, she massaged her right arm by bending her elbow in a 90-degree angle with her fist clenched and pointed upward. This gesture was received by those passing her in the street by a similar gesture or a line in Italian, which she could not understand. Completely baffled and wondering why Italians were so rude, she continued walking in the street massaging her arm. (Christopher C., USA)

Why were the Italians reacting like this?

6.5.19 Invited guests in Croatia

I am British but my husband is originally from Croatia. Last year we were there, and we invited a number of his relatives to the house near the beach we had rented for the Summer. I cooked dinner for them and when the guests arrived, we all had a nice meal together outdoors in our garden.

Afterwards, however, my husband pointed out that I had been very impolite and that, no doubt, his relatives would have been shocked by my behavior (Joan J., UK).

Why was Joan's behavior inappropriate in Croatia?

6.5.20 Gender roles in the mountains of Southern Italy

I was participating in a Summer camp in the South of Italy, in a small and remote village in the mountains of Calabria. We were working with the poor youngsters of the village and for the last evening, we decided to organize a small theatre play for the children. But soon, our plans for the play led to a serious disagreement with the local boys, who did not want the Calabrese girls to participate in the theatre. Since the play was set on a street, they could appear only at the doors pretending to clean the houses. (Rosa C., Italy)

How should Rosa react now?

6.5.21 "There are three elements…" in Kosovo

While I was working for Europe Aid, the international aid office of the European Union, I participated in a meeting that was taking place in Kosovo. As I wanted to express that in my opinion there were three main problems to solve, I said "There are three points" and simultaneously showed my right hand with three fingers stretched. I immediately felt that the Kosovars deemed my behavior inappropriate. (Marc F., Belgium)

Why are the Kosovars so upset by Marc's seemingly innocent gesture?

6.5.22 Body language in Greece

During my first year in Greece, I had some minor acclimatization problems because of the language barrier: English is not spoken as fluently as in some other European countries. As a consequence I relied on a lot of body language and simply pointing to things I either wished to buy or have more information about.

At one point I was in a bakery, and among the things I was purchasing were five buns. The attendant didn't understand how many I wanted, so my natural reaction was to hold out my hand (my palm facing towards her) and show her five outstretched fingers. Her reaction was most unexpected. She looked at me as if I had just killed her baby and literally threw the bag with its contents across the counter in my direction. I asked for additional items but I was ignored. I tried to pay the items I had by putting the money onto the counter.

The attendant snatched the money out of my hands before I could do so and again threw the change in my direction. This time most of it landed on the floor.

I was the only customer in the store and I was baffled. I couldn't really communicate with the lady so I didn't ask for an explanation of her behavior. I also didn't want to make things any worse. Whatever I had done seemed to upset her a great deal. (Moritz H., Austria)

Why was the Greek shopkeeper so upset with Moritz's gesture?

6.5.23   *Preparations for the 2004 Olympics in Athens*

Architecturally speaking, the "jewel in the crown" of the 2004 Olympic Games in Athens was to be the opening and closing roof on the main stadium. The roof uses innovative technology and consists of two giant arcs with a total span of 304m and a maximum height of 80m. They provide the support for the cables that hold the polycarbonate panels comprising the roof. The roof's total weight is 16,000 tons and it covers an area of 10,000 sq.m. This means that almost 95% of the seats will be covered when the roof closes.

However, about a month before the opening ceremony the roof was still not in place, and journalists started writing that it would be the jewel in the crown "either by its presence or its absence." Jacques Rogge, the (Belgian) president of the International Olympic Committee (IOC), declared that the games could possibly take place without the roof being installed.

More generally, preparation for the games fell so far behind schedule that the IOC started considering contingency plans to withdraw the games from Athens. An insurance policy was taken out to protect against the cancellation of the multi-million dollar event. Bill Martin, an IOC member, suggested that the IOC would not have chosen Athens "knowing where they would be today."

In reality, on the day of the opening ceremony everything was ready and the roof on the stadium was in place, and at the closing ceremony Jacques Rogge called the 2004 Athens Olympics "unforgettable, dream games", praising the Greek organizers who had been criticized earlier (source: printed press and various Internet sites).

Which cultural difference helps explaining what went on here?

6.5.24   *Denying a handshake in Antwerp*

One day I was at a cocktail party in Antwerp with my (female) secretary and we were introduced to diamond broker, let's call him Mr. Goldstein. When we both extended our hand for a handshake, to our astonishment Mr. Goldstein reciprocated with a friendly handshake to me, but he refused to shake my secretary's hand. She was very upset because she thought Mr. Goldstein refused to shake hands with her because of her lower social status (K.V.D., Belgium).

Could there be a different explanation for Mr. Goldstein's behavior?

6.6 Americas and Caribbean

6.6.1 *In a hurry, in a restaurant?*

When I first arrived in Maastricht my friends and I went into town to get something to eat at a local restaurant.

When we sat down we waited ten minutes for the waitress to give us menus. When we got them we quickly decided what we wanted. After fifteen minutes the waitress came over and took our order. After we finished eating we waited for thirty minutes for the check. Finally we had to call the waitress over and then she handed us the bill.

We were appalled that service could be so poor, and blamed it on the fact that the tip is included in the fare, so the waiter has no incentive to provide optimal service (Tiffany C., USA)

Was Tiffany right to blame what had happened on the fact that the waiter in Europe does not expect an extra tip if offering "good" service?

6.6.2 *Will dinner be ready on time?*

Two American students named Bill and Larry were studying at the University of Maastricht. They were living at the Guesthouse dorms where the majority of the foreign students at the University stay.

One day, one of Bill's neighbors, an Italian girl named Maura, told him that they were going to have a pasta party later on that night around 9: 00pm, and that they would like for him and his roommate to come. Bill accepted the invitation even though he thought by himself that 9: 00pm was late for dinner, since he was accustomed to eating at 6: 00pm; but for an authentic Italian dinner, the wait would be worth it!

At 9: 00pm, Bill and his roommate gathered up their plates, silverware and cups, and ventured into the kitchen for an Italian dinner. When they arrived, they noticed that the dinner had not even begun to be prepared. It was obvious to the two that it was going to take over an hour before it would be served.

Twenty minutes later the majority of the party showed up, but by this time Bill and Larry were growing impatient and hungry. To make things worse, they had made plans with friends that they were to meet at 10: 00pm. Bill and Larry ended up leaving the party around 9: 45pm without having dinner, but still wanting to keep their engagement (Bill C., USA)

How is Bill and Larry's reaction likely to be received by Laura?

6.6.3 *Excelling above your peers at school*

As an American undergraduate student studying finance, I came to Maastricht University to gain deeper insight in the workings of international financial markets. Of course, being a fourth-year student, the material covered in class was relatively difficult. On several occasions, a number of Dutch students would ask me if I wanted to participate in study groups outside of class. Though I would thank them for inviting me, I always declined. (Christopher H., USA)

Why does Christopher decline the invitation of the Dutch students to rehearse the course materials together?

6.6.4 Getting acquainted with Americans (1)

In the first semester of this year, in Antwerp I took a class called *Language, Culture and Management*, a class mostly taught to foreign students. In this class there was a group of the American students. During one of the first lessons, we were put in groups all with people of different nationalities and were asked to discuss some questions together. The two American girls were very friendly and clearly the most open people in the group. We all exchanged names and talked about a number of things together. During the next class though, which was two weeks later, they didn't seem to remember any of us, and they didn't talk to any of us again during any of the next classes. I felt fairly disappointed about this (Vanessa B., France).

How might you explain Vanessa's disappointment?

6.6.5 Getting acquainted with Americans (2)

The first semester of this academic year I studied abroad, more specifically in Vienna, Austria. There were plenty of other exchange students and the mix of cultures was very interesting. Among them was an American girl called Elina. She was always very excited about everything and she always "loved" everything we did.

One day we went to a concert of David Bowie, and of course again she "loved" it and she told me "Oh, you're such a great guy, we should hang out more often"; but when I arranged a party with her in mind, she did not show up.

I talked about it with a Norwegian friend and he told me he had experienced the same.

A Canadian girl I met in Vienna as well, had discovered this difference during her first week in Europe and had adapted her behavior to "less excited" because she noticed that otherwise Europeans do not trust you.

In fact the Canadian girl made many more European friends than Elina during her stay in Vienna. Even now I still have contact with the Canadian girl once a week through MSN chat, but not with Elina although she is in my chatbox as well (Maarten P., Belgium)!

How could you explain Maarten's interpretation of Elina's behavior?

6.6.6 Group orientation in Mexico

My sister was planning a trip to Mérida, Mexico one Summer. She talked to a man who owned a small hotel in Mérida on the phone, and when she provided her last name, he seemed to be pleased and more helpful. My sister is of anglo ethnicity but she married a Hispanic man whose last name is Pérez, and she now takes it as her own. Pérez is a very common Mexican last name and in fact was the hotel owners name as well. He was willing to give my sister a 20% discount and a nicer room because of this. But when my sister arrived in Mérida the hotel owner saw the light color of her skin. (John E., USA)

How is the Mexican hotel owner possibly going to react when John's sister arrives?

6.6.7 A customs agent in Mexico

Working in Mexico, I received a shipment of goods from Belgium which were needed urgently, so insisted with the local customs agent asking that he complete the necessary paperwork to clear the goods through customs as quickly as possible.

The customs agent promised that everything would be ready the next day, but when I returned that was not the case, and this scenario repeated itself several times, before I finally managed to clear the goods through customs more than a week later. (Marcel S., Belgium)

Was there anything Marcel could have done to speed up things?

6.6.8 Fixing the air conditioning in Mexico

A few years ago I spent a vacation at Playa del Carmen, Mexico. It was very hot, usually above 30° C.

One day the air conditioning system in our hotel room broke down. We called the hotel receptionist who promised that the problem would be fixed the same day, but that did not happen.

The next morning we called the front desk again, asking if perhaps they had forgotten about our problem. They had not forgotten, they said, and again a promise was made to fix the air conditioning "today".

Eventually we complained to the American (US) manager of the hotel and the repairman arrived a few hours later that same day (Dimitri L., Belgium).

Which cultural difference might explain what happened here?

6.6.9 Rotating jobs in Mexico

One of my clients recently bought and implemented a system that is supposed to maximize personnel efficiency. A central feature of this software program is that teams are ever-changing, so that people will work with different co-workers every other week. The implementation of the system went fairly smoothly in various European subsidiaries and in the US, but ran into grave difficulties in Mexico. (Elisabeth F., Belgium)

Why was this scheme harder to implement in Mexico than in the US and Europe?

6.6.10 *A small tip for the customs agent*

Upon arrival into Guatemala City's international airport, Dean wanted nothing more than to find his Guatemalan friend and get started with his long-planned vacation. Dean had a substantial amount of baggage for a two-week trip because he was bringing gifts for his friend and his friend's family in addition to his mountain bike and photographic equipment.

After getting his baggage from the belt, Dean proceeded to the customs counters where the agent eyed Dean's baggage and asked for "a small tip" to send him quickly on his way. Not understanding what he meant, Dean proceeded to wheel his cart forward thinking all was OK. After all, the agent had smiled when he uttered what he said. (Al A., USA)

What is likely to happen next?

6.6.11 *Going to the movies together in Honduras*

I spent a year as an exchange student in Honduras, during which time I also met the man who would become my husband. Early on in our relationship, I suggested we go see a movie together I was interested in, but my fiancé appeared clearly embarrassed. Although he did not say so, I immediately felt perhaps he could not afford to buy two tickets, even though they seemed very inexpensive to me (about 1.5 euro each at the time!).

I therefore proposed that I pay for our visit to the movies this time, but he got very mad when I made that suggestion, and we wound up not going to the movies at all (Evelien S., Belgium).

Why did Evelien's boyfriend get mad at her?

6.6.12 *An appointment with some Brazilians*

I spent last Summer in London. I was staying with my (female) Polish friend in a house where a few Brazilians were also living.

One day two Brazilian boys invited me and my friend to the Salsa club, in order to show us what a "real Brazilian" party looked like. As my friend and I had planned a city tour that day, we were supposed to meet the Brazilians at the club itself.

We arrived there 20 minutes late, and feeling a little embarrassed because of it. But to our surprise, the boys hadn't come yet. They arrived about 40 minutes later and they seemed not to find anything inappropriate about this. (Malgorzata K., Poland)

Why does the behavior of the Brazilians not correspond to Malgorzata's expectations?

6.6.13 *Leaving a meeting and returning, Brazil*

I used to work for a company that made parts for big earth-moving machines, traveling all around the world meeting with prospective clients.

One time I was in Brazil trying to persuade a company to sign a contract with my firm. My partner and I had prepared a presentation for the top executives of the Brazilian company. When the presentation started there were eight executives in the room.

The meeting had been going on for about an hour when some people started to get up and leave. They were gone for over an hour and then came back in, acting as if they had only been gone for a few minutes. My partner and I were shocked by the behavior of these people. I had no idea why they got up and left for such a long period of time. In fact I never found out about this strange behavior during a presentation but I did land the account.(Brooke H., USA)

Which cultural concept might help explain the behavior of the Brazilians in this story? Why did their behavior upset the Americans from the US?

6.6.14 Hissing you

When I first moved to the island of St. Lucia in the Caribbean I felt very uncomfortable and sexually harassed because everywhere I went men were "hissing" at me. As a reaction I would ignore them completely, assuming that they were just being rude. (Amy B., Canada)

Was Amy's initial reaction appropriate in this case?

6.6.15 Immigrants in the USA more literate than the natives?

In 1950, William Robinson computed the literacy rate and the proportion of the population born outside the USA for each of the 48 states in the USA, on the basis of figures from the 1930 census. Robinson showed that these two figures were associated with a positive correlation of 0.53 – in other words, the greater the proportion of immigrants in a state, the higher its average literacy.

Does that mean that immigrants had indeed a positive influence on the literacy rate of the states where they settled?

6.7 Africa

6.7.1 An African student at Cornell University

Two years ago my best friend took a Summer program at Cornell University in the USA. One of the African students who was in her class one day received a telephone call informing him that his sister had died unexpectedly in his home country. As soon as this was known, the other African students, from different countries, started collecting money in order to enable the student whose sister had died to return to his home country for the funeral (Ellen N., Belgium).

Which cultural features help explaining the behavior of the African students who started collecting the money?

6.7.2 A vegetarian in Kenya

Sanne, a Dutch student, arrives in Kenya to study abroad for the semester. She is a vegetarian and has heard that this will not be a problem because some Africans who are Muslims do not eat meat. Her reasons for being a vegetarian are mostly moral: she does not eat animals that are caged. This includes cows, pigs, chickens and other animals taken to a butcher shop. In her country being a vegetarian is not that unusual.

Arriving in Kenya, she was immediately served a typical English breakfast of eggs, sausages and toast. When they offered her sausage she said no thank you and explained that she was a vegetarian. But the waiter kept bringing more plates of sausage even though she was not eating them. Getting frustrated, she tried to explain to him that she does not eat animals that are caged such as pigs and cows, the kind of meat that typically makes up sausage. The waiter still tried to serve her sausage and looked dejected when she did not eat it. He could not understand why Sanne was not eating the sausage.

The woman at the next table saw what was happening. Curious, she asked Sanne why she did not want sausage, but when Sanne explained about caged animals the woman did not seem to understand. Sanne then tried to explain it in a different way: she said she did not eat meat because of moral reasons. The woman nodded and said, "oh it is religious". Even more frustrated, Sanne said, "no it is not religious, it is just moral". (Stephanie A., USA)

Why is it difficult for the Africans to fully understand what Sanne is saying to them in this story?

6.7.3   Hiring someone in Congo (formerly Zaïre)

The Head of Personnel Office (a local African person) of a Belgian company in Congo wants to hire a member of his own village community, with very low qualifications for the job, rather than a person from another region with much higher qualifications.

What should the reaction of the Belgian general manager be in this case?

6.7.4 Congo (formerly Zaïre): a minister in town

On the occasion of a visit by a government minister to the town in Congo where a Belgian company is located, the mayor requests the use of the company's flagship car, a brand-new Mercedes 500 SEL, for two weeks, without compensation.

Should the Belgian company accept this request?

References

Note: Following Belgian rather than Dutch conventions, Dutch names beginning with *Van* or *van* are to be found under the letter *v*, and those beginning with *de* under the letter *d*.

Abramson, N.R. & J.X. Ai. 1999. Canadian companies doing business in China: Key success factors. *Management International Review* 39: 1, 7-35

Adams, Francis & Charles Osgood. 1973. A Cross-Cultural Study of the Affective Meanings of Color. *Journal of Cross-Cultural Psychology,* 4: 2, 135-56

Adler Nancy. 1984. Expecting International Success: Female Managers Overseas. *Columbia Journal of World Business* 73: 5, 79-85

Adler Nancy. 1992. *International Dimensions of Organizational Behavior.* Belmont (California), Wadsworth (4th edition 2001)

Alexander, Caroline. 2004. *The Bounty. The True Story of the Mutiny on the* Bounty. London, Penguin Books

Allport, Gordon. 1954. *The nature of prejudice.* Cambridge, Mass., Perseus Books

Ambler, Tim & Morgen Witzel. 2004. *Doing Business in China.* London, Routledge

Anderson, Philip, Leigh Lawton & Richard Rexeisen, Ann Hubbard. 2006. Short-term study abroad and intercultural sensitivity: A pilot study. *International Journal of Intercultural Relations* 30: 4, 457-469

Armstrong, Karen. 1999. *A History of God.* London, Random House

Ashkenazi, Michael & Jeanne Jacob. 2000. *The Essence of Japanese Cuisine. An Essay on Food and Culture.* Philadelphia, University of Pennsylvania Press

Badinter, Elisabeth. 1980. *L'amour en plus. Histoire de l'amour maternel, XVIIe-XXe siècle.* Paris, Flammarion

Barbara S. Schouten. 2008. Compliance behavior and the role of ethnic background, source expertise, self-construal and values, *International Journal of Intercultural Relations* 32, 515-523

Barkema Harry & Freek Vermeulen. 1997. What Differences in the Cultural Backgrounds of Partners are Detrimental for International Joint Ventures? *Journal of International Business Studies,* 845-864

Barrette, Geneviève, Richard Bourhis, Marie Personnaz & Bernard Personnaz. 2004. Acculturation orientations of French and North African undergraduates in Paris, *International Journal of Intercultural Relations* 28: 5, 415-438

Bartlett, C.A. & S. Ghoshal. 1992. What is a global manager? *Harvard Business Review,* Sept-Oct., 124-132

Bartnett, S. T. 1997. Foreign subsidiary manager selection: An information processing approach. *Business and the contemporary world* 9: 1, 77-93

Barzun, Jacques. 2000. *From Dawn to Decadence. 500 years of Western Cultural Life, 1500 to the Present*. New York, HarperCollins

Bassett, Kath & Christine Vasey. 1996. China from Both Sides of the Wall. In: David Killick & Margaret Perry editors, *Developing Cross-Cultural Capability*, Leeds Metropolitan University, 177-180

Batiste, Pierre & Thierry Zephir (sous la direction de). 2009. *Dvāravatī. Aux sources du bouddhisme en Thaïlande*. Paris, RMN, Musée Guimet

Beals, Ralph & Harry Hoijer. 1971. *An Introduction to Anthropology*. New York, MacMillan

Beldona, Sam, Andrew C. Inkpen & Arvind Phatak. 1998. Are Japanese Managers More Long-Term Oriented than United States Managers? *Management International Review* 38: 3, 239-256

Bennett, John, editor. 1995. *Towards the next Millenium: Challenges and Opportunities in Language Training, Business and Multicultural Contexts*. University of St Gallen

Berlin, Brent & Paul Kay. 1969. *Basic Color Terms: Their Universality and Evolution*. Berkeley, University of California Press

Bernstein, William. 2008. *A Splendid Exchange. How Trade Shaped the World*. London, Atlantic Books

Berry, J.W. 2008. Globalisation and acculturation. *International Journal of Intercultural Relations* 32: 4, special issue "Globalization and Diversity: Contributions from Intercultural Research", 328-336

Berry, John W. 2005. Acculturation: Living successfully in two cultures. *International Journal of Intercultural Relations*, 29, 697-712

Bidney, David. 1953. *Theoretical Anthropology*. Berlin, Schocken Books (new edition, 1995, with Martin Bidney, Piscataway, New Jersey, Transaction Publishers)

Biguma, Constantin & Jean-Claude Usunier. 1991. Gestion culturelle du temps: le cas bantou. In: Franck Gauthey & Dominique Xardel, *Management interculturel. Modes et modèles*, Paris, Economica, 95-114

Black, J. Stewart & Hal Gregersen. 1999. The Right Way to Manage Expats. *Harvard Business Review* 77: 2, 52-63

Black, J.S. & M. Mendenhall. 1990. Cross-cultural Training Effectiveness: A Review and a Theoretical Framework for Future Research. *Academy of Management Review* 15, 113-36

Blackman, Carolyn. 1997. *Negotiating China. The whos and whys of successfully negotiating with the Chinese*. Crows Nest, NSM, Australia, Allen & Unwin

Blom, Herman. 2008. *Interculturele samenwerking in organisaties*. Bussum, Coutinho

Blommaert, Jan & Jef Verschueren, editors. 1991. *The Pragmatics of Intercultural and International Communication*. Amsterdam, John Benjamins

Blommaert, Jan & Jef Verschueren. 1992. *Het Belgische migrantendebat. De pragmatiek van de abnormalisering*. Antwerp, International Pragmatics Association (IPrA)

Blommaert, Jan & Jef Verschueren. 1994. *Antiracisme*. Antwerp, Hadewijch

Blommaert, Jan & Jef Verschueren.1993. The Rhetoric of Tolerance or, What Police Officers are Taught About Migrants. *Journal of Intercultural Studies* 14: 1. 49-63

Boorstin, Daniel. 1983. *The Discoverers. A History of Man's Search to Know his World and Himself*. New York, Random House

Boorstin, Daniel. 1993. *The Creators. A History of Heroes of the Imagination*. New York, Random House

Boski, Pawel. 2008. Five meanings of integration in acculturation research. *International Journal of Intercultural Relations* 32: 2, special issue "Convergence of Cross-cultural and Intercultural Research"

Bosman, Femke, Rudy Richardson, Joseph Soeters. 2007. Multicultural tensions in the military? Evidence from the Netherlands armed forces. *International Journal of Intercultural Relations* 31, 339-361

Bourdieu, Pierre. 1979. *La Distinction*. Paris, Editions de Minuit

Bradford, Ernle. 1972. *The Shield and the Sword*. London Penguin Books

Brett, J.M. & T. Okumura. 1998. Inter- and intra-cultural negotiations: US and Japanese negotiators. *Academy of Management Journal*, 41: 5, 100-112

Brew, Frances P. & David R. Cairns. 2004. Do culture or situational constraints determine choice of direct or indirect styles in intercultural workplace conflicts? *International Journal of Intercultural Relations* 28: 5, 331-352

Bucknall, Kevin. 2002. *Chinese Business Etiquette and Culture*. Raleigh, Boson Books

Buls, Charles. 1994. *Siamese Sketches* (originally published as *Croquis siamois*, Brussels, 1901). Translated and edited by Walter Tips. Bangkok, White Lotus

Burgoon, Judee, David Buller & W. Gill Woodall. 1996. *Nonverbal Communication. The Unspoken Dialogue*. New York, McGraw-Hill

Byrne, Donn. 1971. *The Attraction Paradigm*. New York, Academic Press

Cartwright, S. & C.L. Cooper. 1993. The Role of Culture Compatibility in Succesfull Organizational Marriage. *Academy of Management Executive* 7: 2, 57-70

Cassiday, Patricia A. 2005. Expatriate leadership: An organizational resource for collaboration. *International Journal of Intercultural Relations* 29, 391-408

Celli, Nicoletta. 2006. *Le Bouddhisme*. Paris, Hazan

Chaney, Lilian & Jeanette Martin. 1995. *Intercultural Business Communication*. Englewood Cliffs, Prentice Hall

Chang, Wei-weng. 2009. Schema adjustement in cross-cultural encounters: A study of expatriate international aid service workers. *International Journal of Intercultural Relations* 33, 57-68

Chen, Min. 1993. Understanding Chinese and Japanese Negotiating Styles. *The International Executive* 35: 2, 147-159

Chen, Yi-feng, Dean Tjosvol & Sofia Fang Su. 2005. Goal interdependence for working across cultural boundaries: Chinese employees with foreign managers. *International Journal of Intercultural Relations*, 29 , 429-447

Chirkov, Valery I., Martin Lynch & Sora Niwa. 2005. Application of the scenario questionnaire of horizontal and vertical individualism and collectivism to the assessment of cultural distance and cultural fit. *International Journal of Intercultural Relations* 29, 469-490

Cingöz-Ulu, Banu, Richard N. Lalone. 2007. The role of culture and relational context in interpersonal conflict: Do Turks and Canadians use different conflict management strategies? *International Journal of Intercultural Relations* 31, 443-458

Claes, Marie-Thérèse & Marinel Gerritsen. 2002 (2nd edition 2007). *Culturele waarden en communicatie in internationaal perspectief*. Bussum, Coutinho

Close, Frank. 2000. *Lucifer's Legacy: The Meaning of Asymmetry*. Oxford, Oxford University Press

Cohen, Raymond. 1997 [1991]. *Negotiating Across Cultures. International Communication in an Interdependent World*. Washington DC, United States Institute of Peace Press

Cole, Michael. 1998. *Cultural psychology: A once and future discipline*. Cambridge, Mass., Harvard University Press

Condon, John & Fathi Yousef. 1985 [1975]. *An Introduction to Intercultural Communication*. New York, Macmillan

Condon, John. 1984. *With Respect to the Japanese.* Yarmouth (Maine), Intercultural Press

Cooper, Robert & Nanthapa Cooper. 1990 [1982]. *Culture Shock! Thailand.* Singapore, Times Books International

Cooper, Robert. 1991. *Thais Mean Business. The Foreign Businessman's Guide to Doing Business in Thailand.* Singapore, Times Books International

Copeland, Lennie & Lewis Griggs. 1985. *Going International. How to Make Friends and Deal Effectively in the Global Marketplace.* New York, Random House

Corbin, Alain (volume dirigé par). 2005. *Histoire du Corps. 2. De la Révolution à la Grande Guerre.* Paris, Seuil

Courbage, Youssef & Philippe Fargues. 2005. *Chrétiens et Juifs dans l'islam arab et turc-* Year: 2005. Paris, Payot

Coveney, Peter & Roger Highfield. 1990. *The Arrow of Time.* London, Flamingo

Crystal, David. 1980. *A First Dictionary of Linguistics and Poetics.* London, André Deutsch

Cusher, Kenneth. 2008. Editorial for *International Journal of Intercultural Relations* 32: 2, special issue "Convergence of Cross-cultural and Intercultural Research"

d'Iribarne, Philippe. 1989. *La logique de l'honneur.* Paris, Seuil

Davies, Norman. 1996. *Europe. A History.* London, Pimlico

Dawkins, Richard, 2004. *The Ancestor's Tale.* London, Weidenfeld & Nicolson

De Mooij, Marieke, & Geert Hofstede. 2002. Convergence and divergence in consumer behavior: implications for international retailing. *Journal of Retailing,* 78: 1, 61-69

De Mooij, Marieke. 2003. *Consumer Behavior and Culture. Consequences for Global Marketing and Advertising.* Newbury Park, Sage

De Mooij, Marieke. 2010. *Global Marketing and Advertising. Understanding Cultural Paradoxes.* Newbury Park, Sage

Dekker, Daphne M., Christel G. Rutte, Peter T. Van den Bergh. 2008. Cultural differences in the perception of critical interaction behaviors in global virtual teams. *International Journal of Intercultural Relations* 32, 441-452

Dennett, Daniel C. 2006. *Breaking the Spell. Religion as a Natural Phenomenon.* London, Allen Lane

Deresky, Helen. 2010 (7th edition). *International Management. Managing Across Borders and Cultures.* New York, HarperCollins

Deshpande, Satish P. & Chockalingam Viswesvaran. 1992. Is Cross-cultural Training of Expatriate Managers Effective: a Meta Analysis. *International Journal of Intercultural Relations* 16, 295-310

Doing Business Internationally. The Resource Book to Business and Social Etiquette. 1997. Princeton, Princeton Training Press

Dubois, Jean et alii. 1973. *Dictionnaire de linguistique.* Paris, Larousse

Duggan, Christopher. 2007. *The Force of Destiny. A History of Italy Since 1796.* London, Allen Lane

Dun & Bradstreet *see* Morrison et alii

Dundes Renteln, Alison. 1990. *International Human Rights: Universalism vs. Relativism.* Newbury Park, Sage

Dunung, Sanjyot. 1995. *Doing Business in Asia. The Complete Guide.* New York, Lexington Books

Easterly, William. 2006. *The White Man's Burden.* New York, Penguin Group

Ekman, Paul & Wallace Friesen. 1969. The repertoire of nonverbal behavior: Categories, origins, usage, and coding. *Semiotica, 1,* 49-98

Ekman, Paul & Wallace Friesen. 2003. *Unmasking the Face: A Guide to Recognizing Emotions From Facial Expressions.* Cambridge, Mass., Malor Books

Eliseeff, Danielle. 2003. *Confucius. Des mots en action.* Paris, Gallimard

Engholm, Christopher. 1991. *When Business East Meets Business West. The Guide to Practice and Protocol in the Pacific Rim.* New York, Wiley & Son

Eppink, Derk-Jan. 2004. *Avonturen van een Nederbelg.* Tielt, Lannoo

Ergeneli, Azize, Raheel Gohar & Zhanar Temirbekova. 2007. Transformational leadership: Its relationship to culture value dimensions. *International Journal of Intercultural Relations* 31: 6, 703-724

ESOMAR. 1993. *(Seminar on) Marketing Integration of East and West Europe: Transition and Evolution.* Budapest, 12-15 May 1993. Amsterdam, Esomar

Euwema, Martin C., IJ. Hetty van Emmerik. 2007. Intercultural competencies and conglomerated conflict behaviors in intercultural conflicts. *International Journal of Intercultural Relations* 31, 427-441

Evanoff. 2004. Univeralist, relativist and constructivist approaches to intercultural ethics. *International Journal of Intercultural Relations*, 28, 439-458

Evanoff. 2006. Integration in intercultural ethics. *International Journal of Intercultural Relations*, 30, 421-37

Evans, David, editor. 1996. *Communicative Ability and Cultural Awareness: A Key to International Corporate Succes.* (=8th ENCODE Conference). Nice, Groupe EDHEC

Evans, Vyvyan. 2003. *The Structure of Time.* Amsterdam, John Benjamins

Eylon, Dafna & Kevin Au. 1999. Exploring Empowerment Cross-Cultural Differences Along the Power Distance Dimension. *International Journal of Intercultural Relations* 23: 3, 373-385

Fage, J.D. 1988. *A History of Africa.* London, Unwin Hyman

Fang, Tony. 1999. *Chinese Business Negotiating Style.* Thousands Oaks, Sage

Faure, Guy & Jeffrey Rubin, editors. 1993. *Culture and Negotiation. The Resolution of Water Disputes.* Newbury Park, Sage

Feghali, Ellen. 1997. Arab Cultural Communication Patterns. *International Journal of Intercultural Relations* 21: 3, 345-378

Fernández-Armesto, Felipe. 2001. *Civilizations. Culture, Ambition and the Transformation of Nature.* New York, The Free Press

Ferraro, Gary. 1994. *The Cultural Dimension of International Business.* 2nd edition. Englewood Cliffs, Prentice Hall (3rd edition 1998)

Finkelstein, Barbara, Anne Imamura, Joseph Tobin (eds.). 1991. *Transcending Stereotypes. Discovering, Japanese Culture and Education.* Yarmouth, Intercultural Press

Fisher, Glen. 1980. *International Negotiation. A Cross-Cultural Perspective.* S.l., Intercultural Press

Fisher, Roger & Scott Brown. 1988. *Getting Together. Building Relationships As We Negotiate.* New York, Penguin Books USA

Fisher, Roger & William Ury. 1981. *Getting to Yes. Negotiating an Agreement without Giving in.* London, Business Books Limited

Fisk, Robert. 2006. *The Great war for Civilisation. The Conquest of the Middle East.* London, Harper Perennial

Fox, Robin Lane. 2005. *The Classical World.* London, Peguin Books

Francis, June. 1991. When in Rome? The effects of cultural adaptation on intercultural business negotiations. *Journal of International Business Studies*, 22: 3, 403-428

Fukuyama, Francis. 1992. *The End of History and the Last Man.* London, Penguin Books

Gallien, Chloé. 1996. "You Can't Get a Word in Edgeways!"; Acquiring Intercultural Competence in the Language Class. In: David Killick & Margaret Perry editors, *Developing Cross-Cultural Capability*, Leeds Metropolitan University, 60-66

Gauthey, Franck & Dominique Xardel. 1991. *Management interculturel. Modes et modèles*. Paris, Economica

Ge Gao & Stella Ting-Toomey. 1998. *Communicating Effectively with the Chinese*. Thousands Oaks, Sage

Ge Gao. 1998. "Don't Take my Word for it." – Understanding Chinese Speaking Practices. *International Journal of Intercultural Relations* 22: 2, 163-186

Geertz, Clifford. 1973. *The Interpretation of Cultures. Selected Essays*. New York, Basic Books

Geertz, Clifford. 2000. *Available Light. Anthropological Reflections on Philosophical Topics*. Princeton, Princeton University Press

Gellner, Ernest. 1983. *Nations and Nationalism*. Cornell University Press (2nd edition, 2009)

Gibson, Robert, editor. 1998. *International Communication in Business. Theory and Practice*. Sternenfels, Verlag Wissenschaft & Praxis

Glazer, Sharon. 2006. Social support across cultures. *International Journal of Intercultural Relations* 30, 605-622

Goulemot, Jean, Paul Lidsky & Didier Masseau. 1995. *Le voyage en France. Anthologie des voyageurs européens en France, du Moyen Age à la fin de l'Empire*. Paris, Robert Laffont

Gourevitch, Aron. 1989. Le Marchand. In: Jacques Le Goff, *L'homme médiéval*. Paris, Seuil, coll. Points-Histoire n° H183, 267-314

Grant, Michael. 1979. *History of Rome*. London, Faber & Faber

Grieten, Els. 1994. *Interculturele problemen bij internationale communicatie met leveranciers en klanten, toegespitst op Oost-Europa*. University of Antwerp (RUCA-TEW) (Unpublished thesis)

Gruzinksi, Serge. 2004. *Les quatre parties du monde. Histoire d'une mondialisation*. Editions de la Martinière

Gudykunst William & Young Yun Kim. 1992. *Communicating with Strangers. An Approach to Intercultural Communication*. New York, Mc-Graw-Hill, 2nd edition

Gumperz, John & Celia Roberts. 1991. Understanding in Intercultural Encounters. In: Jan Blommaert & Jef Verschueren, *The Pragmatics of Intercultural and International Communication*, Amsterdam, John Benjamins, 51-90

Hall, Christopher. 1996. *Intercultural Communication as a Component of University Modern Language Courses*. In: David Killick & Margaret Perry editors, *Developing Cross-Cultural Capability*, Leeds Metropolitan University, 39-47

Hall, D.G.E. 1995 [1955]. *A History of South-East Asia*. London, Macmillan

Hall, Edward T. 1959. *The Silent Language*. New York, Anchor Books Doubleday

Hall, Edward T. 1976. *Beyond Culture*. New York, Anchor Books Doubleday

Hall, Edward T. 1983. *The Dance of Life. The Other Dimension of Time*. New York, Anchor Books Doubleday

Hammer, Mitchell R. 2005. The Intercultural Conflict Style Inventory: A conceptual framework and measure of intercultural conflict resolution approaches. *International Journal of Intercultural Relations*, 29, 675-695

Hampden-Turner, Charles, & Fons Trompenaars. 1997. Response to Geert Hofstede. *International Journal of Intercultural Relations, Volume 21, Issue 1, February* 149-159

Harris, Eddy. 1992. *Native Stranger. A Black American's Journey into the Heart of Africa*. New York, Simon & Schuster

Harris, Philip & Robert T. Moran. 1979. *Managing Cultural Differences*. Houston, Gulf Publishing Company (4th edition 1996)

Harvey, Michael. 1997a. Dual-Career Expatriates: Expectations, Adjustment and Satisfaction with International Relocation. *Journal of International Business Studies*, 627-659

Harvey, Michael. 1997b. "Inpatriation" Training: the Next Challenge for International Human Resource Management. *International Journal of Intercultural Relations* 21: 3, 393-428

Hawking, Stephen. 1988. *A Brief History of Time*. London, Bantam Press

Haworth, Dwight & Grant Savage. 1989. A Channel-Ratio Model of Intercultural Communication: The Trains Won't Sell, Fix them Please. *The Journal of Business Communication* 26: 3, 231-254

Hendry, Joy. 2003. *Understanding Japanese Society*. London, Routledge Curzon

Herfst, Selma L., Jan Pieter van Oudenhoven, Marieke E. Timmerman. 2008. Intercultural Effectiveness Training in three Western immigrant countries: A cross-cultural evaluation of critical incidents. *International Journal of Intercultural Relations* 32, 67-80

Hidasi, Judith. 1995a. Miscommunication: a Two-way or One-way Issue? In: John Bennett editor, *Towards the next Millenium: Challenges and Opportunities in Language Training, Business and Multicultural Contexts,* University of St Gallen, 71-6

Hidasi, Judith. 1995b. Communication Gaps between Euro-American and Japanese Speakers. *Szakmai Füzetek,* Külkereskedelmi Főiskola, Budapest

Higonnet, Patrice. 2002. *Paris, Capital of the World*. Cambridge, Mass., Harvard University Press

Hill, Richard. 1994. *EuroManagers & Martians*. Brussels, Europublications

Hofstede, Geert & Michael Bond. 1988. The Confucius connection: From cultural roots to economic growth. *Organizational Dynamics*, 16: 4, 5-21

Hofstede, Geert. 1980. *Culture's Consequences. International Differences in Work- related Values*. Beverly Hills-London, Sage (2nd edition, 2001: *Culture's Consequences. Comparing Values, Behaviors, Institutions and Organizations Across Nations*)

Hofstede, Geert. 1991. *Cultures and Organizations. Software of the mind*. London, McGraw-Hill

Hofstede, Geert. 1996. Riding the Waves of Commerce: A Test of Trompenaars' "Model" of National Culture Differences. *International Journal of Intercultural Relations* 20: 2, 189-198

Hofstede, Geert. 1998. Think Locally, Act Globally: Cultural Constraints in Personnel Management. *Management International Review* 38: 2, 7-26

Holden, Nigel. 2002. *Cross-Cultural Management*. London, Prentice Hall

Holmes, Richard. 2008. *The Age of Wonder*. London, Harper Press

Hourani, Albert. 1991. *A History of the Arab Peoples*. New York, Warner Books

Hu Wenzhong & Cornelius Grove. 1999. *Encountering the Chinese*. Yarmouth, Maine, Intercultural Press

Huang Quanya e.a. 1997. *Business Decision Making in China*. New York, The Haworth Press

Huntington, Samuel. 1993. *The Clash of Civilizations and the Remaking of World Order*. New York, Simon & Schuster

Hupchick, Dennis. 1994. *Culture and History in Eastern Europe*. New York, St Martin's Press

Israel, Jonathan. 1998. *The Dutch Republic. Its Rise, Greatness and Fall,* 1477-1806. Oxford, Clarendon Press

Jackson, Jane. 2008. Globalization, internationalization, and short-term stays abroad. *International Journal of Intercultural Relations* 32: 4, special issue "Globalization and Diversity: Contributions from Intercultural Research", 349-358

Johnson, Michael & Robert T. Moran. 1992. *Cultural Guide to Doing Business in Europe.* Oxford, Butterworth-Heinemann

Jöns, Ingela, Fabian J. Froese & Yong Suhk Pak. 2007. Cultural changes during the integration process of acquisitions: A comparative study between German and German-Korean acquisitions. *International Journal of Intercultural Relations* 31, 591-604

Kameda, Naoki. 2005. *Managing Global Business Communication.* Tokyo, Maruzen

Kanter, Rosabeth & Thomas Dretler. 1998. "Global Strategy" and its Impact on Local Operations: Lessons from Gillette Singapore. *Academy of Management Executive* 12: 4, 60-8

Kaushal, Ritu, Catherine T. Kwantes. 2006. The role of culture and personality in choice of conflict management strategy. *International Journal of Intercultural Relations* 30, 579-603

Kay, Paul, Brent Berlin e.a. 2009. *World Color Survey.* The University of Chicago Press

Kealey, Daniel & David Protheroe. 1996. The Effectiveness of Cross-cultural Training for Expatriates: an Assessment of the Literature on the Issue. *International Journal of Intercultural Relations* 20: 2, 141-65

Kealey, Daniel, David R. Protheroe, Dough McDonald, Thomas Vulpe. 2005. Re-examining the role of training in contributing to international project success: A literature review and an outline of a new model training program. *International Journal of Intercultural Relations* 29, 289-316

Keay, John. 2000. *India. A History.* London, Harper Perennial

Kenton, Sherron & Deborah Valentine. 1997. *CrossTalk. Communicating in a Multicultural Workplace.* Upper Saddle River, New Jersey, Prentice Hall

Kilani, Mondher. 1992. *Introduction à l'anthropologie.* Lausanne, Payot

Kim, Young Yun & William Gudykunst, editors. 1996. *Theories in Intercultural Communication.* Newbury Park, Sage

Kincaid, D. Lawrence. 1996. The Convergence Theory and Intercultural Communication. In: Young Yun Kim & William Gudykunst, editors, *Theories in Intercultural Communication,* Newbury Park, Sage, 280-298

Kinross, Lord. 1977. *The Ottoman Centuries. The Rise and Fall of the Turkish Empire.* New York, Morrow Quill Paperbacks

Klausner, William. 1993. *Reflections on Thai culture. Collected writings of William Klausner.* Bangkok, The Siam Society

Klausner, William. 1997. *Thai Culture in Transition.* Bangkok, The Siam Society

Kluckhohn, F. & F. Strodtbeck. 1961. *Variations in Value Orientations.* Evanston (Illinois), Row-Peterson

Kohls, Robert L. 1981. *Developing Intercultural Awareness. A Learning Module.* Washington DC, Sietar

Komin, Suntaree. 1990. *Psychology of the Thai People: Values and Behavioral Patterns.* Bangkok, National Institute of Development Administration Research Center

Kraar, Louis. 1993. The Importance of Chinese in Asian Business. *Journal of Asian Business* 9: 1, 87-94

Kremenyuk, Victor. 1991. *International Negotiation. Analysis, Approaches, Issues.* San Francisco, Jossey-Bass Publishers

Kroeber, Alfred & Clyde Kluckhohn. 1952. *Culture. A Critical Review of Concepts and Definitions.* New York, Meridian Books.

Kruzela, Pavla. 1995. Some Cultural Aspects on Czech and Russian Management. In: Bozena Machova & Slava Kubatova editors, *Uniqueness in Unity. The Significance of Cultural Identity in European Cooperation* (5th SIETAR Europa Symposium), Prague, 222-235

Kumayama, Akisha. 1990. Understanding Gift Giving in Japan. *The International Executive*, 19-21

Kustin, Richard Alan. 1994. Marketing Globalization: A Didactic Examination for Corporate Strategy. *The International Executive* 36: 1, 79-93

Landis, Dan & Rabi Bhagat, editors. 1996. *Handbook of Intercultural Training*. 2nd edition. Thousand Oaks, Sage Publications

Landis, Dan. Globalization, migration into urban centers, and cross-cultural training. 2008. *International Journal of Intercultural Relations* 32: 4, special issue "Globalization and Diversity: Contributions from Intercultural Research", 337-348

Lane, Henry, Joseph DiStefano & Martha Maznevski. 2000. *International Management Behavior*. Boston, PSW Kent

Laurent, André. 1983. The Cultural Diversity of Western Conceptions of Management. *International Studies of Management and Organization* 13: 1-2, 75-96

Le Goff, Jacques. 1982. *La civilisation de l'Occident médiéval*. Paris, Flammarion, coll. Champs n°47

Lefeuvre-Déotte, Martine. 1997. *L'excision en procès: un différend culturel?* Paris, L'Harmattan

Leonard, Karen Moustafa. 2008. A cross-cultural investigation of temporal orientation in work organizations: A differentiation matching approach. *International Journal of Intercultural Relations* 32, 479-492

Lévi-Strauss, Claude. 1955. *Tristes Tropiques*. Paris, Plon

Levitt, Theodore. 1983. The Globalization of Markets. *Harvard Business Review*, 92-102

Lewis, David Levering. 2008. *God's Crucible. Islam and the Making of Europe, 570 to 1215*. New York, W.W. Norton

Lin, Carolyn A. 1993. Cultural Differences in Message Strategies: A Comparison Between American and Japanese TV Commercials. *Journal of Advertising Research*, 33: 4, 40-48

Littrell, Romie F. 2007. Influences on employee preferences for empowerment practices by the "ideal manager" in China. *International Journal of Intercultural Relations* 31, 87-110

Lovitt, Carl & Dixie Goswami, editors. 1999. *Exploring the Rhetoric of International Professional Communication: An Agenda for Teachers and Researchers*. Amityville, Baywood

Lowe, Kevin B., Meredith Downes & Galen K. Kroeck. 1999. The Impact of Gender and Location on the Willingness to Accept Overseas Assignments. *The International Journal of Human Resource Management* 10: 2, 223-234

Luijters, Kyra, Karen van der Zee &Sabine Otten. 2008. Cultural diversity in organizations: Enhancing identification by valuing differences. *International Journal of Intercultural Relations* 32: 2, special issue "Convergence of Cross-cultural and Intercultural Research"

Luo, Yadong. 1997. Guanxi and Performance of Foreign-invested Enterprises in China: An Empirical Inquiry. *Management International Review* 37: 1, 51-70

Lustig, Myron & Jolene Koester. 1999. *Intercultural Competence. Interpersonal Communication Across Cultures*. New York, Longman

Maalouf, Amin 1983. *Les Croisades vues par les Arabes*. Paris, JC Lattès

Maalouf, Amin. 1998. *Les identités meurtrières*. Paris, Grasset

Machova, Bozena & Slava Kubatova editors. 1995. *Uniqueness in Unity. The Significance of Cultural Identity in European Cooperation* (5th SIETAR Europa Symposium), Prague

Magala, Sławomir. 2005. *Cross-Cultural Competence*. London, Routledge

Maisonneuve, Christelle & Benoit Testé. 2007. Acculturation preferences of a host community: The effects of immigrant acculturation strategies on evaluations and impression formation. *International Journal of Intercultural Relations* 31: 6, 669-688

Mak, Anita S., Kirsten Buckingham. 2007. Beyond communication courses: Are there benefits in adding skills-based ExcelL sociocultural training? *International Journal of Intercultural Relations* 31, 277-291

Malinowski, Bronislaw. 1978 [1922]. *Argonauts of the Western Pacific*. London, Routledge & Kegan Paul

Martin, Jeannette & Lilian Chaney. 1992. Determination of Content for a Collegiate Course in Intercultural Business Communication by Three Delphi Panels. *The Journal of Business Communication* 29: 3, 267-283

Mead, Richard & Tim Andrews. 2009. *International Management. Cross Cultural Dimensions*. Cambridge, Mass., Blackwell

Mealy, Marisa, Walter Stephan & I. Carolina Urrutia. 2007. The acceptability of lies: A comparison of Ecuadorians and Euro-Americans. *International Journal of Intercultural Relations* 31: 6, 689-702

Merk, Vincent. 1986. Een Franse zakenlunch is geen broodje met koffie. *Taal en Cultuur*, 34-37

Merk, Vincent. 1989. Frankrijk. *Beroepsvervoer* 21, 14-16 (written by Carmen Boersma)

Merkin, Rebecca S. 2006. Uncertainty avoidance and facework: A test of the Hofstede model. *International Journal of Intercultural Relations* 30, 213-228

Miller, Laura. 1991. Verbal Listening Behavior in Conversations Between Japanese and Americans. In: Jan Blommaert & Jef Verschueren, editors, *The Pragmatics of Intercultural and International Communication*. Amsterdam, John Benjamins, 111-130

Mordillat, Gérard & Jérôme Prieur. 1999. *Jésus contre Jésus*. Paris, Seuil

Morris, Desmond et alii. 1979. *Gestures*. New York, Stein & Day

Morris, Desmond. 1977. *Manwatching: a Field Guide to Human Behavior*. London, Cape

Morrison, Terri, Wayne Conaway & Joseph Douress. 1997. *Dun & Bradstreet's Guide to Doing Business Around the World*. Paramus (New Jersey), Prentice Hall

Narayanan, Vasudha. 2006. *Hindouisme*. Paris, Gründ

Nasierowski, Wojciech & Philip Wright. 1993. Perception of Needs: How Cross-cultural Differences can Affect Market Penetration into Central Europe. *The International Executive* 35: 1, 513-24

Nathan, Rebekah (pseud. for Cathy Small). 2005. *My Freshman Year. What a professor Learned by Becoming a Student*. New York, Penguin Books

Nehring, Heather. 1995. Working in the Czech Republic: Management and Communication Styles. In: Bozena Machova & Slava Kubatova editors, *Uniqueness in Unity. The Significance of Cultural Identity in European Cooperation* (5th SIETAR Europa Symposium), Prague, 250-259

Newman, W.H. 1992. Launching a viable joint venture. *California Management Review*, 68-80

Newman, W.H., 1995. Stages in cross-cultural collaboration. *Journal of Asian Business*, 11: 4, 69-95

Ng, Eddy S.W. & Rosalie L. Tung. 1998. Ethno-cultural Diversity and Organizational Effectiveness: a Field Study. *The International Journal of Human Resources Management.* 9: 6

Nisbett, Richard E.. 2005. *The Geography of Thought.* Yarmouth (Maine), Nicholas Brealey Publishing

Nonis, S.A., J.K. Teng, C.W. Ford. 2005. A cross-cultural investigation of time management practices and job outcomes. *International Journal of Intercultural Relations,* 29, 409-428

Norwich, John Julius. 2007. *The Middle Sea. A History of the Mediterranean.* London, Vintage Books

Ntabaza, Kagaragu. 1992. *Emigani Bali Bantu.* Bukavu, Libreza

Nydell, Margaret. 1987. *Understanding Arabs. A Guide for Westerners.* Yarmouth (Maine), Intercultural Press

Odzer, Cleo. 1994. *Patpong Sisters. An American Woman's View of the Bangkok Sex World.* New York, Arcade Publishing

Osgood, Charles, Murray Miron & William May. 1975. *Cross-cultural Universals of Affective Meaning.* Urbana, University of Illinois Press

Osmani-Gani, Ahad & Thomas Rockstuhl. 2009. Cross-cultural training, expatriate self-efficacy, and adjustments to overseas assignments: An empirical investigation of managers in Asia. *International Journal of Intercultural Relations,* 33: 4, 277-290

Oziewicz, Ewa, editor. 1998. *Contemporary Problems of International Economy.* Sopot, University of Gdansk, Institute of Foreign Trade

Paik, Yongsun & Rosalie L. Tung. 1999. Negotiating with East Asians: How to Attain "Win-Win" Outcomes. *Management International Review* 39: 2, 103-122

Palich, L.E. & L.R. Gomez-Mejia. 1999. A theory of global strategy and firm efficiencies: Considering the effects of cultural diversity. *Journal of Management,* 25: 4, 587-606

Pan, Jia-Yan, Daniel Fu Keung Wong, Cecilia Lai Wan Chan, Lynette Joubert. 2008. Meaning of life as a protective factor in acculturation: A resilience framework and a cross-cultural comparison. *International Journal of Intercultural Relations* 32, 505-514

Peterson, Brooks. 2004. *Cultural Intelligence. A Guide to Working with People from Other Cultures.* Yarmouth, Intercultural Press

Phillips, David, Gerge Liu, Kennon Kwok, Jason Jarvinen, Wei Zhang, Ian Abramson. 2001. The *Hound of the Baskervilles* effect: natural experiment on teh influence of psychological stress on timing of death. *BMJ (British Medical Journal)* 323, 1443-1446

Phongpaichit, Pasuk & Chris Baker. 1997. *Thailand. Economy and Politics.* Oxford, Oxford University Press

Pinker, Steven. 2007. *The Stuff of Thought. Language as a Window into Human Nature.* London, Penguin

Pinto D. 1990. *Interculturele Communicatie.* Houten/Zaventem, Bohn Stafleu Van Loghum

Pinxten Rik. 1994. *Culturen sterven langzaam. Over interculturele communicatie.* Antwerp, Hadewijch

Plasseraud, Yves (editor). 2005. *Atlas des minorités en Europe.* Paris, Editions Autrement

Poncini, Gina. 2004. *Discursive Strategies in Multicultural Business Meetings.* Bern, Peter Lang

Popper, Karl. 1959. *The Logic of Scientific Discovery.* London, Hutchinson

Popper, Karl. 1963. *Conjectures and Refutations.* London, Routledge and Kegan Paul

Poyatos, Fernando. 1992. *Advances in Nonverbal Communication.* Amsterdam, John Benjamins

Pye, Lucian W. 1992. The Chinese Approach to Negotiating. *The International Executive* 34: 6, 463-468

Reader, John. 1998. *Africa. A Biography of the Continent*. London, Penguin Books

Reichenbach, Hans. 1958. *The Philosophy of Space & Time*. New York, Dover Publications

Remland, Martin, Tricia Jones & Heidi Brinkman. 1995. Interpersonal distance, body orientation, and touch: effects of culture, gender and age. *The Journal of Social Psychology*

Rémy, François. 1983. *40.000 enfants par jour: vivre la cause de l'UNICEF*. Paris, Laffont

Richmond, Yale & Phyllis Gestrin. 1998. *Into Africa. Intercultural Insights*. Yarmouth (Maine), Intercultural Press

Richmond, Yale. 1995. *From 'da' to 'yes'. Understanding the East Europeans*. Yarmouth (Maine), Intercultural Press

Ricks, David. 1993. *Blunders in International Business*. Cambridge (Mass.), Blackwell

Ritzer. 1993 (5th edition 2008). *The MacDonaldization of Society*. Newbury Park, Sage

Ritzer. 2004 (2nd edition 2007). *The Globalization of Nothing*. Newbury Park, Sage

Roche, Daniel. 2003. *Humeurs vagabondes. De la circulation des hommes et de l'utilité des voyages*. Paris, Arthème Fayard

Sakuragi, Toshiyuki. 2008. Attitudes toward language study and cross-cultural attitudes in Japan. *International Journal of Intercultural Relations* 32, 81-90

Samovar, Larry & Richard Porter. 1997. *Intercultural Communication. A Reader*. Belmont, Wadsworth

Schneider, Susan & Jean-Louis Barsoux. 1997. *Managing Across Cultures*. London, Prentice Hall

Schneider, Susan & Jean-Louis Barsoux. 2002 (2nd edition). *Managing Across Cultures*. London, Prentice Hall

Schnerb, Bertrand. 2005. *L'Etat bourguignon*. Paris, Editions Perrin

Schouten, Barbara C. 2007. Self-construals and conversational indirectness: A Dutch perspective. *International Journal of Intercultural Relations* 31, 293-297

Schwartz, Shalom. 1995. Identifying Culture-Specifics in the Content and Structure of Values. *Journal of Cross-Cultural Psychology*, 26: 1, 92-116

Schwartz, Shalom. 1999. A Theory of Cultural Values and Some Implications for Work. *Applied Psychology: An International Review*, 48: 1, 23-47

Seelye, H. Ned & Alan Seelye-James. 1995. *Culture Clash. Managing in a Multicultural World*. Lincolnwood (Ill.), NTC Business Books

Segaller, Denis. 1993 [1980]. *Thai Ways*. Bangkok, Post Books

Seligman, Scott. 1999. *Chinese Business Etiquette*. New York, Time Warner

Selmer Jan, Ingemar Torbiörn & Corinna T. de Leon. 1998. Sequential Cross-cultural Training for Expatriate Business Managers: Predeparture and Post-arrival. *The International Journal of Human Resource Management* 9: 5, 831-840

Sen, Amartya. 2003. Culture and development. Available online, www.scribd.com

Shadid, W. 1998. *Grondslagen van interculturele communicatie*. Houten, Bohn Stafleu Van Loghum

Shaughnessy, Edward, general editor. 2005. *China*. London, Duncan Baird Publishers

Smet, Ria. 2002. McDonald's: a strategy of cross-cultural approach. *Journal of Language for International Business*, 13: 1-2, 11-21

Sobre-Denton, Mirian & Dan Hart. 2008. Mind the gap: Applications-based analysis of cultural adjustment models, *International Journal of Intercultural Relations* 32, 538-552

Soeters, Joseph L., Coen E. van den Berg, A. Kadir Varoğlu & Ünsal Siğri. 2007. Accepting death in the military: A Turkish-Dutch comparison. *International Journal of Intercultural Relations* 31, 299-315

Soissons, Jean-Pierre. 2000. *Charles Quint*. Paris, Grasset

Sokal, Alan & Jean Bricmont. 1997. *Impostures intellectuelles*. Paris, Odile Jacob [published in English as: *Intellectual Impostures*]

Solnon, Jean-François. 1987. *La Cour de France*. Librairie Arthème Fayard

Søndergaard, Mikael. 1994. Research Note: Hofstede's Consequences: A Study of Reviews, Citations and Replications. *Organizational Studies* 15: 3, 447-56

Strathern, Paul. 2005. *The Medici*. London, Pimlico

Strong, Roy. 2003. *Feast. A History of Grand Eating*. London, Pimlico

Tanaka, Hiroko. 1999. *Turn-taking in Japanese Conversation*. Amsterdam, John Benjamins

Thomas, David. 2002. *Essentials of International Management. A cross-Cultural Perspective*. Thousand Oaks, Sage

Thomas, Hugh. 1980. *A History of the World*. New York, Harper Colophon Books

Thompson, Allan G. 1996. Compliance with Agreements in Cross-Cultural Transactions: some Analytical Issues. *Journal of International Business Studies*, 375-390

Ting-Toomey, Stella. 1994. Managing intercultural conflicts effectively, in Samovar & Porter, *Intercultural Communication: A reader*, 360-372, Belmont, Ca: Wadsworth

Ting-Toomey, Stella. 1999. *Communicating across cultures*. New York, Guilford

Tips, Walter. 1996. *Gustave Rolin-Jaequemyns and the Making of Modern Siam. The Diaries and Letters of King Chulalongkorn's General Adviser*. Bangkok, White Lotus

Tobin, Joseph. 1994. *Re-made in Japan*. Yale, University Press

Trinh, Xuan Kim. 2004. *Interculturele aspecten van het zakendoen met Vietnam*. Unpublished Master's thesis, University of Antwerp

Trompenaars, Fons. 1993. *Riding the Waves of Culture. Understanding Cultural Diversity in Business*. London, Nicholas Brealey

Trompenaars, Fons. 2003. *Did the Pedestrian Die? Insights from the Greatest Culture Guru*. Chichester, Capstone

Tsang, Eric W.K. 1998. Can Guanxi be a Source of Sustained Competitive Advantage for Doing Business in China? *Academy of Management Executive* 12: 2, 64-73

Tung, Rosalie. 1981. Selection and Training of Personnel for Overseas Assignments. *Columbia Journal of World Business* 16: 1, 68-78

Ulijn, Jan. 1995. The Anglo-Germanic and Latin concepts of politeness and time in cross-atlantic business communication: from cultural misunderstanding to management success, *Hermes, Journal of Linguistics*, 63-4

Understanding Asian Values. 1996. Brussels, European Institute for Asian Studies

Ury, William. 1991. *Getting past No. Negotiating with Difficult People*. London, Century Business

Usunier, Jean-Claude. 1996. *Marketing Across Cultures*. London, Prentice Hall

Usunier, Jean-Claude. 1998. *International & Cross-Cultural Management Research*. London, Sage

van de Vijver, Fons, Seger Breugelmans & Saskia Schalk-Soekar. 2008. Multiculturalism: Construct validity and stability. *International Journal of Intercultural Relations* 32: 2, special issue "Convergence of Cross-cultural and Intercultural Research"

Van den Broeck, Omar. 1995. *Islam en het Westen*. Zoetermeer, Uitgeverij Oase

van Oudenhoven, Jan-Pieter. 2002. *Cross-culturele psychologie. De zoektocht naar verschillen en overeenkomsten tussen culturen*. Bussum, Coutinho

Varner Iris. 1996. From Baseball to Football: the Role of Sport Terminology in American Business Communication. In: David Evans, editor, *Communicative Ability and Cultural Awareness: A Key to International Corporate Succes.* (=8th ENCODE Conference) Nice, Groupe EDHEC, 184

Varner, Iris & Linda Beamer. 1995. *Intercultural Communication in the Global Workplace.* Chicago, Irwin

Verluyten, S. Paul 1998c. Power Distance in a Mid-Range Power Distance Culture: Thailand. Paper presented at the conference on *Interdisciplinary Theory and Research on Intercultural Relations,* California State University, Fullerton, March 1998

Verluyten, S. Paul. 1993. Doing Business in the Philippines. In: *Language and Culture: Bridges to International Trade.* Preston, University of Central Lancaster, 277-290

Verluyten, S. Paul. 1997. *Some Cultural Aspects of Thai Companies, with Recommendations for Westerners.* University of Antwerp, Centre for ASEAN Studies

Verluyten, S. Paul. 1998a. Hypercorrection and Other Adaptation Strategies in Intercultural Communication. In: Robert Gibson editor, *International Communication in Business. Theory and Practice,* Sternenfels, Verlag Wissenschaft & Praxis, 109-18

Verluyten, S. Paul. 1998b. Cross-cultural Investigations into Work-Related Values in Central Europe: a Blank Spot on the Map. In: Ewa Oziewicz, editor, *Contemporary Problems of International Economy.* Sopot, University of Gdansk, Institute of Foreign Trade, 85-91

Verluyten, S. Paul. 1999. Cultural Biases in Intercultural Business Communication Courses and How to Avoid Them. In: Carl Lovitt & Dixie Goswami, editors, *Exploring the Rhetoric of International Professional Communication: An Agenda for Teachers and Researchers,* Amityville, Baywood, 191-209

Victor, David A. 1992. *International Business Communication.* New York, Harper-Collins Publishers

Vigarello, Georges (volume dirigé par). 2005. *Histoire du Corps. 1. De la Renaissance aux Lumières.* Paris, Seuil

Vulpe, T., D.J. Kealy, D.R. Protheroe, D. MacDonald. 2001. *A profile of the interculturally effective person.* Edmonton, Canada: Centre for intercultural learning; Canadian Foreign Service Institute

Wang, Mary e.a. 2000. *Turning Bricks into Jade. Critical Incidents for Mutual Understanding among Chinese and Americans.* Yarmouth, Maine, Intercultural Press

Ward, Colleen et alii. 1998. The U-Curve on Trial: a Longitudinal Study of Psychological and Sociocultural Adjustment During Cross-Cultural Transition. *International Journal of Intercultural Relations* 22: 3, 277-291

Ward, Colleen. 2008. Thinking outside the Berry boxes: New perspectives on identity, acculturation and intercultural relations. *International Journal of Intercultural Relations* 32: 2, special issue "Convergence of Cross-cultural and Intercultural Research"

Watson, James & Anne Hill. 1984. *Dictionary of Media and Communication Studies* (entry «Apache silence»). London, Hodder Arnold

Watson, Peter. 2005. *Ideas. A History from Fire to Freud.* London, Weidenfeld & Nicolson

Welty, Roger. 2004. *Thai Culture and Society.* Bangkok, Asia Books

Wibaut, Patricia. 2009. *Zakendoen in India: een snelle evolutie?* Unpublished Master's thesis, University of Antwerp

Wickham, Chris. 2009. *The Inheritance of Rome. A History of Europe from 400 to 1000.* London, Allen Lane

Williamson, Andrew. 2003. *The Chinese Business Puzzle. How to Work More Effectively with Chinese Cultures.* Oxford, How To Books

Winkel, Frans & Aldert Vrij. 1990. Interaction and impression formation in a cross-cultural dyad: Frequency and meaning of culturally determined gaze behavior in a police interview-setting. *Social Behaviour,* 5: 5, 335-350.

Wolpert, Stanley. 2005. *India*. Berkeley, University of California Press

Wong, Y.H. & Thomas Leung. 2001. *Guanxi. Relationship Marketing in a Chinese Context*. York, The Haworth Press

Wyatt, David. 2003. *Thailand. A Short History*. Yale, University Press

Xie, Anping, P.-L. Patrick Rau, Yuchien Tseng, Hui Su, Chen Zhao. 2009. Cross-cultural influence on communication effectiveness and user interface design. *International Journal of Intercultural Relations* 33, 11-20

Yeh, Ryh-song & John Lawrence. 1995. Individualism and Confucian Dynamism: A Note on Hofstede's Cultural Root to Economic Growth. *Journal of International Business Studies* 655-669

Yoshimura, Noboru & Philip Anderson. 1997. *Inside the Kaisha: Demystifying Japanese Business Behavior*. Boston, Harvard Business School Press

Zeldin, Theodore. 1998. *An Intimate History of Humanity*. London, Random House, Vintage Books

Zhang, Hao 2008. *The impact of economic growth on business negotiating behavior: theories, evidence and implications*. Unpublished PhD dissertation, University of Antwerp

Index

Only major occurrences are listed for each term. For discussions which extend over several pages, only the first page is given. Adjectives and other derived forms can be found under the corresponding noun, thus Confucian under Confucius, etc.

Absenteeism 185
Accounting system 169
Acculturation 231
Achievement 162, 178
Acquainted, getting 46, 156
Acquisitions 19
Adaptation 231
Address, forms of 87
Africa 47, 56, 63, 94, 146, 149, 151, 152, 155, 248
African Americans 71, 112, 115
Age 25, 168
Air France-KLM 19
Aizuchi 38
Al-Andalus 214
Alcohol 123
Alfa Romeo 131
Ambition 161
American Indians 115, 207
Andes 64
Anglo-saxon 55, 136, 171, 191
Angry, getting 86
Antipraxis 82
Antwerp 52, 227
Anxiety 167, 171
Apache silence 43
Apology 83
Appointments 66
APS 66
Arabs , Arab countries 47, 51, 53, 58, 72, 81, 84, 94, 109, 123, 140, 153, 156, 249
Area studies 260
Argentina 248

Arizona 64
Arrogance 197
Arrow of time 60
Ascription 178
Ask questions 95
Assimilation 225
Athens 222
Attribution 32
Austria 137, 192
Austro-Hungarian Empire 222
Autonomy 176
Aymara 64

Backchannelling 38
Bali 61, 104
Bangkok 70
Banquets 122, 124
Bantu 63, 65, 67
Barega 65
Barnum 84
Bathing 119
BATNA 252
Battle of the Golden Spurs 222
Beckoning 117
Bed linen 245
Beef 123
Behavior 176
Belgium 22, 53, 71, 94, 115, 133, 137, 142, 146, 159, 167, 170, 178, 192, 222, 247
Bias, cultural 211
Bilateral adaptation 235
Bill 126
Blowing your nose 119

BMW   242
Body language   111
Bosnia   222
Boss   134
Botswana   150
Bowing   73, 120
Brand name   257
Brazil   45, 73, 116, 248
Buddhism   215
Bukavu   64
Bunkhun   155
Burma   69
Bush   31
Bushido   249
Business card   89
Buyer-seller relationship   236
Byzantine Empire   214

Cambodia   81
Canada   225, 226, 229
Career   161
Cases   189
Catholicism   137
Central Europe   48, 198, 126
Change of cultural values   198
Chevrolet Nova   189
Chicken   124
China   11, 42, 45, 47, 48, 49, 50, 52, 55, 62, 64, 66, 77, 81, 83, 101, 113, 119, 122, 124, 128, 130, 131, 139, 147, 151, 152, 155, 156, 216, 217, 249, 258, 262,
Chinese Values Survey   54, 212
Chopsticks   125
Christianity   214
Chulalongkorn   49, 92, 93
Circular time   61
Clash of civilizations   228
Climate   137
Clovis   145
Clusters, cultural   191
Coarse mazed cultures   193
Coca Cola   130, 241
Colonialism   201, 203
Color   257, 259
Color terms   21
Comforters   50
Company, loyalty to   179
Compensation, paying   109
Competition   162
Compliance behavior   139
Confidentiality   147
Conflicts, verbal   85, 182

Confucius   54, 104, 135, 175, 213, 216, 248, 249
Congo   95, 150
Connunitarianism   178
Consensus   185
Conservatism   176
Consonants   80
Constantinople   214
Consultation process   50
Consultative management   140
Contact hypothesis   18
Context   101
Contract   49
Convergence   241
Conversation   38
Conversational analysis   187
Conversion, religious   145
Correlation Power Distance – Individualism   158
Cosmetics   14, 245
Costa Rica   136, 158
Court cases   52, 93
Cravate   28
Criticizing   98
Croat   28
Crusaders   214
Cultural distance   229, 332
Cultural fit   229, 232
Customer satisfaction   181
Cyclical time   61
Cyprus   222

Daimler-Chrysler   19
Damascus   214
Daoism   216
Deciding   52
Decision making   138
Decision making style   134
Delays   53
Denying cultural differences   208
Denying problems   102
Dependency   154, 157
Dialogue, intercultural   203
Diffuse   178
Dimensions, cultural   175
Dining   120
Dinner party   91
Directness   90
Disagreeing with boss   134
Discourse analysis   187
Dispute   52
Distance   35, 71
Divergence   243

Diversity   228
Dominican Republic   60
Drinking   126
Duvets   50

East Asia   56, 91, 215, 248
Eastern Europe   48, 198, 126
Ecological fallacy   23
Economic growth   247
Egalitarianism   176
Embarrassment   114
Emoticons   113
Emotional   178
Emotions, expressing   84, 171
Empowerment   139, 170
English   77
Ethics   201
Ethnocentrism   201
Etiquette   12, 119, 164, 183, 189
Europe   67, 105, 196, 225, 245
Event linked time   62, 68
Exaggeration   82
Expatriates   19, 253
Experts   169
Explanation first   50
Explicitness   90
Expressing emotions   84
Eye contact   35, 114, 187

Face saving   12, 68, 91, 154
Facial expressions   112, 186
Failure rate of expatriates   253
Fairness   183
Family   161, 192
Farang   89
Farsi   81
Feet   33, 212
Female circumcision   208
Femininity   161, 247
Filial piety   213
Fine mazed cultures   193
Finland   69
Firing a worker   182
Fish   125
Flemish   221
Food   218
Ford Mondeo/Contour   243
Fork   125
Formality   87
France   41, 42, 45, 57, 73, 85, 117, 137, 139, 140, 159, 181, 192, 197, 226, 247
Friendship   196

Future   61, 62, 64, 65

Gaijin   89
Gender   24
Gender roles   163
Germany   57, 73, 116, 170, 192
Gestures   116
Gifts   120
Global manager   174
Globalization   241
Globalization of nothing   228
GNP per capita   158
Greece, classical   62
Greetings   120
Groups   208
Growth, economic   247
Guanxi   48, 155
Guilt   153

Hai   38
Handshake,   119, 120
Haptics   73
Harmony   91, 104, 154
Harmony with nature   176
Hassidic Jews   227
Head   127, 129
Head wobble   116
Headscarf   209, 224
Hebrew   62
Hierarchy   133, 176, 186, 200
High context   90, 153
High culture   22
Hispanics   112
Hitotsubashi University   49
Holistic thinking   187, 200
Homogeneity, cultural   220
Homs   214
Honda   244
Hong Kong   124, 131
Honor   94, 159, 181
Honorificals   86
Hopi   64
Hospitality   122
Hugging   74
Hungary   126, 224
Hypercorrection   238

Iceberg model   27
Identity cards   169
Idioms   77
Implementing decisions   52
Implicitness   90
Indebtedness   154

India 43, 45, 59, 116, 123, 135, 137, 140, 206, 243, 248
Indirectness 90, 100
Indivdualism 145, 178
Individual 208
Indonesia 48, 153
Inequality 133
INSEAD 192
Integration 225
Intercultural training 254
Interpersonal distance 35
Interpersonal distance 71
Interpreters 11, 12, 77, 80
Interrupting 40
Intolerance 214
Invitation 91
Iran 81, 231
Iraq 33, 84, 252
Ireland 248
Islam 214
Israel 84, 137
Italy 40, 57, 73

Japan 14, 31, 38, 41, 42, 45, 48, 49, 50, 52, 56, 66, 68, 69, 71, 73, 77, 79, 87, 92, 96, 101, 113, 115, 116, 119, 120, 123, 127, 150, 151, 161, 162, 163, 167, 171, 215, 217, 239, 248
Jews 129
Job security 167
Joint ventures 19, 323
Judaism 214
Judo 94

Kaizen 51
Karaoke 127
KFC 241
Kimchi 247
Kissing 74
Kissing map 28
Koizumi 31
Korea (South) 50, 147, 247, 248
Kosher 123
Krushchev 116
Kuwait 46, 252

Language 77
Latin America 53, 58, 72, 77, 116, 147, 192
Latin countries 63, 168, 171
Left hand 128
Lega 65
Leisure 161, 163

Lek 104
Leveling 162
Lifetime employment 149
Linear time 60, 63
Linguistics 187
Loneliness 152
Long-term orientation 14, 54, 175, 248
Loser 162
Loudness of voice 35, 81, 194, 234
Low context 90, 105, 153, 184
Loyalty 148
LVMH 14

Maastricht 31
Maastricht University 108
MacDonald's 241
MacDonaldization 228
Mai pen rai 92
Malawi 236
Malaysia 140, 146, 243, 249
Management, international 256
Mañana 53
Maquiladoras 150
Marginality 225
Marginalization 225
Marketing, cross-cultural 257
Marriage 146
Masai 218
Masculinity 161
Mastery (over nature) 176
MBO 139
Melanesia 64
Melting pot 225
Menstruation 129
Mergers 19
Mexico 53, 187
Microsoft 12
Middle East 51
Mongols 214
Monochrony 57, 178
Monogamy 205
Moral discipline 213
Moral principles 184
Morocco 48, 57, 115
Multiculturalism 170, 207, 220, 224
Mumbai 227
Muslims 224
Mutitasking 58

Nationalism 220
Native speaker 77
Nature 178
Navajo 64, 65, 71, 115, 151, 206

Negotiating   46
Negotiations   251
Nepotism   148
Netherlands   22, 133, 138, 162, 185, 191, 225
Neutral   178
New-Zealand   83
Nine lucky number   132
No, saying   97
Nodding   116
Non verbal communication   111
Northern Ireland   221
Norway   138, 164
Number symbolism   130, 131
Numerical majority   236

Office space   74
OK-sign   117
Onion model   26
Openness   218
Origin of cultural dimensions   137
Ottoman Empire   222, 224
Overadaptation   238
Overstatement   82
Overtime   184

Packaging   257
Pakikisama   154
Pakistan   137
Parisians   197
Parker Pen   242
Parsi   227
Particularism   148, 177
Past   64
Past, present and future   60
Paying for a meal   126, 155
Pecking order   133
Perfectionism   51
Perfume   14
Personal opinion   146
Philippines   45, 148, 151, 154, 190, 210, 242
Phonology   80
Physical contact   73, 112
Planning system   169
Point with finger   34
Poland   44, 126, 199
Polychrony   57, 63, 178
Polygamy   205
Polynesia   64
Pork   123
Portugal   247
Power Distance   133, 247

Practices   26
Prague   78
Present   66
Pride   94, 182
Privacy   81, 151
Privileges   140, 141
Problems, denying   102
Procedural time   62
Process   51
Progress   62
Pronunciation   78
Prostitution   127, 210
Protection (from group)   148, 150
Protestantism   137
Proverbs   65
Proxemics   71
Psychology, cross-cultural   186
Punctuality   43
Pyramid   192

Qaddafi   115
Quail   124
Quantitative-qualitative research   180
Questionnaire   175
Quitting   233

Rachasap   109
Racism   170
Rank   89
Refrigerators   246
Registration   169
Relativism, cultural   202
Replications of Hofstede   174
Reports   168
Research methods   173
Rhetoric   84
Ringi-sho   50
Risk taking   170
Rituals, Uncertainty Avoidance   168
Rolin-Jaequemyns   49, 92
Roman Empire   228
Romania   129
Rule orientation   167, 171
Rule orientation   171
Russia   199
Rwanda   80, 221

Salad   123
Sapir-Whorf hypothesis   21, 206
Saudi-Arabia   52, 234
Saving money   66, 167
Savings ratio   66
Scandinavia   136, 146, 162, 168, 171, 191

South East Asia   47, 56, 83, 91, 215, 217, 248
Seating arrangements   88
Segregation   225
Self-reference criterion   31
Separation   225
Sephora   14
Service orientation   181
Shake head   116
Shame   153
Sharing   151
Shi   65
Shintoism   215
Shoes   33, 131
Short-term orientation   14, 54, 175
Sikh   226
Silence   42, 153
Similarity-attraction hypothesis   229
Sincerity   104
Singapore   73, 131, 227, 253
SIR   93, 154
Situation   25
Sleeping   119
Slurping   119
Smell   257
Smoking   120, 127
Smooth interpersonal relations   93, 154
Social class   24
Socialist countries   198
Sociology   173
Soles of shoes   33, 128
Solidarity   162
Somalia   226
South Africa   68
Spain   179, 247
Specific-diffuse   69, 178
Spending   66
Spiral   50
Spitting   119
Spontaneity   104
SRC   31, 150
Staring   111
Status   87
Stereotypes   193
Stewardess   34
Stratification, social   86
Stress   167, 171
Subcultures   69
Superlatives   82
Superstition   130
Sushi   96
Sweden   156, 163, 164
Sweden, King of   135
Switzerland   44, 192
Syncretism, religious   214

Tamil   227
Thailand   49, 66, 71, 73, 78, 79, 81, 86, 87, 88, 82, 96, 99, 102, 111, 114, 120, 128, 132, 135, 136, 140, 142, 146, 155, 206, 210, 215, 223, 238, 241, 248, 258
Time   37, 178
Time lag   44
Toilet   119
Tokyo   49, 101
Tolerance   214, 218
Tolerance of silence   42
Toyota   131, 241, 244
Traditions of the profession   182
Training, intercultural   254
Transsexuals   206
Tribe   179
Tunisia   94
Turkey   59, 141
Turn taking   40
Typology   175

UDHR   145, 207
UK   41, 56, 83, 116, 117, 170, 226, 245, 248
Ummayads   14
UN peacekeepers   254
Uncertainty Avoidance   167, 247
Unforeseen circumstances   52
Unilateral adaptation   235
Universalism   148, 177
Universalism, ethical   202
Unofficial networks   182
Unzipping cultural dimensions   179
USA   44, 56, 67, 71, 73, 83, 105, 116, 139, 147, 170, 183, 192, 194, 242
USSR   48
Utang na loob   154

Vacation   161, 163
Value clusters, value types   175
Values   26, 175
Vegetarian   123
Verbal communication   77
Vietnam   45, 66, 156
Village market   191

Wage differential   139
Wai   73, 120
Waiting   63

Waldheim   81
Wales   147
Walesa   44
Well-oiled machine   192
Work   161, 162

Yiddish   222, 227

Yin-yang   217
Yugoslavia   222

Zooming in, zooming out   49
Zoroaster   62
Zoroastrians   227

Gedrukt en gebonden bij Acco, Leuven